Clodia

OKLAHOMA SERIES IN CLASSICAL CULTURE

Clodia

A Sourcebook

Julia Dyson Hejduk

UNIVERSITY OF OKLAHOMA PRESS: NORMAN

Also by Julia Dyson Hejduk

King of the Wood: The Sacrificial Victor in Virgil's Aeneid (Norman, 2001)

Hejduk, Julia Dyson, 1966–
    Clodia : a sourcebook / Julia Dyson Hejduk.
        p. cm. — (Oklahoma series in classical culture)
    Includes bibliographical references.
    ISBN 978-0-8061-3907-4 (pbk. : alk. paper) 1. Clodia, 94–53 B.C.—Relations with
men. 2. Clodia, 94–53 B.C.—In literature. 3. Women—Rome—Biography. 4. Cicero,
Marcus Tullius—Criticism and interpretation. 5. Catullus, Gaius Valerius—Criticism and
interpretation. 6. Love poetry, Latin—History and criticism. 7. Rome—In literature.
I. Title.
    DG260.C6H45   2008
    937'.05'092—dc22
    [B]
                                                                    2007034420

Clodia: A Sourcebook is Volume 33 in the Oklahoma Series in Classical Culture.

The paper in this book meets the guidelines for permanence and durability of the
Committee on Production Guidelines for Book Longevity of the Council on Library
Resources, Inc. ∞

1 2 3 4 5 6 7 8 9 10

For my husband

Contents

PART II. CLODIA'S LEGACY

Preface

This is a book I never intended to write. When Ward Briggs, the Classics editor for the University of Oklahoma Press, requested some ideas for useful sourcebooks, I thought immediately of Clodia. Flamboyant female star of the AP Latin reading list, object of fierce male passions in poetry and prose, paragon of the freedom and power of aristocratic women in the late Roman Republic, she was the only real woman from the ancient world about whom such a splendid variety of sources survived; the field was simply waiting for someone to assemble all these texts into a single volume. I hoped someone would do so, as this was a book I wanted to use both for my Introduction to Roman Civilization course and for my Women in Antiquity course. When an e-mail came back enthusiastically asking me for a proposal, I laughed—it had not occurred to me that I myself might be the one to perform this useful task. But as I thought about it, I decided that reeling in some existing translations, perhaps with an appendix of essays by experts, would not be too onerous.

It was then that I discovered firsthand what a personal thing translation actually is. I had supposed that assembling other people's translations would be like hiring a maid, a welcome (if somewhat expensive) delegation of a chore; I found instead that it felt like giving up a child. My purpose as a classicist has always been to help others experience the kind of astonishing, intimate contact with ancient voices that electrified me the first time I read Homer in Greek. Translations, especially of poetry, muffle those voices. While real modern poets have certainly created stunning and beautiful translations, they often do so by sacrificing fidelity to the literal sense of the original languages. Many sourcebook translations, on the other hand, render the literal sense accurately but make little attempt to convey the beauty of the original. My goal has been to find a middle ground, to produce translations that will please the ear while remaining as close as possible to the meaning of the Latin. In some ways capturing the chatty, elliptical tone of Cicero's private letters was an even greater challenge than poetry: casual conversations are more deeply rooted in the speakers' culture and language than are the sonorous cadences of more formal genres (which are challenging enough). But whether or not the result has been aesthetically successful English poetry and prose, I can at least promise that I have made every attempt to keep the static from my own voice to a minimum.

Along with language, the other enormous barrier between the modern and the ancient world is context: the set of assumptions, empirical knowledge, cultural practices, shared memories, and so on that form what theorists call the "competence" of each member of a society. It is impossible for a modern reader fully to recapture an ancient reader's competence; but the more we know, the closer we will come. The footnotes and glossary in this volume are intended partly to give readers with little or no knowledge of Roman civilization enough information to "get" what the authors are saying. Where this book differs from most sourcebooks, however, is in its copious references to modern scholarship, especially on matters of literary interpretation. Readers who want simply to read and enjoy the primary texts are free to ignore the footnotes, while those who want to follow up on interpretive questions will have some idea of where to start.

The second half of this volume, which is not about Clodia per se, requires some explanation. Catullus' poems to and about Lesbia (his pseudonym for Clodia) are the first in the Western tradition to depict, albeit impressionistically, a sustained affair with a single richly characterized woman; though they owe something to Greek erotic epigram and lyric, they represent the beginning of what most would consider genuine love poetry. In the generations after Catullus, several poets—Gallus (whose work has been lost), Propertius, Tibullus, and Ovid—followed his lead, exploring the delights and miseries of romantic love from every angle. But though these later elegiac poets portray their affairs vividly, even graphically, the differences between their women and Lesbia/Clodia are as illuminating as the similarities: the relationships are cast in terms of power, of "slavery" to a "mistress," but never again in Catullus' terms of equality and friend-ship. To understand who Clodia is, it is important to understand who she is not, and that can best be done by hearing the continuation of the conversation Catullus began. In addition to shedding light on Clodia, of course, these sources on her poetic afterlife happen to be glorious poems and fascinating windows on Roman society, not to mention the human heart.

Many classicists have seen partial or complete drafts in various stages of development and have saved me from countless errors and infelicities. In particular I would like to thank Ward Briggs, Christopher Craig, Elaine Fantham, Peter Knox, Andrew Riggsby, Marilyn Skinner, Jeffrey Tatum, Clifford Weber, and the anonymous reader. I am grateful for the patience and encouragement of the University of Oklahoma Press, especially director John Drayton, special projects editor Alice Stanton, associate editor Julie Shilling, and my wonderfully meticulous copy editor, Sarah Nestor. My mother, Elizabeth Dyson, sacrificed weeks of her life to pore over the entire manuscript. My debt to my husband, Matthew Hejduk, includes among other things his in-house editing on very short deadlines. Any remaining blemishes are my own.

Abbreviations

A&R	*Atene e Roma: rassegna trimestrale dell'Associazione Italiana di Cultura classica*
AC	*L'Antiquité classique*
AHD	*American Heritage Dictionary* (ed. William Morris, Houghton Mifflin, 1976)
AJP	*American Journal of Philology*
Am.	Ovid, *Amores* (Loves/Love Affairs)
ANRW	*Aufstieg und Niedergang der Römischen Welt*
Att.	Cicero, *Epistulae ad Atticum* (Letters to Atticus)
Bell. Cat.	Sallust, *Bellum Catilinae* (War with Catiline)
BICS	*Bulletin of the Institute of Classical Studies*
Cael.	Cicero, *Pro Caelio* (In Defense of Caelius)
Cat.	Catullus
Cic.	Plutarch, *Cicero*
CJ	*Classical Journal*
CP	*Classical Philology*
CQ	*Classical Quarterly*
CW	*Classical World*
d.	death
Dom.	Cicero, *De Domo Sua* (Concerning His House)
Fam.	Cicero, *Epistulae ad familiares* (Letters to Friends)
fr.	fragment
G&R	*Greece and Rome*

GRBS	*Greek, Roman and Byzantine Studies*
Har.	Cicero, *De Haruspicum Responsis* (On the Responses of the Soothsayers)
HSCP	*Harvard Studies in Classical Philology*
Inst.	Quintilian, *Instituto Oratoria* (The Training of an Orator)
JHS	*Journal of the History of Sexuality*
JRS	*Journal of Roman Studies*
LCM	*Liverpool Classical Monthly*
Mart.	Martial
MD	*Materiali e discussioni per l'analisi dei testi classici*
OCD	*Oxford Classical Dictionary* (eds. Simon Hornblower and Antony Spawforth, Oxford, 1996)
OLD	*Oxford Latin Dictionary* (ed. P. G. W. Glare, Oxford, 1982)
PCPhS	*Proceedings of the Cambridge Philological Society*
PLLS	*Papers of the Leeds International Latin Seminar*
Prop.	Propertius
Q. fr.	Cicero, *Epistulae ad Quintum fratrem* (Letters to His Brother Quintus)
QUCC	*Quaderni urbinati di cultura classica*
SB	D. R. Shackleton Bailey, *Letters to Atticus* (letters are numbered sequentially)
Sest.	Cicero, *Pro Sestio* (In Defense of Sestius)
s.v.	sub verbo ("under the word")
TAPA	*Transactions of the American Philological Association*
Tib.	Tibullus

Clodia

Introduction

It is hard to reconcile Catullus' tone in the earlier poems with her being a "little" *puella* weeping over a sparrow and in fear that "old men" would spy on their kisses with the indubitable picture of her elsewhere as an important and ruthless political force and an ostentatiously abandoned hussy.

Thornton Wilder[1]

WHO WAS CLODIA?

"Palatine Medea": the personification of murderous female passion, living in Rome's fashionable quarter. This is Cicero's unforgettable characterization of Clodia Metelli (= "wife of Metellus") in his speech defending her former lover Marcus Caelius Rufus, the *Pro Caelio* (56 B.C.). Cicero depicts her in this speech as a "brazen, dissipated whore" who, he insinuates, poisoned her own husband three years earlier; Caelius should be excused for having an affair with her, because affairs with prostitutes (he argues) are and always have been condoned. Clodia's ability to corrupt the young men of Rome, however, springs not merely from her loose morals, but from her wealth, social status, and powers of persuasion. In that regard it is understandable—if still surprising—that, six years before Cicero's scathing speech

---

1. Letter to *New York Times* drama critic Brooks Atkinson (20 December 1947) about the sources for Wilder's epistolary novel *The Ides of March,* in which Clodia plays a starring role. Quoted in Wilder (1948) 263.

(62 B.C.), he had asked the same woman to speak on his behalf to mollify her husband's brother in a delicate political matter. The change from cordiality to open hostility reflects a similar change in Cicero's relationship with Clodia's half-brother Publius Clodius Pulcher, who in 57 B.C. had pushed a bill through the Assembly ordering Cicero's exile from Rome.

An even more famous and colorful depiction of Clodia appears in the poetry of Catullus, where she is sometimes a whore who "shucks" all comers in back alleys, sometimes a comrade who shares in an "everlasting pact of holy friendship." Although the poet calls her by a pseudonym, "Lesbia," he plants an obvious clue to her identity: the opening of poem 79, "Lesbius est *pulcher*" ("Lesbius is pretty"), refers unmistakably to Clodia's brother Publius Clodius *Pulcher,* with Lesbius/Lesbia mirroring Clodius/Clodia. In her promiscuity, her intelligence, her charm, and her status as the poet's social equal or even superior, the poetic fiction called "Lesbia" would appear to have much in common with the femme fatale of Cicero's speech.

Yet the identification of Lesbia with Clodia Metelli is not quite so simple. Among Cicero's many slurs on Clodia's character is his persistent insinuation of an incestuous relationship with her brother Clodius, an insinuation also found in Catullus' "Lesbius" poem mentioned above. So far so good, but all female members of aristocratic families shared the feminine form of the family name, which means that Clodia's two sisters were also named Clodia. Clodius was said to have slept first with his youngest sister, who was then the wife of Lucullus (they were divorced in 66 B.C.); this accusation was amplified during Clodius' trial for sacrilege in 61 B.C., the incident that gave rise to enduring hostility between Clodius and Cicero. Only after this trial, it seems, was the incest insinuation expanded to include Clodia Metelli, as well as the other sister, wife of Marcius Rex. As T. P. Wiseman, the most eloquent modern opponent of the identification of Lesbia with Clodia Metelli, rightly observes, "If we had a speech against Clodius from 61 B.C. instead of one in defence of Caelius from 56, the identification of Clodia Luculli as Lesbia would seem as self-evident as that of Clodia Metelli has appeared to many modern scholars."[2]

It should be noted that yet another fascinating, little-known source sheds light on a Clodia who may be identical with Lesbia, Clodia Metelli, or both of them. In the months following his daughter Tullia's death (45

2. Wiseman (1969) 56.

B.C.), the greatest grief of his personal life, Cicero's private letters reveal his eagerness to purchase Clodia's property for a shrine to Tullia. He seems to expect success if he can come up with the money. That Cicero can refer to this Clodia as a free agent in full control of her own property is in itself an important indication of the power upper-class women could wield in the late Republic. If this Clodia is also the woman whom he had publicly pilloried eleven years earlier as a whore and a murderess, that is an even more revealing piece of evidence about the reality behind Roman oratory and the public's response to it. The restoration of amicable relations between Cicero and Clodia, that is, might suggest that both she and the public were willing to see a court case as an artificial ritual rather like a play or a sporting event: the players must act their roles to the hilt, must do whatever it takes to win, but afterward they can shake hands and get on with their lives. Although I would not argue for quite this degree of artificiality, it is worth keeping in mind that forensic attacks should not be taken at face value, that they were governed by complex unwritten rules and had sometimes surprising consequences.

In my view the preponderance of evidence suggests that the model for Catullus' Lesbia and the property owner referred to in Cicero's late letters are both Clodia Metelli. But a review of the arguments for and against will give a good idea of the sort of tantalizingly inconclusive investigations that are the delight and the frustration of classical scholarship.

Let us begin with the propositions set out by Wiseman:

(a) Lesbia was one of the three Clodiae.
(b) Lesbia was married.
(c) Catullus' poems, including those on Lesbia, were written c. 56–54 B.C.
(d) None of the Clodiae was married at that time.

At least one of these propositions must be false.[3]

Wiseman goes on to argue that "(d)" must be the culprit: since marriages were one of the key means of cementing political alliances, it is prima facie probable that one or all of the sisters in this tight-knit and politically ambitious clan did remarry, even though we have no specific evidence for

3. Wiseman (1969) 57.

it.[4] Yet the logic holds only if we add one more crucial and, I believe, false proposition: that the poems were invariably written at the time the events they describe were taking place. In poem 68b, a flashback to the beginning of the affair, Lesbia is clearly married; but even if this poem was written in 56–54 B.C., it is perfectly reasonable to suppose that the poet is remembering events from before 59 B.C. (the date of Metellus' death). By deliberately linking his poetic mistress to a real public figure, Catullus limits his freedom to shape the story of the affair: he must have had some sort of involvement with Lesbia's model (if it were pure fiction he would be a laughingstock),[5] and she must have had a husband and various lovers at the time. His technique of deliberately shuffling the sequence of the Lesbia poems, however, placing those about falling in love *after* those about renunciation, allows him to arrange them along thematic lines that frustrate attempts to date them precisely. The poems we have are perfectly consistent with an affair of several years (that is, one that would overlap with both the marriage to Metellus and the affair with Caelius) molded into a "story" whose narrative coherence is emotional, not chronological.

The strongest evidence for connecting Lesbia with Clodia Metelli depends on identifying one of Catullus' rivals as Marcus Caelius Rufus, the defendant in the *Pro Caelio*. Even if Caelius had slept with more than one Clodia (for which there is no evidence whatsoever), the connection of Caelius and Clodia Metelli in this notorious court case, which took place right around the time we believe Catullus was writing (56 B.C.), would have reinforced the identification of Lesbia with Clodia Metelli for Catullus' readers. In fact, although there is nothing quite so specific as "Lesbius est pulcher," several details from Catullus' poems to one "Rufus" (69 and 77) dovetail nicely with elements in Cicero's speech, as J. D. Noonan has pointed out.[6] Briefly, Catullus says that a "goat" dwells in Rufus' armpits, while Cicero mentions that Caelius belonged to the Luperci, a fraternity that ran around with goat-skin loincloths and whips; Catullus accuses Rufus of burning his guts and "poisoning" his life, as Caelius was accused

---

4. Wiseman (1969) 59. Briscoe (1971) notes the improbability of Wiseman's suggestion that Lesbia may be the Clodia who married one A. Ofilius, had fifteen children, and lived to the age of 115.

5. How much of the affair is fictional (indeed, one might argue that all affairs contain a large dose of fiction) is impossible to say. Even if Catullus chose to make it up out of whole cloth, however, the question of which Clodia the story revolves around is still meaningful.

6. Noonan (1979).

of poisoning Clodia; and Catullus calls the armpit goat a *bestia* ("beast"), the *cognomen* of one of the prosecutors in the *Pro Caelio,* who had also been accused of poisoning women.[7] Moreover, while poems 69 and 77 are addressed to a "Rufus," poems 58 and 100—which have several thematic similarities to the "Rufus" poems—are addressed to a "Caelius."

In sorting through the scholarship concerned with identifying the various players in Catullus' poems, one frequently encounters arguments that rely upon apparent contradictions in personality or status as evidence that two characters cannot be the same. It is taken for granted, for instance, that the same person cannot be described as both malodorous and elegant,[8] both friend and enemy,[9] both a prude and a whore.[10] Such arguments neglect a crucial aspect of Catullus' artistry, not to mention human nature: the paradox of "I hate and I love" (85.1), the wild swings of emotion that arise from infidelity, is a predominant theme in his poetry. Catullus addresses the "Rufus" of poem 77 as a former friend who, literally, "burned up my intestines" by stealing his love; he addresses the "Caelius" of poem 100 as a friend who helped him out when an insane passion was burning up his marrow, then wishes Caelius luck and potency in his latest homosexual love affair (always a source of scorn for the Romans if the object of desire was an adult). It is pointless to argue that friendship and enmity are mutually exclusive. If we see that poem 100 is dripping with sarcasm, the climax of a "cycle" of betrayal and jealousy in counterpoint with the Lesbia poems, then it becomes probable that this "Caelius" and "Rufus" are one and the same: Marcus Caelius Rufus, sometime lover of Clodia Metelli.[11] Even if

7. For a more detailed explanation of these similarities, see notes on Cat. 69 and 77.

8. Austin (1960) 148–49: "The Rufus of 69 is a dirty creature, pilloried for his public nastiness: the Rufus of 77 is a one-time friend, who has done Catullus a private, personal wrong by creeping in and stealing away his happiness. If either can be identified with M. Caelius Rufus, the subject of 77 alone is a possibility."

9. Wiseman (1969) 56: "Catullus' Caelius was a trusted friend and confidant of the poet in his affair with Lesbia; Catullus' Rufus was a treacherous rival, one of Lesbia's lovers [and so the identification collapses]." This logic is followed by Arkins (1983) 309.

10. Hillard (1981) takes the sexual frigidity imputed to Clodia Metelli by a famous quip of Caelius to be incompatible with the sexual license of Lesbia: see "Testimonia," *Inst.* 8.6.53.

11. See Dettmer (1997) 151–69 on the coherence of the Caelius Rufus "cycle." The only argument with any weight against seeing all these Caelii and Rufi as the same person is that Catullus 100.2 refers to Caelius as the "flower of Veronese youth," whereas Cicero implies (*Cael.* 5) that Caelius hailed from Interamna, in Picenum (i.e., not Verona). This argument is inconclusive, however, for two reasons: (1) The text in *Cael.* 5 is corrupt—that is, the place-name of Caelius' birthplace is not clear from the manuscripts. (2) As Goold (1983) 211, 262 suggests, Catullus

Catullus' "Caelius" and "Rufus" are different people, if *either one* is Marcus
Caelius Rufus, then the identification of Lesbia as Clodia is all but assured.

As Marilyn Skinner observes in her important article "Clodia Metelli,"[12]
both Lesbia and the Clodia of the *Pro Caelio* are in a sense mythical con-
structions, molded by the demands and conventions of two genres (poetry
and oratory) that often bear a rather tenuous relationship to truth. In
Cicero's letters, by contrast, the passing mentions of Clodia may give us
more of an uncensored glimpse into the reality of her life and the status of
some Roman women. The question of which Clodia owns the property
that Cicero seeks to buy thus becomes an important one. Once again, cir-
cumstantial evidence suggests that it was in fact Clodia Metelli. In an
appendix on "Tullia's Fane," D. R. Shackleton Bailey concludes with the
following observation:[13]

> In 56 Clodia possessed *horti* ["gardens, park, estate"] on the Tiber,
> probably opposite the Campus Martius. . . . [*Cael.* 36, "You have
> gardens on the Tiber, and you have carefully placed them in a location
> where all the youth come to swim."] The situation fits, and there is
> piquancy in the possibility that this *Zaubergarten* ["pleasure garden"]
> might have become Cicero's ἐγγήραμα ["retreat for his old age"].

In another ingenious piece of detective work, Shackleton Bailey notes that
Cicero, after hounding his friend Atticus again to buy Clodia's property,
asks about the divorce of one Lentulus Spinther from a woman who is
elsewhere called Metella—that is, the "daughter of Metellus," and so very
likely the daughter of Clodia Metelli as well. That connection and a few
other elliptical references would make perfect sense if Lentulus were
indeed Clodia's son-in-law.[14]

If it is the case that the Clodia of the *Pro Caelio,* Cicero's letters, and
Catullus' poems are the same woman, then we have a richer selection of
material about this woman than about any other from the Roman Republic.[15]

---

could well be calling Caelius the "pick of Verona's youth" for some other reason than because his
birthplace was Verona.

12. Skinner (1983).

13. Shackleton Bailey (1966) 404–14.

14. See note on *Att.* 2.52.2 **Spinther getting a divorce?**

15. Clodia and Tullia (Cicero's daughter), for instance, are the only women of the Roman
Republic described under the "Lives" section of the essay on "Women in Roman Society" by

Is it possible to reconstruct from these male, inevitably biased and impressionistic sources a meaningful answer to the question, "Who Was Clodia?" Certainly not in the same way we reconstruct the lives of women from the past few centuries, aided by letters, diaries, handiwork, houses, portraits, photographs, and so on. Studying classical antiquity is like trying to solve a puzzle with 95 percent of the pieces missing. We have not a word from Clodia's own pen, nor even a reported speech from her own mouth (beyond Catullus' complaint that she "hurls abuses" at him and the like). The one physical detail we are given is "flaming eyes" (*Har.* 38, *Cael.* 49).

Perhaps the only advantage to having so little information is that it is possible to present *all* the surviving ancient sources on Clodia in the first half of this volume. By good fortune these sources happen to comprise delightful readings from a variety of genres: letters, oratory, love poetry, and biography. Whatever the gaps in our knowledge may be, these readings will shine some light both on an extraordinary woman and on the workings of Roman passion, politics, and poetry.

LOVE AFTER LESBIA

In the second half of this book, a substantial selection of post-Catullan poems epitomizes the brief but splendid flowering of Roman love elegy (also included are a smattering of epigrams alluding to an infamous sparrow eulogized by Catullus). For Clodia lives on, not only in the sensational sources about her directly, but also as a model for the entire genre of erotic poetry.

Roman literature was primarily a process of *aemulatio* ("rivalry"), the self-conscious reworking of earlier texts. The first known work of Latin literature (by Livius Andronicus, 240 B.C.) was the translation of a Greek play; the best known work of Latin literature (Virgil's *Aeneid*, 19 B.C.) is a sustained allusion to Homer's *Iliad* and *Odyssey*. This lack of "originality" in our sense was considered a fatal flaw in the Romantic era, which acknowledged only "Nature" as a legitimate source for true "Art." In recent times,

---

Treggiari (1996), and Tullia's "character and life are seen through the filter of her father" (124). In Fantham et al. (1994) 281–85, Clodia is the example of the "New Woman" of the late Republic; the only other historical figure named is one Sempronia, about whom Sallust writes a single paragraph (see "Testimonia," *Bell. Cat.* 25).

however, the pendulum is starting to swing back, and readers have begun again to see the Romans' relationship with earlier texts as one of enriching dialogue, not slavish imitation. (One might mention that, as we now know, even the poems attributed to Homer were the culmination of a rich, centuries-old oral tradition.) No text is an island: with varying degrees of self-consciousness, authors necessarily draw upon the language and themes of earlier works, thereby conveying a richness of meaning that would be impossible "starting from scratch."[16]

That the Romans created such connections with unusual self-consciousness and skill is beyond doubt. The controversies arise when readers attempt to interpret these connections. For instance, it has long been recognized that the battle between Aeneas and Turnus in Virgil's *Aeneid* recalls the battle between Achilles and Hector in Homer's *Iliad*; the similarities are sustained and deliberate, thus earning the status of "allusion" or "reference." The reader is clearly meant in some sense to "compare and contrast" with the model, and disagreements arise only over what the allusion *means*. While Roman love poets sometimes engage in such allusions, their brand of intertextuality is often more diffuse, drawing upon an entire idiom rather than a specific textual locus. When Ovid declares "Miserable me!" (*me miserum*) in *Am.* 1.1.25, for instance, it would appear that, rather than alluding to a particular model, he is drawing on "poetic memory" to place himself in the tradition of miserable lovers.[17] But when he writes a poem on the death of his mistress's parrot, it would appear that he is alluding specifically to Catullus' poem on the death of his mistress's sparrow (Cat. 3). The hedging phrase "would appear" shields the interpreter from the charge of dogmatism, for the line between "allusion" and "poetic memory" is blurred. The unlovely term "intertextuality," which covers both phenomena, provides additional protection.

One of the aims of this volume is to show Roman intertextuality in action. It would be disingenuous, I should add, to claim that all of the elegies included here are inspired by Clodia/Lesbia in any specific way. Many motifs of Roman elegy are found first in Catullus simply because he is the earliest Roman love poet whose works have survived in quantity, and some elegiac motifs do not appear in Catullus at all. Nevertheless, one

16. See Boyd (1997) 19–48 on the varieties of "Reused Language."
17. See the nuanced discussion of Hinds (1998) 29–34.

of the most exciting aspects of Roman love poetry—paradoxically, for those who crave "originality"—is its interconnectedness: the persistent dialogue among texts opens the way for humor, pathos, and everything in between. Although it would be impossible to present in one volume all of these elegies' literary models (which would include Greek and Roman epics, tragedies, and comedies, to name a few), the present selection can at least give a taste of the conversation among poems of the same genre.

But are these poems not (the reader may wonder) the spontaneous outpourings of a full heart? Does this talk of "calculation" and "intertextuality," this cataloging of common themes, reduce them to a literary exercise and rob them of their power? Are they in any sense *real*?

These fictions do tell us something about male attitudes toward women, but not always in a straightforward or transparent way. The sentiments expressed by the "I" of the poems may in fact be quite opposite to those of the man who held the pen.[18] Ovid, in particular, delights in exposing the lover's rhetoric for what it is, as in the pair of poems where the narrator eloquently protests his fidelity (2.7) and then wonders how his cheating was found out (2.8). Sometimes Ovid creates a sense of his sincerity, but at other times he strives for an appearance of *insincerity,* and readers have faulted him for conveying precisely the effect that he intended. Since we have little evidence outside the texts themselves for assessing what the author (as opposed to the narrator) was "really like," we are frequently subject to what Duncan Kennedy calls "the piquant circularity of extrapolating 'reality' from the text and then using it to assess the viewpoint from which that 'reality' has been presented."[19]

The sources given here unquestionably pose difficulties for the modern student of social history seeking to recover the truth about women in antiquity. And yet these poems open a window, however clouded, on the ancient mind and heart—and perhaps the modern as well. The power of art does not depend upon its accurate depiction of "reality." As George Goold observes,

> The structure and traditions of Roman society did not make it easy
> for highborn Roman youths to meet, fall in love with, and marry

---

18. As Gotoff (1974) 238 observes of Tibullus, "the poems are charming instead of banal precisely because the speaker is not the poet."

19. Kennedy (1993) 15.

highborn Roman girls in a natural sequence; what *was* natural, therefore, was that the dream liaisons depicted in the Roman elegiac poets should be invested with a universal appeal. Escapist literature, yes! But then, how much of literature, how much of mankind's nobility, springs from the heart's irrepressible yearning to transcend the reality by which we unhappy mortals are fettered![20]

It is also worthwhile to remember the power of literature to transform both its readers and its creators. Jasper Griffin's essay on "Augustan Poetry and the Life of Luxury" is a useful corrective to those who would set up a firm dichotomy between art and reality. As he remarks, "not only does literature reflect, at whatever remove and with whatever stylisation, the experiences of life, but also in its turn it affects actual behavior; and can do so with great force."[21] Many of the sources presented in this volume, for good or ill, have had a profound effect on the experience of romantic love in the Western world.

Themes in Roman Love Poetry

Love poetry must work hard to appear to be the spontaneous outpouring of a full heart. Of all the love objects in Roman poetry, Lesbia has the greatest claim to "reality": she can at least be identified fairly securely with an actual person, whatever the real nature of the relationship between Catullus and Clodia may have been. As the tradition develops, the girlfriends become more obviously fictional, even if they are described in more concretely physical terms.

The collection in this book attempts to show the progress of certain themes from Catullus to Propertius, Tibullus, and Ovid. Some of these motifs have a universal feel, such as Catullus' taut "I hate and I love." Ecstasy, jealousy, renunciation and counter-renunciation—these emotions do not change much over the centuries. But there are some motifs that may appear strange to a modern audience and which cannot be appreciated fully without an awareness of the cultural circumstances of ancient Rome. These will

---

20. Goold (1990) 11.
21. Griffin (1985) 3.

emerge most clearly from reading the poems themselves, but a brief introductory sketch may prove helpful.

love as slavery (servitium amoris). The reality of slavery gives a certain pungency to the idea of the poet as his woman's "slave." What for most modern readers is not a living metaphor meant for the Romans a radical reversal of power relationships that they observed and participated in every day.[22] See "Slavery" below.

love as war. While the idea of love as a "war between the sexes" is certainly not unique to Rome, an admixture of physical violence in romantic love is quintessentially Roman. This was a society that reveled in watching people kill each other (the movie *Gladiator* is accurate in this respect). Kissing often involved biting; bruised necks and torn clothing appear frequently in erotic poems. On a more metaphorical level, Roman poets often claim to consider anger and abuse toward themselves a sure proof of true love.

love as military service (militia amoris) (not to be confused with the preceding).[23] Part of the countercultural tendency of Roman elegy involved seeing love as an arduous activity comparable to serving as a soldier;[24] either the girl herself or Venus, the goddess of love, is like a general leading her lover on a difficult campaign. For the Romans military service represented virility and virtue, and those in other professions wished to cash in on its masculine cachet (Cicero, similarly, liked to compare the practice of oratory to military service). There is perhaps a precursor to this idea in Cat. 11, but it becomes more fully developed in Prop. 2.7, then expounded to the point of absurdity in *Am.* 1.9.

love as disease. The idea that love can be sickening, infecting the lover against his will, is an ancient commonplace. Whereas philosophers may

---

22. Copley (1947) 300 points out that "the concept of *servitium amoris* as it is found in Roman elegy, is almost entirely the invention of the Roman writers themselves, the fruit of their own imagination." Lyne (1979) argues that Propertius was the first poet to develop the idea at length, but it rapidly proved contagious: "The formalization of 'servitium amoris' happened quickly. By the time of Prop. Book II and certainly by Tib. Book II it seems a convention, albeit a fresh and challenging one. In Ovid's *Amores* it is a conceit" (128).

23. See Gale (1997) on both *militia amoris* and "love as war" more generally.

24. See Hallett (1984).

make a bona fide attempt to find a "cure," poets rather transparently cherish their "misery" as a fruitful source of poetic inspiration.[25]

love as foedus ("pact"). Another concept no longer celebrated in modern poetry is that of the *foedus,* properly a formal agreement between two parties. Legal formulas used in a romantic context tend to become softened by repetition and habituation. One might compare the traditional wedding ceremony's familiar and beautiful phrase "to have and to hold," which originated in the strict language of legal contracts designating the transfer of ownership ("have") and possession ("hold") of a piece of property.

The word *foedus* means a binding agreement of some kind, but it can have quite different nuances: a "pact" between equal individuals or a "treaty" between unequal powers. Catullus' last Lesbia poem calls their love "an everlasting *foedus* of holy friendship." Propertius turns this on its head in his final Cynthia poem: the *foedus* there is not a "pact" between equals (*foedus aequum*), but a "treaty" between entities of unequal power (*foedus iniquum*), one victorious (Cynthia) and one conquered (Propertius).

love as amicitia. Our understanding of this theme is complicated by the gendering of Latin nouns and the nuances of modern English. *Amicus* is properly translated "friend"—that is, "male friend" (since what we have is males writing mainly for other males). *Amica,* the feminine form of this noun, is best translated not simply as "(female) friend," but as "girlfriend." The lopsidedness of the terminology here has a parallel in the different semantic spheres of our "girlfriend" and "boyfriend" (women routinely say "I saw a movie with my girlfriend," but men . . . ?). The relationship between a man and his *amica,* that is, would be a romantic attachment quite different from the *amicitia* between *amicus* and *amicus.*

Catullus' idea of true *amicitia* existing between members of the opposite sex is revolutionary.[26] In poem 72, for instance, Catullus compares his love for Lesbia to that of a father for his sons *and his sons-in-law.* Comparing romantic love to filial or parental love is striking and perhaps hyperbolic,

25. See Caston (2006).

26. See Ross (1969) 80–94 on "Lesbia and the Vocabulary of Political Alliance." Lyne (1980) 26, followed by Fitzgerald (1995) 117–20, modifies "political alliance" to "aristocratic obligation"; yet however one formulates the idea, it is clear that Catullus is applying terms from a peculiarly *male* sphere to his relationship with Lesbia.

but not exactly radical; such emotions are primal, spontaneous, and fierce, qualities one can easily see a passionate lover seeking to convey. But love for *sons-in-law* is something else entirely, a cultivated affection arising from a contractual relationship with political repercussions. So radical is this idea that we see little trace of it in Propertius, Tibullus, or Ovid.[27]

It is in this, perhaps, that Clodia stands apart from the rest—and that the letters of Cicero and the love poems of Catullus strangely converge. Lesbia may be a goddess (like Ovid's Corinna), a sexually rapacious femme fatale (like Propertius' Cynthia), but she is also an equal, not only intellectually, but as a participant in the male sphere of *amicitia*. Cicero asks her to negotiate on his behalf; he pumps Atticus for her glimpses into political events; he wants to purchase her property. Cynthia dazzles her lover with her artistic and intellectual achievements, but Clodia, it seems, was a power to be reckoned with in the male world of politics and finance. Amid all the various metaphors for love—as slavery, as military service, as war, as mythological fantasy, as worship—the most radical Catullus offers is that of love as friendship.

Some Translation Issues

Translating poetry is invariably frustrating, especially when one language is ancient and the other modern.[28] English conveys meaning primarily by word order: consider, for instance, the significant difference between "dog bites boy" and "boy bites dog." Latin, by contrast, conveys meaning primarily by the "inflections" or endings placed on words: *puer* ("boy") *canem* ("dog") *manducat* ("bites") means "boy bites dog," whereas the words in the same order but with different endings, *puerum canis manducat,* mean "dog bites boy." This allows for a flexibility of word order—with attendant surprises, nuances, and ambiguities—impossible to replicate in English. Furthermore, the rhythm of Latin poetry depends on a complex system of metric

27. Oliensis (1997) shows how the elegists employ sexual *amor* in their depiction of male *amicitia*. But none of them, as far as I can tell, pick up on Catullus' strategy of employing male *amicitia* in the depiction of sexual *amor.* On the complexities of *amicitia* in the late Republic, see Brunt (1965).

28. Gaisser (2001) provides an excellent overview of centuries of translations of Catullus, demonstrating that translations can exhibit nearly as much variety as original poetry can.

"quantity" something like our musical notation of half-notes and quarter-notes, not simply (as in English) on stressed and unstressed syllables. The translations in this volume employ meters that approximate the rhythm of the Latin, but the interplay of "quantity" and "stress" is inevitably lost.

Other difficulties arise from the different usage of Latin words, even if their meanings seem straightforward. For instance, the Romans often used first person plural forms, "we/us/our," to stand for first person singular forms, "I/me/my" (like our "editorial we"). Since the first person singular forms were also available in Latin and were widely used, it is sometimes difficult to explain why in a particular case the plural form is chosen to convey singular meaning. Though it is usually clear when "we/our" is standing for "I/my," sometimes the usage presents a real and important ambiguity difficult to convey in English. Cat. 58.1 declares (literally), "Caelius, our Lesbia [does very wicked things]": is the "our" here standing for "my," as it often does, or is Catullus calling Lesbia "*our* Lesbia" because she was the lover of both himself and Caelius? Although it is tempting simply to translate the plural pronouns and possessives as plural, the sense in English is sometimes so jarring that "I/my" seems preferable (e.g., where Catullus clearly means "I love you," not "we love you").

A single word can sometimes establish an intertextual connection, either by pointing the reader to a specific passage ("allusion") or by evoking a poetic idiom ("poetic memory"). Such connections are often obscured by translations, which generally use a variety of English words to translate the same Latin one. In this collection several key Latin words (or cognates) are always mapped to the same English words (or cognates):

candidus (here = "radiant"). This word, meaning "shining" or "white," can be used to describe everything from the sun to a woman's skin to the toga of a political "candidate" (scrubbed white for the occasion). Its connotations include beauty, divine power, and favorable omens.[29]

carmen (here = "song"). The Romans had the same word for "song," "poem," and "magical charm/spell/incantation." Words arranged in a particular order, that is, were believed to have a quasi-magical power, whether or not they were actually set to music. Roman poets—especially Ovid—frequently exploit this rich ambiguity.

29. See Clarke (2003) 52–66 on the connotations of *candidus* and its cognates.

cura (here = "care"). Like English "care," Latin *cura* represents a feeling of concern, anxiety, and tenderness; it can also, more frequently than in English, refer to the object of this feeling.

deliciae (here = "cherished delight"). The essential meaning is "something that gives pleasure"; translations include "toy," "luxury," "sweetheart," "self-indulgence," and "whim." Cicero uses the term pejoratively in *Cael.* 44 to refer to the sort of foolish "lovemaking" Caelius has outgrown.[30] The word's appearance in the famous first line of the "Lesbia cycle" (Cat. 2.1, "Sparrow, cherished delight of my girl") causes it to recall, in a sense, the whole genre and set of values that the cycle represents.

miser (here = "miserable" or "in misery"). This becomes the standard epithet of the unhappy lover ensnared against his will (see, e.g., Cat. 8.1, Prop. 1.1.1, *Am.* 1.1.25), almost a technical term for "lovesick" (lovers generally seem to enjoy wallowing in this kind of "misery").

pietas/pius (here = "righteousness/righteous"). Although this word does include our concept of religious "piety," its application is far broader: it denotes responsibility, dutifulness, and fulfilling one's obligations both to inferiors (e.g., children, clients) and superiors (e.g., parents, patrons, gods).[31]

venustus (here = "attractive"). Etymologically, this means "having the attractive qualities of Venus," though the word is frequently used in nonerotic contexts (like English "lovely").[32]

ROMAN CIVILIZATION

Since the imagined audience for this volume is an intelligent English-speaking reader with no prior knowledge of ancient civilization, the following section provides a very brief introduction to some of the topics

30. Quinn (1970) 92.
31. As Ross (1975) 14 observes, "Roman piety (*pietas*) was essentially concerned with human, not divine, affairs: Roman religion did not explore celestial spheres but was concerned, typically, with the here and now, with the efficient and orderly functioning of the everyday world."
32. See the rich and nuanced discussion by Krostenko (2001) of *venustus* and several related terms (*elegans* ["elegant"], *bellus* ["pretty"], *facetus* ["witty"], *lepidus* ["charming"], and *festivus* ["amusing"]) in Catullus and Cicero. Krostenko argues that such terms embody the "social performance of identity through aesthetic means" (1) and were "the primary lexical expression of a

most relevant to the sources presented in this book. Unless otherwise noted, the information here is derived either from common knowledge or from the *Oxford Classical Dictionary*, the best one-volume reference work on classical antiquity. Further aid is to be found in the glossary (which defines all proper names and a few key Latin words), the footnotes, and the bibliography.

Women

In the world of the late Republic and early Empire (the time period covered by this volume), a woman's lot in life was determined in large measure by her birth.[33]

Upper-class women were defined by and representatives of the clan to which they belonged (see "Names" below). Although they could not vote or hold office, Cicero's letters attest to the more informal ways in which they could influence political events. They also played an important role in religion: some religious ceremonies were, or were supposed to be, confined entirely to women, such as the rites of the Bona Dea or "Good Goddess" (which Clodia's brother illegally infiltrated in drag). Unlike their counterparts in ancient Greece, noble Roman women were active participants in mixed-sex dinner parties; they could attend public meetings, trials, sporting events, and the theater; they were often highly literate. Their marriages, however, were generally arranged by their fathers in order to cement political alliances. Girls in their teens frequently were married to men fifteen or twenty, sometimes even fifty, years older. Affairs were common and divorces were easy; either partner simply informed the other in the presence of witnesses that the marriage was over. Children were routinely placed in custody of the father.

Women of the demimonde—foreigners, courtesans, and women of uncertain parentage—are abundant in Roman love poetry. In many ways they had more freedom than their upper-class counterparts, even if they had fewer

---

conceptual category in which aestheticism, formerly opposed to 'real' social worth in Roman culture, was now constructed as its complement" (3). These words reflect a shift in Roman values to embrace Greek culture and aesthetics, but not in an unproblematic way; for instance, Cicero may use the same word as a term of approbation or disapprobation in different rhetorical contexts.

33. Standard works on women in antiquity include Sarah B. Pomeroy (1975), Treggiari (1991), and Fantham et al. (1994).

rights (e.g., they could not appear in court or contract legal marriages with upper-class Roman citizens). The Ipsitilla of Cat. 32, for instance, apparently has a house of her own and the liberty to invite whatever male guests she pleases at any time of day. Such women are often endowed with an attractiveness more than merely physical, like the "little whore" of Cat. 10, "not entirely uncharming or unrefined," who demolishes Catullus in a contest of wit. Because our knowledge of such women is even more the product of male fantasy than our knowledge of noblewomen, it is difficult to say whether the poets' frequent emphasis on their mercenary, grasping nature is a reflection of reality or a literary artifice.[34] Often it is also difficult to say whether a given poetic mistress, such as Propertius' Cynthia or Tibullus' Delia, belongs to this class or to the nobility. In some poems the dramatic situation demands the presence of a husband, which would imply the woman's status as a social equal; in other poems the theme is instead the woman's lower social status rendering her ineligible for marriage with an upper-class Roman citizen. On slave women, who also appear not infrequently as love objects, see "Slavery" below.

Social Classes

The highest social class was that of senators, who were required to possess one million sesterces; the next was that of knights, required to possess four hundred thousand sesterces. The knights, who could be as powerful and wealthy as senators, were closest to the modern "business class." Senators were technically forbidden to engage in business ventures (relying for their wealth on land holdings), though in practice they often became silent partners of businessmen. The remaining Roman population consisted of the *plebs* (see "Patricians and Plebeians"), who were full citizens but generally poor, and slaves and freedmen (see "Slavery").

Slavery

Something like one-third of the population of the ancient Roman world consisted of slaves. Unlike those in the American antebellum South, slaves were not distinguished by physical characteristics, and manumission (freeing)

---

34. See James (2001).

was common, especially if directed by will upon an owner's death. Freed slaves (called "freedmen") had a special social status: though their former owners remained their "patrons" (see "Patrons and Clients"), freedmen had many of the rights of citizens, and if a freedman (or freedwoman) married a citizen, their children received full citizen status. It was permissible and common for men to sleep with their own slaves of either sex. Women, who were responsible for maintaining the purity of the family line, were not allowed to do so (hence Cicero's cutting slurs about Clodia's intimacy with her slaves) and even risked becoming enslaved themselves if found violating this taboo.

Patrons and Clients

One of the most important political and social institutions in Rome was the highly complex system of "patronage." A patron was "a man who gave assistance and protection to another person, Roman or non-Roman, who thereby became his client. In return, clients gave their patrons respect, deference and services, which included personal attendance and political support" (*OCD* s.v. *patronus*). The system seems straightforward enough when involving truly hierarchical relationships; complications arise when those who would appear to be social equals refer to one another as "patron," sometimes in an ironic or mock-complimentary way (as in, e.g., Cat. 1 and 49). Like "slavery," "patronage" can refer both to real and to metaphorical power relationships.

Patricians and Plebeians

The "patricians" belonged to families whose ancestors, according to tradition, were *patres* or "fathers" in the first Senate; "plebeians" were everyone else. Although the word *plebs* generally refers to the urban poor, "plebeians" could be quite wealthy. The early days of the Republic were characterized by various struggles between these classes (the "Struggle of the Orders"), which resulted in the gradual increase of plebeian power. One of the concessions granted to plebeians was that only plebeians could be tribunes; in the late Republic the tribunate became increasingly important, because tribunes could summon the plebeian assembly to pass legislation and could veto measures put forth by other magistrates. Clodia's half-brother Clodius, though born a patrician, got himself adopted by a plebeian in order to be eligible for the tribunate. (Most adoptions in Rome were of adults and were for reasons of inheritance or politics.)

Names

By the time of the late Republic, Roman names for male members of the upper classes consisted of a *praenomen* ("first name"), a *nomen* ("family name"), and sometimes a *cognomen* ("nickname"). There were only about a dozen *praenomina* in common use, and hence they were generally abbreviated (see Glossary, "*Praenomen*," for a list). The *nomen* designated the *gens* or family. The *cognomen* originally designated some distinguishing characteristic of a man—anything from an insult like "Stupid" (Brutus) to a compliment like "Beautiful" (Pulcher)—but was then passed down to his offspring. Women were called by the feminine form of the *nomen*, which can lead to some confusion in the case of multiple offspring—such as the three Clodiae.

Political Offices

Politics was considered the proper occupation for upper-class Roman males. By the late Republic most political offices were filled by election and lasted for one year. Campaigning involved both informal networking among one's peers and wooing the populace with shows (plays, gladiatorial contests) and gifts; the boundary between acceptable largesse and electoral bribery (*ambitus*) was blurred.[35] At the age of thirty, a man became eligible to enter the *cursus honorum* or "sequence of elected offices" (quaestor, aedile, praetor, consul), which gained him admission to the Senate for life. After holding office, ex-praetors and ex-consuls ("consulars") generally became governors of provinces, where they often amassed great wealth. Tribunes were outside of this sequence (see "Patricians and Plebeians"). Voters were divided into groups; the majority within each group determined that group's vote, and the majority of groups determined the winner. For

35. See Riggsby (1999) 21–49.

the highest offices, voting was done in such a way that the wealthiest men voted first, and thus elections were often decided before the poorer citizens could cast their votes.[36]

Patria Potestas ("Father's Power")

The patriarchal nature of Roman society was codified in law. The *paterfamilias,* or "father of the household," had legal power over his offspring until they were officially "emancipated" and became *sui iuris* ("under their own authority"); this could happen only through the father's death, through a fictitious "sale" to a third party (resembling the sale of slaves), or, for a woman, through a particular kind of marriage (called *manus*) that transferred her to her husband's household. When the *paterfamilias* died, all his male heirs who had not previously been emancipated became *patresfamilias,* regardless of their age. According to the ancient law code known as the "Twelve Tables" (c. 450 B.C.)—which schoolboys had to memorize—fathers had the right of life and death over their children, and there are some famous examples of fathers in the early Republic killing their own sons as punishment. People *in potestate* ("under [the father's] power") could not legally make wills or own property. With their father's permission, they could administer a portion of his goods (called a *peculium*), which in practice often comprised substantial wealth.

The Circulation of Books

As Raymond Starr demonstrates, the circulation of literary texts in the ancient world had little to do with formal "publishing," "bookstores," or "libraries."[37] Authors frequently read their works in progress to one another at dinner parties and other informal gatherings—to which, of course, only friends and social equals would be invited. When a text was sufficiently polished, the author would generally send it to one or two friends for comments; he might then send a revised version to a slightly larger circle, but only to people he knew personally. These friends could then make copies (or allow copies to be made) for their own friends, who might or might not

---

36. On some of the socioeconomic realities of elections in Rome, see Tatum (2003–2004).
37. Starr (1987).

be known to the author; at this point the work could be considered "public," as strangers had access to it. The first public library in Rome was founded in the 30s B.C. Bookstores did exist, but they handled only current works and were patronized only by those who could not obtain texts through private copying. Cicero never mentions going to a bookstore.

Textual Criticism

Since few words from the pens of ancient authors have survived as originally written, a large part of the study of antiquity involves "textual criticism," the art of figuring out what the authors actually wrote and how that text was transmitted.[38] Papyri buried in the dry sands of Egypt preserve a more or less random assortment of ancient documents, many of them in tatters. The earliest surviving manuscripts are copies of copies made hundreds of years after the original, and each stage provided an opportunity for new errors to be introduced. The text of Catullus, for instance, survived antiquity in a single copy (now lost, so that all we have is two copies of that lost copy) from which all our manuscripts derive; these manuscripts are "corrupt" (incorrect or incomplete) in many places, requiring "emendation" (correction based on educated guesswork) by editors. Disagreements abound.[39]

In this volume, <> indicates text to be inserted, {} indicates text to be excised, *** indicates text that is missing or impossibly garbled, and [ ] indicates words not in the Latin but added to the translation for the sake of clarity.

---

38. For the textual history of each Latin author, see Reynolds (1983). For a survey of textual transmission in general, see Reynolds and Wilson (1991).

39. See, for instance, the note on Cat. 1.9 **for its patron's sake**.

Part I

Clodia

Cicero

INTRODUCTION

Why Read Cicero's Letters?

It should be admitted immediately that, of all the sources in this book, Cicero's letters are the toughest nut for modern readers to crack. A line like Catullus' "Let us live, my Lesbia, and let us love" is immediately accessible, at least on the surface; not so a sentence like Cicero's "Let Publius send some men to sign and seal it; I'll swear that our friend Gnaeus, the colleague of Atius Balbus, told me he assisted at the auspices." Because of this kind of frequently recurring opacity, Cicero's letters are usually neglected entirely or excerpted beyond recognition in sourcebooks. Yet they are in some ways the closest thing we have to the "real" voice of a person from the ancient world. Preserved in part by Cicero himself (who kept copies) and in part by their recipients, these letters—especially those to his best friend, Atticus—are our richest cache of day-by-day assessments of the political situation in Rome during the thrilling and tragic days of the late Republic. They also give us a unique insight into the psyche of a man whom many would consider the world's greatest orator, who played an important role in Roman history (even if not quite as important as he himself maintained), and who transmitted to the Middle Ages and beyond the intellectual heritage of the Greco-Roman world.[1] As Shackleton Bailey, Cicero's finest modern editor, observes:

1. In the words of John Henry Cardinal Newman (1999) 253, "Neither Livy, nor Tacitus, nor Terence, nor Seneca, nor Pliny, nor Quintilian, is an adequate spokesman for the Imperial City. They write Latin; Cicero writes Roman."

No other Greek or Roman has projected himself into posterity like Cicero in his extant correspondence. Socrates and Horace have left sharper images; but how much of our Socrates is Plato's artifact, and how much of our Horace is Horace's? No similar suspicion can arise with Cicero, because the letters that reveal him were never meant to become public property—his state of mind if anyone had told him that this would one day happen hardly bears imagination. Nothing comparable has survived out of the classical world: not the "literary" letters of Plato, Seneca, and Pliny; not Fronto's correspondence with imperial pupils or patrons, the prosings of a hypochondriac pedagogue in a dull epoch; not the flotsam of papyrus finds. In Cicero's letters we see a Roman Consular, on any reasonable estimate one of the most remarkable men of his eventful time, without his toga.[2]

The selection given here includes the complete text of all the letters that mention Clodia, with her name in **boldface** for easy reference. None of these letters is specifically *about* Clodia; nevertheless, it is precisely because they are *not* focused on her that they give us some of the most fascinating insights into a woman's role in an ostensibly male world. For instance, in his response to the angry letter by Clodia's husband Metellus, Cicero observes,

> When I'd discovered that the whole intent of [your brother's] tribunate was to scheme and devise mischief against me, I appealed to your wife **Claudia** and your sister Mucia (whose devotion to my cause through my connection with Gnaeus Pompeius I'd seen in many situations) to discourage him from doing me that injury.

---

2. Shackleton Bailey (1971) xi–xii. Of course, Cicero did write some of his letters with his toga on, so to speak; he intended to publish a selection, and just how private any given letter was meant to be is a matter of debate. Stowers (1986) 19 cautions that the difference between "private" and "public" letters is "a distinction more appropriate to modernity than antiquity." Trapp (2003) 14 observes that Cicero "was never truly off duty, as stylist or as self-presenter." Rosenmeyer (2001) 3 calls Cicero's letters "quasi-public compositions, clearly written with a view to eventual publication." Yet although this is an accurate characterization of *some* of the letters, many of them are too candid, too elliptical, and (frankly) too mundane for us to suppose that Cicero intended them for public viewing. See Nicholson (1994) 63 on the "Delivery and Confidentiality of Cicero's Letters": "Though Cicero apparently never resorted to using a cipher as some of his contemporaries did, we often find him using Greek, code-words and nicknames, or carefully veiled language to protect his private correspondence from prying eyes."

What does it say about Cicero, about Clodia (here politely called "Claudia"), and about the potential role of women that he would ask her to intervene in such a delicate political matter? Our modern inclination is to simplify the description of personal relationships among historical figures; we might say, for instance, "Atticus was Cicero's best friend, Clodius was Cicero's worst enemy. Since Clodius and Clodia were close, Clodia must have been Cicero's enemy and the enemy of his enemies." The letters give us a glimpse of a more complex reality: Clodia at a drunken dinner party whispering to Atticus about her brother (who is plotting Cicero's downfall), Atticus hinting at the juicy gossip he's got for Cicero, Cicero dying to hear. . . . The stuff of history, perhaps, but also of Hollywood.

Historical Background

Ever since supporters of the reformer Tiberius Gracchus were clubbed to death in the Forum (133 B.C.), Rome had been torn by various forms of civil unrest, with military power increasingly concentrated in the hands of a few men (such as Marius and Sulla) who turned their armies against Rome itself. Catiline, an impoverished aristocrat, attempted to overthrow the Republic during Cicero's Consulship (63 B.C.); Cicero's speeches against him were responsible for getting five of Catiline's top conspirators executed without trial (Catiline was defeated in battle several months later). The next year, Clodius was accused of infiltrating the all-female rites of the Bona Dea ("Good Goddess") in drag—allegedly to carry on an affair with Caesar's wife—but was acquitted despite Cicero's evidence exploding his alibi. Relations between Cicero and Clodius, which had been characterized by distrust mingled with banter (see *Att.* 2.1.5), became overtly hostile and remained so ever after. With Pompey's help Clodius got himself adopted into a plebeian family and became tribune, thus allowing him to move a bill exiling anyone who had executed Roman citizens without trial. In March 58 B.C. this caused Cicero to flee from Rome. He returned in September 57 B.C., and his speeches in the year that followed (such as the *Pro Caelio*) included virulent attacks on Clodius—and his sister.

Events in the eleven years between the last pre-exile letter and the first post-exile letter given here (February 56 B.C. and May 45 B.C., respectively) brought Cicero much disappointment. When Pompey, Caesar, and Crassus—the so-called First Triumvirate—were reunited at Luca in 56

B.C., Cicero (who, despite his bravado, depended on Pompey's protection) was forced to recant his public criticism of Caesar; he grieved inwardly and turned away from politics. Clodius was murdered by Milo's gangs in 52 B.C., but Cicero's speech in defense of Milo was unsuccessful, apparently because military troops in the Forum intimidated him too much for him to deliver it properly. When open war broke out between Pompey and Caesar, Cicero refused Caesar's overtures and joined Pompey in Greece (49 B.C.); when Pompey was defeated and killed in 48 B.C., Caesar pardoned Cicero, but Cicero never was happy with Caesar's reign. The death of Cicero's daughter Tullia in February of 45 B.C., the greatest grief of his personal life, caused him to throw himself into philosophical writing. After the assassination of Caesar (March 44 B.C.), Cicero returned enthusiastically to politics with his *Philippics,* a long series of speeches attacking Mark Antony and supporting Octavian (later Augustus). But when Antony and Octavian teamed up in 43 B.C. and Antony put Cicero's name on the proscription list, Octavian did not protect him. Antony had the great orator decapitated and pinned his head and hands to the Rostra, a gruesome symbol of the death of the Roman Republic.

CICERO: LETTERS

This letter from Clodia's husband, Quintus Metellus Celer (the only letter in this volume written by someone other than Cicero), shows Celer's anger at Cicero for attacking Celer's brother, Quintus Caecilius Metellus Nepos. Nepos had become tribune on 10 December 63 B.C., five days after the execution of the Catilinarian conspirators (which Cicero had pushed through), and threatened Cicero with prosecution. The Senate passed its "Ultimate Decree" to remove Nepos, but he was reinstated shortly afterward. Celer seems to have written before he had heard of the reinstatement.

Letters to Friends 5.1
from Celer, Cisalpine Gaul, January 62 B.C.

[1] I hope you are well.

I had thought, on the basis of our reciprocal understanding and renewed goodwill, that I would not be made an object of ridicule in my absence, and that my brother Metellus would not have his person and property attacked by you on account of a phrase.[1] If his own propriety was not enough to defend him, either the prestige of our family or my own devotion to you and to the Republic should have been enough to support

---

The notes on Cicero's letters are based upon the commentaries of Shackleton Bailey (1965–70, 1980). Unless otherwise noted, citations of "*SB*" refer to the corresponding place in his commentary.
    1. *Fam.* 5.1.1 **on account of a phrase**: Probably something said during Nepos' *contio* ("public meeting"), in which he attacked Cicero; Cicero counterattacked with his own speech, *Against the Contio of Quintus Metellus*.

him. Now I see that he has been thwarted, and I have been deserted, by those for whom such conduct was least appropriate.

[2] And so I am in mourning and squalor[2]—I who am leading a province, I who am leading an army, I who am waging a war![3] Since you have dealt these things out with neither the reasonableness nor the clemency of our ancestors, it will be no wonder if you regret them. I did not expect you to be of such shifting mind toward me and my family. Meanwhile, neither grief for my family nor injury by any man will drag me away from my public duties.

Cicero's response to the preceding letter seems to have brought about the desired reconciliation with Celer. It is the only passage in Cicero's writings that depicts Clodia in a wholly positive light, as a friend (or at least friendly acquaintance) whom Cicero asks to negotiate on his behalf with her brother-in-law. As such, it gives us a rare glimpse into the sort of informal yet essential role that women could play in the male world of politics.

Letters to Friends 5.2
to Celer, Rome, January or February 62 B.C.
[1] I hope you and the army are well.

You write me that you "had thought, on the basis of our reciprocal understanding and renewed goodwill, that you would never be made an object of ridicule" at my hands. I can't quite figure out what this means. But I suspect it's gotten back to you that, as I was arguing in the Senate that many people were unhappy about my saving the Republic, I said that your relatives, to whom you couldn't say no, had prevailed upon you to keep back the praises of me you had previously decided to proclaim in the Senate. As I was saying this, I added that the duty of preserving the Republic's safety had been divided between us in such a way that I was to defend the City from domestic plots and civil crime, you to defend it from armed enemies and secret conspiracies; and that our alliance in such a great and illustrious cause had been undermined by your relatives, who had feared that, as I had showered you with such abundantly honorific praise, you too might show me some token of our mutual goodwill.

---

2. *Fam.* 5.1.2 **in mourning and squalor**: Relatives of people threatened with public disgrace dressed in mourning garb; compare note on *Cael.* 4 **gloom and squalor of his father**.

3. *Fam.* 5.1.2 **waging a war**: Celer was currently in command of one of the two armies opposing Catiline.

[2] As I was talking in this vein, revealing what my eager expectation of your speech had been and how utterly wrong I was, my speech struck some people as funny, and it raised a few laughs—not at you, but at my mistake, and because I was confessing so openly and sincerely how much I longed for your praise. Now, this can hardly be construed as anything but a compliment to you, that even in my most stunning triumph I should feel the need of some commendation from your lips.

[3] As for "our reciprocal understanding," I don't know what you'd say "reciprocal" means in friendship; for my part, I'd say it means when equal goodwill is received and given. If I were to say I'd renounced a province[4] for you, you'd undoubtedly think me a bit disingenuous; my own reasons led me to this decision, and it brings me greater pleasure and reward daily. But I will say this, that as soon as I'd renounced the province at the public meeting, I began at once to plan how to hand it over to you. I say nothing about your lottery;[5] I only want you to imagine that nothing here was done by my colleague without my knowledge. Remember, further, how quickly I convened the Senate that day after the lots had been assigned, and how much I said about you: you yourself told me my speech had been not only a compliment to you, but even an insult to your colleagues!

[4] Now, the preamble of the decree the Senate passed that day is such that, while it exists, my friendly service to you can't be in the dark. And later, after you had set out, I'd like you to remember what I did for you in the Senate, what I said at public meetings, what letters I sent you. I'd like you to judge for yourself whether your recent arrival in Rome offered a "reciprocal" response to all these things put together.

[5] As for "our renewed goodwill," I don't see how you can say something is "renewed" that has never been diminished.

[6] As for "it is not appropriate for Metellus, my brother, to be attacked by you because of a phrase," I'd like you to realize, first, that I strongly approve of your sentiment and your brotherly feeling, full of humanity and loyalty; second, that if I oppose your brother in anything for the sake

---

4. *Fam.* 5.2.3 **renounced a province**: Consuls and praetors generally became governors of provinces after their terms expired. *SB* (1980) notes that Cicero's decision not to do so "may have been one of the worst mistakes of his career."

5. *Fam.* 5.2.3 **lottery**: The praetors drew lots to determine which province each would receive; the presiding consul (here Gaius Antonius, Cicero's "colleague") apparently had some way of stacking the cards.

of the Republic, you must forgive me (for I am a friend of the Republic second to none). But if I've defended my own safety against his extremely cruel attack on me, you should be content that *I* have not complained to *you* about the injury done me by your brother. When I'd discovered that the whole intent of his tribunate was to scheme and devise mischief against me, I appealed to your wife **Claudia**[6] and your sister Mucia (whose devotion to my cause through my connection with Gnaeus Pompeius I'd seen in many situations) to discourage him from doing me that injury.

[7] And yet that man—as I'm sure you've heard—on December 31 inflicted upon me, the consul and the savior of the Republic, an injury greater than any that has been inflicted on the most wicked citizen holding the lowest office in the State: he deprived me of the right to hold a public meeting as I was leaving office. This injury, however, brought me the greatest honor; for when he allowed me nothing except to swear an oath, I swore in a loud voice an oath most true and beautiful[7]—and the people in an equally loud voice swore that I had sworn it truly.

[8] Though I'd received such an egregious injury, yet that same day I dispatched some common friends to Metellus to beg him to abandon his plan. He answered them that in his mind the matter was closed; and in fact, shortly before, he'd said at a public meeting that one who had inflicted capital punishment on others without a hearing[8] ought to be denied the right

---

6. *Fam.* 5.2.6 **Claudia**: An alternate spelling of Clodia. The implications of this alternation are a subject of unresolved scholarly debate. The following facts are fairly certain: (1) "o" for "au" was a variation characteristic of the Umbrian dialect and gave words a rustic, nonelite flavor; (2) the fact that Clodius and Clodia both adopted this spelling indicates their closeness; (3) both patrician and plebeian branches of the family used "Claudius"; (4) the spelling "Clodius" predates Clodius' adoption into a plebeian family in 59 B.C. Riggsby (2002a) attributes the spelling to Clodius' wish to curry favor with the populace by using a nonelite form; Tatum (1999) 247–48 speculates that Clodia's "faddism" was responsible. In any event it is notable that Cicero, in writing to the husband of Clodia/Claudia, tactfully chooses the spelling that recalls her distinguished ancestry rather than her fashionable slumming or her brother's revolutionary leanings.

7. *Fam.* 5.2.6 **an oath most true and beautiful**: As *SB* (1980) notes, "Nepos and another Tribune used their constitutional power of 'blocking' (*intercessio*) to stop Cicero addressing a public meeting after laying down his office as Consul. They would only allow him to take the customary oath—that as a magistrate he had done nothing against the law. Cicero turned the tables by changing the usual form of the oath and swearing that he and he alone had saved the state and the City. He was fond of recalling this incident in after years."

8. *Fam.* 5.2.8 **inflicted capital punishment on others without a hearing**: Cicero maintained until the end that he had done the right thing in having Catiline's co-conspirators executed without trial (63 B.C.), claiming that by making war on the State they had relinquished their rights as Roman citizens, who were entitled to due process. Clodius would soon have Cicero exiled (March 58 B.C.) on the basis of this allegedly illegal action.

to speak himself. What a worthy human being and outstanding citizen, opining that the punishment decreed by the Senate with the consensus of all good men for those who wanted to burn the City, slaughter the magistrates and the Senate, and ignite the most terrible war—that this punishment was right for the man who freed the Senate from slaughter, the City from flames, Italy from war! And so I stood up to Metellus, your brother, in person. For on January 1 I argued with him in the Senate about the Republic in such a way that he could tell he had a strong and stubborn man to contend with. On January 3, when he began to develop his proposal [to recall Pompey], with every other word of his speech he challenged me, threatened me; and his greatest scheme was to get rid of me in any way he could, not by legal procedure but by violent assault. If I hadn't resisted this attack of his with courage and spirit, who wouldn't have thought my strength during my consulate came from chance rather than wisdom?

[9] If you were unaware that Metellus was scheming against me, then you should realize that your brother has been concealing extremely important affairs from you; if, on the other hand, he let you in on his plan at all, you should consider me quite gentle and easygoing for not complaining to you about these same affairs. And if you now understand that I've been moved to action not by Metellus's "phrase," as you say, but by his deliberate, scheming hostility, please also recognize my humanity—if "humanity" is the word for laxity and weakness of spirit in the face of bitterest injury! I never spoke a word in the Senate against your brother; whenever some proposal was made, I kept my seat and assented to whoever seemed to me to take the most lenient position. I'll say this too, that although I shouldn't at that point have lifted a finger, yet I endured without ill will—and even for my part helped bring about—that my personal enemy, because he was your brother, should by decree of the Senate be released from penalties.

[10] Therefore, I did not *fight* against your brother, I *fought back* against your brother; nor, as you say, was I of "shifting mind" toward you, but rather of such constant mind that I remained firm in my goodwill toward you even when I no longer received your favors. And at this very moment, in response to your letter, which is practically an open threat against me, I reply: Not only do I forgive your grief, but I even give you the highest praise (for my own sensibility reminds me how great is the strength of brotherly love); I beg you, too, to be a fair-minded judge of my own grief; and, if I have been attacked by your relatives bitterly, cruelly, and without

cause, to recognize that I should not only have refused to yield, but even have employed your help and that of your army in such a serious cause.

I've always wanted you to have friendly feelings toward me, and I've always tried to make you understand that I have the friendliest feelings toward you. I stand fast and, if you'll let me, shall keep standing fast in my goodwill; and I'd rather cease hostilities with your brother through my love for you than see our friendship cool in any way because of my hostility toward him.

Written over a year after the Bona Dea trial, this letter shows a phase in Cicero's relationship with Clodius characterized by barbed witticisms: Clodius is a "boor" who must be "taught to behave" but not yet the deadly enemy he would soon become. It is also the first appearance of the slur about incest with Clodia.

Letters to Atticus 2.1 (*SB* 21)
Antium (?), c. June 3 (?) 60 B.C.

[1] As I was going to Antium on June 1, eager to leave Marcus Metellus' gladiators behind, your boy intercepted me. He gave me a letter from you and a sketch of my "Consulship" in Greek. I was happy that, some time before, I'd given Lucius Cossinius a book on the same topic, likewise in Greek, to pass on to you; for if I'd read yours first, you would say I'd plagiarized from you. Although those verses of yours (for I was glad to read them) struck me as a bit shaggy and unkempt, nevertheless they were adorned by the very fact that they had neglected all ornament, and, like women, seemed to smell good precisely because they didn't smell at all. My book, on the other hand, soaked up the whole box of Isocratean perfume, plus the little boxes of his disciples, and even a good deal of Aristotelian rouge.[9] You skimmed it at Corcyra, as you indicate to me in another letter, but afterward, I suppose, you received it from Cossinius.

---

9. *Att.* 2.1.1 **Isocratean perfume . . . Aristotelian rouge**: As *SB* (1965) notes, Isocrates and Aristotle represented "the two main traditions of rhetorical study as opposed to hack teaching." Cicero also wrote Latin verse on the subject of his own consulship, with regard to which the poet Juvenal, quoting one of Cicero's infamous lines, made the following observation:

> Because of his genius his hand and neck were severed, nor have
> puny pleaders ever stained the Rostra with blood.
> "Oh Rome, so fortunate to be born when I was consul!"
> He could have scorned the swords of Antony, if he had
> always spoken that way. (*Satire* 10.120–24)

[2] I wouldn't have dared to send it to you if I hadn't scrutinized it slowly and scrupulously. Though Posidonius wrote me back from Rhodes that when he read my little memoir, which I had sent him so he could write more ornately on the same topic, not only was he not spurred on to write, he was positively scared away! What more can I say? I've confounded the Greek nation. Those who were pressing me on all sides to give them something to adorn have now stopped pestering me. If you like the book, you'll make sure it appears in Athens and the other towns of Greece. For it seems it could shine some light on my achievements.

[3] I'll also send you my little speeches, both the ones you ask for and more besides, since you too enjoy what I write spurred on by the enthusiasm of my young fans. Seeing how in those speeches called "Philippics" that compatriot of yours, Demosthenes, shone brilliantly, and how he distanced himself from that pugnacious, forensic speaking style in order to appear more august and statesmanlike, I decided it would be to my advantage to make sure I too had some speeches that could be called "Consular."[10] Of these, (1) is in the Senate on January 1, (2)[11] to the people about the Agrarian Law, (3) on Otho,[12] (4) in defense of Rabirius,[13] (5) on the children of proscribed persons,[14] (6) when I resigned my province in public assembly,[15] (7) when I sent Catiline away,[16] (8) when I addressed the people the day after Catiline fled, (9) in the public assembly the day the Allobroges informed on

Less flamboyant but equally damning is the assessment of Cicero's poetry put forth by *SB* (1971) ix: "not much survives, but enough."

10. *Att.* 2.1.3 **some speeches that could be called "Consular"**: As Cape (2002) 119 notes, "Cicero's selection of a few of his own speeches as a coherent and aesthetic unity is the first evidence we have for such a phenomenon in antiquity."

11. *Att.* 2.1.3 **(1) . . . (2)**: When Publius Servilius Rullus (tribune 63 B.C.) introduced a bill (supported by Crassus and Caesar) to redistribute public land in Rome and the provinces, "Cicero, presenting himself as a *popularis* (see OPTIMATES) and as defending Pompey's interests, secured the withdrawal of the bill by his (largely extant) speeches *De lege agraria* ["On the Agrarian Law"]" (*OCD*).

12. *Att.* 2.1.3 **on Otho**: Lucius Roscius Otho (tribune 67 B.C.) carried a law assigning the first fourteen rows in the Theater to knights; when the general public hissed him during his praetorship in 63 B.C., Cicero wrote a speech defending him (only a fragment survives).

13. *Att.* 2.1.3 **Rabirius**: Rabirius had been accused of treason (*perduellio*).

14. *Att.* 2.1.3 **on the children of proscribed persons**: "In opposition to a tribunician proposal inspired by Caesar for the removal of the political disabilities imposed by Sulla on the children of his victims" (*SB* [1965]). Nothing of this speech survives.

15. *Att.* 2.1.3 **when I resigned my province in public assembly**: See note on *Fam.* 5.2.3 **renounced a province**. Nothing of this speech survives.

16. *Att.* 2.1.3 **when I sent Catiline away**: This and the next three speeches constitute the four surviving "Catilinarians."

him, (10) in the Senate on December 5. There are also two short ones, fragments, so to speak, of the ones on the Agrarian Law. I'll make sure you have this whole corpus. And since you enjoy both my writings and my doings, from the same books you'll see both what I've done and what I've said—or else you shouldn't have asked! I wasn't forcing myself on you.

[4] You ask why it is I'm summoning you, and at the same time you suggest that you're tied up with business—though you don't refuse to come running, not only if I need you but even if I just want you. To be honest, there's no real need, but still, it seems to me you could have arranged your travel times more conveniently. You're gone too long, especially since you're really quite close, but I'm not enjoying your company and you're missing mine! And of course everything's quiet right now, but if Little Beauty's[17] insanity were able to progress a little further, I'd surely be fetching you from there. However, Metellus[18] is holding him back brilliantly, and will continue to hold him back. What more can I say? He's a patriotic consul and, as I've always maintained, a good man by nature.

[5] He [Clodius], on the other hand, is not pretending, but really wants to become a tribune of the people.[19] When this issue was being handled in the Senate, I crushed the man and rebuked his fickleness for seeking a tribunate in Rome when he had repeatedly said he was seeking an inheritance in Sicily. And I said we really didn't have to trouble ourselves, since he'd have no more chance of wrecking the Republic as a plebeian than his kindred spirits among the patricians had when I was consul. Now, when he said that he had come on the seventh day from the Straits and that no one had been able to greet him and that he had entered by night, and he flaunted this in the public assembly, I said that this was nothing new for him. From Sicily to Rome in a week: but from Rome to Interamna in three hours.[20] Entry by

17. *Att.* 2.1.4 **Little Beauty's**: Latin *Pulchellus*, a contemptuous diminutive of Pulcher ("Beautiful"), the *cognomen* of Clodius.

18. *Att.* 2.1.4 **Metellus**: Clodia's husband. Although Metellus had at first reluctantly supported his brother-in-law Clodius' scheme to become tribune, by this point he had turned against it.

19. *Att.* 2.1.5 **to become a tribune of the people**: See introduction, "Patricians and Plebeians." Clodius tried by various means for a "transfer to the *plebs*" (*transitio ad plebem*) in order to become tribune. The Senate debate Cicero refers to probably concerns whether Clodius' *sacrorum detestatio*, or "abjuration of [his family's] sacred rites," was sufficient to establish this transfer. See Tatum (1999) 96–102.

20. *Att.* 2.1.5 **from Rome to Interamna in three hours**: Cicero testified that he saw Clodius in Rome the evening of the Bona Dea incident; Clodius claimed that he was at Interamna (about forty miles from Rome) at the time.

night: same as before. "No one came in your way: not at that time, either,
when it was most crucial for someone to get in your way." What more can I
say? I'm making this boor behave, not only through the constant gravity of
my orations, but also through this sort of witticism. And so now even with
the man himself I trade banter and jokes. Yes, when we were introducing a
candidate to the Forum, he asks me whether I'd been in the habit of giving a
place to the Sicilians[21] at the gladiatorial shows. I said No. He said, "Yet I,
as their new patron,[22] shall institute that practice. But **my sister**, who has so
much consular space,[23] gives me just one foot." "Don't complain about one
foot[24] from your sister," I said; "you can always hoist the other one!" You'll
say, "Not a very consular witticism": I confess it. But I really can't stand
that consular woman: "for she is mutinous, she wages war with her man,"[25]
and not only with Metellus but also with Fabius,[26] because he's annoyed at
their worthlessness.[27]

[6] You mention the Agrarian Law; it really seems to have cooled down.
As for your reproaching me "with gentle arm" about my friendship with
Pompey, I wouldn't want you to think I've joined up with him for my own
safety's sake; but things had fallen out in such a way that if there were any
dissension between us, there would necessarily have been tremendous dis-
cord in the Republic. I'd foreseen and taken precautions against this, not by
departing from that excellent conduct of mine, but by his becoming better
and casting aside some of his crowd-pleasing frivolity. And know that he
proclaims more glorious praise of my deeds—which many had encouraged
him to attack—than of his own; for he testifies that the Republic was well

21. *Att.* 2.1.5 **giving a place to the Sicilians**: Cicero was the quaestor in charge of Sicily in
75 B.C., Clodius in 61 B.C. (after his acquittal in the Bona Dea incident). The seating at gladiatorial
shows was carefully segregated by rank (and gender), reinforcing the social hierarchy.

22. *Att.* 2.1.5 **new patron**: As *SB* (1965) notes, "at least in his own estimation"; this is the sort
of conceited remark Cicero made a career of deflating.

23. *Att.* 2.1.5 **consular space**: As consul, Clodia's husband would have seating at his disposal;
that this space is referred to as belonging to *Clodia* tells us something about the distribution of
power in their relationship.

24. *Att.* 2.1.5 **one foot**: In English as in Latin, "foot" is both a unit of measurement and a body
part, thus setting up one of Cicero's innumerable jokes about incest between Clodius and Clodia.

25. *Att.* 2.1.5 **"for she is mutinous, she wages war with her man"**: This appears to be a line
from a (lost) Roman comedy. On the importance of comedy in Cicero's treatment of Clodia, see
note on *Cael.* 1 **public festivals and games**.

26. Att. 2.1.5 **Fabius**: Fabius must have been Clodia's lover; possibly he is Quintus Fabius
(Maximus) Sanga, who helped reveal the plans of the Catilinarians to Cicero.

27. *Att.* 2.1.5 **their worthlessness**: That is, the worthlessness of Clodius and Clodia.

served by him, but preserved by me. I don't know what advantage I get from his saying this; but surely there's great advantage for the Republic. What if I make even Caesar, who's enjoying quite favorable winds right now, a better man? I suppose I'm doing great harm to the Republic?

[7] Why, even if no one bore me ill will, and if all were on my side (as they should have been), still, the medicine that healed the corrupted parts of the Republic should have been no less worthy of praise than that which amputated them. But now, seeing as the knights I'd stationed on the Capitol Rise[28] with you as their standard-bearer and leader have deserted the Senate, while the leaders of our order think they're reaching out and touching heaven if the bearded mullets in their fishponds[29] eat out of their hands, while they ignore everything else—doesn't it seem to you that I'm doing enough good if I make sure those capable of doing harm choose not to?

[8] I love our Cato just as much as you do; but still, even with his excellent soul and his outstanding integrity, he sometimes does harm to the Republic. For he pronounces his opinions as if he were in the Republic of Plato,[30] not the Sewer of Romulus. What could be more just than for jurors to be prosecuted for taking bribes? Cato made this motion and the Senate agreed. So knights are at war with the Senate (not with me, since I dissented). What could be more irresponsible than tax farmers[31] defaulting on their contracts? And yet, to retain the loyalty of that order, it was worth the loss. Cato opposed this and won. And so now, with a consul locked in prison[32] and one riot after another, not one of those men whose joined forces I and all consuls after me used to count on to defend the Republic

28. *Att.* 2.1.7 **knights I'd stationed on the Capitol Rise**: During the exposition of the Catilinarian conspiracy, the knights gathered on the road from the Forum to the Capitoline Hill, where the Senate was meeting, to protect the senators.

29. *Att.* 2.1.7 **bearded mullets in their fishponds**: Both Cicero and Clodius make fun of the upper class's passion for pisciculture (see note on 2.9.1 **"Those Tritons of the Fishponds"**). See Syme (1939) 23: "Secluded like indolent monsters in their parks and villas, the great *piscinarii* ['fishpond fanciers'], Hortensius and the two Luculli, pondered at ease upon the quiet doctrines of Epicurus and confirmed from their own careers the folly of ambition, the vanity of virtue." Griffin (1985) 7 observes that these fishponds became a "symbol for Rome of plutocratic inertia." For further references, see Holland (2003) 175–85, "Shadows in the Fishpond," and D'Arms (1970) 40–42.

30. *Att.* 2.1.8 **Republic of Plato**: Plato's *Republic* (fourth century B.C.) depicts an ideal totalitarian state run by perfectly wise philosopher-kings.

31. *Att.* 2.1.8 **tax farmers**: Latin *publicani* (our "publicans") would essentially purchase from the state the right to extract taxes from the provinces; they would realize as profit whatever exceeded the amount they promised the state. They were little loved.

32. *Att.* 2.1.8 **a consul locked in prison**: Metellus (Clodia's husband) had been sent to prison for obstructing the Agrarian Law.

has lifted a finger. You'll ask, "What are you saying? Are we to keep these men on as mercenaries?" What else can we do, if it's impossible otherwise? Or should we be slaves to our own freedman and slaves? But, as you would say, enough angst.

[9] Favonius carried my tribe[33] more handsomely than his own but lost Lucceius' tribe. He prosecuted Nasica unhandsomely, and nastily at that; from his speech it seemed that at Rhodes he'd thrown his effort into the mills, not Molo.[34] He was slightly annoyed with me for taking the defense. But now he's running for office again, for the sake of the Republic. I'll write you about what Lucceius is doing when I see Caesar; he'll be here in two days.

[10] As for the harm the Sicyonians are doing you,[35] you can chalk that up to Cato and his emulator Servilius. What do you expect? Doesn't that blow fall upon many good men? But if such was their pleasure, let's applaud, and then be left all to ourselves when the quarrels begin.

[11] My Amalthea[36] waits for you and needs you. I'm really happy with my properties at Tusculum and Pompeii, except that they've buried me— yes me, the avenger of *aes alienum*[37]—not in Corinthian bronze but in that vulgar kind. We hope all's quiet in Gaul. Expect my "Weather Signs"[38] along with my little speeches any day now, but still, write me your thoughts about when you'll return. For Pomponia had word sent me that you'd be in Rome in the month of Quintilis. That didn't agree with the letter you'd sent me about your census.[39]

33. *Att.* 2.1.9 **tribe**: The electorate was divided into thirty-five "tribes," with the majority within each tribe determining its vote.

34. *Att.* 2.1.9 **the mills, not Molo**: Molo was a highly regarded teacher of rhetoric in Rhodes; "mills" in Latin is *moli.*

35. *Att.* 2.1.10 **the harm the Sicyonians are doing you**: Atticus, a prosperous businessman, was involved in some financial transactions with the people of Sicyon (a Greek city in heavy debt to Rome); at Cato's prompting, Servilius introduced a decree that helped the Sicyonians at the expense of Roman knights. See *SB* (1965) on *Att.* 1.13.1, 1.19.9.

36. *Att.* 2.1.11 **Amalthea**: Atticus had a shrine of Amalthea (a nymph who nursed the infant Zeus) on his estate; Cicero wanted to create a similar one on his own estate at Arpinum, and had asked Atticus for architectural and mythological details (*Att.* 1.16.18).

37. *Att.* 2.1.11 **aes alienum**: The Latin phrase for "debt," meaning literally, "bronze [money] belonging to another." "Corinthian bronze" refers to statues (such as wealthy Romans would like to show off in their homes).

38. *Att.* 2.1.11 **"Weather Signs"**: Cicero in his youth did a Latin translation of part of the famous poem by Aratus (*Phaenomena*) on astronomy and weather.

39. *Att.* 2.1.11 **your census**: This has something to do with Atticus' being present in order to be enrolled on the list of citizens, though it could sometimes be done through representatives (why Atticus had to be present himself is not entirely clear).

[12] Paetus, as I wrote you before, donated to me all the books his brother had left him. This gift from him now depends on your attention. If you love me, make sure they're preserved and sent along to me. Nothing could please me more than this. I'd like you to preserve carefully not just the Greek ones, but the Latin ones too. Then I'll feel this little gift is truly yours.

I sent a letter to Octavius. I hadn't spoken with him at all in person; for I didn't think that that business of yours was a province matter, nor did I reckon you among the usurers. But I wrote, as I ought, attentively.

In the following three letters to Atticus, we see Cicero's increasing fear for his position (and the Republic) now that Clodius has been adopted into a plebeian family and is thus eligible to become tribune. Clodia—who, despite her enmity with Cicero, remained friends with Atticus—appears not only as a source of sensitive information, but as the "bugle blower" for her brother (i.e., leading the charge in what Cicero would characterize as Clodius' attacks on the Republic).

Letters to Atticus 2.9 (*SB* 29)
Antium, 16 or 17 (?) April 59 B.C.

[1] Since Quaestor Caecilius had suddenly told me he was sending a boy to Rome, I wrote this quickly in order to *** <thank you for> your wonderful conversations with Publius, both the ones you write about and the one you hide and say it's too long to set down all the responses you had to it. But as for the one that hasn't yet taken place, which the infamous **Ox-Eyes**[40] is going to report to you[41] when she gets back from Solonium—please realize I'm so eager for that one that nothing could please me more! However, if such agreements as have been made concerning myself are not honored, I'm on cloud nine, as long as our dear Jerusalemarian bestower of plebeian status[42] finds out what fine recompense he's made for those stinking speeches

40. *Att.* 2.9.1 **Ox-Eyes**: Cicero's favorite nickname for Clodia. The word, which Cicero usually writes in Greek, is an epithet of Hera in Homer's *Iliad*. (It designates large, beautiful eyes, not a bovine insult.) It was appropriate (in Cicero's view) for Clodia because, like Hera, she had striking eyes, was involved in an incestuous relationship with her brother (Hera and her husband Zeus were siblings), and henpecked her husband. See Griffith (1996) 381–82.

41. *Att.* 2.9.1 **report to you**: As *SB* (1965) notes, "It looks as though Atticus and Clodius conducted their 'dialogues' only or mainly through her as go-between."

42. *Att.* 2.9.1 **Jerusalemarian bestower of plebeian status**: Pompey, who had captured Jerusalem in 63 B.C. Plebeian status allowed Clodius to become a tribune; see introduction, "Patricians and Plebeians."

of mine. Look out for a magnificent palinode![43] And in fact, so far as I can prophesy by guesswork, if that scoundrel is to be in favor with these ruling powers, he's not going to be able to puff himself up with either "The Canine Consular"[44] or "Those Tritons of the Fishponds."[45] For we can't possibly be unpopular if we're stripped of resources and that "senatorial sway."[46] But if he has a break with them, it'll be ridiculous for him to rail against us. But let him rail. Very prettily, believe me, and with less noise than I'd thought, this political wheel has come full circle[47] much faster than seemed possible. This is Cato's fault, but it's also through the sleaziness of those who ignored the auspices,[48] the Lex Aelia, and the Junia-Licinia, and the Caecilia-Didia;[49] who threw out all remedies for the Republic; who have bestowed kingdoms on tetrarchs like private estates, gobs of money on a handful of men.

[2] I now see which way the wind of ill will is blowing and where it's going to settle. You may conclude that I learned nothing either from experience or from Theophrastus[50] if you don't see longing for that era of mine

43. *Att.* 2.9.1 **palinode**: That is, a recantation of previous praise of Pompey. *SB* (1965) notes, "Once again C. tries to blind himself to the mortifying truth, that his security really depended upon Caesar's forbearance and Pompey's protection."

44. *Att.* 2.9.1 **"The Canine Consular"**: Clodius' scornful nickname for Cicero. "Canine" translates Latin *cynicus*. "Cynic" (the name of a Greek philosophical school) is derived from the Greek word for "dog"; the implication of the nickname here (apparently) is that Cicero's rhetoric was biting, sycophantic, and shameless.

45. *Att.* 2.9.1 **"Those Tritons of the Fishponds"**: Another coinage by Clodius (it seems), referring to the upper classes (see note on *Att.* 2.1.7 **bearded mullets in their fishponds**).

46. *Att.* 2.9.1 **"senatorial sway"**: As in the previous sentence, Cicero appears to be quoting scornful sobriquets from the opposition.

47. *Att.* 2.9.1 **political wheel has come full circle**: *SB* (1965) interprets, "Time was when the Senate stood firm, based on the *concordia ordinum* ["harmony among the social classes"]. Then the alienation of the *equites* led to the collapse of its authority. Now it is back in favour. The first half of the revolution (the speed of it anyhow) was Cato's fault, the second can be put down to the misdeeds of the dynasts. Such is the sense, but the metaphor . . . will not stand too much pressure. The power of the Senate had not been restored, and as for popularity, the masses, who (allegedly) hated the 'Triumvirs' now, had not loved the Senate in 61."

48. *Att.* 2.9.1 **ignored the auspices**: Before important undertakings, Romans took a reading on the gods' attitude by having "augurs" (one of many classes of religious official) observe the behavior of birds in various quarters of the sky—a complex psuedoscience. The tribune Vatinius had willfully ignored the auspices in the matter of Clodius' adoption, among other things.

49. *Att.* 2.9.1 **Lex Aelia . . . Caecilia-Didia**: Caesar and Vatinius had disregarded these laws when summoning the assembly to ratify Clodius' adoption.

50. *Att.* 2.9.2 **Theophrastus**: This successor of Aristotle wrote extensively on political topics and in particular on how policies needed to be manipulated to suit changing times (see Cicero, *De Finibus*, 5.11).

soon. Indeed, if the Senate's power was a cause of ill will, what do you think will happen when that power has been transferred, not to the people, but to three exorbitant men?[51] So let them make whomever they want consuls and tribunes of the people—let them even wrap Vatinius' scrofula[52] in a priest's double-dyed toga; you'll soon see not only those who never stumbled become heroes, but even Cato, the very one who blundered.

[3] As for me, if your pal Publius will allow it, I'm planning to sophisticize; if he forces me, then I'll just defend myself, and, as befits the sophistic art, I profess "to ward off the man who is the first to attack."[53] May the fatherland be with me! It's gotten from me, if not more than it was owed, at least more than it demanded. I'd really rather be a passenger on someone else's ship than a fine captain with such ungrateful passengers. But this more easily in person.

[4] Now to answer your question. I'm planning to return to Antium from Formiae on May 3. From Antium I want to set out for Tusculum on May 7. But when I get back from Formiae (I want to be there until April

---

51. *Att.* 2.9.2 **three exorbitant men**: In 60 B.C. Caesar, Pompey, and Crassus had formed what is called the First Triumvirate ("Group of Three Men"), though this alliance had no official legal status. Cicero had been invited to join in as the group was being formed; he was tempted, but declined. He describes his response to overtures by Cornelius Balbus, one of Caesar's intimates (*Att.* 2.3.3 = *SB* 23, December 60 B.C.):

> He assured me that Caesar would follow my and Pompey's advice in all things and that he would make an effort to unite Crassus with Pompey. Here's the plus side: the greatest intimacy with Pompey—with Caesar too, if I want it; a return to grace with my personal enemies; peace with the multitude; leisure in my old age. But I'm moved by that finale of mine in the third book [of the poem on his consulship: see note on *Att.* 2.1.1 **Isocratean perfume . . . Aristotelian rouge**]:
>
>> "Meanwhile the course that from the very first in your youth,
>> the one you sought with virtue and spirit when you were consul—
>> stay that course and increase your fame and the praise of good men."
>
> Since Calliope herself has prescribed these things to me in that book containing many aristocratic sentiments, I don't think I can hesitate to make this my motto: "The one best bird-sign is to fight for the fatherland" [*Iliad* 12.243, a famous statement by Hector—the Trojan hero who, in his courage, ignored unfavorable bird-signs and lost the war].

52. *Att.* 2.9.2 **Vatinius' scrofula**: On the continual references by Vatinius' opponents to his *strumae* ("glandular swellings of pus and blood"), see Corbeill (1996) 45–56. The Romans considered physical deformities as prima facie evidence of moral failings.

53. *Att.* 2.9.3 **"to ward off the man who is the first to attack"**: *Iliad* 24.369. The Sophists (an intellectual movement popular in late fifth–century Athens) answered questions but did not initiate arguments.

29), I'll let you know right away. Terentia sends you her greetings and "Cicero the Small salutes Titus the Athenian."[54]

Letters to Atticus 2.12 (*SB* 30)
Tres Tabernae, 19 April 59 B.C.

[1] So they'd deny that Publius has been made a plebeian?[55] Really, this is tyranny, and absolutely not to be put up with! Let Publius send me some men to sign and seal it; I'll swear that our friend Gnaeus, the colleague of Atius Balbus,[56] told me he assisted at the auspices. Oh, sweet letters of yours, given to me both at once! I have no idea what glad tidings I can give in return, though I certainly confess they're owed you.

[2] But look at this coincidence. I'd just come out from the Antium district onto the Appian Way at Three Taverns, on the very Festival of Ceres, when my friend Curio runs into me on his way from Rome. Right then and there, your boy arrives with the letters. Curio asked me whether I'd heard anything new. I said "No." He says, "Publius is running for tribune of the people." "What are you saying?" "Yes, and as Caesar's arch-enemy," he says, "and so he can get rid of all those laws." "What about Caesar?" says I. "He says he had nothing to do with his [Clodius'] adoption." Then he declared his own hatred and that of Memmius and Metellus Nepos. I embraced the youth and sent him off and rushed to the letters. What are they talking about with this "living voice"? I saw so much better what was really going on from your letters than from his conversation—about the

54. *Att.* 2.9.4 **"Cicero the Small salutes Titus the Athenian"**: These words, in Greek, were probably written by Cicero's son. "Titus" was Atticus' *praenomen*; "Atticus" is a *cognomen* meaning "living in Athens" ("Attica" is the region in which Athens lies).

55. *Att.* 2.12.1 **So they'd deny . . . plebeian**: Atticus had reported that Caesar and Pompey were threatening to declare Clodius' adoption illegal. Cicero's tone here is, of course, ironic. After his exile he attempted, unsuccessfully, to make the case that Clodius' adoption had in fact been illegal and that therefore his tribunate was invalid: see Tatum (1999) 105.

56. *Att.* 2.12.1 **our friend Gnaeus, the colleague of Atius Balbus**: The precise point of this sarcastic reference is difficult to pin down: see *SB* (1965). As we know from Suetonius (*Augustus* 4), Balbus was the grandfather of Augustus, was related on his mother's side to the family of Pompey ("our friend Gnaeus" here), and sat on the Board of Twenty (*Vigintiviri*) set up by Caesar in connection with the Agrarian Law. *SB* conjectures that Balbus "was the 'triumviral' choice for the vacant Augurate [a quasi-political priesthood]. . . . His close family ties with Pompey and Caesar would more than atone for absence of *nobilitas*, when even such a parvenu as Vatinius could be seriously considered; on the other hand its lack would give point to C.'s sneer; Atius Balbus might be a suitable Vigintivir, but for the Augural College he was socially well below standard."

daily gossip-gathering, about Publius' ruminations, about **Ox-Eyes'** bugle,[57] about Athenio the standard-bearer,[58] about the letter sent to Gnaeus, about Theophanes' and Memmius' talk! And more, how much you excite me about that lascivious dinner party! I'm ravenous with curiosity, but still, I'll happily allow you not to write me about that symposium; I'd rather hear it in person.

[3] As for your urging me to write something, my material grows daily, as you say, but even now the whole thing is in ferment, raw wine in autumn. Once it settles down, what I write will be more clarified. If you can't get it from me right away, still, you'll be the first to have it, and for a while the only one.

[4] You're right to like Dicaearchus.[59] He's a splendid fellow, and a much better citizen than those unjust rulers of ours.

I wrote this letter at four o'clock on Ceres' Day, just as soon as I'd read yours, but I thought I was going to give it the next day to whoever came my way. Terentia enjoyed your letter. She wishes you all the best, and "Cicero the Philosopher sends greetings to Titus the Politician."[60]

Letters to Atticus 2.14 (*SB* 34)
Rome, c. 26 April 59 B.C.

[1] What longing you arouse in me to hear about the conversation with Bibulus, about the chat with **Ox-Eyes**, about that luscious dinner party as well! So please hurry and quench my thirsty ears, though I think we have nothing more to fear than that our dear friend Sampsiceramus[61] may run amuck when he senses that he's getting a lashing from every man's tongue

57. *Att.* 2.12.2 **Ox-Eyes' bugle**: Clodia is humorously depicted as blowing the *lituus* or war trumpet to sound the charge for her brother's "army." Such symbolism is applied to women rarely, to say the least.

58. *Att.* 2.12.2 **Athenio the standard-bearer**: Athenio was the leader of the Sicilian slave revolt of 104–100 B.C. Cicero is insinuating that Clodius' following consisted largely of slaves; his lieutenant Sextus Cloelius, who is probably the one nicknamed "Athenio" here, may also have borne the family *cognomen* Siculus or "Sicilian." As *SB* (1965) notes, "According to C. his relations with Clodia . . . were even less respectable than her brother's"; see *Dom.* 25.

59. *Att.* 2.12.4 **Dicaearchus**: A student of Aristotle, Dicaearchus wrote on a variety of topics (politics, philosophy, literature, geography, etc.) and was a favorite with Atticus. "Dicaearchus" means "just ruler."

60. *Att.* 2.12.4 **"Cicero the Philosopher sends greetings to Titus the Politician"**: Like the end of the previous letter, this tag was written in Greek, presumably by Marcus Cicero (Cicero's son).

61. *Att.* 2.14.1 **Sampsiceramus**: A ruler in Syria whom Pompey had confirmed as such, "Sampsiceramus" becomes Cicero's nickname for Pompey.

and sees that these proceedings are easy to overturn.[62] For my part, I'm so washed out that I'd rather be tyrannized over in this leisure[63] we're rotting away in than fight with the most supreme hope.

[2] As for that composition you're always urging me to do, it's hopeless. I have a chamber of commerce here, not a villa, so many Formians ***. But never mind the crowd; after ten o'clock the rest are not too troublesome. Gaius Arrius is my next-door neighbor—no, call him my tent mate: he even says he's avoiding going to Rome expressly so he can philosophize with me all day long! Then on the other side there's Sebosus, that friend of Catulus. Whither should I turn? I declare, I'd go to Arpinum at once, only it's clear it would be the most convenient to wait for you at Formiae—provided it's no later than May 6. See to what sort of men my ears are held hostage! What a splendid opportunity for anyone who might want to buy the Formian estate from me, with them right on the premises! And yet you say, very properly, "Let us attempt some great thing worthy of much leisurely contemplation." At any rate, my promise will be made good, no labor will be spared.

The following two letters were probably written after Clodius had become tribune-elect, and they clearly reflect Cicero's increasing anxiety. Clodia appears once again as a source of sensitive information. Clodius, whom Cicero invariably calls by various nicknames, is mocked as the "blood-brother of our dear Ox-Eyes."

Letters to Atticus 2.22 (*SB* 42)
Rome, August (?) 59 B.C.

[1] How I wish you were in Rome! Surely you would have stayed if we'd thought these things would come about. For then we'd be holding onto our Little Beauty very easily, or at least, we'd be able to find out what he was about to do. Now this is how the matter stands: he flits about, he rages; he's sure of nothing, he threatens all kinds of people with all kinds of things; he seems to be about to do whatever Chance puts in his

---

62. *Att.* 2.14.1 **sees that these proceedings are easy to overturn**: Caesar's legislation on land for Pompey's veterans and the ratification of Pompey's arrangements in the East were of questionable legality. Cicero fears that Pompey may turn to violence if these "proceedings" are "overturned."

63. *Att.* 2.14.1 **leisure**: Latin *otium*, a problematic concept for the Romans: see D'Arms (1970) 70–72, "Leisure and Politics," on the changes in Cicero's attitude toward *otium* as the Republic deteriorated and he found that "he had more of it than he could bear" (72).

way. When he sees how the current regime is hated, he seems on the point of attacking those who brought it about; but when on the other hand he recalls their wealth, their power, their armies, he turns against good men;[64] more, he threatens me myself both with violence and with legal action.

[2] Pompey[65] had a talk with him, and as he told me himself (for I have no other witness), he [Pompey] dealt with him quite strongly, in that he said that he [Pompey] would be in utter disgrace for his treachery and wickedness if danger were to come to me from the one he himself had armed by letting him become a plebeian. But that both [Clodius] and Appius had given him their word about me. That if [Clodius] did not keep it, he [Pompey] would make sure everyone understood there was nothing more deeply engrained in him than our friendship. When [Pompey] had said this and much else to the same effect, he said that [Clodius] at first, of course, had offered much resistance, but finally gave up and agreed to do nothing against [Pompey's] will. But afterward, even so, [Clodius] did not stop saying the ugliest things about me. Even if he weren't doing that, I still wouldn't trust him in the least, and I'd be making all preparations, just as I'm doing.

[3] Now, I'm conducting myself in such a way that both my popularity and my wealth are increasing daily. I don't so much as dip a finger in politics; I apply myself to lawsuits and to my work in the Forum with the greatest diligence, which I think ingratiates me very much, not only with those who make use of such services but with the crowd as well. My house is thronged, people come up to me, the memory of my consulship is renewed, enthusiasm for me is made clear. My hopes are getting so high that occasionally it seems to me that I shouldn't even avoid the impending conflict.

[4] Now I need both your advice and your affection and your loyalty; so hurry! Everything will be made easier for me if I have you. Much can be done through our friend Varro[66] that will be still more secure with pressure from you, much can even be extracted from Publius himself, much be known that cannot stay hidden from you, much too—but it's ridiculous to list these things one by one when I need you for everything.

---

64. *Att.* 2.22.1 **good men**: See note on *Cael.* 77 **one of the good men**.

65. *Att.* 2.22.2 **Pompey**: In the rest of this paragraph, the names "Pompey" and "Clodius" do not appear at all in the Latin; they have been added to the English for the sake of intelligibility.

66. *Att.* 2.22.4 **Varro**: Marcus Terentius Varro, a polymath who produced some 620 books (only the ones on "The Latin Language" and "Agriculture" survive), was a supporter of Pompey.

[5] I wish you could be persuaded of this one thing: if I see you, everything will be straightened out for me; but all depends upon this happening before he enters his magistracy. I think under pressure from Crassus Pompey may <waver, but> if you're here—you who can find out from the man himself through **Ox-Eyes** how genuine their intentions are[67]—I'll be either free from harassment, or at least free from error. You don't need my prayers and exhortations. You know what my desire, the time, and the gravity of the situation call for.

[6] About politics, I have nothing to report to you other than people's utter hatred of those who have all the power. Yet there's no hope of a change. But, as you can well believe, Pompey himself is sick of it and regrets it passionately. I can't foresee clearly what outcome I should expect; but things are surely bound to blow up at some point.

[7] I'm sending you back the book of Alexander,[68] a careless person and not a good poet, but still not without his uses. I'm glad to have become friends with Numerius Numestius,[69] and I've found him a serious person and responsible and worthy of your recommendation.

Letters to Atticus 2.23 (*SB* 43)
Rome, August (?) 59 B.C.

[1] Never before, I think, have you read a letter of mine that wasn't written by my own hand. From this one you'll be able to gather how terribly preoccupied I am. For since I had no free time at all and I had to take a walk to refresh my poor little voice, I dictated this[70] while walking.

[2] First, then, I want you to know that our friend Sampsiceramus deeply regrets his position and longs to be restored to the place from which he fell, and is sharing his grief with me and sometimes asking openly for a remedy, which I don't think can be found by any means. Second, the leaders and allies of that whole party are getting feeble, even

---

67. *Att.* 2.22.4 **from the man himself . . . intentions are**: That is, Clodia can report to Atticus what the intentions of Clodius and Pompey are with regard to Cicero (among other things).

68. *Att.* 2.22.7 **Alexander**: Probably a contemporary of Cicero, this Alexander wrote poems on astronomy and geography; Cicero was apparently still gathering materials for his own book on geography.

69. *Att.* 2.22.7 **Numerius Numestius**: A friend of Atticus, who had recommended him to Cicero (*Att.* 2.20.1 = *SB* 40)—Roman networking in action.

70. *Att.* 2.23.1 **I dictated this**: It is a convention of Roman epistolary style to view time from the standpoint of the reader, not the writer. We would more likely say "I am dictating this."

though there's no opposition; never has there been greater unanimity of will and opinion.

[3] I, however (I really want you to know this!), am taking part in no political deliberations whatsoever and have devoted myself entirely to the work and business of the court. Consequently, as can easily be imagined, I'm the subject of much reminiscence about and nostalgia for my former achievements. But the blood brother of our dear **Ox-Eyes**[71] is flinging about no small terrors and making threats—he denies it to Sampsiceramus, flaunts and parades it to everyone else. Therefore—if you love me as much as you do in fact love me—if you're sleeping, wake up! If you're standing still, walk! If you're walking, run! If you're running, fly! It's incredible how much I depend on your advice and wisdom and, most of all, your love and loyalty. The enormity of this matter perhaps demands a lengthy discourse, but the intimacy of our minds is content with a short one. It's terribly important to me that you be at Rome, if not for the voting, then at least after he's been elected.[72] Take care of yourself.

This letter, written six months after Cicero's return from exile, shows the sort of violent disorder into which the Republic had degenerated. Incest with Clodia has become a weapon in the battle—both verbal and physical—between what Cicero would characterize as Clodius' gangs and the supporters of the true Republic.

Letters to His Brother Quintus 2.3
Rome, 12 and 15 February 56 B.C.

[1] I wrote you before about what happened earlier; now hear what was done next. On February 1 the embassies were postponed until February 13. That day they didn't take place. On February 2 Milo was present [for

---

71. *Att.* 2.23.3 **blood brother of our dear Ox-Eyes**: Latin *Boopidis nostrae consanguineus.* This is the one place where Clodia's nickname is written in Roman letters, not Greek (perhaps because the letter was dictated). The word *nostrae* literally means "our," but with connotations (here ironic, of course) of affection. There may be some (presumably obscene) pun in *consanguineus,* which literally means "blood relative"; compare the description of Sextus Cloelius (*Dom.* 25) as a "sharer in your [Clodius'] blood" (*socius tui sanguinis*).

72. *Att.* 2.23.3 **after he's been elected**: It is not entirely clear when the elections for tribune took place; this passage seems to imply that they had not yet been held, but *Att.* 22.5, "before he enters his magistracy," seems to imply that they had: see Tatum (1999) 111. In any case, Clodius' tribunate was regarded as a certainty once he assumed plebeian status. Three months after he took office (December 59 B.C.), Cicero went into exile: see note on *Fam.* 5.2.8 **inflicted capital punishment on others without a hearing**.

his trial].[73] Pompey came as supporting counsel. Marcus Marcellus spoke, at my request. We came off creditably. The trial was adjourned until February 6. Meanwhile, since the embassies were put off until the 13th, the provinces for the quaestors and the equipping of the praetors came up. But with the interruptions of multiple complaints about public affairs, nothing was accomplished. Gaius Cato[74] proposed a law abrogating Lentulus' command. His son changed clothes.[75]

[2] On February 6 Milo was present. Pompey spoke—or at least he wanted to; for as he stood up, the Clodian gangs started yelling; and so it happened that throughout his whole speech, he was impeded not only by shouting, but by abuse and curses. As he reached his conclusion—for he was really brave despite it all, he wasn't deterred, he delivered the whole thing, and from time to time he even commanded silence through his personal authority[76]—but as he reached his conclusion, Clodius stood up. There was such an outcry against him from our side (for it was a pleasure to return the favor) that he kept his composure neither of mind nor of tongue nor of countenance. That went on from the time Pompey had finished his speech, around noon, until about two o'clock, when all kinds of curses and even some extremely obscene verses about Clodius and **Clodia** were recited. Enraged and pale with fury, he was asking his supporters, right in the midst of the shouting, who it was who was murdering the people through hunger.[77] His gangs responded, "Pompey." Who wanted to go to Alexandria? They answered, "Pompey." Whom did they want to go there? They answered, "Crassus." He was present then, with no friendly intent toward Milo. About three o'clock, as if at a signal, the Clodians began to spit on our men. Our rage flared up. They pressed against us to move us from the place. An attack by our side: flight of the gangs! Clodius was thrown off the Rostra; I fled then too, in case something should happen in

73. *Q. fr.* 2.3.1 **Milo was present [for his trial]**: Clodius, who had just been elected curule aedile, accused Milo of seditious violence (*vis*).

74. *Q. fr.* 2.3.1 **Gaius Cato**: Tribune in 56 B.C.; not related to the famous Cato (Uticensis).

75. *Q. fr.* 2.3.1 **changed clothes**: That is, changed into mourning garb; see note on *Fam.* 5.1.2 **in mourning and squalor**. It was a rare and disgraceful event for a magistrate to be relieved of command. Father and son were both named Cornelius Lentulus Spinther. The father was consul in 57 B.C.; on the son, see note on *Att.* 12.52.2 **Spinther getting a divorce**.

76. *Q. fr.* 2.3.2 **personal authority**: Latin *auctoritas* designates not legal power, but rather the personal qualities that inspire respect; when a man with *auctoritas* talks, people listen.

77. *Q. fr.* 2.3.2 **murdering the people through hunger**: Pompey was *curator annonae* or superintendent of the grain supply.

that riot. The Senate was summoned to the courthouse; Pompey went home. Still, I didn't go to the Senate, to avoid either keeping silent about such atrocities or offending the minds of good men by defending Pompey (for he was being harried by Bibulus, Curio, Favonius, Servilius Junior). The matter was postponed until the next day. Clodius put off the day until the Quirinalia [February 17].

[3] On February 7 the Senate was convened in Apollo's temple, so that Pompey could be there.[78] The matter was handled gravely by Pompey. Nothing was accomplished that day. On the 8th, at Apollo's temple, a Decree of the Senate was handed down: "That which was done on February 6 was done against the State." That same day [Gaius] Cato railed against Pompey vehemently and throughout his speech accused him as if he were a criminal. About me—against my will—he said much that contained the highest praise. When he denounced Pompey's treachery toward me, my ill-wishers listened to him in deep silence. Pompey answered him with vehemence and alluded to Crassus, and said plainly that he would be better equipped to guard his own life than Africanus[79] had been, whom Gaius Carbo had murdered.

[4] And so it seems to me that important things are happening. Pompey realizes this, and he shares with me his suspicion that a plot is being hatched against his life; that Gaius Cato is being supported by Crassus; that money is being supplied to Clodius; that both of them are being strengthened both by him and by Curio, Bibulus, and the rest of his detractors; that he absolutely must make sure he is not overwhelmed, with that assembly-loving populace practically alienated from him, the nobility hostile, the Senate unfair, the youth traitorous. And so he's arming himself, he's calling up men from the fields. But Clodius is strengthening his own gangs. A troop is being gathered for the Quirinalia; for that, we are far superior, with Pompey's own forces. But a great troop is expected from Picenum and Gaul, so that we can resist even [Gaius] Cato's motions about Milo and Lentulus.

---

78. *Q. fr.* 2.3.3 **Apollo's temple, so that Pompey could be there**: The temple was outside the city boundaries (*pomerium*). It was unlawful for military commanders to enter the city proper without special dispensation.

79. *Q. fr.* 2.3.3 **Africanus**: Publius Cornelius Scipio Aemilianus Africanus Numantinus (grandson of the Publius Cornelius Scipio Africanus who defeated Hannibal), a ruthless military leader. Though the facts of his case are not entirely clear, it seems that he was murdered (129 B.C.) on account of his opposition to the reforms of Tiberius Gracchus.

[5] On February 10 Sestius was indicted for bribery by the informer Gnaeus Nerius, of the Pupinian clan, and the same day for seditious violence by one Marcus Tullius.[80] He was sick. I came to him at home (as I should) right away and put myself entirely at his disposal; and this I did beyond the expectation of men who thought I was right to be angry at him; so that I appeared most decent and most amiable both to him and to everyone; and so I will act. But this same Nerius the informer also gave the names of Gnaeus Lentulus Vatia and Gaius Cornelius as additional intermediaries. The same day a Decree of the Senate was passed: "The political fraternities and caucuses shall depart; and the condition shall be imposed upon them that whoever does not depart will be liable to the same punishment as that for seditious violence."

[6] On the 11th I defended Bestia on a charge of bribery before the praetor Gnaeus Domitius, to a huge throng in the middle of the Forum. I happened upon that point in my speech when Sestius, having received many wounds in the temple of Castor, was saved by Bestia's intervention. Here I conveniently preempted some of the charges that are being trumped up against Sestius, and I embellished him with true praises, to the great applause of all. That was extremely gratifying to the man. I write this to you because you have often admonished me in your letters to retain Sestius' goodwill.

[7] On the 12th of February I wrote this before dawn. That day, I was to dine with Pomponius for his wedding feast.[81] Everything else about my affairs (as you predicted to me, though I scarcely believed you) is characterized by prestige and goodwill; which, my brother, have been restored to you and to me through your patience, virtue, righteousness, and even charm. A Licinian house near Piso's lake[82] has been rented for you. But I hope in a few months, after July 1, you'll move back into your own.[83] The Lamiae, respectable tenants, have leased your house in the Carinae. I've gotten no letter from you after that one from Olbia. I'm eager to know what you're doing and how you're enjoying yourself, and most of all to see you

---

80. *Q. fr.* 2.3.5 **one Marcus Tullius**: This man's identity is not known. Some editors read "Publius Tullius."

81. *Q. fr.* 2.3.7 **Pomponius for his wedding feast**: Atticus (here "Pomponius") was marrying Pilia.

82. *Q. fr.* 2.3.7 **Licinian house near Piso's lake**: The text here is uncertain, as is what is meant by "Licinian [Lucinian?] house" and "Piso's lake [grove?]."

83. *Q. fr.* 2.3.7 **your own**: Quintus had a house on the Palatine next to Cicero's.

in person as soon as possible. Take care of your health, my brother; and although it's winter, still remember it's Sardinia.[84]

February 15.

The remaining letters given here were written in the wake of the death of Cicero's daughter, Tullia, in the middle of February 45 B.C. (her baby son, born in January, died a few months later).[85] For a few weeks Cicero stayed with Atticus, then he retired to his retreat at Astura. These letters touch on his obsession with building a shrine to Tullia, for which he considered buying the horti *(variously translated "gardens," "estate," or "pleasure grounds") of Clodia.[86] The letters are remarkable both for the power and autonomy Cicero ascribes to Clodia and for the apparent absence of animosity between them.*

Letters to Atticus 12.38a (*SB* 279)
Astura, 7 May 45 B.C.

[1] So you say you think the soundness of my mind now needs to be made clear, and certain men are talking about me in harsher terms than either you or Brutus use in your letters. Well, if those who think I'm mentally shattered and decrepit should find out what kind and quantity of writing I'm producing, I believe—if they have any human decency—they'd decide either that I shouldn't be criticized, if I'm sufficiently recovered to bring a clear mind to write on a difficult subject, or that I should be praised, if I've chosen the distraction from grief most appropriate for a man of culture and learning.

[2] But since I'm doing everything I can to help myself, make sure you bring about what I see is a concern for you no less than for me. It seems to me that I owe this, and that I won't be able to recover unless I either pay the debt or see that I'm able to pay it—that is, find the sort of place I want. If Scapula's heirs are thinking of dividing the property in four parts and auctioning them, as you say Otho told you, obviously there's no place for a buyer; but if they'll sell, we'll see what can be done. That Publician place now belonging to Trebonius and Cusinius[87] had been mentioned to me;

---

84. *Q. fr.* 2.3.7 **although it's winter, still remember it's Sardinia**: Sardinia was unhealthy at all times, but especially in summer.

85. On Cicero's grief and his search for a "practical" cure, see Erskine (1997).

86. On the probability that this Clodia was in fact Clodia Metelli, see introduction, "Who Was Clodia?"

87. *Att.* 12.38a.2 **Trebonius and Cusinius**: These men were probably in Spain with Caesar at the time.

but you know it's just an empty field. I don't like it at all. **Clodia's** place is quite nice, but I don't think it's for sale. As for Drusus' property, though you dislike it, as you say, still I'll have to resort to it if you don't find something else. The building doesn't concern me. For I'll be building the same thing I'd build even if I don't get those properties.

I liked "Cyrus II" as much as the other works of Antisthenes, a fellow with more cleverness than learning.

Letters to Atticus 12.42 (*SB* 282)
Astura, 10 May 45 B.C.

[1] I didn't want any "letter day" from you; for I saw what you say in your letter, and anyway I suspected, or rather understood, that there was nothing for you to write. As for the 8th, I of course supposed you were gone and saw clearly that you had nothing to say. Still, I'll send to you pretty much every day; I'd rather do that for nothing than have you have no one to give your letter, if anything should happen to come up that you think I should know about. So on the 10th I received your letter with nothing in it. For what did you have to write about? Still, it didn't bother me to have that one such as it was—if nothing else, I knew you had no news.

You did however say something or other about **Clodia**. Where is she then, or when will she come back? I like the idea so much that, after Otho, nothing would please me more.

[2] But I don't think she'll sell (for she enjoys the place and she's rich), and it doesn't escape you how difficult the other option is. But I beg you, let's work hard to come up with something to get what I desire.

[3] I think I'll leave here on the 16th, but I'll go either to the Tusculan place or home, then maybe to Arpinum. I'll write you when I know for sure.

Letters to Atticus 12.41 (*SB* 283)
Astura, 11 May 45 B.C.

[1] I had nothing to write. But I still wanted to know where you were, and if you're gone or are planning to be gone, when you were going to return. So let me know. And since you wanted to know when I was leaving here, I decided to stay at Lanuvium on the 16th, then go to the Tusculan place or Rome the next day. You'll know on the day itself which I plan to do.

[2] You know how misfortune loves to find fault, very little with you, of course, but still, I'm longing deeply for the shrine. If it's not—I won't

say "accomplished," but such that I can see it under way (I'll be bold to say this and you, as usual, will understand), my grief will turn itself upon you, not of course justly; but still you'll put up with this I'm writing as you put up with everything of mine and always have. I wish you'd turn all your consolations toward this one matter.

[3] If you're asking what I want, first Scapula's, then **Clodia's**, then (if Silius is unwilling and Drusus is being unreasonable) that of Cusinius and Trebonius. I think there's a third owner; at least I know Rebilus used to be. But if you like the Tusculan place, as you indicated in one of your letters, I'll defer to you. In any case you'll get this done if you want me to be comforted, me whom you scold even more harshly than your usual practice allows—but you do this with the greatest affection and, perhaps, overcome by my fault—but still, if you want me to be comforted, this is the greatest comfort, or if you want to know the truth, the only one.

[4] Once you've read Hirtius' letter, which seems to me like a sort of rough draft of that criticism Caesar wrote about Cato,[88] let me know what you think, if it's convenient.

I come back to the shrine. If that obligation is not fulfilled this summer—you see the entire season remains—I'll consider myself guilty of a crime.

Letters to Atticus 12.43 (*SB* 284)
Astura, 12 May 45 B.C.

[1] It had occurred to me to advise you to do exactly what you're doing. For I thought you could do the same thing more comfortably at home, with no interruptions.

[2] As I wrote you before, I decided to stay at Lanuvium on the 16th; from there, either Rome or Tusculum—you'll know which one beforehand.

You do well in saying that you know this project will be a comfort to me; believe me, it's a greater comfort than you can imagine. Just how much I desire it is clear from the fact that I'm daring to confess it to you, who I don't think are entirely in favor of it. But in this matter you should put up with my deviance. Put up with it? No, you should even help it along.

---

88. *Att.* 12.41.4 **rough draft of that criticism Caesar wrote about Cato**: Cicero had written a book (now lost) in praise of Cato; Caesar responded with a two-book "Anti-Cato." Of Hirtius' pamphlet, Cicero observes (*Att.* 12.40.1 = *SB* 281), "Hirtius catalogues the faults of Cato, but along with the greatest praises of *me.*"

[3] I'm not confident about Otho,[89] perhaps because I desire it. But also, the place is beyond my resources, especially with an opponent who's eager and rich and an heir. My second choice is **Clodia's** place. But if those are less possible to attain, get whatever. I consider myself under a greater religious obligation than anyone ever constrained by a vow. You'll see about Trebonius' place, too, even if the owners are absent. But, as I wrote you yesterday, you'll take Tusculum into consideration too, so that the summer doesn't slip away; that definitely mustn't be allowed to happen.

Letters to Atticus 12.44 (*SB* 285)
Astura, 13 May 45 B.C.

[1] I'm both happy that Hirtius wrote you something sympathetic about me (it was decent of him) and far happier that you didn't send me his letter; that was even more decent of you. I want that pamphlet of his[90] he sent me about Cato to be circulated by your people, so that from that lot's abuse, his eulogy will be even greater.

[2] As for your dealings with Mustela, you have in him quite a suitable fellow and one very much in my camp ever since Pontianus. So get something established. And what better move than making an opening for a buyer? That can be done through any of the heirs. But I think Mustela will put it through, if you ask. I think you'll actually be giving me both the place I want for our present purpose and also a retreat for my old age. For those places of Silius and Drusus don't seem to me the right thing for a paterfamilias. As if I'm going to sit around in the villa all day long! So I'd prefer the other two, first Otho's, then **Clodia's**. If nothing happens, we'll either have to get Drusus into the game or use the Tusculan place.

[3] You were right to shut yourself in at home; but please, finish it up and make yourself available to me. From here, as I wrote before, I'll stay at Lanuvium on the 16th, then to Tusculum the next day. I've pulverized my spirit and perhaps conquered it, if I can just remain firm. So you'll know tomorrow, maybe, the day after at the latest.

But what is this, please? Philotimus says that Pompey isn't detained at Carteia (about which Oppius and Balbus had sent me a copy of the letter to Clodius Patavinus and said they thought it was the case), and that no small

89. *Att.* 12.43.3 **about Otho**: That is, "about my ability to outbid Otho in an auction."
90. *Att.* 12.44.1 **that pamphlet of his**: See note on *Att.* 12.41.4 **rough draft of that criticism Caesar wrote about Cato.**

war remains. He [Philotimus] tends to be an utter faux-Favonius.[91] But still, whatever you have. I also want to know what's up with Caninius' shipwreck.

[4] Here, I've finished two big sections; for in no other way am I able to stray away from my misery, so to speak. But you, even if you have nothing to write me (which I see will be the case), still, I'd like you to write this very thing—"I had nothing to write"—just not in those exact words!

Letters to Atticus 13.26 (*SB* 286)
Astura, 14 May 45 B.C.

[1] About Vergilius' share, I quite approve. So act accordingly. And indeed, that one will be first, **Clodia's** second. But if neither one, I'm afraid I may be distraught and rush to Drusus. I'm reckless in my desire for this thing, as you know. And so every day I keep turning back to the Tusculan place. Anything rather than not have this resolved this summer.

[2] As my situation is now, I've got no place where I can be happier than at Astura. But because those who are with me—I think because they can't bear my gloom—are hurrying home, even if I could stay, still, as I wrote you, I'll set out from here so I don't appear abandoned. Where, then? From Lanuvium I'm trying, anyway, for Tusculum. But I'll let you know at once. Please finish the letter. As for me, it's incredible how much I write, at night, too; sleep is out of the question. Yesterday I even did a letter to Caesar,[92] since you thought it was a good idea. It wasn't a bad thing to write, if you might possibly think it's useful; as things stand now, of course, there's certainly no need to send it. But whatever you think best. I'll send you a copy anyway, perhaps from Lanuvium, unless I happen to go to Rome. But you'll know tomorrow.

Letters to Atticus 12.47 (*SB* 288)
Lanuvium, 16 May 45 B.C.

[1] As for Mustela, it's as you say, even if it's a big project. So I'm inclining more toward **Clodia**. Though in either case, Faberius' debt[93]

---

91. *Att.* 12.44.3 **faux-Favonius**: As *SB* (1966) observes, "since Cato's death Favonius stood as the type of a republican zealot."

92. *Att.* 13.26.2 **letter to Caesar**: In *Att.* 12.40.2 (*SB* 281), Cicero says that he is trying to write a "Letter of Advice" to Caesar on the model of Aristotle's and Theopompus' letters to Alexander the Great. It was never sent or published.

93. *Att.* 12.47.1 **Faberius' debt**: Faberius was Caesar's secretary (*scriba*) and handled some of his finances. Caesar (through Faberius) owed Cicero a great deal of money.

needs to be looked into. It won't hurt for you to talk about him a bit with Balbus and tell him that in fact, as the matter stands, we want to buy and can't without that money and don't dare while it's uncertain.

[2] But when is **Clodia** going to be in Rome and how much do you guess she wants? I'm definitely looking that way, not that I'd prefer it, but because it's a big thing and tough to compete with an eager man, a rich man, an heir. Even if I'm second to none in eagerness, I'm the loser as regards the other things. But more on this in person.

Letters to Atticus 12.52 (*SB* 294)
Tusculum, 21 May 45 B.C.

[1] You know Lucius Tullius Montanus, who set out with [Marcus] Cicero. I got a letter from his sister's husband saying that Montanus owes Plancus[94] twenty thousand sesterces as a surety for Flaminius, and that you'd received a request about this from Montanus. I'd certainly like you to help him, whether by making a request to Plancus or by helping him in some other way. If you happen to know more about this than I do, or if you think a request should be made to Plancus, I'd like you to write me, so I'll know how the matter stands and what request should be made.

[2] I'm waiting to hear what you did about the letter to Caesar. I'm really not so concerned about Silius. You need to get me either Scapula's place or **Clodia's**. But you seem to have some doubt about **Clodia**; is it about when she's coming or about whether she'll sell? But what's this I hear about Spinther getting a divorce?[95]

---

94. *Att.* 12.52.1 **Montanus owes Plancus**: *SB* (1999) 23: "As City Prefect, nominated by Caesar before he left for Spain, L. Munatius Plancus was concerned with the disposal of confiscated property. Flaminius Flamma owed money on the purchase of such property and called upon Montanus as his surety."

95. *Att.* 12.52.2 **Spinther getting a divorce?**: This question may be a clue to determining whether the property Cicero seeks to buy is that of our Clodia Metelli or of one of her sisters: see introduction, "Who Was Clodia?" Here is a slightly more detailed summary of the complex argument of *SB* (1966) 412–13:

That Cicero mentions Lentulus Spinther's divorce right after discussing Clodia would suggest that Spinther was connected with her in some way. In *Att.* 13.7 (*SB* 314), Cicero says he has heard that "Lentulus [i.e., Lentulus Spinther] has definitely divorced Metella"—that is, a woman whose father was named Metellus, like our Clodia's husband; Metella may well be Clodia's daughter. Furthermore, in *Att.* 12.40.4 (*SB* 281), while discussing the possibility of purchasing various properties, Cicero writes, "As for what you write me about Lentulus, it doesn't rest with him." It is probable that, in response to Cicero's statement in 12.38a.2 (*SB* 279) that "Clodia's place is quite nice, but I don't think it's for sale," Atticus had said something to the effect that Lentulus might

[3] About the Latin Language,[96] put your mind at ease. You'll say, "What's that compared to your writings?" These are mere copies, they come about with rather little work; I just supply words, of which I have an abundance.

Letters to Atticus 13.29 (*SB* 300)
Tusculum, 27 May 45 B.C.

[1] I've learned about the property from your letter and from Chrysippus. In the house, whose awkwardness I was well acquainted with, I see little or no change; but he approves of the bigger baths and says the smaller ones could be made into winter apartments. So a little covered path should be added; if I make it the same size as the Tuscalan, it will be almost cheaper by half than the one there. As for the model temple I want, nothing looks more suitable than the grove, with which I was familiar; it used to get no traffic at all, but now, I hear, it gets a great deal. There's nothing I'd like more. By the gods, indulge my fever[97] about this! As for the rest, if Faberius settles that debt[98] with me, don't ask how much; I want you to beat out Otho. Yet I don't think he'll go crazy—I believe I know the fellow. I hear he's been so badly pummeled that I don't think it's likely he'll be the buyer.

[2] For why else would he be letting it happen? But why am I making a case? If you settle Faberius, let's buy it, no matter how expensive; if you don't, we can't, no matter how cheap. **Clodia** then. I think there's some hope of getting it from her directly,[99] both because it's a lot cheaper and because Dolabella's debt[100] now seems to be on its way to settlement, so I'll be sure I can pay even in cash. Enough about the property. Tomorrow, either you or your excuse; I think it'll be a Faberian one. But do what you can.

---

have some pull with Clodia—which would make perfect sense if Lentulus was indeed married to Clodia's daughter.

96. *Att.* 12.52.3 **the Latin Language**: The text and the sense of this paragraph are uncertain. Cicero may be referring to the work on the Latin Language by Varro, to some contemplated work of his own, or to the Latin language itself.

97. *Att.* 13.29.1 **By the gods, indulge my fever**: Cicero writes these words in Greek. The word "fever" (Greek *typhos*) could also be translated as "foolish passion" or "hobby"; it would seem that Cicero realizes the folly of his obsession even as he begs Atticus to put up with it.

98. *Att.* 13.29.1 **Faberius settles that debt**: See note on *Att.* 12.47.1 **Faberius' debt**.

99. *Att.* 13.29.2 **getting it from her directly**: Cicero hopes to be able to buy directly from Clodia without having to bid at an auction.

100. *Att.* 13.29.2 **Dolabella's debt**: Dolabella divorced Cicero's daughter in 46 B.C. and never did repay the dowry, despite Cicero's confidence here that he will.

[3] I've sent you back Quintus Cicero's letter. Oh thou man of iron, who art not moved by his perils![101] He accuses me too—I'm sending the letter with yours. That other one about the campaign I think is a copy. I sent a courier to Cumae today. I gave him your letter to Vestorius, which you'd given through Pharnaces.

This is the only one of Cicero's "Clodia" letters written after the assassination of Julius Caesar (15 March 44 B.C.).

Letters to Atticus 14.8 (*SB* 362)
Sinuessa, 16 April 44 B.C.

[1] When you wrote, you thought I was at my beach house; but actually I got your letter on the 15th in my little Sinuessan lodge. That's great about Marius,[102] grieved as I am about Lucius Crassus' grandson! Best of all, though, that Antony has the approval of even our friend Brutus. You say that Junia brought a mild and friendly letter, yet Paulus gave me one sent to him by his brother,[103] at the end of which he says that a plot is being made against him, and that he discovered this from reliable sources. That pleased me little and him much less. I'm not worried about the queen's flight.[104] I'd like you to write me what **Clodia** has done.[105] As for the Byzantines, please take care, among other things, to send for Pelops.[106] As per your request, I'll write you as soon as I figure out about the Baiae characters[107]

101. *Att.* 13.29.3 **perils**: Cicero's nephew Quintus Cicero was on military campaign in Spain.

102. *Att.* 14.8.1 **Marius**: This imposter claimed to be the grandson of the great Gaius Marius and Lucius Licinius Crassus; he gained a large following on the strength of this lineage and was banished by Caesar. He seems really to have been one Gaius Amatius (Herophilus?), perhaps a runaway slave. When he returned from exile after Caesar's death and agitated against Caesar's assassins, he was thrown into prison and executed by Antony in April of 44 B.C. Atticus' letter had mentioned the imprisonment and possibly the execution (Cicero's "grief" here is sarcastic).

103. *Att.* 14.8.1 **Junia . . . his brother**: Junia was Lepidus' wife; both of the letters were from Lepidus. Paulus' suspicion of a plot against himself would be borne out when his brother Lepidus allowed (or caused) him to be proscribed.

104. *Att.* 14.8.1 **the queen's flight**: Apparently, Cleopatra had just left Rome. Many Romans had been distressed when Caesar had brought her there.

105. *Att.* 14.8.1 **what Clodia has done**: Presumably, about selling her estate—but we can only guess.

106. *Att.* 14.8.1 **Byzantines . . . Pelops**: Plutarch (*Cic.* 24.7) singles out Cicero's letter to Pelops as "petty and whining, since Pelops had neglected to bring about certain honors and decrees [for Cicero] from the Byzantines."

107. *Att.* 14.8.1 **Baiae characters**: Caesarians (such as Hirtius and Balbus) currently staying at Baiae.

and that song and dance you want to know about, so you won't be in the dark about anything.

[2] I'm dying to hear about what the Gauls, the Spaniards, and Sextus are doing. No doubt you'll relate all that along with the rest. I'm glad your little sickness has at any rate given you an excuse to rest; it seemed to me as I read your letter that you were resting for a little while. Do always write me everything about Brutus, where he is, what he's planning; I really hope he can now roam safely throughout the whole City. But in any case.

CICERO: SPEECHES (EXCERPTS)

*The three Cicero speeches cited here were delivered after his return from exile
(September 57 B.C.) and before the* Pro Caelio *(April 56 B.C.).*[1] *During Cicero's
exile, Clodius had destroyed Cicero's house and consecrated the site as a
shrine to Liberty; with his speech "Concerning His House," Cicero persuaded
the pontiffs to have the shrine taken down and his house rebuilt. When soothsayers interpreted some strange noises heard outside the city early in 56 B.C.
as revealing the gods' anger at various sacrilegious acts, Clodius argued that
Cicero's rebuilding and reoccupation of his house was responsible; Cicero
countered with his speech "On the Responses of the Soothsayers." Shortly
afterward, Cicero successfully defended the ex-tribune Sestius on charges of
various violent acts aimed at Clodius.*

De Domo Sua [Concerning His House] [57 B.C.]
25: You, of course, to that thoroughly revolting glutton—the sampler of your
lusts, the most despicable and criminal of men, Sextus Cloelius, the sharer
in your blood, who with his tongue has alienated even your own sister
from you—through your law you handed over to him all grain supplies
private and public, all the bread-basket provinces, all the contractors, all the
keys to the granaries!
26: That measure you say you passed—killer of father, brother, sister![2]—
didn't you pass it by an irregular procedure?

---

1. On Cicero's rhetorical strategies in the so-called *Post Reditum* ("After the Return")
Speeches, see Riggsby (2002b).
2. *Dom.* 26 **killer of father, brother, sister!**: Cicero is exaggerating a bit here.

92: You say that I frequently call myself Jupiter, and that I also keep saying Minerva is my sister. My insolence in calling myself Jupiter is nothing compared to my ignorance in thinking that Minerva is Jupiter's sister! But at least I claim that my sister is a virgin: you didn't let your sister remain a virgin.

De Haruspicum Responsis [On the Responses of the Soothsayers] [56 B.C.]
9: What's the difference whether, banished from the most sacred ceremonial altars, he complains about sacred rites and ceremonies—or whether, exiting his sister's bedroom, he pleads on behalf of modesty and chastity?
38: Don't you even realize this, that those blind eyes of your great-grandfather[3] were more to be desired than these flaming eyes[4] of your sister?
39: You, when you send forth those rabid speeches in public meetings, when you overturn the houses of citizens, when you pelt the best men with stones in the Forum, when you hurl flaming torches onto the roofs of your neighbors, when you set fire to sacred temples, when you incite the slaves, when you throw rituals and games into confusion, when you fail to distinguish between wife and sister, when you don't realize what bedroom you are entering—then you are a bacchant, then you are raving mad, then you pay that penalty which alone has been ordained by the immortal gods against the crimes of men.
42: After his father's death, he offered that first flower of his tender youth to the lusts of wealthy rakes; after sating their intemperance, he wallowed in domestic adulteries with his own siblings.
59: What spendthrift ever cavorted as freely with whores as this man does with his sisters?

Pro Sestio [In Defense of Sestius] [56 B.C.]
16: As tribune of the people he was successful in overthrowing the Republic, through no strength of his own (for what strength could a man have who had lived that sort of life—a man exhausted by scandals with his brothers, incest with his sisters, and every unheard-of lust?).
39: I did not have to deal with Saturninus, who with great pugnacity of spirit sought to compensate his own grief, because he knew that the supervision

---

3. *Har.* 38 **blind eyes of your great-grandfather**: Appius Claudius Caecus ("The Blind"); compare his cameo in *Cael.* 33–35.
4. *Har.* 38 **flaming eyes**: See note on *Cael.* 49 **flaming eyes**.

of the grain supply had been insultingly transferred from himself (the quaestor at Ostia) to Marcus Scaurus, the leader of the Senate and the State; but I had to deal with a male whore of wealthy rakes, with the adulterer of his sister, with a priest of perversions, with a poisoner, with a forger of wills, with an assassin, with a bandit.

116: That arch-comedian [Clodius] himself, not only a spectator but an actor and virtuoso, who knows all his sister's interludes,[5] who is introduced into a gathering of women as a harp girl, saw neither your shows in that fiery tribunate of his nor any others except those from which he scarcely escaped alive.

5. *Sest.* 116 **all his sister's interludes**: For Clodia as "composer," see notes on *Cael.* 31 **author** and 64 **little drama**.

CICERO: *PRO CAELIO*

This closing speech from the trial of Marcus Caelius Rufus, delivered eight months after Cicero's return from exile, is such a masterpiece of evasion that we do not even know what the five charges against Caelius involved.[1] *Caelius spoke first in his own defense, Crassus second, and Cicero last; Cicero tells us that "the sedition at Naples, the assault on the Alexandrians at Puteoli, and the property of Palla" were dealt with by Crassus (§23), and we know little more about them than these phrases. The remaining accusations were of collusion in the murder of the philosopher Dio (see note on §18* **arrival of King Ptolemy***) and of scheming to poison Clodia. Cicero's brilliantly effective strategy is to argue that Clodia's bitterness toward her ex-lover is the real motivation for the whole trial, but that Clodia's whorelike behavior makes her testimony worthless and Caelius' affair with her excusable.*

The inserted headings (my own addition) are intended to help the reader navigate this long, complex, and eminently rewarding exemplar of Ciceronian rhetoric. Numbers of the sections that speak directly or indirectly about Clodia (1–2, 18–20, 30–38, 47–70, 75–76, and 78) are in **boldface***.*

INTRODUCTION: SETTING THE COMIC STAGE

[1] If some person happened to be here now, gentlemen of the jury, who knew nothing about our laws, courts, and way of life, he would certainly marvel at the atrocity of this case—atrocity so great that on days set aside

---

The notes presented here are based upon the commentary of Austin (1960); unless otherwise noted, citations of "Austin" refer to the corresponding place in his commentary.

1. On oratory as the "Art of Illusion," see Gotoff (1993).

for public festivals and games,[2] when all legal business is suspended, this one case is being tried; nor would he doubt that the defendant is in the dock for a crime so great that the State could not stand if it were overlooked. When the same person heard that there's a law ordering seditious, conspiratorial citizens to be tried at any time—men who have besieged the Senate under arms, done violence to the magistrates, assailed the Republic—he wouldn't disapprove of the law, but would ask what crime is being handled in this case. When he heard that no crime, no recklessness, no seditious violence is being tried, but rather that a young man of brilliant wit, industry, and prestige[3] is being accused by the son of a man whom he himself both is preparing to prosecute and has prosecuted already,[4] and moreover that this young man is under attack through a whore's wealth . . . ? He would applaud the accuser's righteousness, he would think woman's lust ought to be reigned in—and he would consider you, gentlemen of the jury, extremely hardworking, who are not allowed to relax even on a public holiday!

[2] In fact, if you want to attend diligently and form an accurate opinion of this whole case, you'll recognize, gentlemen of the jury, that no one who had any choice would stoop to this accusation—nor, having stooped, would

2. 1 **public festivals and games**: The *Ludi Megalenses,* in honor of Cybele, held 4–10 April and consisting of various sporting events and theatrical performances. Salzman (1982) discusses, among other things, how Cicero alludes to the plot of one of these dramas in constructing his own: the jealous wrath of Cybele (implicitly, Clodia) over the infidelity of Attis (implicitly, Caelius). More generally, Cicero pervasively casts the events and characters in his speech as those in a comedy: see Geffcken (1973) and Leigh (2004). As Leigh points out, "To redimension the matters at issue in the trial of Caelius as if they were the plot of a comedy is peculiarly effective for its ability to suggest that this is all rather less significant than the prosecution would have the jury believe, for the compromising central role [of *meretrix,* "prostitute"] that the unfortunate Clodia is now obliged to play, and for the implications that the defendant's role as comic *adulescens* [see note on §2 **youth**] has for his inevitable return to sobriety" (333).

3. 1 **young man of brilliant wit, industry, and prestige**: To establish the character of the defendant was of crucial importance in Roman trials; see Riggsby (2004) on the "Rhetoric of Character." As Craig (1995) 411 observes in his useful summary of Roman court procedures, "there was a real danger that a defendant was innocent until proven obnoxious." The word "brilliant," Latin *illustris,* literally means "shining"; as Ramage (1985) 1 observes, Cicero "sets up a dichotomy in the speech whereby Clodia and everyone connected with her are characterized by concealment and other qualities that follow from this (vagueness, darkness, anonymity, dissimulation, deception, ambush), while Caelius and his allies show a visibility in the broadest sense of the term (clarity, brilliance, honesty, candor)."

4. 1 **son of a man . . . prosecuted already**: The son is Lucius Sempronius Atratinus; the father is Lucius Calpurnius Bestia, whom Caelius had prosecuted for bribery—and Cicero had successfully defended—only weeks before (11 February). The present trial prevented Caelius from prosecuting Bestia a second time.

he have any hope at all, were he not relying on *someone's*[5] intolerable lust and excessively bitter hatred. But I forgive Atratinus—a most cultured and excellent youth[6] and my dear friend—since he has the excuse of righteousness, or necessity, or tender age. If he wanted to make the accusation, I attribute this to righteousness; if he was commanded to, to necessity; if he had any hopes of winning, to childishness. The others not only shouldn't be forgiven, but should be sharply resisted.

CHARACTER WITNESS #1: CAELIUS' FATHER

[3] And indeed, it seems to me, gentlemen of the jury, that the most appropriate way to open the defense of Marcus Caelius' youth would be to respond first to what his accusers have said to defame him and to disgrace and despoil his dignity. His father has been made a reproach to him in differing ways: the man is said to be either insufficiently distinguished himself, or treated with insufficient righteousness by his son. Concerning his own dignity, Marcus Caelius [the Elder] replies himself—silently, effortlessly, and indeed without any oration from me—to those who know him and to the elder among us. Those men, however, to whom because of his old age he is not so well known, since he has long been spending less time in the Forum and in our company—let them rest assured that, whatever dignity it is possible for a Roman knight to possess (which, certainly, can be very great), Marcus Caelius always has been held to possess in the highest measure and is so held today, not only by his own friends, but by all who have for any reason had the opportunity to make his acquaintance.

[4] I might add that to be the son of a Roman knight shouldn't have been made grounds for reproach by the accusers, given the present jury and myself the counsel for the defense.[7] As for what you said about his righteousness, I

---

5. 2 *someone's*: Clodia's, that is.

6. 2 **youth**: Latin *adulescens*, unlike our "adolescent," denoted roughly the period of life between the donning of the *toga virilis* (fifteen or sixteen) and the minimum age for election to public office (thirty). Atratinus was said to be seventeen at the time of the present trial. The contrast between youthful inexperience (especially of the young Caelius) and mature wisdom (especially of Cicero himself and the jury)—another stock theme of comedy—runs throughout the speech. May (1988) 106 notes in Cicero's treatment of Atratinus "an overbearing tone of condescension that must have caused even the bystanders to wince."

7. 4 **myself the counsel for the defense**: Cicero was the son of a knight.

can form an opinion, to be sure, but his father can judge with certainty. What I think, you will hear from the witnesses on oath; what his parents feel is proclaimed by the tears of his mother, the incredible gloom and squalor of his father,[8] and this mourning and grief you see here before you.

CHARACTER WITNESS #2: CAELIUS' TOWNSPEOPLE

[5] As for your reproach that the young man is not approved of by his own townspeople, gentlemen of the jury, the Praetuttians have bestowed greater honors[9] upon Marcus Caelius in his absence than upon anyone else in person; even in his absence they elected him to the most eminent rank and gave him who wasn't seeking them things they denied to many who did seek them. And these same townspeople have now dispatched to this trial, with a most weighty and elegant speech of commendation, a deputation both of the most distinguished men of our order[10] and of Roman knights. In my opinion I've now laid the foundations of my defense, which are firmest if they rest upon the judgment of a man's own people. Nor, indeed, could this young man be sufficiently commended to you if he were displeasing not only to his father (a man of such quality), but also to such a distinguished and upstanding group of townspeople.

[6] For my part, to speak of myself, it's from such springs that I've flowed forth into people's notice, and my work here in the courts and the conduct of my life have streamed down into people's good opinion somewhat more broadly through the approval and commendation of my friends.

DISMANTLING THE "MORALITY" ARGUMENT

As for the reproach about his morals, which all the accusers have harped on with insinuations and slander rather than concrete charges, Marcus Caelius will never take this so hard that he'll regret not having been born ugly. For such slanders come from all sides against everyone

---

8. 4 **gloom and squalor of his father**: It was standard practice in Roman law courts for the defendant and his relatives to garner pity by appearing in mourning garb looking as shabby and miserable as possible.

9. 5 **greater honors**: Caelius had been elected a *decurio*, a member of the local Senate.

10. 5 **men of our order**: Senators.

whose form and appearance in their youth was fine.[11] But it's one thing to slander, another to bring a real accusation. Accusation needs an actual charge in order to specify the matter, mark off the man, prove by argument, confirm by witness; slander, on the other hand, has no purpose other than insult. It's called "abuse" if done aggressively, "urbanity"[12] if done wittily.

[7] I was amazed, and annoyed, that this part of the accusation was allotted mainly to Atratinus. It wasn't decent and it wasn't necessary for his tender years to make such accusations, and—as was undoubtedly evident to all of you—the modesty of that excellent youth scarcely allowed him to feel comfortable with such a speech. I could wish that one of the more seasoned among you had undertaken the task of speaking slander; in that case I could refute that slanderous license of yours more freely, more vehemently, and more in my own character. With you, Atratinus, I shall deal more gently, both because your modesty puts a damper on my speech and because I must preserve my good offices toward you and your father.

[8] Nevertheless, I want to admonish you, first—so everyone can judge you to be what you in fact are—to cut yourself off as thoroughly from license in words as you do from baseness in deeds; second, not to speak against another man things you would blush to hear falsely spoken about yourself. For who is there to whom this path does not lie open? Who is there who couldn't speak slander against that youth and dignity of yours as aggressively as he pleased—without any genuine grounds for suspicion, perhaps, yet not entirely without basis? But the blame for those parts of your speech lies with the men who wanted you to plead the case. It's a credit to your integrity that we saw you say these things unwillingly, and to your wit that you said them with such elegance and polish.

[9] However, the rebuttal to this whole speech of yours is brief. For insofar as the youth of Marcus Caelius could have offered a place for that

11. 6 **fine**: Latin *liberalis,* literally, "befitting a free man (i.e., not a slave)." Appearance and ancestry were thought to be linked to moral qualities. Those who were freeborn and good looking were automatically considered "better" in every sense of the word; see Corbeill (1996) 14–56. Cicero is drawing attention to Caelius' looks not only to suggest that criticisms of him spring from envy, but also to make a sort of prima facie case that Caelius is a "fine" young man in other ways.

12. 6 **"urbanity"**: On the meaning of *urbanitas,* see the extensive note of Austin (1960). The ways of the *urbs* or "city" (which, without further qualification, invariably meant "Rome") were considered sophisticated, witty, "smart," and "cool"; the ways of the country (*rus*) were considered the opposite. As is also evident from Catullus, any degree of nastiness was excusable if it was sufficiently witty.

suspicion, it was fortified against attack, first, by his own integrity, and second, by the diligence and discipline of his father. When he gave Caelius the toga of manhood—I say nothing here about myself; let my role be such as you judge it to be, but let me say that the young man was handed over to me at once by his father.[13] No one laid eyes on this Marcus Caelius in the flower of his youth except when he was in his father's company, or mine, or in the most chaste house[14] of Marcus Crassus, where he was educated in the most honorable arts.

ANOTHER CHARGE: CAELIUS' RELATIONSHIP WITH CATILINE

[10] Now as for the reproach about Caelius' intimacy with Catiline, he should be far removed from that kind of suspicion. For you all know that when Caelius was a young man, Catiline ran for consul against me.[15] If Caelius ever joined him or parted company with me—though many good young men supported that wicked and dishonest man—then let Caelius be judged to have been excessively intimate with Catiline. "But afterward," you say, "we know and see that this man was numbered among Catiline's friends!" Who denies it? But right now my defense is concerned with that youthful time of life which is naturally weak itself, and easy prey for the passions of others. He was constantly with me when I was praetor; he didn't know Catiline, who was then governor of Africa. A year followed; Catiline spoke in his own defense against charges of extortion.[16] Caelius was with me; he never went to Catiline even when summoned as a supporter in court. Then came the year I ran for consul; Catiline ran against me. Caelius never joined with him, never broke with me.

13. 9 **handed over to me at once by his father**: As Burnand (2004) 281 observes, "By presenting himself as a father-figure, Cicero offers himself as a much needed character witness for his own client."

14. 9 **most chaste house**: The contrast between Clodia's corrupting *house* and the chaste, honorable houses run by decent men (not women) is powerfully developed throughout the speech: see Leen (2000–2001). On the role of Roman women (as opposed to Greek women) within the house, see Wallace-Hadrill (1996). Cicero's emphasis on the constant chaperoning of the teenage Caelius has partly to do with the perceived vulnerability of that age to sexual advances from adult males; see Richlin (1993) 537–38.

15. 10 **Catiline ran for consul against me**: In 64 B.C. Caelius was about eighteen.

16. 10 **charges of extortion**: In 65 B.C. Catiline was acquitted.

[11] After spending so many years in the Forum without suspicion, without disgrace,[17] Caelius supported Catiline when he ran for consul a second time. For how long, then, should that season of youth have been protected? In my day, indeed, a single year was allotted for "keeping our arms inside the toga"[18] and to undergo exercise and training on the Campus in tunics;[19] if we'd begun serving in the army right away, that same time was for learning the ways of military camps and campaigns. In that stage of life, if a man didn't defend himself through his own uprightness and purity, through both the discipline of his household and a certain innate goodness of his own, then he couldn't escape true disgrace no matter how closely he'd been guarded by his family and friends. But a man who'd presented those first beginnings of youth unstained and undefiled—no one would utter a word about his reputation and integrity, when he'd grown up at last and was a man among men.

[12] Yes, Caelius did support Catiline, but it was when Caelius had been active in the Forum for several years. And many men of every rank and every age did the same. For that man, as I believe you recall, gave abundant signs—not full blown, but in outline—of having the greatest virtues. He made use of many wicked men; and he pretended he'd devoted himself to the best of men. In him there were many incitements to lust; there were also certain incentives to industry and labor. Lustful vices blazed in him; zeal for military pursuits flourished as well. I don't think the world has ever seen such a portent,[20] such a conflation of natural inclinations and desires contrary, contradictory, and at war among themselves.

---

17. 11 **disgrace**: Latin *infamia.* One who was *infamis* not only had a "bad reputation" informally, but also was subject to various legal sanctions, such as not being allowed to appear on another's behalf in court. See Edwards (1997) on *infamia* and its consequences.

18. 11 **"keeping our arms inside the toga"**: Literally, this means refraining from extravagant gestures; figuratively, it means being "on probation."

19. 11 **exercise and training on the Campus in tunics**: Oratory was an aerobic business in ancient Rome. The Campus Martius, which lay outside the *pomerium* or official boundary of the city, was used for training and mustering military troops (it was illegal to enter the city under arms). Cicero likes to emphasize the parallel between military service and oratory.

20. 12 **portent**: Latin *monstrum* can mean "monster" in our sense of an unnatural, wicked creature, but also means an evil "omen, portent, or prodigy"; such portents were a sign of the gods' wrath and demanded expiation by religious rites (chiefly sacrifice). By depicting Catiline as a *monstrum,* Cicero "models the communication situation" so as to lead his audience to the inevitable conclusion that Catiline had to be "expiated" by quasi-religious means. See Axer (1989), Corbeill (2005).

[13] Who, at times, was pleasanter to the more illustrious men, who closer to the more disgraceful? What citizen had better political sympathies at one time, what enemy was more loathsome to this State? Who was more corrupt in his pleasures, more patient in his labors? Who was more rapacious in stealing, more generous in giving? These traits in that man, gentlemen of the jury, were truly astonishing:[21] to embrace many with his friendship; to protect them with his devotion; to share what he possessed with everyone; to slave for all his friends in times of need with money, influence, bodily labor, even crime, if need be, and recklessness; to adapt his own nature and mold it for the occasion and twist and bend it this way and that; to live properly with the upright, loosely with the lax, gravely with old men, agreeably with young, recklessly with the criminal, wantonly with the lustful.

[14] Through this nature so shifting and versatile, that man had gathered all wicked and reckless men from every land, but also held many brave and good men in his sway through a certain appearance of simulated virtue. Nor would there ever have arisen from him such terrible momentum for destroying this Empire, if such monstrous and excessive vices hadn't been rooted in some kind of skill and patience. Therefore, gentlemen of the jury, let that line of argument be spat back, and let friendship with Catiline not stand as a reproach. For this is something shared with many men, and even with some good ones. Even I, I say, I myself was almost taken in by him,[22] when he seemed to me both a good citizen and eager for every excellence and a firm and faithful friend; I had to see his crimes with my own eyes before I'd believe them, seize them with my own hands before I'd even suspect them. So if Caelius was once in the great throng of that man's friends, he should rather be annoyed at

---

21. 13 **astonishing**: Latin *admirabilis* can mean both "admirable" and "paradoxical."

22. 14 **I myself was almost taken in by him**: From Cicero's letters to Atticus on this subject, we get some tantalizing glimpses into both the shifting alliances of Roman politics and the irrelevance of actual guilt or innocence in Roman court cases. In July 65 B.C., when Catiline was about to be prosecuted for extortion, Cicero writes to Atticus that "Catiline will certainly be a candidate [for consul in 63 B.C., along with Cicero himself] if the jury decides the sun doesn't shine at noon" (*Att.* 1.1.1). Yet in the next letter, Cicero writes, "At this time I'm planning to defend Catiline, my fellow candidate. We've got the jury we want, and the full cooperation of the prosecution [i.e., the prosecutor Publius Clodius Pulcher, Cicero's future enemy, was in collusion with the defense]. If he's acquitted, I hope he'll be more closely allied with me in conducting the campaign; but if it turns out otherwise, I'll bear it philosophically" (*Att.* 1.2.1). Why Cicero changed his mind about defending Catiline is not known.

his mistake (just as I too sometimes regret my own error about that man) than fear reproach for that unfortunate friendship.

[15] And so your speech has slid downhill from slanders about impurity to a slur about conspiracy. For you've alleged—though hesitantly and on tiptoe—that because of his friendship with Catiline this man was a participant in the conspiracy; not only did this reproach not hold water, but this eloquent youth's speech barely held together. Was Caelius so insane, so crippled either in his character and nature or in his property and fortune? Finally, when did the name of Caelius ever come under suspicion? I'm saying too much about something not the least in doubt. But I will say this: not only if he'd been a conspirator himself, but even if he'd been less than completely hostile to that hateful crime, he never would have wished to gain distinction in his youth by accusing another man of conspiracy.[23]

ANOTHER FALSE CHARGE: BRIBERY

[16] Now, since I've come to this point, I don't know whether I should bother responding about buying votes and those reproaches of yours about political clubs[24] and bribery agents. For Caelius would never have been so insane as to accuse the other man of bribery if he'd defiled himself with the unbounded bribery you claim, nor would he have sought to bring suspicion upon the other man for that very deed he wanted free rein to do himself. If he thought he himself might ever run the risk of being prosecuted for bribery, he never would have summoned the other man on that charge.[25] As for that, although he does it unwisely and against my

---

23. 15 **accusing another man of conspiracy**: In 59 B.C., Caelius successfully prosecuted (and Cicero unsuccessfully defended) Gaius Antonius Hybrida, Cicero's colleague as consul in 63 B.C. On this complex issue, see Austin (1960) 158–59. The exact charge is unclear: it appears to have been either treason (*maiestas*) or extortion (*repetundae*), with conspiracy (*coniuratio*) "a side issue, even if it was that which really ruined Antonius" (159).

24. 16 **political clubs**: Latin *sodales*. A *sodalicium* (its members were *sodales*) was a "club" or "fraternity" gathered for religious, social, or political purposes; in this context it refers to a private political club assembled to influence elections by bribery and other means. In February 56 B.C., shortly before the present trial, a senatorial decree attempted to suppress these clubs; a law followed shortly afterward (in 55).

25. 16 **If he thought . . . that charge**: Cicero never explains *why* a man could not accuse someone else of a crime that he himself had committed or hoped to commit. On the blurriness of the line between acceptable "gifts" to the electorate and unacceptable "purchasing" of votes, see Riggsby (1999) 21–49; the distinction was essentially one of perception, not reality.

wishes, nevertheless he would appear to be overly eager to prosecute an innocent man, rather than worried about his own affairs.

ANOTHER FALSE CHARGE: DEBT

[17] As for your reproaching him with debt, criticizing his spending, demanding his account books, see how little I have to say. Whoever is under his father's power[26] keeps no account books. He has never borrowed any money whatsoever. One kind of expenditure in particular has been objected to, that for his rent; you said he paid thirty thousand. Now at last I understand: Publius Clodius' block is for sale, one of whose apartments, I believe, Caelius rents for ten thousand. However, since you wanted to make yourselves agreeable to Clodius, you've crafted this lie of yours to help him out!

THE UNFORTUNATE MOVE TO CLODIA'S NEIGHBORHOOD

[18] You criticized him for moving away from his father. In fact, at Caelius' age that should not be criticized at all. When in a criminal case he'd achieved a victory that annoyed me,[27] to be sure, but was glorious for him, and he'd reached the age to run for a magistracy, Caelius moved away from his father—not only with his father's permission, but even with his encouragement. Since his father's house was far from the Forum, he rented an inexpensive house on the Palatine so he could more easily reach my house and be visited by his own friends. At this juncture I could well say what that most illustrious man Marcus Crassus said a little earlier when he was complaining about the arrival of King Ptolemy:[28]

---

26. 17 **under his father's power**: See introduction, "*Patria Potestas.*"

27. 18 **victory that annoyed me**: See note on §15 **accusing another man of conspiracy**.

28. 18 **arrival of King Ptolemy**: Ptolemy XII, nicknamed "Auletes" ("Fluteplayer"), father of the last and most famous Cleopatra. All the Macedonian kings of Egypt (following the death of Alexander the Great in 323 B.C.) were called "Ptolemy," and all but the first married their sisters, usually named "Cleopatra," in imitation of the gods Isis and Osiris (sister/brother and wife/husband). In 59 B.C. Auletes, the son of a concubine, gave Julius Caesar and Pompey an enormous bribe (six thousand talents) to get them to support his kingship (Suetonius, *Caesar* 54); this did not endear him to his own subjects, who expelled him from Alexandria (the capital of Egypt) in 58 B.C. Auletes then appealed to Rome for help, requesting that Pompey lead the necessary army (the task was given to someone else). When the enraged Alexandrians sent an embassy of a hundred

"Would that never in the Pelian grove . . ."[29]

and in fact I could go further with these verses:

"For never would the lady wandering" have caused us this annoyance,
"Medea, sick at heart, wounded by savage love."

For thus, gentlemen of the jury, you'll find out what I'll reveal when I finally come to this issue: that this Palatine Medea and this move were the cause of all the young man's troubles—or at least of all the gossip.

ANOTHER FALSE CHARGE: EXPELLING A SENATOR FROM THE PONTIFICAL ELECTION

[19] Therefore, those parts of the accusers' speech which I understand are now being fabricated and built up as a fortification—relying upon your common sense, gentlemen of the jury, I'm not afraid of these at all. They were saying a senator would be testifying that he'd been expelled by Caelius from the pontifical election.[30] I'll ask this man, if he'll step forward, first, why he did nothing at the time; second, if he preferred to complain

---

citizens led by the philosopher Dio to Rome, Auletes had the ambassadors murdered. Before Dio could testify to the Senate about this atrocity, Auletes had him murdered as well by one Publius Asicius (57 B.C.), who was tried and acquitted thanks to Cicero's defense (56 B.C.).

29. 18 **"Would that never in the Pelian grove . . ."** This line and the quotation that follows are from the opening of the *Medea Exul* ("Medea in Exile"), a tragedy by Ennius adapted from the *Medea* of Euripides (most Roman tragedies are translations/adaptations of Greek ones). The full quotation from Ennius is this:

Would that never in the Pelian grove
had the maple trunk been cut and fallen to earth,
nor had the rudiments of the ship to be created
ever been begun, which now is called by name
"The Argo," because in her selected Argive men
were carried to seek out the Golden Fleece of the ram
of Colchis, by king Pelias' order, through guile.
For never would my lady, wandering, have set foot from home,
Medea, sick at heart, wounded by savage love.

Crassus, presumably, chose the quotation because of what happened to the "selected men" (comparing the Argonauts to the embassy murdered by Ptolemy); Cicero picks up on the Medea theme instead.

30. 19 **expelled by Caelius from the pontifical election**: *Pontifices,* or religious officials who oversaw the state cult, were elected by a special popular assembly.

rather than prosecute, why he had to be brought forward by you rather than coming of his own accord, and why he preferred to complain so long after the event rather than right away. If he replies to me cleverly and eloquently, then I'll ask, finally, from what spring that senator of yours flows forth. For if he arises and springs to birth from his own self, then perhaps, as usual, I'll be impressed; if, however, he's but a rivulet summoned and diverted from the wellspring of your accusation, I'll rejoice that, despite all the influence and wealth propping up your accusation, only a single senator could be found who was willing to do you a favor!

ANOTHER FALSE CHARGE: ACCOSTING OTHER MEN'S WIVES (AND A DIG AT CLODIA)

[20] And I don't, in any case, fear that other kind of witness-of-the-night. For they said there would be men to testify that their wives had been molested by Caelius on the way back from dinner. What upstanding men these will be, who'll dare to say this under oath, when it means they'll have to confess that they never attempted to seek legal satisfaction for such great injuries, not even by a private meeting and settlement out of court! But this whole line of attack, gentlemen of the jury, you already foresee in your minds and must repel when it's launched. For Caelius' accusers are not his real opponents; spears are hurled at him openly, but supplied in secret.

CICERO DISCREDITS THE WITNESSES

[21] And I'm not saying this to stir up ill will against those for whom this case should even be a source of pride. They're fulfilling their duty, defending their own friends, doing what the bravest men always do: wounded, they grieve; angered, they flare up; challenged, they fight. But even if these brave men have just cause for attacking Marcus Caelius, it's up to your wisdom, gentlemen of the jury, not to think on that account that *you* have just cause for catering to someone else's resentment rather than your own duty. For you see what a multitude there is in the Forum, what classes, what passions, what a variety of men. Out of this swarm, how many do you think there are who'd be willing to offer themselves, furnish untiring labor, and promise their sworn testimony to men who are powerful, influential, and eloquent, when they think such men want something?

[22] If any of this kind happen to have injected themselves into this trial, shut out their ambition, gentlemen of the jury, by your wisdom, so you'll be seen at the same time to have cared for this man's safety, for your own conscience, and for the security of all citizens against dangerously influential men. For my part, I'll draw you away from witnesses[31] and not allow the truth of this case—which can't in any way be altered—to be grounded upon witnesses' whims, which can be very easily molded, and turned and twisted around with no trouble at all. I'll argue with concrete evidence, I'll rebut the charges with proofs clearer than any light; fact will fight with fact, argument with argument, reason with reason.

THE SERIOUS CHARGES: SEDITION, MURDER, ROBBERY (?)

[23] Consequently, I'm quite pleased that Marcus Crassus has pleaded with gravity and polish that part of the case[32] pertaining to the sedition at Naples, the assault on the Alexandrians at Puteoli, and the property of Palla. I could wish that the part about Dio[33] had also been pleaded by him. About Dio himself, however, what would you expect to hear—seeing as the one who did it either isn't afraid or openly confesses (for he's a king), and the one said to have been his aid and abettor, Publius Asicius, was acquitted in court? Therefore, since this crime is such that the one who committed it doesn't deny it and the one who denied it has been acquitted, should this man be afraid who was far removed not only from the deed, but even from the suspicion of complicity? And if the case did Asicius more good than the ill will from it did him harm, will your slander hurt Caelius, who was tainted not only by no suspicion of that deed, but also by no disgrace?

---

31. 22 **I'll draw you away from witnesses**: Later in the speech (§55), Cicero declares the testimony of a certain witness to be sufficient proof of his argument. See Craig (1989) 314.

32. 23 **that part of the case**: Though the three charges listed in this sentence may well have been valid and significant, Cicero's successful strategy of brushing them off as trivial leaves us in ignorance about what they really were: see Austin (1960) on §23 and pp. 152–54. The sedition at Naples was "probably some local dispute." The assault on the Alexandrians was probably connected with the intrigues involving Ptolemy Auletes (see note on §18 **arrival of King Ptolemy**). The "property of Palla" is mysterious, but it is possible that this Palla was the mother or stepmother of Lucius Gellius Poplicola, probably the "Gellius" whom Catullus attacks as a rival for Clodia's love. If so, it would seem that the prosecution of Caelius was, as Gardner (1958) 432 observes, "a family affair."

33. 23 **the part about Dio**: See note on §18 **arrival of King Ptolemy**.

[24] "But Asicius," you say, "was acquitted through collusion."[34] It's very easy to reply to this point, especially for me, by whom the case for the defense was pleaded. Caelius thinks Asicius' case is excellent; however that may be, he thinks it has nothing to do with his own. And not only Caelius, but also these most cultured and learned youths, endowed with the finest literary training and most outstanding accomplishments, Titus and Gaius Coponius. These of all men were most grieved at Dio's death, since they were won over not only by Dio's zeal for learning and for culture, but also by his hospitality. Dio, as you've heard, lived at Titus' house; he'd met him in Alexandria. What he or his brother, a man of the highest distinction, think of Marcus Caelius you'll hear from them in person if they'll step forward.

THE ISSUE CICERO REALLY WANTS TO ADDRESS: CAELIUS' ALLEGED LOOSE LIVING

[25] Therefore, let these matters be cast aside, so we can at last proceed to those on which this case really turns. I noticed, gentlemen of the jury, that you listened to my friend Lucius Herennius very attentively. Although you were enchanted for the most part by his wit and his particular style of speaking, yet I sometimes feared that that speech, presented to incriminate subtly, might indeed insinuate itself gradually and insidiously into your minds. For he said a lot about luxury, a lot about lust, a lot about the vices of youth, a lot about character and morals; and though in ordinary life he's mild, and usually behaves very agreeably, with that culture and courtesy nearly everyone likes—in *this* case he sounded like a curmudgeon,[35] a censor, a schoolmaster; he scolded Marcus Caelius as father has never scolded son; he delivered a diatribe on incontinence and intemperance. What more can I say, gentlemen of the jury? I excused your rapt attention, seeing as I myself had to shudder at a speech like that—so grim, so grating.

[26] And yet the beginning was the part that impressed me least, where it was said that Caelius was intimate with my friend Bestia, dined with

---

34. 24 **collusion**: For an example of collusion between prosecution and defense, see note on §14 **I myself was almost taken in by him**.

35. 25 **curmudgeon**: Latin *patruus*, "paternal uncle," proverbially harsh and censorious, like our "Dutch uncle." A *maternal* uncle (*avunculus*), on the other hand, was proverbially benevolent, whence our "avuncular." To say "sounded like an uncle" would be fatally ambiguous.

him, often came to his house, supported his candidacy for the praetorship. Things that are manifestly false don't impress me; for he said that those men dined with him who either aren't here or have to tell the same tale out of necessity. Nor, indeed, did it trouble me when he said that Caelius was his companion in the Luperci. What a fierce fraternity, those brothers Luperci, quite primitive and savage, with their infamous woodland pack banded together before culture and laws—seeing as the brothers not only inform against each other, but even mention the fraternity when making an accusation, so that it appears they're afraid someone might possibly be unaware of it!

[27] But I pass over these things; let me respond to the ones that troubled me more. The criticism of his luxurious lifestyle was long but also fairly calm, with more argument than bitterness, so that it was received all the more attentively. For my good friend Publius Clodius,[36] when he was beating the air with great vigor and vehemence, all fired up and pleading everything with the sternest of language, at the top of his lungs—even though I applauded his eloquence, I wasn't terribly afraid of it; for I'd seen him lose quite a few cases.[37] To you, Balbus, with your kind permission, I'll respond first, if it's right and proper for me to defend a man who's never said no to a dinner party, who's been to the park, who's worn perfume, who's seen Baiae.[38]

36. 27 **Publius Clodius**: This is almost certainly not Publius Clodius Pulcher, but some more obscure member of the family.

37. 27 **for I'd seen him lose quite a few cases**: As Gotoff (1986) 132 notes, "No one would know better than Cicero that on occasion these words might be said of any powerful orator."

38. 27 **who's seen Baiae**: Compare §35, in which dalliance at Baiae (a resort on the Bay of Naples) is one of the many reproaches thrown at Clodia. That Baiae is acceptable for a man but damning for a woman is a choice example of the pervasive double standard on which Cicero's argument rests.

It appears that Baiae figured prominently in an earlier quarrel between Cicero and Clodius. In his speech *Against Clodius and Curio* (probably 61 B.C.; only fragments survive), Cicero complains that Clodius has unfairly criticized him—a harmless middle-aged man on summer vacation—for enjoying Baiae's healing waters:

First, this harsh and old-fashioned man railed against those who were at Baiae in the month of April and enjoyed the warm waters. What do I have to do with this man so grim and severe? *These* morals can't withstand such an austere and imperious schoolmaster, according to whom men who are his elders aren't allowed to attend to their delicate health with impunity—even on their own property, at a time when nothing is going on at Rome. But of course, it's fine to excuse the others, just not the one who has property there, no way. "What," he says, "does a man of Arpinum, a hayseed and a rube, have to do with Baiae?" (Cicero fr. 20 Schoell)

[28] For my part, I've both seen and heard of many men in this State who have not only tasted this sort of life with their lips and touched it, as they say, with their fingertips, but have in fact surrendered their entire youth to sensual pleasures—and have then at some point emerged from the depths and borne good fruit, as they say, and become men of substance and renown. For by common concession this age is allowed a certain amount of fun, and nature itself lavishes desires upon youth. If these erupt in such a way that they ruin no one's life, overturn no one's house, then they're generally considered harmless and acceptable.

[29] But you seemed to me to be stirring up some special ill will against Caelius out of the disgrace attaching to all youth. And so all the silence that greeted your speech was for this reason: though only one man was being accused, we were thinking about the vices of many. It's easy to attack luxury. Daylight would fail me if I were to attempt to express all that can be said on that subject: about seduction, about adultery, about promiscuity, about extravagance, an enormous speech could be made. Though you set as your theme no specific defendant but rather those terrible vices, yet the topic itself can be the target of copious and weighty accusation. But it's up to your wisdom, gentlemen of the jury, not to be sidetracked from the defendant at hand and not to unleash against the man in the dock that sting of your grave severity which the accuser has aroused against the situation, against the vices, against the morals, against the times we live in—when this man is called into undeserved disrepute not for his own crime, but for the vices of many.

[30] Therefore I don't dare respond to your severity as it deserves. For my plan was to beg a little leeway for youth and seek forgiveness. As I say, I don't dare; I offer no excuse on the basis of age, I waive the rights that are conceded to all. This alone I ask: if at this moment there's any common hatred of the debt, the willfulness, the lusts of youth—which I recognize are great—then at least let this man not be injured by the sins of others, by the vices of youth and of the times. In turn, I who make this request shall not neglect to respond very carefully to the accusations brought specifically against the man himself.

See D'Arms (1970) 42–43 and Geffcken (1973) 70–74 on Cicero's permutations of the Baiae theme, especially the ironic difference between this speech (Baiae harmless, Clodius puritanical) and the *Pro Caelio* (Baiae dangerous, Clodius degenerate).

The Specific Charges Concerning Clodia: Gold and Poison

Now, there are two accusations, about gold and about poison.[39] In these charges one and the same character[40] is at work. The gold was taken from Clodia, the poison sought in order to be given to Clodia, as they say. All the other things are not accusations but slanders, belonging to an emotional quarrel rather than a political trial. "Adulterer, pervert, middleman"—this is abuse, not accusation. There's no basis, no foundation for these accusations; they're insulting phrases rashly hurled out by an angry prosecutor, with no one taking responsibility for them.

[31] I see the author[41] of these two accusations, I see the source, I see the true identity and wellspring. He needed gold; he took it from Clodia, took it without witness, and kept it as long as he wanted. I see here the greatest evidence of a remarkable sort of intimacy. He wanted to kill her; he sought poison, bribed the slaves, prepared the potion, chose the place, brought it secretly. Again, I see here the great hostility arising from a really bitter breakup. The whole substance of this case, gentlemen of the jury, is with Clodia, a woman not only noble, but also notorious;[42] I'll say nothing about her except what's necessary to refute the accusation.

[32] But you understand, Gnaeus Domitius, in keeping with your outstanding insight, that the whole affair for us turns upon her. If she doesn't say she provided the gold for Marcus Caelius, if she doesn't claim he

---

39. 30 **about gold and about poison**: Cicero goes into more detail about these charges in §§51–53.

40. 30 **character**: Latin *persona*, literally "mask" and hence "character (in a play)." See note on §1 **public festivals and games**.

41. 31 **author**: Latin *auctor*, which (as in English) means both "originator" and "author [of a literary work]." Cicero likes to cast Clodia as the "composer" of a farce; compare notes on §64 **little drama** and *Sest.* 116 **all his sister's interludes**.

42. 32 **not only noble, but also notorious**: The exact force of the wordplay here is hard to render in English. Latin *nobilis* can mean "noble" in our sense of both "aristocratic" and "heroic," but it can also mean "well known" (not necessarily in a good way). Latin *nota* means, literally, "known," with possible connotations of personal acquaintance, widespread familiarity, and notoriety (in an unflattering sense). Cicero is implying that the flamboyant, aristocratic Clodia is intimately "known" to more men than a decent matron should be. As the Greek historian Thucydides has Pericles observe in his famous Athenian funeral oration, "There will be great glory for her who is least spoken of among men, for good or ill" (*Peloponnesian War* 2.46). Despite the gap between Periclean Athens and late Republican Rome, there was still a lingering sense that for a woman to be widely "known" was not a virtue.

prepared the poison for her, then we're acting with undue aggression in naming a materfamilias[43] in a manner other than that which the sanctity of matrons demands. But if, with that woman removed, they've got no accusation or resources left with which to assail Marcus Caelius, what choice do I have, as his defending counsel, but to repel those who are attacking him? And indeed, I'd be doing that even more vigorously, were I not held back by my enmity with that woman's husband—brother, I meant to say;[44] I always make that mistake. Now I'll proceed with moderation and go no further than my duty and the case itself compel: for I've never thought it seemly for me to engage in enmity with a woman, especially with one everyone has always considered to be the (girl)friend of all men rather than the enemy of any.[45]

APPIUS CLAUDIUS THE BLIND ACCUSES CLODIA

[33] Nevertheless, I'll inquire of Clodia herself beforehand whether she'd rather I deal with her in a severe, grave, old-fashioned way or in a relaxed, smooth, urbane manner. If she chooses that austere manner and style, then I'll have to resurrect from the Underworld one of those bearded characters[46]—not with the little goatee she adores, but with that bristly one we see on ancient statues and busts—to scold the woman and speak in my place, lest by chance she get angry with me. Therefore, let someone rise up from her own family—best of all, the famous Appius Claudius the Blind; for it'll cause him the least pain who won't be able to see her.[47]

---

43. 32 **materfamilias**: Literally, "mother of the family/household," mate of the *paterfamilias*. See introduction, "*Patria Potestas*."

44. 32 **that woman's husband—brother, I meant to say**: This is a choice example of the rhetorical device known as "self-correction," *reprehensio* (Latin) or *epanorthosis* (Greek). As Austin (1960) observes, "Cicero's wit is not always in good taste."

45. 32 **(girl)friend of all men rather than the enemy of any**: See introduction, "love as *amicitia*."

46. 33 **bearded characters**: In the early Republic, long, full beards were in style; in Cicero's day, most mature men were clean shaven. The "little goatee" was a fashion for the self-consciously elegant.

47. 34 **Appius Claudius the Blind . . . see her**: As Osgood (2005) 356–57 points out, Cicero's humorous *prosopopoeia* ("role playing") here alludes to the crusty censor's most famous speech, which apparently began "with Appius noting that, having been pained by his blindness before, he now wished that he were deaf also, because he never expected to see or hear the senate considering such counsels [about making peace with Pyrrhus]." Dufallo (2001) 135 suggests that

[34] He, indeed, if he'll rise up, will thus plead and thus speak forth: "Woman, what do you have to do with Caelius, with a man so very young, with a man who doesn't belong to you?[48] Why were you either so great a friend that you provided gold or so great an enemy that you feared poison? Had you not seen that your father, your uncle, and your grandfather, had you not heard that your great-grandfather, your great-great-grandfather, and your great-great-great-grandfather were consuls? Finally, were you not aware that you were held by the bonds of matrimony to Quintus Metellus, a man most brilliant, brave, and patriotic, who surpassed nearly all citizens in virtue, glory, and dignity the moment he stepped out the door? When you had married out of the most exalted bloodline into the most brilliant family, why were you so intimate with Caelius? Was he your blood relative, your in-law, a friend of your husband?[49] None of these. What was it, therefore, aside from a certain recklessness and lust? If our male ancestors did not impress you, did not even my daughter, the famous Quinta Claudia,[50] inspire you to rival her family renown in the sphere of womanly glory? What about the famous Claudia the Vestal who, embracing her father as he celebrated his triumph, prevented him from being dragged from his chariot by a hostile tribune of the people? Why did the vices of your brother impress you rather than the virtues of your father, and grandfather, and both male and female ancestors all the way back to me? Did I dissolve the peace with Pyrrhus so that you might daily forge pacts[51] of the most shameful love affairs? Did I build the aqueduct so that you might use it for

---

by becoming in his performance a sort of "surrogate" for Appius, "Cicero reproduces many of the cultural values that Appius embodies at the same time that he re-creates gossip as 'truth' and these values themselves as open to a newly selective application rather than rigid imitation."

48. 34 **who doesn't belong to you**: Latin *alienus* means, literally, "belonging to someone else" but can also mean "alien," "a stranger," "estranged," and "inappropriate."

49. 34 **your blood relative, your in-law, a friend of your husband**: These are the three categories of male acquaintances with whom it was acceptable for respectable Roman women to converse.

50. 34 **Quinta Claudia**: When the Romans were attempting to drag a statue of Cybele up the Tiber River (in order to "import" the goddess to Rome), it got inextricably stuck; Quinta Claudia, a matron who had been accused of unchastity, proved her innocence by moving the statue easily after praying to the goddess to vindicate her. See Ovid *Fasti* 4.305–44. As Salzman (1982) 301 points out, this drama was enacted on stage as part of the *Ludi Megalenses* festivities displaced by Caelius' trial; see note on §1 **public festivals and games**. For a compendium of well-known "Claudias" both before and after our Clodia, see Kleiner and Matheson (2000) 1–3.

51. 34 **pacts**: See introduction, "love as *foedus*."

indecencies? Did I build the road so that you might tread it in the company of other women's men?"[52]

CICERO ACCUSES CLODIA

[35] But why, gentlemen of the jury, have I brought on stage such a grave character that I must fear the same Appius may suddenly turn around and begin to accuse Caelius with that censorial gravity of his? But I'll see to that later on, gentlemen of the jury, and in such a way that I'm confident I can justify Marcus Caelius' life to even the most severe of judges. You, however, woman—for now I myself speak to you with no mask between us—if you plan to justify what you do, what you say, what you pretend, what you connive, what you claim, then you must render and explain the reason for such friendship, such intimacy, such connection. For the accusers are bandying about lusts, love affairs, adulteries, Baiae,[53] beaches, dinner parties, trysts, songs, symphonies, boating parties—and these same men indicate that they're saying nothing against your wishes. Since you've wanted these things to be dragged out into the Forum and the court, according to some insane and reckless plan, you should either rebut them and demonstrate that they're false or admit that no credence whatsoever ought to be given to either your accusation or your testimony.[54]

CLODIUS ACCUSES CLODIA

[36] If, on the other hand, you'd rather I proceed in a more urbane fashion, I'll deal with you thus. I'll remove that harsh and almost savage old man; then I'll put on one of the men of today, and best of all your youngest brother, the most urbane in that respect, who loves you so very much— who because of some sort of timidity and groundless fears in the night always used to sleep with you, his big sister, when he was a tot. Suppose

---

52. 34 **other women's men**: See note on §34 **who doesn't belong to you** (the Latin here is *alienus* again).

53. 35 **Baiae**: See note on §27 **who's seen Baiae**.

54. 35 **no credence . . . your testimony**: As Austin (1960) 167–68 points out, in a law passed shortly after the present case, prostitutes were forbidden to testify in court; Cicero's implication that Clodia belongs to this category "must have been something more damaging than mere abuse."

he speaks with you thus: "Why are you in an uproar, sister? Why are you raving mad?

> Why do you raise a shout with your words and make a mountain out of a molehill?[55]

You spied your neighbor, a tender youth; his radiance and his height, his face and his eyes knocked you out; you wanted to see him more often; you found yourself in the same park sometimes; a noblewoman, you want to ensnare this son and heir of a miserly and grasping father[56] with your wealth and hold him captive. You can't; he kicks back, he rejects you, he pushes you away, he doesn't think your gifts are worth it. Take yourself to another man! You've got gardens on the Tiber, and you've carefully placed them in a location where all the young men come to swim; you can choose your matches from here any day of the week. Why are you pestering this man who rejects you?"

COMIC FATHERS ACCUSE CAELIUS

[37] Now, in turn, I come back to you, Caelius, and take upon myself a father's authority and severity. But I can't decide which father is best to put on—some imperious and pitiless Caecilian one:[57]

> "For now at last my spirit burns, my heart is swelling with anger,"

or one like this:

> "Oh unhappy one, oh accursed one!"

Those fathers are made of iron:

55. 36 **Why do you raise a shout . . . molehill**: This line is from a comedy that would have been known to Cicero's audience but is lost to us.

56. 36 **son and heir of a miserly and grasping father**: Two stock comic characters.

57. 37 **Caecilian one**: Caecilius Statius was a comic poet of the second century B.C. who, as Austin (1960) points out, "seems to have specialized in surly old men." In the passage that follows, Cicero contrasts the "imperious and pitiless" father with the lenient and forgiving one (both were stock figures in comedy).

"What should I say, what should I wish? Since you
with your foul deeds make all my wishes vain,"

they're scarcely tolerable. Such a father would say: "Why did you betake
yourself to the vicinity of a whore? Why didn't you flee when her snares
became evident?

> Why have you known any woman belonging to another? Scatter and
>   squander;
> you have my permission. If you become poor, you'll be the one to
>   suffer, not me.
> I'll be satisfied if I can just enjoy what life is left me."

[38] To this grim and outspoken old man Caelius would respond that
he didn't stray from the path at all in following his desire. What proof?
There was no expenditure, no losses, no borrowing. "But," you say, "there
was that nasty rumor!" How rare the man who can escape *that,* especially
in such a gossipy City! Are you surprised that a neighbor of this woman
has gotten a bad reputation when her own full brother[58] wasn't able to
escape the whisperings of the wicked? For a mild and merciful father
such as this one—

"He broke down the doors: they'll be rebuilt. He tore
his clothing: it'll be resewn,"

Caelius' case is a very simple one. For what point was there on which he
could not defend himself easily? Now, I'm not speaking a word against
that woman. But if there were some woman—not like this one in the
least—who prostituted herself to all and sundry, who'd always got some
man openly declared as her lover, to whose gardens, house, Baiae, the
lusts of all men moved as they pleased, who even supported young men
and made up for the stinginess of their fathers by her own expenditures—
if this widow were living freely, this hussy lecherously, this moneybags
extravagantly, this slut in the lifestyle of a whore—should I consider a
man improper if he may have taken a few liberties in addressing her?

---

58. 38 **full brother**: Clodius and Clodia were actually half-siblings (different mothers).

Let's Lighten Up

[39] Someone will say: "Is this your idea of discipline, then? Is this how you instruct the youth? It was for this that his father entrusted and handed over his boy to you, to station his youth amid love affairs and sensual pleasures, and for you to defend this lifestyle and these pursuits?" If any man, gentlemen of the jury, had been endowed with a character so virtuous and restrained that he rejected all sensual pleasures and spent the whole course of his life in labor of body and development of mind, who took pleasure in no rest, no relaxation, no amusements of his friends, no sports, no dinner parties, who thought nothing in life was worth seeking except what pertained to praise and dignity, then in my opinion I consider this man to be equipped and adorned with divine virtues of some kind. In this class, I believe, were the Camilli, the Fabricii, the Curii, all those men who brought the State from its humblest beginnings to its present greatness.

[40] But this class of virtues is scarcely to be found, not only in the *mores* of our own day, but even in books. Even the volumes recording that ancient severity have become obsolete, and not only among us [Romans], who pursued this code of action and manner of life in deed rather than word. Even among the Greeks, most learned of men, who, though they could not act, yet were allowed to speak and write in honorable and distinguished ways, certain other precepts became prominent when the times changed for Greece.

[41] And so some have said that the wise do everything for the sake of pleasure,[59] and educated men have not shied away from this shameful turn of speech. Others have thought that virtue ought to be combined with pleasure,[60] so that through their skill in speaking they've combined the things that contradict each other most of all. Those who've commended the single straight path to glory through labor[61] are practically left alone in

---

59. 41 **the wise . . . pleasure**: A caricature of Epicurean philosophy, to which Cicero was not sympathetic. Ancient Epicureanism did elevate the importance of "pleasure" (Greek *hedone*) but rejected the intemperate sensualism we call "hedonism."

60. 41 **Others have thought . . . pleasure**: The Academic philosophers (named after Plato's Academy), to whom Cicero was sympathetic, advocated a path somewhere between Epicureanism and Stoicism.

61. 41 **Those who've commended . . . labor**: Stoicism was actually quite influential in the Roman thinking of Cicero's day; he is downplaying its significance for the sake of his present argument.

the schools. For Nature herself has produced for us many temptations for Virtue to yawn, from time to time, and shut her eyes; she's shown young men many slippery paths on which she could scarcely set foot and go forward without some fall and tumble; she's given us a great variety of highly agreeable things by which not only this tender age may be captivated, but even the more seasoned.

[42] Accordingly, if you find any man who spurns with his eyes all beauty in things, who's captivated by no scent, no touch, no taste, who shuts out every sweet sound from his ears, I, perhaps, and a few others will suppose that the gods are showing this man their special favor—but most will suppose they're showing him their wrath. Therefore, let that deserted and uncultivated and secluded path be left to the leaves and brambles. Let youth be allowed a little fun; let young manhood be a little freer; let pleasures not always be told "No"; let that true and upright conduct not always win out. Let desire and pleasure occasionally conquer reason, as long as the following precept and moderation in these matters are maintained: Let youth preserve its own integrity, let it not steal someone else's wife, let it not squander its patrimony; let it not be ruined by interest payments; let it not invade someone else's home and household; let it not bring unchastity to the chaste, dishonor to the decent, disgrace to the good; let it not frighten anyone with violence; let it not participate in treachery; let it be free of crime. Finally, when it does bow to sensual pleasures and give some time to youthful fun and to these frivolous desires of young manhood, let it call itself back at some point to care for affairs of the home, the Forum, and the Republic, so it can be seen to have thrown off through satiety and scorned through experience what it hadn't previously rejected through reason.

[43] And indeed, both in our recollection and in that of our fathers and ancestors, gentlemen of the jury, many of the most outstanding people and illustrious citizens were those whose excellent virtues stood out at a mature age, when the desires of youth had simmered down. I'd rather not mention any of these by name; you can bring them to mind yourselves. For I don't want to combine even the smallest peccadillo with the supreme glory of any brave and brilliant man. But if I did want to, I could broadcast the names of many of the best and most distinguished men, who were marked partly by too much freedom in youth, partly by excessive luxury, enormous debt, extravagance, love affairs. Since these things were later

covered up by many virtues, anyone who wanted to excuse them could do so on the grounds of youth.

Caelius' Nearly Sterling Character as Evidenced by His Lack of Debt and His Oratorical Skill

[44] However, in the case of Marcus Caelius—for I'll now speak more confidently about his honorable pursuits, since I dare to make certain confessions freely, relying upon your wisdom—no luxury will be turned up, no extravagance, no debt, no passion for dinner parties and brothels. And indeed, age not only does not diminish in people this vice of greed and gluttony, but even increases it. Moreover, what we call "loves" and "cherished delights," which generally don't continue to bother those endowed with a firmer mind—for they quickly ripen and wither—never did besiege him or hold him captive.

[45] When he was speaking in his own defense, and before that when he was prosecuting—I say these things to defend him, not to boast[62]—you heard his manner of speech, his eloquence, his wealth of expressions and language; in your wisdom, you perceived these things thoroughly. And in him you saw not only his native wit shining forth, which often thrives through its own strength even if not nourished by industry; rather, unless by chance I was deceived by my own bias toward him, he possessed the light of reason, instilled by good education and enhanced by care and diligence. Yet know this, gentlemen of the jury, that those lusts which are imputed to Caelius and these pursuits[63] about which I'm arguing can't easily coexist in one man. For it's impossible for a mind surrendered to passion, hampered by lust, by desire, by greed, often by excessive wealth, sometimes even by poverty, to be able to sustain whatever this is that we do in public speaking, however it is we do it, not only by physical, but also by mental exertion.

[46] Now can you think of any reason why, when there are such rewards for eloquence, such pleasure in speaking, such praise, such influence, such honor, there are and always have been so few who occupy themselves with this pursuit? It's because all sensual pleasures must be blotted out, all pursuits

---

62. 45 **boast**: Cicero had been Caelius' instructor.

63. 45 **those lusts . . . and these pursuits**: The modern reader may doubt that lust and rhetorical skill are in fact incompatible. Yet Cicero adamantly maintains throughout his works that success in oratory requires personal virtue.

of amusement left behind, sports, jokes, parties, practically even the con-versation of friends abandoned. Consequently, in this matter the sheer labor is a stumbling block for people and discourages them from the quest, not a lack of native wit or childhood education.

[47] Now would this man, if he'd given himself over to the sort of life you describe, have prosecuted an ex-consul while still in his youth? If this man were running away from labor, if he were held captive by pleasures, would he be entering this sort of battle daily, would he invite personal enmities, would he prosecute, would he risk a capital trial, would he himself fight for so many months under the very eyes of the Roman people either for salvation or for glory? Therefore, doesn't that neighborhood smell at all suspicious, and the rumors people are spreading—doesn't Baiae itself speak out? In fact, not only does it speak out, it positively bellows that the lust of one woman has debased itself this far: not only does she not seek seclusion and shadows to conceal her scandalous behavior, but she positively exults in the most shameful deeds among teeming crowds and in the clear light of day.

BACK TO CLODIA, THE WHORE

[48] But if there's anyone who would think even affairs with prostitutes should be forbidden to youth, certainly that man is quite severe—I can't deny it—but he's at odds not only with the license of the present genera-tion, but also with the customs and concessions of our ancestors. For when was this not common practice, when was it criticized, when was it not permitted, when, in short, was it the case that what is allowed was not allowed? Here I'll just outline the situation itself, I'll mention no woman by name; just so much I'll leave ambiguous.

[49] If some unmarried woman throws open her house to the lust of all men and openly establishes herself in a whorish lifestyle; if she makes a habit of enjoying dinner parties with men who are complete strangers; if she were to do this in the City, in the park, among those crowds at Baiae; if, finally, not only in her bearing, but also in her dress and the company she keeps, not only by flaming eyes[64] and licentious speech, but also by

---

64. 49 **flaming eyes**: This is the only detail in any ancient source about Clodia's appearance (other than the indirect ones in Cat. 43). See Griffith (1996) on Clodia's flaming eyes as evidence of her sexual immorality.

embraces, osculations,[65] beach parties, boating parties, dinner parties, she were to conduct herself in such a way that she was seen to be not only a whore, but a brazen and dissipated whore: if, by chance, some young man should have been with this woman, would he appear in your eyes, Lucius Herennius, to be a predator or a lover—to have wanted to conquer her chastity or to satisfy her lust?

[50] I'm forgetting about the injuries you've done, Clodia, I'm putting away the memory of my own grief; I'm paying no mind to your cruelties to my friends and family in my absence. Let these words I've spoken not be aimed at you. But I ask the following specifically of you, since the accusers say they've got both the accusation from you and you yourself as its witness. If there should be any woman of the type I depicted a little earlier—not at all like yourself—with the lifestyle and behavior of a whore, if a young man should have some dealings with her, would this seem to you to be particularly shameful and scandalous? If you're not that woman—as I prefer to think—then what charge can they make against Caelius? But if they'll have it that you *are* that woman, then why should we be afraid of this accusation, if you don't care about it?[66] Accordingly, please show me the path and the strategy for my defense. For either your modesty will protest that nothing too scurrilous was done by Marcus Caelius, or your immodesty will offer a splendid line of defense both for this man and for all the rest.

BACK TO THE GOLD ISSUE

[51] Now that my speech appears to have emerged from the shallows and sailed past the cliffs, the remainder of my voyage[67] looks free and clear. For the two accusations of the most serious crimes revolve around a single woman: the gold, which is said to have been taken from Clodia, and the poison, which Caelius is charged with having obtained to murder this same Clodia. According to you, Caelius took gold to give to Lucius Lucceius'

---

65. 49 **osculations**: See note on Cat. 48.6 **osculations**.

66. 50 **If you're not that woman . . . care about it?**: This is a classic example of the "dilemma," a rhetorical device in which the victim is offered a choice between two jointly exhaustive propositions (i.e., no other option is possible), both of which are damning. On Cicero's frequent and masterful use of "dilemma" in this speech, see Craig (1993) 105–21.

67. 51 **voyage**: Roman authors frequently compare the process of writing to a sea voyage.

slaves, by whom Dio the Alexandrian, then living with Lucceius, was to be murdered. A great accusation indeed, either ambushing ambassadors or inciting slaves to murder their master's guest—a plan full of wickedness, full of audacity!

[52] With regard to the former accusation, I ask this first: Did he tell Clodia why he took the gold, or didn't he? If he didn't tell her, then why did she give it? If he did tell her, then she has convicted herself of complicity in the same crime. Did you dare to produce gold from that treasury of yours, to despoil of her ornaments that Venus of yours,[68] despoiler of others, when you knew the magnitude of the crime for which this gold was being sought—for the murder of an ambassador, for the indelible stain of a crime against Lucius Lucceius, the most sacrosanct and honorable of men? In such an enormous wickedness your generous mind should not have been a conspirator, nor your popular house an assistant, nor that hospitable Venus of yours an accomplice.

[53] Balbus saw this; he said that Clodia was kept in the dark, and that Caelius had conveyed to her that he was seeking gold for the expenses of some games. If he was as intimate with Clodia as you claim when you speak so profusely about his lust, then surely he told her why he wanted the gold; if he wasn't so intimate, then she didn't give it to him. So if Caelius told you the truth, you crazy woman, then you knowingly gave him gold for a crime; if he didn't dare tell you, then you didn't give it.

Why should I now refute this accusation with arguments, which are innumerable? I can say that Marcus Caelius' character is utterly alien to the atrocity of so great a crime; it's scarcely believable that it wouldn't have occurred to a man so clever and prudent that the conduct of such a crime shouldn't be entrusted to slaves unknown to him and owned by someone else. I could also ask some other questions of the accuser, as is my custom and that of other counsels for the defense: Where did Caelius meet with Lucceius' slaves? How did he get in touch with them? If it was on his own, how rash! If it was through someone else, then whom? I can verbally hunt down all the secret lairs of suspicion: no motive, no opportunity, no means,

---

68. 52 **that Venus of yours**: Clodia apparently had a statue of Venus in her home, adorned (Cicero implies) with ornaments taken from her various lovers. As Leigh (2004) 303–305 notes, Clodia's wealth would have made the "despoiling" of her lovers unnecessary, but Cicero's insistence on casting her as a prostitute causes him to insert this implausible detail: "The one thing that Clodia's personal situation permits her not to do is forced onto her by her new generic denomination" (305).

no accomplice, no hope either of completing or of concealing the evil deed, no reason at all, no trace of this heinous crime will be turned up.

[54] But every one of these arguments, which are the orator's stock in trade, and which—not because of my native wit, but because of my culti-vated skill and experience in speaking—could have brought me some advan-tage, since they'd appear to be worked up on my own responsibility[69] and adduced as evidence, I relinquish for the sake of brevity. For I have here, gentlemen of the jury, a man you'd easily allow to share in your sacred duty and your oath: Lucius Lucceius, a most sacrosanct man and an upstanding witness, who would neither have failed to hear that such a crime against his reputation and fortunes had been attempted by Marcus Caelius, nor have ignored it, nor have put up with it. Would such a man, endowed with such culture, such learning, such arts and education, have been able to ignore a danger to the very man he loved because of these same interests? And a crime he would have been shocked to hear of against a stranger, would he have neglected to prevent this against his own guest? A crime he would have grieved to find out had been committed by men he didn't know—would he have neglected to realize that this had been committed by his own slaves? What he would have censured if it had been done out in the fields and on public land—would he have put up with this calmly when attempted in his own city and his own house? What he wouldn't have passed over if some yokel had been at risk—would he, a man of learning, have seen fit to cover this up when a most educated man was in peril of treachery?

[55] But why, gentlemen of the jury, am I keeping you any longer? Hear the solemn oath and authoritative statement of the sworn witness himself, and perceive carefully every word of his deposition. Read it out. [LUCIUS LUCCEIUS' DEPOSITION.] What more are you waiting for?[70] Do you suppose the case itself, the truth itself, can send forth a speech in its own behalf? This is the defense of Innocence, this is the speech of the case itself, this is the one and only word of Truth. In the accusation itself there are no grounds for suspicion, in the facts there is no shred of proof, in the

---

69. 54 **worked up on my own responsibility**: Cicero here plays on the distinction, observed in rhetorical theory since Aristotle, between "inartificial" and "artificial" proofs. Whereas the "inartificial" variety (e.g., physical evidence or the testimony of witnesses) exist independently, "artificial" proofs depend upon the orator's powers of deduction and persuasion.

70. 55 **What more are you waiting for?**: See note on §22 **I'll draw you away from witnesses**.

business that's said to have been transacted there is no trace of a conversation, a place, a time; no one is named as a witness, no one as an accomplice; the entire accusation is brought forth from a hostile, a disgraceful, a cruel, a criminal, a lustful *house*. On the other hand, the house that's said to have been assailed by that nefarious wickedness is full of integrity, dignity, responsibility, sacred duty. From this house an authoritative statement bound by oath has been read out for you, so that the matter in question is subject to no doubt whatsoever: whether it is more likely that a rash, impudent, wrathful woman has trumped up a false accusation, or that an upstanding, wise, and temperate man has given a scrupulous deposition.

BACK TO THE POISONING SCHEME

[56] Thus, the only remaining accusation is the one about poison; of this I can neither find the entrance nor discover the exit. For what was the reason Caelius supposedly wanted to give poison to that woman? To avoid returning the gold? But did she ask for it? To escape accusation? But did anyone make one? Would anyone, in fact, have even mentioned Caelius, if he had prosecuted no one? Indeed, you've even heard Lucius Herennius say explicitly that he never would have sought to cause trouble for Caelius, if Caelius hadn't prosecuted Lucius' friend a second time for the same offense after the friend had been acquitted. Is it believable, then, that so great a crime was committed for no reason? And don't you see that the accusation of an enormous crime has been trumped up in order to appear to be the reason for undertaking another crime?

[57] To whom did he confide, what abettor did he use, what ally, what accomplice, to whom did he entrust so great a crime, to whom his person, to whom his own safety? To the woman's slaves? So it's been charged. And was this man—whom you surely at least credit with native wit, even if you take away everything else because of his enemy's speech—was he so insane as to entrust his own fortunes completely to someone else's slaves? But, I say, to what sort of slaves? For this very point makes a big difference: Was it to those he realized were not experiencing the usual conditions of slavery, but were living too licentiously, too freely, too intimately with their mistress? For who doesn't see, gentlemen of the jury, or who doesn't acknowledge, that in the kind of house where the materfamilias lives like a whore, where nothing that's done is fit to see the light of day,

where outlandish passions, luxuries, in short, all vices and scandals simply unheard of are milling about—that in such a house slaves are not slaves, to whom all these things are entrusted, through whom they're performed, who are involved in the same pleasures, to whom secrets are confided, to whom, even, some part of the daily expenditure and luxury flows back? Did Caelius, then, not see this?

[58] For if he was as intimate with that woman as you claim, then he knew that those slaves, too, were intimate with their mistress. But if his connection with her was not as close as you allege, then how could his intimacy with her slaves be so close? Moreover, what theory is trumped up about the poison itself? Where was it acquired, how was it prepared? How, to whom, in what place was it handed over? They say he had it at home and tested its potency on a certain slave obtained for that very purpose; through that slave's speedy demise the poison was found acceptable by Caelius.

Insinuation That Clodia Poisoned Her Husband

[59] Oh, immortal gods! Why do you sometimes either turn a blind eye to men's greatest crimes or reserve punishment of present villainy until the appointed time? For I saw it, I saw it and drained that cup of sorrow, the bitterest in my life, when Quintus Metellus[71] was wrenched from the embrace and the bosom of his fatherland, when that man who felt himself to have been born for this Empire, two days after he'd shown his vigor in the Senate, on the Rostra, in public affairs, was snatched away, for all his robust youth, his excellent bearing, his supreme strength—snatched most unworthily from all that is good, from the entire State. At that moment— at the very point of death—though now in all other ways his mind was growing dark, this man reserved his final thought for the memory of the Republic, as he watched me weep and signified with choked and dying words what a gale loomed for me, what a storm for the State;[72] knocking several times on the wall he'd shared with Quintus Catulus, he kept calling

---

71. 59 **Quintus Metellus**: The sudden death of Clodia's husband in 59 B.C. led to rumors that she had poisoned him. Although Cicero never accuses her directly—an actual accusation would require concrete evidence—he gets as much mileage or more out of his insinuation that she is in fact her husband's murderess (what George Eliot calls "the superior power of mystery over fact").

72. 59 **what a gale loomed for me, what a storm for the State**: Cicero sees his own exile as a national calamity.

on Catulus' name, often on mine, most often on the Republic, so that it was clear he was grieving not so much that he was dying as that both the fatherland and I were being robbed of his protection.

[60] If the violence of a sudden crime had not destroyed this man, what resistance he, as a man of consular rank, might have put up against his mad cousin—especially since he [Celer] as consul said in the Senate's hearing that he would kill him [Clodius] with his own hand, back when he [Clodius] was beginning to go berserk and stir up trouble! So will that woman, coming forth from this house, dare to say a word about the *celerity*[73] of poison? Will she not be afraid of the house itself proclaiming a speech? Will she not shudder at the walls that know her secrets, at the night full of mourning and grief? But let me return to the accusation; for even this brief reference I've made to that most illustrious and courageous man has weakened my voice with weeping and shackled my mind with pain.

DETAILS OF THE POISONING SCHEME: COMEDY IN THE BATHHOUSE

[61] So at any rate, it's not said where this poison came from or how it was obtained. They say it was given to Publius Licinius here,[74] a decent young man and good, a friend of Caelius; an agreement was made with the slaves that they would come to the Senian baths;[75] Licinius was to go there and hand over to them a small box of poison. At this point I would ask first: What good did it do to have the poison brought to a designated location? Why didn't those slaves just come to Caelius at home? If Caelius still had such a connection, such intimacy with Clodia, what suspicion would be aroused if the woman's slave had been seen at Caelius' house? But if a quarrel had already taken place, if that connection was extinct, if there had been a breakup, then no doubt "this is the source of those tears,"[76] and this is the reason for all these crimes and accusations.

---

73. 60 *celerity*: Clodia's husband's *cognomen* was Celer, "The Swift." Once again, Cicero finds punning innuendo both safer and more effective than open accusation.

74. 61 **Publius Licinius here**: Apparently, Licinius was present in court, but he was never called as a witness. Nothing else is known of him.

75. 61 **Senian baths**: These are "probably baths run as a private speculation . . . such as one often reads of in Martial; the adjective may conceal the name of the manager or builder of the baths" (Austin [1960]).

76. 61 **"this is the source of those tears"**: A line from a comedy, Terence *Andria* 129.

[62] "But no," says the accuser, "when the slaves had squealed to their mistress about this whole affair and Caelius' wickedness, the cunning woman instructed them to promise Caelius everything; but so that Licinius could be caught red-handed when the poison was handed over by him, she ordered the Senian baths to be designated as the place, so she could send her friends to hide out there, then suddenly jump out and catch Licinius when he'd arrived and was handing over the poison." All these allegations, gentlemen of the jury, can be very easily refuted. For why had she designated the public baths, of all places, in which I can find no possible hiding place for men in togas? For if they were in the vestibule of the baths, they wouldn't be hidden; but if they wanted to slip inside, they could hardly do so conveniently in boots and clothes, and might not be admitted at all—unless by chance that powerful woman, by the usual three-penny exchange,[77] had gotten on intimate terms with the bathman.

[63] And I, for my part, was dying to see what sort of fine fellows were to be summoned as witnesses to this poisoning scheme caught in the act; for none have been named thus far. However, I have no doubt that they're highly respectable, who, first, are intimate friends of such a woman, and second, accepted the assignment of being shoved into the baths, which she never would have obtained except from men most honorable and full of dignity, however powerful she might be. But why do I speak of those witnesses' dignity? Observe their virtue, and their diligence. "They hid out in the baths." Outstanding witnesses! "Then they audaciously jumped out." Paragons of self-control! For this is their story: When Licinius had come, was holding the box in his hand, was trying to hand it over, had not yet handed it over, then, suddenly, out flew those brilliant anonymous witnesses; but Licinius, though he'd already stretched out his hand to give over the box, drew it back and took to his heels after the men's sudden attack. O great power of Truth, which easily, all by itself, defends itself against men's cleverness, craftiness, cunning, and all the treachery anyone can dream up!

---

77. 62 **usual three-penny exchange**: Latin *quadrantaria illa permutatione,* a pun whose exact significance is hard to pin down. The usual price of admission to the baths was a *quadrans,* a small copper coin. Caelius called Clodia a *quandrantaria Clytemnestra (Inst.* 8.6.53). As Plutarch explains (*Cicero* 29.5), "They called her 'Quandrantia,' because one of her lovers had put copper coins in a purse and sent them to her as silver (they used to call the smallest copper coin a 'quadrans')." Whether or not Plutarch's etymology of the epithet is correct, the implication is that Clodia was both undiscriminating and inexpensive.

[64] For example, take this whole little drama,[78] by an experienced poetess of countless dramas—how lacking in plot, how incapable of finding a finale! What can we say? Those men, numerous as they were—for there must have been not a few, both so Licinius could be easily caught and so the thing would be better attested by the eyes of many—why did they let Licinius slip through their fingers? And how could it have been harder to seize Licinius after he drew back, in order *not* to hand over the box, than if he *had* handed it over? For they were in position to seize Licinius, so that Licinius would be caught red-handed either when he was holding the poison or when he'd handed it over. This was the woman's entire plan, this was the assignment of these men who were summoned—though I'm still in the dark about why you say they jumped out rashly and prematurely. This was why they'd been summoned, this was the very reason they'd been stationed there: for the poison, the plot, in short, the crime itself, to be caught in the act.

[65] Could they have jumped out at any better time than when Licinius had arrived, when he was holding the box of poison in his hand? If the woman's friends had suddenly emerged from the baths and seized Licinius when it had already been handed over to the slaves, then he'd be begging for protection from bystanders and denying that the box had been handed over by himself. How could they prove him wrong? Would they say they'd seen him? First of all, they'd be calling down upon their own heads an accusation for a most terrible crime; moreover, they'd be saying they'd seen something they couldn't possibly have seen from where they'd been stationed. Therefore, they revealed themselves at the perfect moment, when Licinius had arrived, was getting out the box, was stretching out his hand, was handing over the poison. This is the finale not of a drama, but of a mime—in which, when a suitable ending can't be found, someone gives the slip, then the clapper sounds and the curtain goes up.[79]

[66] And so I ask why it is that this womanly squadron of yours let Licinius—who was faltering, hesitating, backing away, attempting to flee—slip through their fingers; why they didn't seize him; why they didn't mold

---

78. 64 **little drama**: Latin *fabella,* diminutive of *fabula*; see notes on §31 **author**, §69 **most obscene story**, and *Sest.* 116 **all his sister's interludes.**

79. 65 **the clapper sounds and the curtain goes up**: The "clapper" was a clicking device worn like a shoe, used to mark time for dancers or (as here) to signal that the performance was ending. In Cicero's day the curtain was *raised* to conceal the stage and *lowered* to reveal it (there was a slot for the curtain at the front of the stage floor).

the accusation for such a terrible crime by his own confession, by the eyes of many witnesses, by the very voice, in short, of the heinous deed. I suppose they were afraid that so many men would be unable to overcome just one, strong men a weak one, swift men a man scared out of his wits? No evidence will be found in this affair, no grounds for suspicion in this case, no conclusion from this accusation. And so this entire case has been steered away from evidence, from logic, from those tangible proofs by which Truth is so often illumined, toward witnesses. For my part, gentlemen of the jury, I'm awaiting these witnesses not only without any fear, but even with some hope of a good laugh.

[67] My mind is already itching to see, first, elegant young fellows who are intimate friends of this wealthy and noble woman, then brave men stationed by their commandress in ambush within the bunker of the bathhouse. I'll ask them how they lay hidden and where, whether it was a tub or a Trojan Horse[80] that carried and covered so many unconquered heroes waging womanish war. Moreover, I'll compel them to answer why it was that men so numerous and valiant didn't seize this man, all by himself and as weak as you see him here, or pursue him when he fled; without a doubt, they'll never be able to explain themselves if they come to that point. However witty, glib, sometimes even eloquent they may be over their wine, there's one kind of power in the Forum, another in the dining room; one skill among these benches, another among couches; jurors and carousers don't share the same perspective; the light of the sun, in short, is quite different from the light of a lamp. And so, if these men will step forward, we'll shake out all their "cherished delights,"[81] all their idiocies. But they should hear me out in this: Let them turn their energies elsewhere, let them curry favor some other way, let them show off in other venues; let them ingratiate themselves with that woman through their charm, let them conquer her through their extravagance, let them cling to her, lie at her feet, be her slaves; but let them spare the life and fortunes of an innocent man.

---

80. 67 **a tub or a Trojan Horse**: Cicero combines a stock situation from Roman comedy, an adulterer hidden under a tub, with the most famous ambush in martial epic. See Wiseman (1985) 29.

81. 67 **"cherished delights"**: The use of *deliciae* here to mean "effeminate affectations" could hardly be more derogatory.

CLODIA'S SLAVES AND AN OBSCENE RUMOR INVOLVING A BOX

[68] "But those slaves were manumitted on the advice of her relatives, most noble and illustrious people." At last we find something that that woman can be said to have done on the advice and authority of her family,[82] the bravest of men. But I'm longing to know what sort of evidence this manumission provides: it means either that a charge was trumped up against Caelius, or that the possibility of examination by torture[83] was removed, or that a reward was given with good reason to the slaves who were her accomplices in all kinds of affairs. "But the relatives," I'm told, "approved it." Why wouldn't they approve it, since you said[84] you were reporting to them something not brought to you by others, but discovered by you yourself?

[69] Is it any wonder if a most obscene story[85] has latched onto that imaginary box? It seems that nothing fails to fall in with a woman of that sort. The thing has been heard and repeated endlessly as gossip. You've long since recognized in your minds, gentlemen of the jury, what I want to say— or rather, what I don't want to say. Even if this thing was done, it certainly wasn't done by Caelius—for what would it have to do with him?—but by some youth, perhaps, lacking not so much in cleverness as in shame. But if this was a fiction, then it was a lie, not exactly proper perhaps, but still not without wit. Certainly public opinion and gossip would never have given it the stamp of approval, were it not that everything that smacks of the gutter appears to *square*[86] so well with that woman's character.

---

82. 68 **advice and authority of her family**: Technically, a woman was unable to engage in legal transactions without the formal approval of a male guardian (*tutor*); Clodia seems to have summoned a council of her male relatives in order to manumit her slaves. In practice a powerful woman could simply choose a pliable guardian to serve as a rubber stamp.

83. 68 **examination by torture**: Slaves could be examined in court only under torture.

84. 68 **you said**: The "you" addressed here must be Clodia (the ending on *ipsa*, "yourself," is feminine); what the sentence refers to is obscure.

85. 69 **most obscene story**: The word *fabula* can mean "story," "rumor," or "drama." What the *fabula* of the box (*pyxis*) was we can only guess; it seems to have involved some sort of off-color practical joke on Clodia.

86. 69 *square*: Latin *quadrare*, probably a pun on Clodia's nickname; see note on §62 **usual three-penny exchange**.

First Attempt at a Conclusion

[70] My case, gentlemen of the jury, has been pleaded and concluded. Now, you understand how great a judgment faces you, how great a commission has been given you. You are trying a case of seditious violence. This is the law that pertains to the authority, the majesty, the status of the fatherland, the safety of all people; the law that Quintus Catulus carried in what were nearly the final days of the Republic, during the armed rebellion of its citizens; the law that, when that raging fire had been tamed during my consulate, extinguished the smoking remnants of the conspiracy: is it under this same law that the youth of Caelius is now being called to trial, not for a penalty owed the Republic, but for the depraved lust and "cherished delight" of a woman?

[71] And at this point, what's more, the condemnation of Marcus Camurtius and Gaius Caesernius is being brought up.[87] O stupidity! Should I call it stupidity or unparalleled impudence? Do you dare, when you're coming from that woman, to mention those men? Do you dare to stir up the memory of so great a punishment, not yet extinguished, indeed, but dampened by passage of time? For through what charge, what wrong, did they perish? To be sure, they avenged this same woman's spite and resentment with a wicked Vettian assault. Therefore, so the name of "Vettius" could be heard in this case, so that old penny story[88] could be recalled—was *that* why the case of Camurtius and Caesernius was revived? Although they certainly weren't liable under the law concerning seditious violence, yet they were implicated in such evildoing that it seemed they shouldn't be released from the noose of any law whatsoever.

Caelius' Nearly Exemplary Career

[72] Marcus Caelius, on the other hand—why is he in the dock here? No charge appropriate to this court is being brought against him, nor even

---

87. 71 **the condemnation of Marcus Camurtius and Gaius Caesernius**: Austin (1960) notes, "a case, otherwise unknown, presumably quoted by the prosecution as a precedent for extending the *Lex de vi* [law about seditious violence] to cover a case of immorality; Clodia had been concerned in it, and Cicero intends to deplore the imprudence of its mention in the present context, with all that it implied about her."

88. 71 **wicked Vettian assault . . . old penny story**: What these phrases refer to is unknown. It has been conjectured that there is a connection with the story of coin substitution related by

anything that would be beyond the reach of law but subject to your keen scruples. His early youth was devoted to education and to the arts by which we're prepared for this activity in the Forum, for engaging in politics, for honor, for glory, for prestige. Moreover, he was devoted to such friendships with older men whose industry and temperance he would most want to imitate, and to such pursuits shared by his peers, that he would appear to be seeking the same path of glory as the best and noblest.

[73] Furthermore, when a bit of maturity had been added to his youth, he set out for Africa[89] as the aide-de-camp of the proconsul Quintus Pompeius, a man of great propriety and diligence in every duty; Caelius' father had business and holdings in this province, and moreover some experience with provincial administration was quite reasonably deemed suitable by our ancestors for this period of life. He departed from there with the highest commendation from Pompeius, as you'll learn from the latter's own testimony. According to time-honored practice and the example of those youths who later emerged as the highest men and most illustrious citizens in the State, he wanted his diligence to be recognized by the Roman people through prosecuting some brilliant case.

[74] I could wish his desire for glory had led him down a different path; but the time for such complaints has passed. He prosecuted Gaius Antonius,[90] my colleague, a miserable man for whom the memory of his outstanding service to the Republic did no good and the suspicion of intended evildoing did much harm. Afterward, not one of his peers ever attained more prominence in the Forum, in business, in pleading cases for his friends; not one gained more influence among his own people. All the things that no men can achieve unless they're vigilant, sober, industrious—he gained these things through labor and diligence.

Excusing Caelius' Affair with Clodia

[75] At this bend in the course, so to speak, of youth (I'll cover nothing up, relying as I do on your culture and wisdom), the young man's reputation

---

Plutarch (see note on §62 **usual three-penny exchange**), but no external evidence supports this theory.

89. 73 **set out for Africa**: In 61 B.C.

90. 74 **prosecuted Gaius Antonius**: See note on §15 **accusing another man of conspiracy**.

got a bit stuck on the turning post[91] through his new acquaintance with that woman, his unfortunate neighborhood, and his inexperience with pleasures, which, when they've been bottled up too long and repressed and restricted in early youth, sometimes suddenly erupt and pour out in every direction. From this life, or I should say, from this gossip—for it wasn't nearly so egregious as people were saying—anyway, from whatever it was, he has emerged and completely escaped and freed himself and is so far removed from the disgrace of that intimacy that he's now warding off the same woman's enmity and hatred.

Excusing the Prosecution for Bribery of Cicero's Colleague

[76] And then, to quell the gossip that kept getting in his way about his "cherished delight" and laziness—he did this against my wishes, by Hercules, and with much resistance from me, but he did it nonetheless— he brought a charge of bribery against my friend.[92] He keeps pursuing him, prosecutes him again after his acquittal; he pays no mind to any of us, he's more violent than I would wish. But I'm not talking about wisdom, which isn't suited to that period of life; I'm talking about impetuosity of spirit, about the ambition to win, about the mind's burning desire for glory; such pursuits in *our* particular time of life ought to be more circumscribed, but in youth they prefigure in the leaf, as it were, what ripeness of virtue and what fruits of industry are to come. And indeed, young men of great natural talent must always be reined in from glory rather than spurred on; there's more need for pruning than for grafting at that age, if it's blossoming with praises for its talent.

Another Apparent Summation

[77] Therefore, if anyone feels that this man's energy, aggressiveness, and obstinacy in conceiving or conducting enmities have boiled up too high, if anyone's been offended by one of these trivialities, by his brand of

---

91. 75 **stuck on the turning post**: Chariot races (Rome's most popular sport) required the competitors to turn sharply around a post (*meta*) at the halfway point.

92. 76 **charge of bribery against my friend**: Bestia (see note on §1 **son of a man . . . prosecuted already**).

purple, by his throngs of friends, by his sparkle, by his glamour—soon those things will have simmered down, soon age and experience and time will have mellowed them all. Preserve, then, for the Republic, gentlemen of the jury, a citizen of good education, of good political inclinations, one of the good men.[93] I promise you this and pledge it to the Republic: If I myself have done right by the Republic, this man will never be estranged from my way of thinking. I promise this both relying on your friendship and because he himself has now bound himself by the sternest of obligations.

ONE MORE DIG AT CLODIUS' HENCHMAN

[78] The kind of man who prosecuted an ex-consul because he [Caelius] said that the Republic had been violated by him [Antonius] cannot himself be a citizen itching for revolution in the Republic; a man who wouldn't even let someone acquitted of bribery stay acquitted can't possibly be an unpunished briber himself. The Republic holds these two prosecutions by Marcus Caelius, gentlemen of the jury, as either hostages preventing dangerous behavior or pledges of his good intentions. Therefore I beg and beseech you, gentlemen of the jury, that in the same State where just a few days ago Sextus Cloelius was acquitted, whom you saw for two years to be either an assistant or a leader in sedition; a man without property, without faith, without hope, without home, without fortunes; a man corrupt of face, of tongue, of hand, of life altogether; a man who set fire with his own hands to sacred buildings,[94] to the wealth of the Roman people, to a public memorial; a man who struck down the monument of Catulus,[95] destroyed my own house, and burned that of my brother; a man who on the Palatine and under the eyes of the City incited the slave population to bloodshed and to burning the City: in this same State I beg you not to allow that man to have been acquitted through a woman's influence and Marcus Caelius to

---

93. 77 **one of the good men**: "Good" (Latin *bonus*) in this sentence is a code word for politically conservative "Optimate." As Riggsby (1999) 92–93 notes, "to accuse one of the *boni* of *vis* (seditious violence) was *ipso facto* nonsensical. Various individuals of proper political leanings might be subject to occasional lapses of moral or practical judgment which would lead to other crimes, but they could not, by definition, be involved in *vis*."

94. 78 **sacred buildings**: The Temple of the Nymphs, where the censors' records were kept.

95. 78 **monument of Catulus**: Not the friend of Cicero referred to in §59, but a war hero who was consul in 102 B.C. This monument adjoined Cicero's house, which Clodius burned in 58 B.C.; Cicero's brother's house was burned the following year.

be sacrificed to a woman's lust—lest the same woman with her husband-
and-brother be seen to have rescued the most vile bandit and to have crushed
the most honorable young man.

FINAL APPEAL: BACK TO CAELIUS' FATHER

[79] But when you picture to yourself this man's youth, conjure up also
before your eyes the old age of this miserable man here,[96] who leans upon
this, his only son, relying on his hope for him, dreading only misfortune for
him; shore up this man who is a supplicant of your mercy, a slave of your
power, cast down not so much at your feet as at your character and your
sensibilities, so that in seeing another's pain you may bow either to your
righteousness or to your pity. Do not wish, gentlemen of the jury, either
that this man now declining through Nature herself meet his death through
a wound delivered by you sooner than through his own fate, or to uproot as
if by some whirlwind or sudden storm this man in the flower of his youth,
now that the trunk of virtue has been made firm.

[80] Preserve the son for his father, the father for his son, lest you appear
either to have scorned an old man now nearly without hope, or to have not
only failed to nourish but even struck down and destroyed a young man full
of the greatest promise. If you preserve this man for us, for his family, for
the Republic, you will hold him bound, devoted, dedicated to you and your
children, and you most of all, gentlemen of the jury, will reap from all his
strength and his labors fruits that are abundant and lasting.[97]

96. 79 **this miserable man here**: See note on §4 **gloom and squalor of his father**.

97. 80 **fruits that are abundant and lasting**: As Winterbottom (2004) 228 notes, "Cicero's
promise that in future Caelius will mend his ways and bear rich fruit for the state is a substitute
for pointing to such fruit in the past."

Catullus

Gaius Valerius Catullus (c. 84–54 B.C.), author of a long book of poems in various meters and genres,[1] is best known for those that capture his passionate affair with "Lesbia," a pseudonym for Clodia.[2] Rather than a linear narrative, Catullus gives us a jumbled series of snapshots from different stages of the affair, interspersed with poems that tell of his other loves and hates. Readers have increasingly come to see the initially baffling arrangement as an essential part of a complex, carefully crafted "story" with Lesbia at its core. Or perhaps it is two stories, for the Polymetric Lesbia (of poems 1–60) differs from the Elegiac Lesbia (of poems 65–116) as much as a puella *("girl") differs from a* mulier *("woman"): the first ends in utter degradation, the second in an ecstatic vow of eternal friendship.[3]*

The selection here, which includes all the pieces specifically about Lesbia and a sampling of others, attempts to give a sense of how the poet's odd juxtapositions and intratextual references enhance the meaning and richness of individual poems. Poems that appear to concern Lesbia specifically, though she is often not mentioned by name, have their numbers in **boldface***.*

1. The Catullan corpus is generally considered too large to have fit on a single scroll, and modern scholars often divide it into three parts: the "Polymetrics" (poems in a variety of meters, 1–60), the "Longer Poems" (61–68, all of which touch on the theme of marriage in some way), and the "Epigrams" (shorter poems in elegiac couplets, 69–116). Skinner (2003) xxvii argues that Catullus "was responsible for issuing the tripartite collection" but that "this final collection was not made from materials previously undisseminated, but instead put together from works originally circulating as single poems or in self-contained *libelli* ["booklets"]"; poems 1–60 and poems 65–116 would have constituted two such *libelli*.

2. See introduction, "Who Was Clodia?"

3. See introduction, "love as *foedus*" and "love as *amicitia*," and Dyson (2007).

Catullus 1

To whom do I present the charming new booklet[4]
polished smooth, just now, with dry pumice stone?[5]
To you, Cornelius: for you were the one
who used to think my trifles *were* something,
back when you alone of the Italians   5
dared to unroll all history in three scrolls,
learned—Jupiter!—and full of labor.[6]
Therefore, take for yourself this slip of a booklet,
such as it is—so it may, for its patron's sake,[7]
remain enduring more than one generation.   10

---

4. 1.1 **charming new booklet**: With this apparently simple question, Catullus inaugurates a new era in Latin poetry. Cicero branded Catullus and his circle the "new poets," *poetae novi,* sometimes also called "neoteric" from the Greek word *neoteroi* or "newer"; see Quinn (1999) 44–69 on "The Characteristics of the New Poetry." Catullus' short, "charming," elegant poems stand in self-conscious contrast to the lengthy, "shaggy," weighty epics of his predecessors.

5. 1.2 **polished smooth . . . pumice stone**: The uneven ends of a scroll were literally polished smooth with pumice stone, but the "polish" figuratively extends to the content (just as "new" in the previous line means both "recently written" and "of a new style"). Fear (2000) 219, citing Fitzgerald (1995) 40–41, notes that the use of pumice as a depilatory also contributes to the personification of the *libellus* as a "poetic prostitute. [Catullus] creates a poem that will seek public circulation through the merits of the attractiveness created by depilation both within the text (emendation) and on its surface (polish)."

6. 1.7 **learned—Jupiter!—and full of labor**: A double-edged compliment, subject to opposing interpretations. Is Catullus commending Nepos for the "learned" elegance and polish characteristic of his own "new poetry," or is he mocking the historian for his "laborious" tomes? Perhaps both. Rauk (1997) 325 rightly emphasizes the ironic yet affectionate humor that pervades the poem: "The pompous exaggeration of Nepos' accomplishment and the studied diminishing of Catullus' own work can be seen as a kind of role-playing, a joke between close friends who are amused at the view that the outside world has of them."

7. 1.9 **for its patron's sake**: This is a translation of the emendation *qualecumque quidem, patroni ut ergo*. The vulgate reading (i.e., the one most commonly printed) is *qualecumque, quod, <o> patrona virgo*; this would change the translation of line 9 to "such as it is; O patron Virgin, may it." In my opinion a sudden, impassioned prayer to an unnamed Muse would contrast strangely with the self-deprecating tone of "trifles," "slip of a booklet," and "more than one generation" (Muses are accustomed to being asked for immortality). The personification of the *book* as Cornelius' "client," thus making the poem a sort of "letter of recommendation," and the playful assertion that only Nepos' patronage will keep it afloat, are more in Catullus' line. This does not imply that Nepos was the patron of *Catullus* in any real sense (pace Tatum [1997] 486): the tone here is not humility but mock humility, as in poem 49, a thank-you note to another impressive "patron." On the elusive concept of literary patronage, see White (1993), especially 27–34. For a summary of the impressive array of arguments for and against *patrona virgo* and *patroni ut ergo,* see Dettmer (1997) 14–20 and Gratwick (2002); Gratwick suggests *patrocini ergo,* "in witness of your advocacy."

Catullus 2[8]

Sparrow,[9] cherished delight of my girl,[10]
she plays with you, she holds you in her bosom,
she gives your eagerness a fingertip
and often instigates your stinging bites,
whenever my gleaming object of desire   5
is pleased to trifle with some beloved toy—
a little solace also for her pain,[11]
I think, that thus her burning heat may rest:
If only I could play with you as she does,
and lighten the sad cares that press my spirit!   10
***
It[12] is as pleasing to me as they say the little
golden apple was to the swift-footed girl,[13]
which loosed the girdle that had long been tied.

Catullus 3

Mourn, oh Venuses and Cupids, and all
people there are of the more attractive sort:
the sparrow of my girl has passed away,

8. **Catullus 2**: This poem takes the form of a hymn to a divinity: a long list of attributes (1–8) is followed by a sort of "prayer" (9–10).

9. 2.1 **Sparrow**: The reader of Catullus is confronted at once with a major interpretative problem—as Ferguson (1988) 24 designates it, a "potent ambiguity": Is this simply a tender poem about his lover's pet bird, or is "sparrow" meant to be recognized also as a slang term for "penis"? Controversy still rages, but most modern translations and interpretations accept the double entendre. For a brief discussion and bibliography, see Arthur J. Pomeroy (2003) 50–51.

10. 2.1 **girl**: Catullus' *puella* was a married woman about ten years his senior.

11. 2.7 **pain**: Pain (*dolor*) and heat (*ardor*) often refer to sexual passion.

12. 2.11 **It**: The second major interpretive problem in this poem is grounded in a textual problem: What does "It" refer to? Most editors indicate a lacuna (missing lines) in the text or even print "2b" (lines 11–13 here) as a fragment of a separate poem. Fitzgerald (1995) 43 makes the case for seeing the poem as complete (no lacuna): "The suggestive ambiguity of Catullus' interest in playing with the sparrow is compared to the ambiguous interest of the virgin Atalanta in the apple: was it a girlish delight in bright things; a desire that fully comprehended the erotic symbolism of the apple; a confused, virginal combination of both?"

13. 2.12 **swift-footed girl**: Atalanta. This is the first of several similes throughout his poems in which Catullus, explicitly or implicitly, is compared to a recently deflowered young woman (see 11.22–24, 68.91). On the important theme of gender role reversal in Catullus and other poets, see Skinner (1997) for analysis and bibliography.

the sparrow, cherished delight of my girl,[14]
whom she used to love more than her own eyes.   5
For honey-sweet he was, and knew his own
"herself"[15] as well as a girl knows her mother.
And he would not budge himself from out her lap,
but frolicking about now hither, now thither,
ever would twitter to his mistress alone: 10
now he travels along the path of shadows,
that path they say none travel in return.
But you—curses on you! wicked shadows
of Orcus, who devour all pretty things:
such a pretty sparrow you've robbed from me.   15
Oh, wickedly done! Oh, miserable little[16] sparrow!
Now, because of you, the darling eyes
of my girl are red and swollen with her weeping.[17]

Catullus 4[18]

That little clipper,[19] the one you see there, passersby,[20]
claims that it used to be the speediest of ships,
and that it was not incapable of surpassing

---

14. 3.4 **sparrow, cherished delight of my girl**: In the Latin this line is identical to 2.1 (on which see notes).

15. 3.7 **"herself"**: A Roman slave referred to his or her mistress as *ipsa*, "herself."

16. 3.16 **miserable little**: Latin *miselle*, diminutive of *miser*. The persistent association of *miser* with unhappiness in love may support the obscene reading of "sparrow" summarized in the note on 2.1 **Sparrow**.

17. 3.18 **weeping**: Consider the final stanza of Dorothy Parker's "From a Letter from Lesbia":

That thing he wrote, the time the sparrow died—
(Oh, most unpleasant—gloomy, tedious words!)
I called it sweet, and made believe I cried;
The stupid fool! I've always hated birds . . .

18. **Catullus 4**: As Putnam (1972) 16 notes, the ship depicted in this poem "is both real and symbolic at the same time," introducing the themes (to be further developed in poems 31 and 46) of travel, homecoming, and the poet's quasi-erotic love for places and objects.

19. 4.1 **little clipper**: Latin *phaselus* (literally "bean pod"), a small ocean-going ship. In this poem it tells its life story, including bringing its "master" (presumably Catullus) back from Bithynia.

20. 4.1 **passersby**: Epigrams on tombstones, "speaking" in the voice of the deceased, often addressed passing strangers.

the rapid thrust of any floating timber, whether
the need arose to fly with oar blades or with canvas.   5
And it affirms that the shore of the menacing Adriatic
dares not deny this, or the islands of the Cyclades,
and celebrated Rhodes, and the blood-curdling Thracian
Propontis, or the gloomy gulf of the Black Sea
(where that future little clipper was previously   10
a long-haired forest—for on the Cytorian ridge
its eloquent tresses would often whisper a sibilant sigh).
Pontic Amastris and Cytorus rich in boxwood,
the little clipper claims that these things were and are
most intimately known to you; it says that from its   15
earliest origin it stood upon your mountain peak,
that it was in your waters its oars were first baptized.
And thence, through so many uncontrollable seas, it bore
its master, whether the breeze was calling from the left
or from the right, or whether following Jupiter[21]   20
had fallen simultaneously on both the sheets;[22]
and also that it had not made any frantic vows[23]
to the gods of the seashore, as it was coming from the sea
most recently traveled all the way to this crystal lake.
But this was in its former life; now, hidden away,   25
it peacefully ages and dedicates itself to you,
twin brother Castor, and to you, twin brother of Castor.

Catullus 5

Let us live, my Lesbia, and let us love,
and let us calculate all the mutterings of
curmudgeonly old coots to be worth one cent.[24]

21. 4.20 **following Jupiter**: The sky god here, uniquely in Latin poetry (Fordyce [1961] on 4.20), represents "wind." A "following" wind was "favorable" (Latin *secundus* means both).
22. 4.21 **both the sheets**: The "sheets" were ropes or chains holding down the lower corner of the sails.
23. 4.22 **had not made any frantic vows**: That is, it had sailed confidently, making no desperate prayers or promises to the gods.
24. 5.3–4 **calculate . . . worth one cent**: The language here is that of accounting—a trade one might suppose to be inimical to the lovers' wild passion.

Suns have the power to set and rise again;
our brief light, when once it has set, leaves only   5
one night we must sleep for all eternity.
Give me kisses, a thousand,[25] then a hundred;
then another thousand, then a second hundred;
then still another thousand, then a hundred.
Then, when we will have made so many thousands,   10
we'll garble them up, so that we may not know,
nor any wicked man have power to give us
the evil eye, knowing the quantity of kisses.[26]

Catullus 6[27]

Flavius, you'd be wanting to tell Catullus—
you couldn't keep quiet—about your cherished delight,
if she were not devoid of charm and refinement.
But you're enjoying some scrap of syphilitic[28]
whore or other: this you're ashamed to confess.   5
That you're not sleeping a widower's lonely nights
the bed (so what if it's silent) screams out loud,
fragrant with garlands and Syrian olive oil,

25. 5.7 **Give me kisses, a thousand**: This word order, "kisses, a thousand" (*basia mille*)
rather than simply "a thousand kisses" (*mille basia*), further develops the poem's mercantile
imagery: when requesting goods from a merchant, the Romans specified first the item and then
the quantity. See Quinn (1970) on 5.7.

26. 5.13 **the evil eye, knowing the quantity of kisses**: The wicked man might not simply be
envious of so many kisses, but might also be able to practice some sort of black magic if he knew
the number (an idea developed more explicitly in poem 7).

27. **Catullus 6**: Why did the tender poet of 5 and 7 (the reader may wonder) place them on
either side of 6? See the excellent discussion of Wray (2001) 152–59, especially 159: "What Poem
6's Catullus personates and carries out is precisely what the Catullus of Poems 5 and 7 simultaneously wards off and invites: a stern, severely moralizing public exposure fueled by personal envy,
prurient curiosity and pure malice."

28. 6.4 **syphilitic**: Latin *febriculosi*, "feverish." As Wray (2001) 156 points out, the interpretation of the poem depends upon the meaning of this word: is the fever from sexual excitement (so
Martin [1992], "hotblooded") or from genuine disease? The one appearance of the word in Latin
poetry before Catullus (Plautus *Cistellaria* 406) is in a "comic (but roundly damning) inventory of
the attributes of the lowest class of prostitutes. The 'fever' that Flavius' *scortum* ["whore"] has to
offer him is decidedly not that of constant sexual excitation." (Though the disease and the word
"syphilis" did not exist per se in the ancient world, the translation should convey that the woman's
"feverishness" is due to her lifestyle.)

and the bolster dented equally on the right
and on the left, and the quivering couch's rattled,   10
raucous commotion—and rapid locomotion.
No use keeping that stuff quiet, none at all.
Why? You wouldn't be sporting such fucked-out flanks[29]
if you weren't up to a bit of idiocy.[30]
Therefore, whatever you've got, for good or ill,   15
tell me. I want to summon you and your love
to the heavens with my charming poetry.

Catullus 7

You ask how many of your kissations,[31] Lesbia,
would be enough for me and more than enough.
How great the quantity of Libyan sands
lying upon Cyrene, rich in silphium,[32]
between the oracle of steamy Jove[33]   5
and the sacred sepulcher of ancient Battus;[34]

29. 6.14 **fucked-out flanks**: The Romans considered physical appearance to be a reflection of character; ugliness of body betokened ugliness of soul. Whereas obesity was generally seen as a sign of prosperity, skinniness was seen as a sign of profligacy. See Corbeill (1996), especially chap. 4, "Appearance in Action: Effeminacy."

30. 6.14 **idiocy**: The theme of "idiocy" (Latin *ineptiae*) unites poems 6, 8 (line 1 "being idiotic" = Latin *ineptire*), and 12 (line 4 "idiot" = Latin *ineptus*). In poem 10 the word "idiot" does not appear, but Catullus calls a "dimwit" (line 33, Latin *insulsa*) the woman who has just made him look like one.

31. 7.1 **kissations**: Latin *basiatio*, which Catullus apparently invented, takes the word for "kiss" (*basium*, which also appears first in Catullus) and adds the Latin equivalent of our "-ation" ending. This mock-learned word and the philosophical question in which it appears give the poem a pseudointellectual tone that contrasts ironically with its subject. Catullus employs such "-ation" words for two other sex objects: *fututio* ("fuckation") in 32.8 for Ipsitilla and *osculatio* ("osculation") in 48.6 for Juventius. In each case the *quantity* of acts is emphasized ("nine" and "thicker than a ripened cornfield," respectively). Lesbia may be the poet's only love, but she is certainly not his only lust.

32. 7.4 **rich in silphium**: Silphium was an expensive medicinal plant used as a highly effective contraceptive. Catullus would seem to be calling attention to a rather unromantic aspect of his and Lesbia's affair.

33. 7.5 **steamy Jove**: The king of the gods is "steamy" because the climate around his oracle is hot and also because he himself is perpetually lustful.

34. 7.6 **ancient Battus**: Battus was a king of Cyrene; Callimachus, the Greek model for Catullus' "new poetry," was a native of Cyrene and called himself a "son of Battus." Catullus is calling attention to his own allusiveness by alluding to the prince of allusiveness.

or how many stars, when night is silent, gaze
upon the furtive love affairs of men:
for you to kiss so many kisses is
enough and more than enough for crazed Catullus—   10
too many for snoops to be able to reckon up
completely, or an evil tongue to bewitch.[35]

Catullus 8[36]

Miserable Catullus, please stop being idiotic[37]
and recognize that what you see has died is dead.
Suns blazed for you radiantly once upon a time,[38]
when you would come and go wherever that girl led,
loved by me as no other ever will be loved;   5
at the time when all those fun and games were going on
which you wanted, and the girl was not unwilling,
suns blazed for you radiantly, without a doubt.
Now she doesn't want them: don't you want them either,
crazy fool—and don't chase her as she flees, and live in misery,   10
but suffer it with obstinate mind, harden your heart.
Girl, farewell! Now Catullus hardens his heart,
and he won't seek you out, or ask you against your will.
But you'll be sorry, when you aren't asked at all.
Worse luck for you, damned bitch![39] What life remains for you?   15
Who will go to you now? To whom will you seem pretty?

35. 7.12 **an evil tongue to bewitch**: As in poem 5, the idea is that an ill-wisher might have power to cast a spell if he knew the exact quantity. Latin *fascinare* (here = "bewitch") literally means "to bind"; binding spells required specific information about the victim. See Gager (1992).

36. **Catullus 8**: Day (1938) 87 notes that this poem is the "first indication of the use made of New Comedy [Greek comedy of the fourth–third century B.C.] by the Latin erotic poets"; "in composing a soliloquy as a lover determined to break away from his mistress whilst conscious of his weak and fearful hope of reconciliation, Catullus is repeating a theme which was almost a commonplace of comedy."

37. 8.1 **being idiotic**: See note on 6.14 **idiocy**.

38. 8.3 **Suns blazed ... time**: Perhaps a reminiscence of poem 5, in which the recurrence of "suns" is contrasted with humans' eternal sleep of death.

39. 8.15 **Worse luck for you, damned bitch!**: Latin *scelesta* (here = "damned bitch") implies that Lesbia has committed a *scelus*, a crime that makes her "accursed" or "damned" (i.e., subject to religious taboo), as well as "unfortunate."

Whom will you love now? Whose will you be said to be?
Whom will you kiss? Whose little lips will you nibble?
But you, Catullus, be resolved and harden your heart.

Catullus 9

Veranius, in my eyes taking pride of place
out of all my friends—three hundred thousand[40] of them—
have you returned home to your own hearth gods
and brothers of one mind and aged mother?
You have returned. Oh, lucky news for me!   5
I'll visit you safe and sound and hear you relating
the places, deeds, and peoples of the Spaniards,
as is your custom, and hanging on your neck
I'll sweetly kiss[41] your pleasant mouth and eyes.
Oh, all people there are of the luckier sort,   10
what is happier or luckier than I?

Catullus 10

My Varus had led me from the Forum, when I was
at leisure, to pay a visit to his love:
a little whore[42] (as she struck me then at once)
not wholly devoid of charm and attractiveness;
when we'd got there, various topics of conversation   5
came up for us—among them, what Bithynia
was these days, how it was getting on,
and what sort of profit I had gotten there.
I told it like it was: there was no reason—

---

40. 9.2 **three hundred thousand**: Romans often used "three hundred" to designate "an indefinite large number" (they had a word for "thousands" but not one for "hundreds"). Multiplying three hundred by a thousand makes the exaggeration gargantuan.

41. 9.9 **sweetly kiss**: It was not considered effeminate for Roman men to express their affection for one another thus.

42. 10.3 **little whore**: Latin *scortillum*, diminutive of *scortum* ("whore"); the OLD defines *scortillum* as "a young prostitute," but since this is the word's only appearance in classical Latin, it is difficult to pin down its exact implications (which may be closer to "bimbo"). On connections and contrasts between this "not uncharming" whore and the "uncharming" whore of poem 6, see Dettmer (1997) 29–33.

not for themselves,[43] nor the praetors,[44] nor their staff—   10
for anyone to bring back an oilier head:[45]
especially those whose praetor was a facefucker[46]
and didn't think his staff was worth a hair.[47]
"But surely, even so," they said, "the thing
that's said to have started there—you got some men   15
for a litter." I (so I could make myself out,
to the girl, as the only one who'd gotten luckier)
replied, "For me, it didn't go so badly
that, just because a bad province had come up,
I wasn't able to get eight sturdy men."   20
(In fact there was no one, neither here nor there,
who would have been able to put the broken foot
of my old moth-eaten cot[48] upon his shoulder.)
Here she, as you'd expect from the faggier sort,[49]

43. 10.10 **themselves**: The native Bithynians.

44. 10.10 **praetors**: Governors sent to administer provinces; it was normal for them to extort as much money as they could. Catullus was on the staff of the praetor Memmius.

45. 10.11 **oilier head**: A head made sleek by profits and dripping with the "oil of gladness," as at a celebration.

46. 10.12 **facefucker**: Latin *irrumator,* somewhat misleadingly defined by the OLD as "one who submits to *fellatio.*" To force another man to perform oral sex was an act of aggression, not lust; it was considered shameful to be penetrated (orally or anally) but manly to be the penetrator. See Richlin (1981), Adams (1982) 123–25, and Walters (1997). (For the present translation of *irrumator* I am indebted to Wray [2001].) One might note that Memmius was a great patron of the arts (e.g., Lucretius' *De Rerum Natura* is addressed to him); whether Catullus here is teasing a friend or attacking an enemy is not clear.

47. 10.13 **didn't think . . . worth a hair**: A conventional expression of worthlessness, conveniently punning on "oilier head" in 10.11.

48. 10.23 **old moth-eaten cot**: Catullus was wealthy; his protestation of poverty is a poetic conceit (poets are supposed to be poor).

49. 10.24 **faggier sort**: Latin *cinaedior,* "rather like a *cinaedus*" (a Greek borrowing, like most words the Romans used for deviant sexual behavior: see MacMullen [1982] 486–87). On this elusive term (and what it meant to be a "real man" in Rome), see Craig A. Williams (1999) 160–224; as he notes, "a *cinaedus* is a man who fails to live up to traditional standards of masculine comportment, and one way in which he may do so is by seeking to be penetrated; but that is merely a symptom of the deeper disorder, his gender deviance" (174). This is the only place in extant classical literature where the insulting term is applied to a woman. Most translators and commentators tone it down to "sluttier" or some more gender-appropriate term; I prefer to preserve the strangeness and let readers speculate on its implications. As Skinner (1989) 17 suggests, the narrator's "impotent rage at Memmius takes on aspects of another stock comic and satiric situation, the fury of the *cinaedus* cheated of his pay"; it becomes apparent that "the speaker him

said, "Please, my dear Catullus, for a bit,   25
lend them to me: for I would like to be carried
down to Serapis."⁵⁰ "Hold on," I said to the girl,
"as to what I said I had just now . . .
it slipped my mind: my good friend—Cinna, that is,
Gaius Cinna—he got them for himself.   30
But whether his or mine, what's that to me?
I use them just as much as if I owned them.
But you're a real dimwit⁵¹ and a pain in the neck,
never allowing a guy to lower his guard!"

Catullus 11

Furius and Aurelius, Catullus' comrades,⁵²
whether he penetrates to deepest India,⁵³
where on the shore the Eastern wave resounding
    endlessly echoes,

or to the Hyrcani, or the soft Arabs,   5
or the Sagae, or Parthians skilled in archery,
or to where the Nile of seven branches
    colors the waters,

---

self is far more suited to the deeply gendered and politicized part of the *cinaedus* than the young woman he has miscast wantonly."

    50. 10.27 **down to Serapis**: That is, to the temple of the Egyptian deity, a god of healing (perhaps for a disease like that of Flavius' girlfriend: see note on 6.4 **syphilitic**). As Garrison (2004) on 26–27 notes, "The reference helps to characterize her as a working girl: there had been popular agitation in 58 B.C. for shrines of Isis and Serapis on the Capitoline hill, which the Senate resisted."

    51. 10.33 **dimwit**: Latin *insulsa*, literally "without salt" (*sal* means both "salt" and "wit"). She is, of course, anything but, as her request cleverly exposes Catullus' fib. See note on 6.14 **idiocy**.

    52. 11.1 **Furius and Aurelius, Catullus' comrades**: In six other poems (15, 16, 21, 23, 24, and 26), Furius and Aurelius, separately or together, are subjects of Catullus' humorous abuse: he pokes fun at their poverty, pederasty, constipation, etc. Critics disagree about whether this is to be taken as banter among friends or attacks on enemies and consequently about whether their designation in this poem as "comrades" is meant to be ironic. Latin *comites* ("comrades") generally means not simply "friends," but companions or attendants on a journey, especially a military campaign.

    53. 11.2 **India**: "An ill-defined region of Asia, extending from the present subcontinent of India to the borders of China; popularly confused with Ethiopia, Arabia, etc." (*OLD*).

or if he marches across the lofty Alps
visiting great Caesar's monuments,[54]   10
the Gallic Rhine, the horrid sea, the Britons
    furthest of all men,

ready to undertake all these together
with him, wherever the will of heaven will bear him—
give a message to my girl,[55] these words   15
    few and not pretty:

Let her live, and fare well,[56] with her perverts,
whom she clasps three hundred[57] at a time,
loving none truly, but grinding the groins of all of them
    over and over;[58]   20

and let her not, as before, look for my love,
which through her wrong has fallen like a flower[59]

54. 11.10 **great Caesar's monuments**: Caesar's campaigns alluded to in this stanza took place in 55 B.C.; this poem must have been written after that date, at least a year after Catullus returned from Bithynia.

55. 11.15 **give a message to my girl**: The poem's real subject, after three stanzas of "romantic travelogue" (Quinn [1970] on 11), is at last revealed. It may seem, as some readers have objected, that the first half of the poem is disproportionate or irrelevant to the second. The poetic strategy, however, is a variant of the powerful rhetorical device known as a "priamel": a long list of "foils" is presented in apparent contrast to the subject to be praised (or, as here, blamed), and the reflected light from the foils ultimately illuminates the subject. Here, the "travelogue" encompassing the whole known world serves to underscore the intensity of the poet's love and hate. (For a modern example of the priamel form, compare the Beach Boys song "California Girls.")

56. 11.17 **Let her live, and fare well**: Latin *valeat*, like English "farewell," literally means "do well, thrive" but is also the conventional formula for "good-bye." There is perhaps an ironic reminiscence of 5.1, "Let us live, my Lesbia, and let us love."

57. 11.18 **three hundred**: See note on 9.2 **three hundred thousand**.

58. 11.20 **over and over**: See note on 51.4 **over and over**.

59. 11.22 **fallen like a flower**: In Greek and Latin literature, the image of a flower being broken, plucked, or mowed down evokes two symbolically linked events: the defloration of a virgin and the premature death of a young warrior. On Catullus' assumption of a "female" role in his similes, see note on 2.12 **swift-footed girl**. As Miller (2002) 428–29 observes, "Poem 11 is all about power, whether Lesbia's over Catullus, Caesar's over the world, Roman ideology's power to dictate masculine and feminine sexual roles, or Catullus' power rhetorically to frame and carica-ture Lesbia by inverting those sexual norms, so that Lesbia becomes the voracious monster and Catullus the passive flower."

at the meadow's edge, once it is touched by a plough blade
   heedlessly passing.

Catullus 12

Marrucinian[60] Asinius, you use your
left hand not prettily over jokes and wine:
you filch the napkins of the more off guard.
You think that this is clever?[61] You're clueless, idiot![62]
The thing is utterly shabby and unattractive.   5
You don't believe me? Then believe Pollio,
your brother, who would want your thefts paid off
even for a talent;[63] now that boy
is stuffed chock-full of charm and witticisms.
Therefore, either look for three hundred nasty   10
verses,[64] or else send me back my napkin—
which doesn't bother me because of the cost,
but because it's a souvenir from my good friend.
For Fabullus has sent to me, as a gift,
and Veranius, Saetaban handkerchiefs   15
from Spain; it's necessary that I love these
as I love dear Veranius and Fabullus.

Catullus 13

You will dine well at my place, my Fabullus,
in a few days, if the gods are smiling on you—
provided that you bring with you a fine, large

---

60. 12.1 **Marrucinian**: As Quinn (1970) on 12.1 notes, "gauche behavior was perhaps to be expected of a man connected with such a remote part of Italy. (The Marrucini lived on the Adriatic coast close to the river Sangro; for the connexion with that area of the family of the Asinii see Fordyce [1961].)" As Clausen (1988) 13 suggests, "The *cognomen* is probably a fiction, invented by Catullus for this poem and put first to emphasize the contrast between Asinius 'Marrucinus', the provincial boor, and Asinius Pollio, his urbane and witty brother." The contrast between urbanity (always good) and rusticity (always bad) is a major theme throughout Catullus' poems.

61. 12.4 **clever**: Latin *salsum*, literally "salty" (see note on 10.33 **dimwit**).

62. 12.4 **idiot**: See note on 6.14 **idiocy**.

63. 12.8 **talent**: A large unit of weight and money. (The modern meaning "ability," not applicable here, derives from the parable of the talents in Matthew 25:14–30.)

64. 12.10–11 **nasty verses**: Latin *hendecesyllabi* (verses consisting of eleven syllables), "the satirical policemen of high society" (Garrison [2004] on 12.10).

dinner, not without a radiant girl
and wine and salt[65] and every sort of laughter.   5
I say, if you'll bring these things, my attractive friend,
you will dine well; for your own Catullus'
wallet is overflowing with spiderwebs.
But you'll receive in return pure essence of love,[66]
and something, if possible, smoother and more refined: 10
for I'll provide a perfume that the Venuses
and Cupids have bestowed upon my girl.
Once you get a whiff of this, you'll beg
the gods, Fabullus, to make you totally nose.

Catullus 16[67]

I'll fuck your asses and I'll fuck your faces,[68]
Pervert Aurelius and Furius the Fag[69]—
you who've thought I'm insufficiently decent
because of my poems, since they're a little soft.[70]
Yes, it's right that a righteous poet be chaste   5
himself: his *poems* have no such obligation.
At the end of the day, they've only got salt and charm
if they're a bit soft and insufficiently decent,
and have power to prick up the part that itches—

65. 13.5 **salt**: See note on 10.33 **dimwit**.

66. 13.9 **pure essence of love**: Latin *meros amores*. The reader who saw "pure" would initially expect "pure wine" (*merum [vinum]*, i.e., wine unmixed with water). *Amores* literally means "loves" but is often used in the sense of "love affairs," as in 7.8.

67. **Catullus 16**: As Gaisser (1993) 209 notes, this poem was "invoked incessantly by the Renaissance poets to justify writing obscene verse."

68. 16.1 **I'll . . . faces**: See note on 10.12 **facefucker**.

69. 16.2 **Pervert . . . Fag**: Both terms (*pathicus* and *cinaedus*) refer to passive partners in a homosexual relationship. See note on 10.24 **faggier sort**.

70. 16.4 **a little soft**: Latin *molliculi*. As Kennedy (1993) 31 notes, "The Latin adjectives *durus*, 'hard', and *mollis*, 'soft', were so gender-specific, male and female respectively, that the noun *mollitia*, 'softness', could be used without more ado to describe derogatively male behavior that was thought to contain characteristics essentially female." Yet *mollis* can also mean "amorous" or "erotic," and in fact the word soon becomes a tag for the genre of erotic elegy (and its poets). The present poem seeks to prove that one connotation of *mollis*, "erotic," does not entail the other, "effeminate." On the complex of associations evoked by *mollitia*, see Edwards (1993) 63–97. Zetzel (1996) 78 refers to "the conventional elegiac pairing of *mollis* and *durus* referring with equal relevance to beds, women, weapons, or poetry."

not in boys, I mean, but those hairy types[71]   10
who can't get action out of their stubborn[72] loins.
Because you've read about the "many thousands
of kisses," *you* think I'm not a real man?[73]
I'll fuck your asses and I'll fuck your faces.

Catullus 22

That Suffenus, Varus, the one you know really well,
is an attractive person, and witty, and urbane,
but the man composes an inordinate number of verses.[74]
I think there have been ten thousand lines, or more, completed
by him, and not the way it's usually done, written on   5
recycled paper:[75] royal pages, brand new books,
brand new end caps, scarlet thongs, protective covers,
all ruled straight with lead and evened with pumice stone.
When you read these, that charming and urbane Suffenus
seems, in contrast, to have turned into some goat-milker   10
or ditchdigger: it's such a discrepancy and change.
What should we make of this? He who just now seemed
a wit, or something (if possible) cleverer than that—
the man is now more boorish than the boorish country,
as soon as he touches poetry, yet that man is never   15
so blissful as when he's writing a poem: so much does he

71. 16.9 **hairy types**: The growth of body hair was what separated men from boys. Adolescent male love objects in erotic poetry are frequently threatened that they will lose their attractiveness once hairs arise: see Richlin (1992) 35–38.

72. 16.10 **stubborn**: Latin *durus* (see note on 16.4 **a little soft**).

73. 16.12–13 **many thousands of kisses**: Whether this refers to the "kiss" poems to Lesbia (5 and 7) or to the boy Juventius (48) is not clear. As Richlin (1992) 39 points out, "to a Roman reader there was no practical difference between desiring a thousand kisses from your mistress or from your *puer* ["boy"]. Both are expressions of masculine desire—it is the elegance of the poetry and the romantic attitude of mind that are *mollis*." Thomson (1997) 250 notes that the phrase *parum pudicum* (here = "insufficiently decent") is "usually appropriated to homosexuality," suggesting that the reference is to Juventius.

74. 22.3 **inordinate number of verses**: A cardinal sin in the eyes of the "new poets" (see note on 1.1 **charming new booklet**).

75. 22.6 **recycled paper**: Latin *palimpsestus* (Greek "rescraped"), the first appearance of this word in extant literature. Most ancient literature was written with reed pens on papyrus scrolls, which could be washed for reuse; wax (which was common for ephemeral documents) and parchment (which was rare) could be literally "rescraped."

rejoice in himself and fill himself with admiration.
No doubt we all make the same mistake, nor is there anyone
whom, in some respect, you couldn't see as a
Suffenus. Everyone has got his own share of error;   20
but we don't see what kind of knapsack is on our back.[76]

Catullus 27 [77]

O server of fine old Falernian,
bring me in some tarter[78] wine cups, boy,
as the law of our leader Postumia[79]
commands (she's boozier than a boozy berry).
But you, go away,[80] wherever you please, O Waters,   5
you bane of wine, and to the curmudgeonly
betake yourselves. This here is pure Thyonian.

Catullus 31 [81]

Jewel[82] of the peninsulas, O Sirmio,
and islands, all the ones that either Neptune[83] bears

---

76. 22.21 **what kind of knapsack is on our back**: A reference to Aesop's fable in which a man carries one bag on his front containing his neighbor's faults, another on his back containing his own.

77. **Catullus 27**: As Wray (2001) 170–71 notes, wine and water are (among other things) traditional symbols for two kinds of poetry and poets: the wine-drinking, aggressive Archilochus versus the water-drinking, refined Callimachus (see note on 7.6). The poems that follow this (28–60) do indeed contain some harsh invective in the manner of boozy Archilochus.

78. 27.2 **tarter**: Perhaps "drier," "more pungent."

79. 27.3 **law of our leader Postumia**: Roman drinking parties were presided over by a leader who decided how much and what kind of wine was to be drunk. "Postumia" suggests an aristocratic matron; though such women in Catullus' day did sometimes attend men's parties (if not without raising eyebrows), it was unusual for a woman to be the leader. It is unclear who "Postumia" is and why she is chosen here, though a real Postumia who was once a mistress of Julius Caesar has been suggested; see Dettmer (1997) 57.

80. 27.5 **go away**: Perhaps a faint echo of the religious formula banning profane observers from sacred mysteries. Compare Tib. 1.1.76 **go far hence**, Am. 2.1.3 **Stay far, far hence, ye serious**, and Mart. 11.6.6 **Go away**.

81. **Catullus 31**: The poet is celebrating his return from Bithynia to his villa overlooking Lake Benacus (Lago di Garda); see note on **Catullus 4**.

82. 31.1 **Jewel**: Latin *ocellus,* literally "little eye," a term of endearment (like "apple of my eye") and a stumbling block for the translator. Throughout this poem, Catullus personifies his homeland Sirmio as a sort of girlfriend: see Baker (1983).

83. 31.2 **either Neptune**: Probably Neptune in his capacity as god of seas and god of inland waters (see Fordyce [1961] on 31.3).

in crystal lakes or in the unfathomable sea,
how willingly I greet you, and how happily,
hardly believing my own eyes that I've left behind   5
Thynia and the Bithynian fields and see you safe!
Oh, what is luckier than when the mind lays down
its burden, its cares dissolved, and though exhausted by
the labor of travel, we have returned to our own hearth,
and are resting quietly on our long-desired bed?   10
This it is that's the sole reward for such great labors.
Hello, attractive Sirmio! Rejoice in your
rejoicing master; and you, O waves of the Lydian lake,[84]
laugh whatever merriment you have at home.[85]

Catullus 32

I will love you,[86] my sweet Ipsitilla,[87]
my cherished delight, my captivating charm:
bid me come to you to take a siesta!
And if you bid me, help in this way too:
don't let anyone put the bolt in the door,   5
and don't be pleased to go away outside,
but you remain at home, and prepare for me
nine continuous, uninterrupted fuckations.[88]
But if you're going to be busy, bid me at once:

84. 31.13 **Lydian lake**: The Etruscans, an ancient people who came from Lydia before the founding of Rome (eighth century B.C.), had an early settlement there.

85. 31.14 **you have at home**: That is, "you have with you," "you have in stock," but the literal meaning "at home" (Latin *domi*) is essential in this homecoming poem.

86. 32.1 **I will love you**: This formula (Latin *amabo te*) is the conventional way of saying "please" before a request; here Catullus is punningly reactivating its literal meaning.

87. 32.1 **Ipsitilla**: The identity of this woman is unknown; as Godwin (1999) 149 points out, "The name Ipsitilla may even be an obviously invented name as being the diminutive feminine form of *ipsa* ('mistress'; see *OLD* s.v. 'ipse' 12)" (see note on 3.7 **"herself"**). Some commentators assume that she is a professional prostitute who owned her own house. The Romans, for the most part, did not frown on liaisons with such women: extramarital sex was condemned only if it threatened the integrity of an aristocratic house and the legitimacy of aristocratic children. Cicero's strategy in the *Pro Caelio* is to demonstrate that Caelius should not be too sternly reproached for his affair with Clodia, because her behavior places her in Ipsitilla's category. On the poets' reticence about mentioning uncharming realities associated with prostitution (pimps and the exchange of money), see Griffin (1985) 112–41, "*Meretrices,* Matrimony and Myth."

88. 32.8 **fuckations**: See note on 7.1 **kissations**.

for I'm lunched and lying here, and sated, supine,   10
I'm poking a hole through my tunic and my cloak.

Catullus 34

In Diana's care are we,
girls and boys inviolate:
Of Diana, inviolate
    boys and girls, let us sing.[89]

O Latona's daughter, great   5
offspring of greatest Jupiter,
whom her mother brought to birth
    near the Delian olive,[90]

that you might be mistress of mountains
and of forests leafy green   10
and of sacred groves sequestered
    and of sonorous rivers:

you[91] are called Lucina Juno[92]
by those in childbirth's agony,
you are called powerful Trivia,[93] and   15
    with counterfeit light, Luna.[94]

89. 34.4 **boys and girls, let us sing**: This hymn to the virgin goddess is supposedly "sung" by
a chorus of virgin boys and girls, though it is unlikely ever to have been performed in this manner.

90. 34.8 **near the Delian olive**: When Juno's wrath debarred Latona from bearing Jupiter's
illegitimate children anywhere on earth, Latona finally found refuge on the floating island of Delos.

91. 34.13 **you**: The repetition of "you" at line beginning (13, 15, 17) is typical of hymns to
divinities.

92. 34.13 **Lucina Juno**: Roman deities had different epithets to designate their various func-
tions; "Lucina" referred to Juno as a goddess of childbirth. On this poem as an illustration of
Roman "polymorphism"—that is, gods "possessing more than one form or aspect"—see King
(2003) 292–93. It is nevertheless a bit odd, as Quinn (1970) on 34.13 points out, "for a poet in a
hymn addressed to a goddess to tell her that she is also a quite different goddess."

93. 34.15 **Trivia**: Literally "of the crossroads" (Latin *trivium* = "place where three roads
meet"), which, like other liminal or boundary-marking places (thresholds, rivers, etc.), were
regarded with religious awe in antiquity. Latin *Trivia* is a translation of Greek *Trioditis,* an epithet
of Hecate, the Greek Underworld goddess with whom Diana was identified.

94. 34.16 **with counterfeit light, Luna**: That is, with the reflected light of the sun (Luna =

You, goddess, with your monthly course
measuring the path of the year,
fill with harvest excellent
    the rustic house of the farmer.   20

May you be hallowed by whatever
name is pleasing to you, and the race
of Romulus, as you have of old,
    preserve with excellent power.

Catullus 35

To the tender poet,[95] my good friend Caecilius,
O papyrus, I would like you to say
that he should come to Verona, leaving behind
the walls of New Comum and the Larian shore.
For I am wanting him to listen to certain   5
cogitations of his friend and mine.[96]
Therefore, if he's smart, he'll eat up the road,
even though his radiant girl should call him
back a thousand times as he goes, and throwing
both hands around his neck implore him to stay;   10
who now, if the report I'm hearing is true,
is dying for him with uncontrollable love.
For when she read the opening of his Mistress
of Dindymon,[97] since then for the miserable little
darling[98] flames have been eating her inmost marrow.   15
I don't blame you, girl more learned than

Moon). Latin *nothus* primarily means "bastard," "illegitimate," and by extension "spurious" or "counterfeit." One again wonders how flattered Diana would be to be told that her light is appropriated from another deity.

95. 35.1 **tender poet**: That is, a poet who writes on "tender" subjects, a love poet.

96. 35.6 **his friend and mine**: As Garrison (2004) on 35.6 notes, "probably = Catullus. The poet is slyly mysterious, like a conniving slave in a comedy."

97. 35.13–14 **Mistress of Dindymon**: A cult title of Cybele, the subject of Caecilius' poem; "Mistress of Dindymon" may have been its opening words and hence its title.

98. 35.14–15 **miserable little darling**: Latin *misella*, feminine diminutive of *miser.*

the Sapphic muse;[99] certainly, Caecilius'
"Great Mother" is attractively begun.[100]

Catullus 36 [101]

"Annals" of Volusius, sheets of shit,
be ye a votive offering[102] for my girl.
For she vowed to holy Venus and to Cupid
that if I would be reconciled to her
and cease to hurl my fierce poetic curses,   5
then she would offer to the gimpy god[103]
the choicest writings of the worst of poets,[104]
to be scorched by an inauspicious bonfire.
And the girl saw that she was wittily vowing
these, the very worst, to the merry gods.   10
Now, O goddess born of the turquoise sea,[105]
you who dwell upon holy Idalium,
and open Urii, and Ancon, and sandy
Cnidus, and Amathus, and Golgi, and
Durrachium,[106] the Inn of the Adriatic,   15

99. 35.17 **Sapphic muse**: Sappho was the most celebrated female poet in antiquity (she was called "the tenth Muse"). For Sappho's importance to Catullus, see note on **Catullus 51**.

100. 35.18 **attractively begun**: Catullus himself wrote a poem (63, not translated here) about Cybele. As Copley (1972) 184 notes, the implication of "begun" is that his friend's poem "must be carefully reworked before it will be acceptable as good poetry."

101. **Catullus 36**: As Wray (2001) 75 notes, this and poem 37 form a pair: each is "an invective message directed at a named individual male enemy" and "each poem is situated under the sign of a ruling excretory 'element': Poem 36 is a shit poem aimed at Volusius, Poem 37 a piss poem aimed at Egnatius."

102. 36.2 **votive offering**: Roman religion consisted mainly of "contracts" with the gods: humans would offer gods various sorts of gifts in hopes of receiving benefits in return.

103. 36.6 **gimpy god**: Vulcan (i.e., fire).

104. 36.7 **choicest writings of the worst of poets**: Lesbia, presumably, was referring to Catullus' own "fierce poetic curses"; Catullus chooses to interpret her words differently.

105. 36.11 **goddess born of the turquoise sea**: Venus. The list of attributes and cult sites that follows is typical of a hymn to a divinity.

106. 36.15 **Durrachium**: This town has little known connection with Venus. Wiseman (1969) 42–45 suggests that Catullus included it and two others ("open Urii" seems not to have had a Venus cult, and "Ancona" only a minor one) primarily because he had been there himself on his trip home from Greece.

let this vow be rendered and accepted,
if it is not devoid of charm and attractiveness.
But you, meanwhile, proceed into the flames,
ye paragons of boorish fatuosity,
"Annals" of Volusius, sheets of shit.   20

Catullus 37

Smutty tavern,[107] and you all, its comrades-in-arms,[108]
nine columns down the street from the cap-wearing Brothers,[109]
you think that you're the only ones in possession of pricks?
that you alone are free to fuck whatever girls
there are, and to think the rest of us are rancid goats?   5
Or, just because you clods all sit there in a row,
a hundred or two hundred, you think I wouldn't dare
to facefuck[110] all two hundred sitting there at once?
Well, you'd better think again: for it is my intention
to scribble you dicks all over the front wall of this inn.   10
For my girl, who has fled away out of my bosom,
loved by me as no other ever will be loved,[111]
for whose sake great battles have been fought by me,
has pitched her tent there. All you fine and fortunate fellows
love her, and what's more—which is totally unfair—   15
all you beggars and buggers skulking around in alleys;
you[112] above all, alone of all the long-haired dandies,
son of Celtiberia, that rabbity land,

107. 37.1 **Smutty tavern**: As McGinn (2004) 15 notes, "generally speaking, inns, lodging houses, taverns, and restaurants of all kinds were associated with the practice of prostitution."

108. 37.1 **comrades-in-arms**: Latin *contubernales,* literally "tent mates," used both of soldiers sharing a tent and of slaves cohabiting (slaves could not contract legal marriages). As Wray (2001) 81–87 suggests, Catullus throughout this poem casts himself as a "Braggart Soldier" (*miles gloriosus*), a stock character in Roman comedy.

109. 37.2 **cap-wearing Brothers**: Castor and Pollux. As the second-century grammarian Festus notes, these Spartan brothers are so depicted because the Spartans customarily fight in felt caps: Catullus is alluding to their military uniform (Wray [2001] 85).

110. 37.8 **facefuck**: See note on 10.12 **facefucker.**

111. 37.12 **loved . . . loved**: A line nearly identical to 8.5 in the first "renunciation" poem.

112. 37.17 **you**: Catullus now switches from a plural to a singular "you," a man identified by name in line 19.

Egnatius, whom a dark, shadowy beard makes fine,
and teeth shined to a sparkle by Iberian piss.   20

Catullus 40

What delusion, miserable Ravidus,
is pitching you headlong into my invective?
What god, imperfectly summoned to your aid,[113]
is gearing up to start a frenzied brawl?
Is it so you'll catch the public eye?   5
What do you want? You're itching for fame, no matter
how or why? You'll get it, seeing as you wanted
to love my Love[114] and pay a lengthy penalty.

Catullus 43 [115]

Greetings, girl of not-the-smallest nose,
nor of pretty foot, nor of dark eyes,
nor of long fingers, nor of mouth undrooling,
nor, in fact, of tongue too elegant,[116]
girlfriend of the bankrupt Formian.[117]   5
The province is declaring *you* are pretty?

113. 40.3 **imperfectly summoned to your aid**: The success of a transaction with the gods depended upon using an exactly correct religious formula; one small mistake would not only render the "contract" null and void (see note on 36.2 **votive offering**), but would cause the gods to be angry until the fault was expiated by another ceremony (sometimes they had to try over thirty times to get it right). See Dyson (2001) 29–49.

114. 40.8 **my Love**: Possibly Lesbia; the previous poem (not printed here) is an attack on the dental practices of her lover Egnatius (see 37.19–20). But Juventius (see poem 48), whom Catullus elsewhere (15.1, 21.4) calls "my love" (*meos amores*), is also a strong candidate.

115. **Catullus 43**: This poem is the closest we have to a physical description of Lesbia: she implicitly *is* everything the poem's unfortunate addressee is *not*.

116. 43.4 **nor, in fact, of tongue too elegant**: Commentators disagree about just what aspect of her tongue is inelegant. Catullus lets us wonder.

117. 43.5 **bankrupt Formian**: Mamurra. From poem 41 (not printed here), we know that the girlfriend of this "bankrupt Formian" (he was in fact quite rich) is named "Ameana." Latin *decoctor* literally means "one who boils down," that is, one who has become bankrupt by frittering away his financial resources through overindulgence in food and sensual pleasures: see Corbeill (1997) 101–104.

My Lesbia is being compared with *you*?[118]
O fatuous and witless generation!

Catullus 44

O my own farm, whether Sabine or Tiburtine[119]
(for those who have no desire to hurt Catullus affirm
that you're Tiburtine; but the ones who *do* desire it
maintain you're Sabine—they'll bet anything, they say),
anyway, whether more truly Sabine or Tiburtine,   5
I was very happy to be in your suburban
villa, and I drove from my chest a wicked cough
my stomach had given me, not undeservedly,
seeing as I was trolling for an expensive dinner.
For while I was wanting to be a Sestian dinner guest,[120]   10
I read his speech against Antius, the office seeker—
a speech just overflowing with poison and pestilence.
Hence a chilly[121] head cold and a constant cough
kept racking me, until I fled into your bosom,
and put myself together again with rest and nettles.[122]   15
Therefore, I, restored, give you the very greatest
thanks, that you did not take vengeance on my sin.
Nor do I now object—if I am to receive
the heinous writings of Sestius—that their chill should bring
a cold and cough, not to me, but to Sestius himself,   20
who invites me only when I've read his nasty book.

---

118. 43.5 **My Lesbia is being compared with *you*?**: This poem, it is at last revealed, is a sort of ironic "priamel" (see note on 11.15 **give a message to my girl**).

119. 44.1 **Sabine or Tiburtine**: Tibur was a desirable place for summer homes; the Sabine area was further out and considered unfashionably rustic. Catullus' property was on the border. The following lines parody a religious hymn, invoking the deity by a variety of names in hopes that one will hit the mark. As George (1991) 249 points out, they also "establish the tone in which the poem is to be interpreted—one of self-bemusement for the vulnerability caused by the poet's desire to belong to the fashionable set."

120. 44.10 **Sestian dinner guest**: A grandiloquent way of saying "a dinner guest of Sestius."

121. 44.13 **chilly**: The poem's point depends on this word. Latin *frigidus* ("chilly") and *frigere* ("to be cold"), as Fordyce (1961) on 44 notes, are "technical terms of literary criticism for the bad taste which shows itself in bombast, affectation, or preciosity."

122. 44.15 **nettles**: A common cough remedy.

Catullus 45

Septimius, while holding Acme, his love,
in his lap, declares, "My Acme, if I do not
love you to perdition, and furthermore
am not prepared to love you constantly
through all the years, absolutely dying for you,   5
then, all alone, in Libya or parched India,
may I step into the path of a grey-eyed lion."
As he said this, Love, on the front and left,
emitted a right favorable sneeze[123] of approval.
But Acme, lightly bending back her head   10
and kissing the inebriated eyes
of the sweet boy with that glowing mouth of hers
declares, "My Life, Septimikins,[124] so may I
ever be a slave to this master alone,
as for me a far greater and a keener   15
flame is burning in my supple marrow."
As she said this, Love, on the front and left,
emitted a right favorable sneeze of approval.
Now, having started out from excellent auspices,
with mutual passion, they love, they are loved.   20
Septimius, miserable little dear, prefers
Acme alone to Syrias and Britains:
faithful Acme makes her cherished delight
and desires of Septimius alone.
Who has ever witnessed any luckier   25
people, who a more auspicious Venus?

123. 45.8–9 **front and left . . . right favorable sneeze**: My translation accepts the textual emendation and interpretation by Cairns (2005) of this vexed passage, *sinistra et ante/dextram sternuit* (as opposed to the commonly printed "sneezed on the left, as before on the right," *sinistra ut ante/dextra sternuit*). In the language of Roman augury, the pseudoscience of interpreting the gods' will by watching for signs in various quarters of the sky, the "front and left" was considered a lucky quarter; ironically, the word for "favorable," *dexter,* means "right-hand," hence my "right favorable" (a sneeze was generally a lucky omen). Since Acme is Greek and Septimius Roman, Catullus is playing on the "racial diversity of the lovers" and "alluding to the well-known fact that for the Romans the left was (usually) the good side for omens, while for Greeks it was usually the right, and also joking about the confusions which could arise in this area" (541).

124. 45.13 **Septimikins**: Latin *Septimelle* is more mellifluous, but the translator must convey the affectionate diminutive somehow.

Catullus 46 [125]

Now the Spring brings back its soothing warmth,
now the equinoctial heaven's frenzy
grows quiet with the pleasant breezes of Zephyr.
Let the Phrygian fields, Catullus, be left behind,
and the rich plain of sweltering Nicaea: 5
let us fly to the brilliant cities of Asia. [126]
Now my trembling heart is greedy for wandering,
now my joyful feet grow strong with zeal.
Farewell, delightful gatherings of comrades,
starting out together far from home,   10
but carried back by myriad winding paths.

Catullus 48

Oh, Juventius, [127] your honey-sweet eyes,
if someone should allow me to keep kissing them,
I would kiss three hundred thousand [128] times,
and I would never, ever be seen to be glutted,
not even if thicker than a ripened cornfield   5
were to grow the crop of our osculations. [129]

Catullus 49 [130]

Most eloquent of Romulus' descendants,
all that are, and all that were, Marcus Tullius,

---

125. **Catullus 46**: See note on **Catullus 4**.

126. 46.6 **brilliant cities of Asia**: Wealthy places such as Ephesus, Miletus, and Halicarnassus, where Catullus hopes to do some sightseeing before returning home from the tour of duty in Bithynia.

127. 48.1 **Juventius**: This adolescent boy is the subject of a series of poems (15, 21, 23, 24, 48, 81, 99, and perhaps 16 and 40—see Garrison [2004] 171) that forms a humorous counterpoint to the more serious "Lesbia cycle." Sex with pubescent boys, even of the noble class (as Juventius seems to have been), was permitted—as long as it ended when the boy became a man.

128. 48.3 **three hundred thousand**: See note on 9.2 **three hundred thousand**.

129. 48.6 **osculations**: See note on 7.1 **kissations**. The only other appearance of *osculatio* in extant Latin texts is at *Cael.* 49, in a long string of nouns describing Clodia's behavior as that of a whore.

130. **Catullus 49**: Readers have seen varying amounts of affection and satire in this thank-you note; compare the tone of poem 1, another ostensibly self-deprecating poem to a "patron." In any case, Catullus is parodying Cicero's (over)use of superlatives and other hyperbole.

and all that after in other years will be,
to you Catullus gives the very greatest
thanks, the poet very worst of all—   5
so much the poet very worst of all
as you are the patron very best of all.

Catullus 50

Yesterday, Licinius, we spent
our leisure playing many a game on my tablets,
since we had agreed to be decadent:
each of us was writing little verses,
playfully turning the meter now here, now there,   5
giving and taking, over jokes and wine.
And from that place I departed so enflamed[131]
by your charm, Licinius, and your witticisms,
that neither did food give any pleasure to me
in my misery, nor did sleep cloak my eyes with peace,   10
but wild with frenzy I tossed and turned all over
the bed, longing to see the light of day,
so I could speak with you and be together.
But after my limbs, exhausted by their labor,
were lying half-dead upon the little bed,   15
delightful friend, I wrote this poem[132] for you,
so from it you could clearly perceive my pain.
Now beware of being reckless, I pray, and beware

---

131. 50.10 **enflamed**: This word, and many others in the remainder of the poem, depict Catullus'
feelings for Licinius in patently erotic terms. Yet the passion he feels is not simply physical lust:
grown Roman men may have expressed such feelings for adolescent boys (as in poem 48), but
not—at least not in print—for one another. Physical passion here appears rather to be a metaphor
for the intellectual intimacy between Catullus and a fellow poet. On Catullus' and other poets'
exploration of "The Erotics of *Amicitia*," see Oliensis (1997).

132. 50.16 **this poem**: Which poem? The traditional interpretation is "the present poem" (i.e.,
50). Wray (2001) 98–99, however, offers persuasive argument that poem 50 is actually a "cover
letter" for the following poem (51). There is a parallel situation in poems 65 and 66 (not translated
here): in poem 65.15–16, the phrase "I send you . . . this song" (*mitto . . . haec . . . tibi carmina*)
refers unambiguously to poem 66, which, like poem 51, is a translation from a Greek model. In
any case, there is good reason to read poems 50 and 51 as a pair: they are united by the "leisure"
(*otium*) with which 50 opens and 51 closes, the depiction of erotic distress in physical terms, and
the emphasis on the ecstasy of conversing with the beloved.

of rejecting my prayers, apple of my eye,[133]
lest Nemesis exact punishment from you;
she's a violent goddess: of doing her harm, beware!

20

Catullus 51[134]

He seems to me the equal of a god,
he seems—if it is right—to surpass the gods,
who sits across from you and sees you and hears you
    over and over[135]

sweetly laughing, which in my misery ravishes
all my senses: for when I have once laid eyes
upon you, Lesbia, then of the voice in my mouth
    nothing is left me,

5

but my tongue grows numb, a slender flame
oozes down within my limbs, my ears with
their own sound are ringing, and my eyes are
    buried in twin night.

10

Leisure, Catullus, is troubling to you;[136]
leisure gets you too excited, too itchy.
Leisure has been known to destroy both kings and
    prosperous cities.

15

133. 50.19 **apple of my eye**: Latin *ocellus* (see note on 31.1 **Jewel**).

134. **Catullus 51**: This poem is a modified translation of a famous poem by Sappho (31) to another woman. Sappho lived on the island of Lesbos, the source both of our word "Lesbian" and of the pseudonym "Lesbia"; by choosing this pseudonym (which has the same rhythm as "Clodia"), Catullus acknowledges his poetic debt to Sappho.

135. 51.4 **over and over**: This phrase (Latin *identidem*) appears in Catullus only here and in exactly the same line position in 11.19 (11.20 in translation), Catullus' only other poem in the Sapphic meter. These two poems clearly form a pair; yet as Janan (1994) 71 observes, "no narrative sequence connects 11 and 51, to tell us which state of mind came first and which later, which is true and which false—as indeed it cannot and still truly reflect the operation of desire implicit in the word 'identidem.'"

136. 51.13 **Leisure, Catullus, is troubling to you**: Compare note on *Att.* 2.14.1 **leisure**. Peter E. Knox (1984) suggests that in playing on the varied associations of *otium*, "erotic *otium* and *otium* the bane of cities and kings" (98), Catullus may well have been developing an idea about the destructiveness of luxury found in the Sappho poem (most of the last stanza of which has been lost).

Catullus 58

Caelius, our Lesbia,[137] that Lesbia,
that Lesbia whom alone Catullus loved
more than himself and all his friends and family,
now at every street corner and back alley
shucks greathearted Remus's descendants.[138]   5

Catullus 62[139]

The Evening Star's come: youths, rise up! The Evening Star[140]
long awaited, finally, barely raises its light on Olympus.
Now is the time to rise, now to leave the luscious tables,
now will the maiden come, now the *hymenaeus*[141] be sung.
Hymen o Hymenaeus, come, *Hymen o Hymenaeus!*   5

Do you see the youths, unmarried girls? Rise up in response;
no doubt the Night-bringer has revealed its Oetaean flames.[142]
Yes, that's for sure; do you see how swiftly they've leapt up?
They haven't leapt up for no reason, they'll have a song we should beat.
Hymen o Hymenaeus, come, *Hymen o Hymenaeus!*   10

137. 58.1 **Caelius, our Lesbia**: This is probably Marcus Caelius Rufus (of the *Pro Caelio*); see introduction, "Who Was Clodia?" The Latin literally says "our Lesbia"; while in most instances this would simply stand for "my Lesbia" (see introduction, "Some Translation Issues"), Catullus may be reactivating its literal sense as he bitterly recalls that the Lesbia once his now "belongs" to Caelius too (not to mention 299 others: see poem 11).

138. 58.5 **greathearted Remus's descendants**: Compare poem 49.1. In the present poem "greathearted Remus" mimics the ironically grandiloquent tone while calling attention to the dark underside of Roman history (Romulus, founder of Rome, killing his brother Remus—before the latter could in fact engender any "descendants").

139. **Catullus 62**: This poem takes the form of a prenuptial singing contest between a chorus of boys (who regard the wedding in a positive light) and a chorus of girls (who see only disadvantages for the bride). As Fraenkel (1972) 206 notes, "The place of this epithalamium is neither in Greece nor in Rome but in a poetic sphere of its own."

140. 62.1 **Evening Star**: Latin *Vesper,* the planet Venus.

141. 62.4 *hymenaeus*: That is, the traditional refrain (in the next line) to Hymen, the god of marriage.

142. 62.7 **Oetaean flames**: Mount Oeta was frequently associated with the rising of the Evening Star. It was also the place where Hercules burned himself to death to escape being tortured by the poison in a cloak given to him by his wife Deianira (the story of Sophocles' *Trachiniae*). Hercules had shot the centaur Nessus, who was assaulting Deianira, with a poisoned arrow; Nessus told Deianira to save his own blood as a love charm, which she then duly employed when Hercules brought back a

No easy palm,[143] comrades, has been prepared for us;
see the unmarried girls going over their plans together?
It's not for nothing they're planning: they've got something memorable;
no wonder, seeing how hard they're straining with all their minds.
We've diverted our minds one way, our ears another;   15
we'll deserve to be beaten, then: victory loves care.
Therefore, now, at any rate, direct your minds:
now they'll begin to speak, now we'll have to make a reply.
Hymen o Hymenaeus, come, *Hymen o Hymenaeus!*

Evening Star, what crueler fire is borne in heaven?   20
You who can tear a daughter from her mother's embrace,
tear a daughter—clinging—from her mother's embrace,
and dedicate a virgin girl to a burning youth.
What crueler thing does the enemy do in a captured city?
Hymen o Hymenaeus, come, *Hymen o Hymenaeus!*   25

Evening Star, what pleasanter fire gleams in heaven?
You who confirm the promised nuptials with your flame,
the pledge the men have made, the parents have made before,
but haven't sealed it until your sparkling blaze has arisen.
What welcomer thing is given by gods in a happy hour?   30
Hymen o Hymenaeus, come, *Hymen o Hymenaeus!*

The Evening Star, comrades, has taken one of our number.[144]
***

***

For at your coming the guardian always takes up his watch;
Thieves[145] lie hidden at night, whom you often catch—the same

---

concubine, unwittingly bringing about her husband's death. The maidens, that is, are alluding to a
well-known story of infidelity, torture, and death as they contemplate the upcoming wedding.
    143. 62.11 **palm**: The palm branch was awarded to the victor in a contest.
    144. 62.32 We are missing most of this stanza and the beginning of the one that follows.
    145. 62.34 **Thieves**: Godwin (1995) 118: "The idea of the bride being stolen by the groom
from the safety of her parental home is linked with the association of night-time with sex: hence
the remark here about thieves in the night."

but with altered name, Evening Star—when you return as the
    Dawn Star.[146]   35
But the unmarried girls like to carp at you with a feigned complaint.
So what, if they carp at the one they desire in their secret heart?
Hymen o Hymenaeus, come, *Hymen o Hymenaeus!*

As a flower is born, hidden away in a fenced garden,
unknown to any cattle, uprooted by no plough,   40
the breezes caress it, the sun makes it strong, the rain makes it grow;
many a boy is longing for it, many a girl:
when the flower, plucked by slender thumb, has lost its bloom,
not one boy is longing for it, not one girl.
So a maiden, while still untouched, is dear to her own;   45
when she has lost her virgin flower,[147] her body spoiled,
she remains neither delightful to boys, nor dear to girls.
Hymen o Hymenaeus, come, *Hymen o Hymenaeus!*

As a vine is born a spinster in a naked field,
it never raises itself, never grows a succulent grape,   50
but bending over its tender body drooping face down
now, now just touches the tip of its whiplike shoot with its root;
not one farmer has tended it, not one yoke of oxen;
but if this vine should chance to be wed to a husband elm,
many a farmer has tended it, many a yoke of oxen.   55
So a maiden, while still untouched, withers untended;
when at the ripe time[148] she's attained a suitable marriage,
she's dearer to her man, and to her parent less hateful.[149]

And you too—do not fight with such a husband, maiden.
It's not right to fight him to whom your father himself has entrusted you,   60
your father himself with your mother, whom you are bound to obey.

    146. 62.35 **Dawn Star**: The Evening Star (the planet Venus) is the same as the Dawn Star: in one season it rises in the evening, in another at dawn. See Garrison (2004) on 62.34.
    147. 62.46 **lost her virgin flower**: See note on 11.22 **fallen like a flower**.
    148. 62.57 **ripe time**: The Latin word *maturus* ("ripe, mature, ready") can refer to both plants and animals; the maiden is now ready for "plucking."
    149. 62.58 **to her parent less hateful**: Unmarried girls were proverbially a nuisance to their fathers.

Virginity is not wholly your own: it's partly your parents'.
A third belongs to your father, a third has been given your mother—
only a third is your own: don't fight against the two,
who have given their son-in-law their rights along with the dowry.   65
Hymen o Hymenaeus, come, *Hymen o Hymenaeus!*

Catullus 68[150]

68A

That you, crushed down by fortune and by bitter chance,
    are sending me this note composed with your tears,
for me to raise and restore from the very threshold of death
    a shipwrecked man cast out on the sea's foaming waves,
whom neither holy Venus allows to rest in gentle   5
    sleep, deserted on his celibate bed,
nor do the Muses with the sweet song of ancient writers
    give pleasure, while anxious thoughts keep him up all night—
it's gratifying to me, since you're saying that I'm your friend,[151]
    and you're asking me for the gifts of the Muses and Venus.   10
But so my troubles, Mallius, won't be unknown to you,
    or you think I'm spurning the duty of hospitality,
hear what waves of fortune I'm drowning in myself,
    so you'll stop seeking happy gifts from a man in misery.

At the time when the pure toga[152] was first handed down to me,   15
    while flowering youth was spending its spring with pleasure,

150. **Catullus 68:** Whether "68" is actually one poem or two is the subject of long and unresolved scholarly debate (see Lowry [2006] 116 for bibliography). The first section (or poem), lines 1–40, takes the form of a letter to the poet's friend Mallius (or Manlius or Manius), who in his grief over losing a woman has written to Catullus asking for consolation from "the Muses and Venus" (love poems? poems and a lover?). The second section (or poem) is written in gratitude to one Allius, possibly identical with Mallius/Manlius/Manius, who supplied his home as a trysting spot during the early days of the affair between Catullus and a woman who can only be Lesbia (though she is not named). See Clauss (1995) for a persuasive reading of 68A and 68B as mirror images.

151. **68.9 since you're saying that I'm your friend**: The implication is that Catullus did *not* consider Mallius a close friend. As Skinner (2003) 149 observes, "Sensitive to urbane nuance, the authorial audience is expected to recognize that the poetic speaker finds Mallius' effusiveness embarrassing."

152. **68.15 pure toga**: That is, the man's toga (*toga virilis*), which had no stripe around the border (unlike the boy's toga or *toga praetexta*). The *toga virilis* was first put on around age fifteen or sixteen.

I played a good game: that goddess is no stranger to me
   who mingles her sweet bitterness[153] with cares.
But my brother's death, through grief, has robbed away from me
   this whole pursuit.[154] Brother, stolen from me in my misery!   20
You, brother, you—in dying you have shattered my comforts,
   our whole house lies buried together with you,
all my joys, together with you, have passed away,
   joys that in life were fed by your sweet love.
At your death, from my whole mind[155] I drove away   25
   these pursuits and all the pleasures of my soul.

So when you write that it's a disgrace for Catullus to be
   in Verona, since anyone here of greater note
must warm his chilly limbs on a deserted bed,
   this is not a disgrace, Manius—it's misery.   30
You'll forgive me, then, if I don't give you these gifts
   that grief has stolen away from me, since I can't.
If I don't have a great wealth of literature here with me,
   it's because my life is at Rome. That is my house,
that is my home, it's there that I enjoy my life;   35
   just one box[156] out of many attends me here.
Since that's the case, I wouldn't have you think I mean
   with ill will or insincerity of heart
not to have both kinds of wealth[157] on hand for you when you ask:
   if I had any wealth, I'd bring it to you on my own.   40

---

153. 68.18 **sweet bitterness**: Not, as we might say, "bitter sweetness" (or "bittersweetness"). The Romans believed that verbal similarities revealed truths about the nature of things, and they were keenly aware of the resemblance between *amarus* ("bitter") and *amare* ("to love"). In line 51 Venus's epithet "Amathusia" also puns on the AMA- root, though the name ostensibly means simply "of Amathus."

154. 68.19 **pursuit**: Latin *studium*, whose primary definition is "[e]arnest application of one's attention or energies to some specified or implied object, zeal, ardour" (*OLD*). The idea of romantic love as a *studium*, an object of zeal on a par with war, politics, or sports, appears to be a Catullan innovation.

155. 68.25 **whole mind**: The threefold repetition of "whole" (Latin *totus*)—"whole pursuit" (20), "whole house" (22), "whole mind" (25)—is Catullus', whether one attributes this to awkwardness or to artistry.

156. 68.36 **one box**: One container of scrolls, that is. The codex, or book with pages, did not come into use until several hundred years after Catullus.

157. 68.39 **both kinds of wealth**: That is, the Muses and Venus.

68B

I can't keep quiet, goddesses,[158] about what Allius
    did for me, or what great favors he did me,
so fugitive time, as the centuries lose their memory,
    will not conceal his pursuit in the blindness of night.
But I shall tell you, you hereafter tell it to many   45
    thousands, and make sure this page speaks as an old lady[159]
***

and become known more and more when he is dead,   48
nor the lofty spider as she's weaving her slender web[160]
    do her work on the deserted name of Allius.   50

For you know the kind of cares Amathusia[161] has given me
    in her treachery, you know the way she's scorched me,
back when I burned as hotly as the Trinacrian crag
    and the Malian spring of Oetaean Thermopylae,
and my mournful eyes never ceased to melt with a stream of unending   55
    tears, nor my cheeks to drip with gloomy rain.
As on the crest of a mountain high in the air a crystal
    rivulet leaps forth from a moss-covered stone,[162]

158. 68.41 **goddesses**: Muses. Catullus now proceeds to do what he just declared himself incapable of doing—that is, to write a love poem (of sorts), and a learned one, at that.

159. 68.46 **this page speaks as an old lady**: The word for "page" (*carta*) is feminine, and presumably this odd metaphor expresses Catullus' wish that his verses will be both long-lived and eager to spread the gossip to "many thousands." The next line is missing, so we do not know exactly how he would have continued that thought.

160. 68.49 **lofty spider as she's weaving her slender web**: As Thomas K. Hubbard (1984) 33 notes, "The spider is a symbol of oblivion and negation. But strangely, it can also be a symbol of the artist (as one is reminded by Ovid's interpretation of the Arachne myth); this identification is underlined by the frequency of *tenuis* ["slender"], *texens* ["weaving"], and *sublimis* ["lofty"] as terms of neoteric and Augustan poetics."

161. 68.51 **Amathusia**: See note on 68.18 **sweet bitterness**.

162. 68.57–58 **As . . . stone**: Ancient Latin texts were unpunctuated (they usually did not even have spaces between words), and it would not have been immediately clear to ancient readers of this poem that the stream simile refers forward to the "sweet solace" provided by Allius rather than backward to Catullus' stream of tears. In addition to lack of punctuation, the flexible word order of Latin poetry often creates such ambiguity: words or phrases appear at first to mean one thing, but as the text progresses the reader is forced to revise his or her interpretation. Rather than argue about whether the stream simile "really goes" with what precedes or with what follows (and scholars do argue about this), one might do better to accept the ambiguity as an integral feature of the poem and its extraordinary concatenation of similes. As Feeney (1992) 35 remarks, the poem's "dense

which when it has rolled headlong down the sloping valley
    crosses right through the path of masses of people,   60
sweet solace to the traveler in sweaty exhaustion,
    when heavy heat has cracked the parched fields open;
and as for sailors tossed about in whirling blackness[163]
    a favoring breeze arrives with gentler breath,
implored by prayer now to Pollux, now to Castor—   65
    such a help has Allius been for me.
He with a broad path laid open a closed field,
    he, he gave his home to me and to my mistress,[164]
a place for us to give expression to the love we shared.

There with supple foot my radiant divinity[165]   70
entered, and resting her gleaming sole on the smooth-worn threshold
    she halted, with her sandal singing shrill,[166]
just as Laodamia once, burning with love,
    arrived at the home of Protesilaus, her husband

---

and bizarre barrage of analogy leaves one with the sensation that similes are no added ornament
to the poem, something additional to what the poem is saying. They *are* the poem, they *are* what
the poem is saying."

163. 68.63 **whirling blackness**: Latin *turbo* can mean either "whirlwind" or "whirlpool."

164. 68.68 **mistress**: Latin *domina* means primarily a female head of a household—that is, a
woman who gives orders to slaves. While the idea of the (male) lover as the slave of his (female)
beloved rapidly becomes a commonplace in Latin poetry, this line apparently marks its first occur-
rence: see Hallett (1984) 250. Catullus' *domina* is partly responsible for the twist of language that
brought English "mistress" to mean both "a woman in a position of authority" (*AHD* s.v. 1) and "a
woman who has a continuing sexual relationship with a man to whom she is not married" (*AHD* s.v.
6); however, no shade of the latter meaning of "mistress" attaches (yet) to the Latin word.

165. 68.70 **radiant divinity**: Lesbia's "epiphany" has many echoes in later elegy. On Ovid's
allusions to this scene (and phrase) in *Amores* 1.5, see Hinds (1987) 8–10.

166. 68.72 **her sandal singing shrill**: Latin *arguta solea* is extremely difficult to translate:
argutus means "emitting a sharp sound" of some sort, but of what sort and with what implications? Two things are perhaps most relevant to the context. First, to stumble on a threshold was a
bad omen (hence the tradition of the groom carrying the bride over the threshold). Second, *argutus*
is often used to describe poets or objects very like poets. For instance, a character in Virgil's
Eclogues (9.36) compares the poets Varius and Cinna to *argutus* swans, and in the *Aeneid* the
sorceress Circe is said to weave with *argutus* comb (the word for "comb," *pecten,* also means
lyrist's plectrum) in a context that makes her sound suspiciously like a "new" poet: see Thomas
(1986) 66, Dyson (1997). Martial (6.34.7) uses *argutus* of Catullus himself, perhaps with particular
reference to the kind of "new" poetry that Catullus pioneered. The sandal thus sings an appropriate
prelude to the allusive tale of unfortunate love that follows. Clauss (1995) sees the "Delicate Foot
on the Well-Worn Threshold" as emblematic of Catullus' conflation of Callimachean (slender,
elite) and non-Callimachean (exuberant, popular) poetics in this poem.

a home commenced in vain[167]—not yet with sacred blood
    had an offering pacified the lords of heaven.   75
May nothing so completely charm me, Rhamnusian maiden,
    that I'd recklessly attempt it against these lords' will.

How thirstily the altar craves its righteous gore
    Laodamia was taught through the loss of her man,   80
forced to send her new husband out of her arms before
    one winter and a second winter again had come
to satisfy her ravenous love in their long nights,
    so she could live even with her marriage cut off.
The Parcae knew that this would be no long time away,   85
    if he should travel to Ilium's walls as a soldier.
For then, because of the rape of Helen, Troy had begun
    to summon to herself the chief men of the Argives,
Troy (hideous!), common grave of Asia and Europe,
    Troy, bitter ash of all virtues and men,   90
which also to my own brother brought a wretched death—[168]
    oh! brother, stolen from me in my misery,
oh! lovely light from a miserable brother stolen,[169]
    our whole house lies buried together with you,

167. 68.75 **commenced in vain**: The Romans believed that the gods required sacrifices (the ritual slaughter of animals) at the beginning of important human undertakings. If these sacrifices were omitted or were performed incorrectly, the undertaking would be a failure—and the failure of an undertaking indicated that the initial offering must have been faulty, so the system was self-confirming. Protesilaus's home was "commenced in vain" because in his eagerness to begin his married life he had omitted this initial sacrifice.

168. 68.91 **which also . . . death**: As Catullus recalls his own brother's death at Troy, he implicitly likens himself to Laodamia (who also lost her loved one at Troy). On the other hand, Catullus' overwhelming passion for Lesbia is similar to Laodamia's for Protesilaus. The correspondences between myth/simile and reality are thus quite complex: Lesbia is like Laodamia (both "brides" entering "homes" in an ill-omened fashion), but Catullus is also like Laodamia longing for Protesilaus, with Protesilaus representing both Lesbia and Catullus' brother. The confusion results partly because love for Lesbia, for his brother, and for Allius—all different kinds of love—pull the poet's emotions in conflicting directions. It is also remarkable that just as Catullus inverts conventional social hierarchies by making himself a "slave" to his "mistress," so he inverts the gender hierarchy by taking on the passive, female role of Laodamia. See MacLeod (1974) 83–85.

169. 68.93 **light from a miserable brother stolen**: As Lowry (2006) 128 notes, this "light" could refer either to the "light of life" taken from Catullus' brother or to the brother himself, a "light" taken from Catullus. The ambiguity is not resolvable: "Both can be true, and true at the same time."

all my joys, together with you, have passed away,   95
   joys that in life were fed by your sweet love.
Whom now so far away, not among familiar graves
   nor close to the ashes of kinsmen laid to rest,
but buried in Troy, in loathsome, in disastrous Troy,
   an alien land holds fast in distant soil.[170]   100

Rushing there (it is said) at that time, the Greek youths gathered
   from everywhere deserted their holy hearths,
so Paris, exulting in the adulteress he stole, wouldn't spend
   his leisure freely in a bedroom at peace.
Because of that sad chance, then, loveliest Laodamia,   105
   your marriage was wrenched from you, sweeter than life
and breath: engulfing you in such a whirlpool of love
   the tide had cast you down the precipitous pit,
like the one (say the Greeks) near Cyllenean Pheneus
   that dries the fertile soil when the swamp is drained,   110
which once, having smashed the mountain's marrow, the
   false-fathered
   son of Amphitryon is said to have dug,
at the time when with unerring shaft he struck the Stymphalian
   monsters at an inferior lord's command,
that heaven's door might be worn smooth by more divinities,   115
   and Hebe not be a virgin very long.

But deeper than that pit was your deep love, which taught you
   to bear the yoke, though you were still untamed.[171]

---

170. 68.100 **alien land holds fast in distant soil**: We might expect "distant land" and "alien soil"; this is an instance of "transferred epithets," or adjectives modifying the "wrong" nouns. A classic example is *Aeneid* 1.7, where Virgil writes "the walls of high Rome" rather than "the high walls of Rome." Translations that elide such distinctions may miss significant nuances.

171. 68.107–18 **engulfing you . . . untamed**: The strange simile of the pit (Latin *barathrum*, a Greek borrowing) and the equally surprising introduction of Hercules have caused scholars much perplexity. Tuplin (1981) 119–36 offers a detailed discussion of this passage, from which I would mention a few highlights: (1) In saying that Laodamia was "taught" to "bear the yoke" (of marriage) "though yet untamed" (a virgin), Catullus implies that love compelled her against her will; she was also unwillingly "taught" a hard lesson about excessive haste (lines 79–80). (2) The image of the pit "was capable of combining suddenness, inevitability and evil" (133)—a dark comment, to say the least, on romantic love's potentially destructive nature, something the ancients in general

For not so dear to a father wasted by age is the face
    of the late-born grandson nursed by his only daughter,   120
when he brings his name in the nick of time to the witnessed tablets
    and finally becomes heir to his grandfather's riches,
mocking his kinsmen and shattering their unrighteous joys
    as he chases the vultures from a head white with age:
nor does the mate of a snowy dove take such pleasure in him,   125
    who (it is said) is always plucking kisses
with her nibbling beak more lasciviously by far
    than any woman who's feverish with lust.
But you alone surpassed the great, mad passions of these
    as soon as you were matched with your golden-haired man.   130

My Light, then, who didn't fall short of her at all—
    or only a little[172]—came into my lap;
Cupid flitting all around her, now here, now there,
    gleamed in his saffron tunic radiantly.[173]
Even if she's not content with Catullus alone,   135
    I'll bear the blushing lady's[174] occasional cheating,[175]

---

and Catullus in particular saw clearly. (3) Hercules seems to serve primarily as a contrast to the
other characters in the poem, real and mythical: his marriage is legitimate and successful (unlike
Paris/Helen, Protesilaus/Laodamia, Catullus/Lesbia); as a real divinity, he goes in and out heaven's
door without stumbling on the threshold (unlike Lesbia and Laodamia); and he chooses a life of
virtue rather than pleasure (unlike Catullus).

    172. 68.132 **or only a little**: With this understated concession, the house of cards begins to
tumble, and as the poem continues we see just how great a gulf lies between Laodamia and Lesbia.
As MacLeod (1974) 86 notes, "in so far as Catullus can liken Lesbia to Laodamia, he thinks of
her, or thought of her, as virtually a bride; but in so far as he faces reality, he plainly denies that
there is any hint of a marriage between them: there is only the loose association of two polished
and sophisticated people."

    173. 68.133–34 **Cupid . . . radiantly**: Ancient vase paintings often depict brides with little
Cupids flitting about their heads, and saffron is the color of a bride's veil and of the tunic worn by
the marriage god Hymen in poem 61 (on correspondences between these "paired" poems, see
Martin [1992] 179–84). The ironic distance between Lesbia and a blushing bride is made explicit
in what follows (especially 143–46).

    174. 68.136 **blushing lady's**: Like *domina* (see note on 68), the word *era*, which I translate as
"lady" (it is the feminine form of *erus*, "lord," which appears in 75, 77, and 113), implies that
Lesbia is in a position of power over Catullus, her "slave."

    175. 68.136 **cheating**: Latin *furtum* (pl. *furta*), whose primary meaning is "theft," is fre-
quently used in love elegy to refer to "love affairs"—that is, something stolen from the lawful
spouse (as in 145–46, where Lesbia's "little gifts" are called *furtiva*). Here the word ironically

so I won't be pestering her too much like some clown.
  Often even Juno, greatest of goddesses,
swallowed down her seething wrath at her husband's wrongs,
  knowing all-lustful Jupiter's rampant cheating.   140
And yet it is not just to compare men with gods
***
  to raise the wearisome load of your trembling parent.[176]
Still, she didn't come to me to a home perfumed
  with Assyrian scent, led by her father's hand,[177]
but gave furtive little gifts in the amazing night,   145
  stolen[178] out of her very man's very lap.
Therefore it is enough, if I alone am granted
  the day she marks with a more radiant stone.[179]

This gift—the best I could do—composed in song for you
  is offered, Allius, for your many favors,   150
so this day, and that, and another, and another,
  won't desecrate your name with scabby rust.
The gods will add to it as much as they can the gifts
  that Themis once used to give to the righteous of old.
May both of you be happy, you and your Life together,   155
  and the house where we had our game, my mistress and I,
and he who <introduced her>[180] to me in the beginning,
  from whom all good things first came into being,
and she who far before all is dearer to me than myself,
  my Light: life is sweet to me while she's alive.   160

---

points up the quasi-marital status of the poet's relationship with Lesbia, who is cheating both with
him and on him.

176. 68.141–42: Some missing lines here make the progression of thought unclear.

177. 68.143–44 **Still . . . father's hand**: That is, with a traditional marriage rite, in which the
bride was led ceremonially to the groom's house.

178. 68.146 **stolen**: Lesbia or the gifts? The Latin (like the translation) is ambiguous.

179. 68.148 **more radiant stone**: When Lesbia first entered, she was a "radiant divinity"
(*candida diva,* 70); now, after the many reflections he has passed through, Catullus is content if
she considers their trysting days special events, marking them with a "more radiant stone" (*lapide
candidiore*). See Hinds (1987) 8.

180. 68.157 **<introduced her>**: The Latin text here has been garbled in transmission.

Catullus 69

Do not wonder why not a single woman, Rufus,[181]
  wants to have placed her tender thigh under yours,
not if you wear her down with a gift of gauzy clothing
  or with the cherished delight of a glittering jewel.
A certain nasty rumor's hurting your case: it is said   5
  that a grim goat dwells beneath the vale of your arms.[182]
All dread him, and no wonder—for he is really a nasty
  beast, not the kind for a pretty girl to sleep with.
Therefore, either slay this gruesome plague to noses,
  or cease to wonder why they run away.   10

Catullus 70

My woman says that there is no man she would rather marry[183]
  than me, not even if Jove were to ask her himself.
She says:[184] but what a woman says to her longing lover
  ought to be written on wind and rushing water.

---

181. 69.1 **Rufus**: This is very likely the Marcus Caelius Rufus of the *Pro Caelio*: see introduction, "Who Was Clodia?" The pestilential malodor pilloried here is associated with self-delusion and boorishness (Catullus' favorite subjects of attack), while the goat is associated with lechery and moral "stench"; see Nicholson (1997). Noonan (1979) suggests that the threat to women posed by the "plague" of Rufus's body odor alludes to allegations that Caelius was a poisoner of women; poem 77.5–6, in which the same Rufus is both "plague" and "poison," supports such a reading. In addition, "beast" (Latin *bestia*, 69.8) was the *cognomen* of Lucius Calpurnius Bestia, whom Caelius initially supported but then twice prosecuted (his son Atratinus was a prosecutor in the *Pro Caelio*); like Caelius, Bestia was accused of poisoning women, and both were members of the Luperci (see *Cael.* 16), a "rustic" fraternity that ran about in goat-skin loin cloths whipping people (especially women) with goat-skin thongs. The poison Bestia supposedly used, aconite, called both "lady-killer" (thelyphonon) and "beast bane" (therophonon), was foul smelling and inserted vaginally—all associations appropriate to the context here.

182. 69.6 **goat . . . vale of your arms**: Hutchinson (2003) 217 notes that in the Epigrams (poems 69–119), physical objects are less prominent than in the Polymetrics (poems 1–60), with the exception of body parts: "a part of someone's body becomes a distinct thing to contemplate, or even generates a creature, or becomes the whole to which a person is reduced."

183. 70.1 **marry**: Presumably (though not necessarily), this poem refers to the time after Clodia was widowed in 59 B.C. On the pseudomarriage of Catullus and Lesbia, see 68.133–41 (with notes).

184. 70.3 **She says**: Commentators compare this repetition of "says" to a similar repetition of "swears" in Callimachus epigram 25.

Catullus 71[185]

If the accursed armpit goat afflicts any man
    most justly, or sluggish gout deservedly stings him,
that rival of yours, who's giving your love some exercise,
    has miraculously contracted both evils from you.
For as often as he fucks, so often he punishes both: 5
    her he slams with stench, he himself dies[186] with gout.[187]

Catullus 72

Once you used to say that you knew Catullus alone,[188]
    Lesbia, and wouldn't want to hold Jove more than me.
I loved you then not just as the crowd love their girlfriend, but
    as a father loves his sons and his sons-in-law.[189]
Now, I know you: so even if I burn more fiercely,   5
    yet you are much cheaper and shallower to me.
How can this be, you say? Because such injury forces
    a lover to love more, but to wish well[190] less.

Catullus 73

Stop wanting to deserve well at all at anyone's hands,
    or thinking that anyone's able to become righteous.
Everything's thankless, it doesn't help at all to have done
    a good turn: no, in fact, it's sickening and destructive—
as to me, whom no one's crushing more heavily or bitterly   5
    than the man who just held me his one and only friend.

---

185. **Catullus 71**: Presumably the addressee is the same as that of poem 69.
186. 71.6 **slams . . . dies**: Latin *affligit* and *perit*, as Quinn (1970) on 71.6 points out, may both have erotic overtones.
187. 71.6 **gout**: This disease was associated with overindulgence in food and drink. Nicholson (1997) offers the attractive suggestion that Catullus is punning on Clodia's name, which literally means "lame, limping" (as one would be who was afflicted with gout).
188. 72.1 **you knew Catullus alone**: The Latin here could also be construed to mean "Catullus alone knew you." Catullus was capable of expressing himself clearly if he chose: the ambiguity is probably intentional and conveys the confusion of subject and object that is (some might say) a quality of romantic love. English, unfortunately, forces the translator to choose.
189. 72.4 **and his sons-in-law**: On this startling sentiment, see introduction, "love as *amicitia*."
190. 72.8 **wish well**: Latin *bene velle,* another term from the vocabulary of political alliance.

Catullus 74

Gellius had heard that his uncle often scolded
    if someone had cherished delights in word or deed.
Lest this should happen to him, he kneaded his uncle's very
    wife, and made his uncle Harpocrates.[191]
He got what he wanted: for, though he should facefuck his very   5
    uncle, his uncle will not breathe a word.

Catullus 75

My mind has been dragged so far down, Lesbia, by your wrong,
    and has so ruined itself by the favors it's done,
that now it could neither wish you well, if you became perfect,
    nor stop loving you, if you did—everything.

Catullus 76

If there is any pleasure for a person remembering
    services past, when he thinks how he is righteous,
and has not broken a sacred trust or abused the power
    of the gods to deceive people in any pact,
then many joys, Catullus, in a long life await you,   5
    joys arising out of this thankless love.
For all things people can kindly do or say to anyone,
    these have been both done and said by you:
and all have gone sour, entrusted to a thankless heart.
    Therefore, why should you torture yourself any more?   10
Why not toughen your heart and bring yourself back from there
    and stop being miserable, since the gods are hostile?
It's hard to cast away a long love all of a sudden;
    it's hard—but do it any way you can.
This is your only salvation, this is the fight you must win;   15
    do this, whether it's possible or not.
O gods, if you have any heart, or if you have ever finally
    given aid to those on the verge of death,

191. 74.4 **Harpocrates**: An Egyptian sun god, depicted holding his finger to his lips as if
commanding silence.

look upon me in my misery, and if I've lived a pure life,
   snatch this plague and pestilence from me,   20
which creeps like numbing torpor[192] into the depths of my limbs
   and utterly drives the happiness from my heart.
I'm not asking anymore that she love me in return,
   or (what is impossible) that she wish to be chaste:
I want to be healthy myself, and get rid of this foul sickness: 25
   O gods, grant me this in return for my righteousness.

Catullus 77

Rufus,[193] considered a friend by me in vain and for nothing
   (for nothing? no, for a high and evil price),
is this how you've snuck up on me, and burned my guts
   and snatched[194] away all our goods[195] from me in my misery?
You've snatched them away, alas, alas! you vicious poison   5
   of our life! alas, alas! you plague on our friendship!

Catullus 79

Lesbius is beautiful.[196] Of course he is! Lesbia would choose him
   over you, Catullus, with your whole family.

---

192. 76.21 **numbing torpor**: Poem 51 also presents physical symptoms of love, but the lover expresses no desire to be free of them; here, he wishes (or claims to wish) to be free of the "disease" entirely. Booth (1997) 167 observes, "Had Catullus presented his condition to a modern doctor, it might well have been diagnosed as a classic case of reactive depression, that is, depression with a clearly identifiable external cause"—not merely the "lovesickness" depicted by previous poets.

193. 77.1 **Rufus**: See note on 69.1 **Rufus**.

194. 77.4 **snatched**: As Dettmer (1997) 180 notes, pointing out the echo in 77.4 of 76.19–20, "The gods appear to have provided an immediate answer to Catullus' prayer in c. 76 to free him from his love affair by having Rufus (in c. 77) appropriate Lesbia."

195. 77.4 **our goods**: On the ambiguity of "our" versus "my," see note on 58.1 **Caelius, our Lesbia**. This translation retains "our" throughout, since both the woman and the friendship "belong" to Caelius and Catullus together.

196. 79.1 **Lesbius is beautiful**: Clodius' *cognomen* was *Pulcher,* "Beautiful"; Clodia/Clodius would naturally give rise to Lesbia/Lesbius. This poem provides the most compelling internal evidence for identifying Lesbia with Clodia, an identification that Catullus clearly intended his readers to see. For the political implications of incest, which implies clannish aristocratic snobbery as well as sexual deviance, see Skinner (1982) and Rankin (1976) 119–21.

But yet this beautiful man would sell Catullus, with family,
 if he could find three kisses from men who know him.[197]

Catullus 82

Quintius, if you want Catullus to owe you his eyes,[198]
 or something—if possible—dearer than his eyes,[199]
do not snatch away from him what to him is far dearer
 than his eyes, or anything dearer than his eyes.

Catullus 83

Lesbia hurls abuses at me in her husband's presence:
 this is the summit of happiness for that dolt!
You ass, don't you get it? If she kept quiet, oblivious of me,
 she would be healed: but now, since she snarls and curses,
not only does she remember, but—something fiercer by far—   5
 she's furious! That is: she burns, and she speaks.

Catullus 84

Hadvantages,[200] Arrius would say, whenever he wanted to say
 "advantages," and for "ambuscade," *hambuscade.*
And then he would hope that he had spoken admirably,
 when he'd said *hambuscade* with all his might.

197. 79.4 **three kisses from men who know him**: Friends often greeted each other in public with kisses. Catullus is simultaneously ridiculing lady-killer Lesbius' (Clodius') lack of male friends, hinting at his homosexual desires (to complement his incestuous desires), and suggesting that *cunnilingus* with his sister—a mark of degenerate effeminacy—makes his mouth unkissable.

198. 82.1 **owe you his eyes**: Roman poetry often makes eyes a symbol of what is most precious and therefore an appropriate object to swear by. For a comic variation on this theme, see *Am.* 3.3.

199. 82.2 **dearer than his eyes**: Presumably, the one thing Catullus considers "dearer than his eyes" is Lesbia, though this is never stated.

200. 84.1 *Hadvantages*: Pronunciation was (and is) a marker of origin, education, and social class. Arrius overcompensates to the point of incorrectness (as if we were to say, e.g., "I know whom you are").

Thus, I think, his mother, thus his freeborn uncle,[201]   5
   thus had his mother's father and mother spoken.
When he'd been sent to Syria, everyone's ears got a break:
   they would hear these things spoken smoothly and lightly,
nor did they find themselves in dread of such words for the future,
   when suddenly the horrible news arrives: 10
The Ionian Sea, after Arrius had traveled thither,
   was now no longer "Ionian" but *Hionian.*

Catullus 85

I hate and I love.[202] Why do I do this, you may well ask.
   I don't know, but I feel it happen and it's torture.[203]

Catullus 86

Quintia is beautiful to many. In my eyes, she's radiant,
   tall, good posture: I grant these single points.
I deny that the whole is beautiful. For no attractiveness,
   not a grain of salt[204] resides in so great a body.
Lesbia is beautiful; she is both entirely lovely,   5
   and alone has robbed all the Venus[205] from all other women.

---

201. 84.5 **freeborn uncle**: The implication is that Arrius' other relatives are *not* freeborn.

202. 85.1 **I hate and I love**: This concise statement of the lover's perpetual dilemma echoes throughout all subsequent love poetry. Ovid, for instance, expands on the idea at great length in *Am.* 3.11b.

203. 85.2 **it's torture**: Latin *excrucior,* literally, "I'm crucified" (a word this translation avoids because the inevitable Christian overtones would be misleading for a modern audience). In the Roman world, only slaves were subjected to this terrible punishment. If Catullus is hinting here at "slavery" to his "mistress," then this is the only trace of the *servitium amoris* in his epigrams (poems 69–116); in general, the ideas of love as political alliance and of love as slavery are mutually exclusive.

204. 86.4 **salt**: See note on 10.33 **dimwit**.

205. 86.6 **all the Venus**: Until the early medieval period (seventh century A.D. or so), Latin writing contained only capital letters. "Venus" was the goddess of sexual love, but what we might call "venus" referred to a range of things in her sphere, such as sexiness, charm, and the act of intercourse.

Catullus 87

No woman is able to say that she's been loved so truly
    as my own Lesbia has been loved by me.
No faith so great was ever found in any pact[206]
    as has been found, from my side, in your love.[207]

Catullus 91

Gellius, I wasn't expecting you to be loyal to me
    in this my miserable, this my hopeless love
because I knew you well, or thought that you were faithful
    or could hold back your mind from scandalous filth,
but because I saw that neither mother nor sister to you[208]   5
    was the woman whose great love[209] was devouring me.
And though I was connected to you by frequent dealings
    I hadn't believed this was reason enough for you.
You thought it was enough: such joy do you find in every
    wrong in which there's any hint of crime.   10

Catullus 92

Lesbia's always cursing me, and never keeps quiet
    about me: damned[210] if Lesbia doesn't love me!
What proof? Because I'm exactly the same: I rail against her
    constantly—but damned if I don't love her!

206. 87.3 **pact**: See introduction, "love as *foedus*."
207. 87.4 **your love**: Latin *amore tuo*. As in English, "your love" can mean "love for you," "love by you," or "love belonging to you." On a similar ambiguity stressing love's confusion of subject and object, see note on 72.1 **you knew Catullus alone**.
208. 91.5 **neither mother nor sister to you**: That is, Catullus had thought (he ironically asserts) that only incest had any appeal for the wicked Gellius.
209. 91.6 **whose great love**: See note on 87.4 **your love**.
210. 92.2 **damned**: Latin *dispeream*, literally, "may I utterly perish." Catullus likes to reactivate the literal meanings of such expressions (see note on 32.1 **I will love you**).

Catullus 93[211]

I'm not especially eager, Caesar, to want to please you,
   or to know whether you're a white man or a black.[212]

Catullus 95

My Cinna's "Smyrna,"[213] finally published after the ninth
   harvest and the ninth winter since it was begun,
as Hortensius, meanwhile, five hundred thousand [lines] in one [year][214]
***
"Smyrna" will be sent far to the Satrachus' deep waves;[215]
"Smyrna" the hoary ages will long unroll.   5
But the "Annals" of Volusius[216] will die right at Padua[217]
   and often provide luxurious tunics for mackerel.[218]
Let my good friend's tiny monument be dear to my heart:
   but let the people exult in swollen Antimachus.[219]

---

211. **Catullus 93**: This poem is sometimes cited as an example of the "free speech" of the late Republic: poets of the Empire would not have spoken so. Three other poems (29, 54, and 57, not translated here) attack Caesar and his supporters in even more virulent terms. Suetonius (*Caesar* 73) relates, "When Valerius Catullus—whose verses about Mamurra Caesar openly declared to have inflicted a lasting stigma upon himself—apologized, Caesar invited him to dinner that very day, and continued friendly relations with Catullus' father as he had before."

212. 93.2 **a white man or a black**: This is simply a proverbial way of saying "I don't care who you are." (Modern issues involving race are not relevant here.)

213. 95.1 **"Smyrna"**: This "epyllion" (short epic), of which only two fragments survive, told of Smyrna's incestuous passion for her father (Ovid tells the story in *Metamorphoses* 10.298–528, but with "Smyrna" called "Myrrha"). Catullus contrasts the constrained, slender elegance of this paragon of "new poetry" with the unpolished bulk of long epics (see note on 1.1 **charming new booklet**).

214. 95.3 **five hundred thousand [lines] in one [year]**: The next line (which would have contained the nouns modified by "five hundred thousand" and "one") is missing.

215. 95.4 **Satrachus' deep waves**: Smyrna/Myrrha's son Adonis spent time by this river in Cyprus.

216. 95.6 **"Annals" of Volusius**: These meet another ignominious fate in poem 36.

217. 95.6 **die right at Padua**: Volusius' verses will not make it past their place of origin at the mouth of the Padus (Po) River.

218. 95.7 **tunics for mackerel**: As Thomson (1964) argues, this refers to the wrapper in which fish would be *cooked* (not sold), thus reinforcing the idea of the incineration of Volusius' poems introduced in poem 36.

219. 95.9 **let the people exult in swollen Antimachus**: Callimachus derided the clumsy, lengthy epic *Lyde* by Antimachus. For Callimachus and his followers, excessive popularity and excessive length were symbolized by a swollen, muddy river; his own poetry he compared to a clear, small, secluded spring. See Clausen (1972) 277.

Catullus 96[220]

If anything pleasing or welcome arising from our grief,
    Calvus, has power to reach the silent tomb,
from the longing with which we live again our former loves
    and weep for friendships that were once let go,
surely Quintilia's grief at her own untimely death   5
    is not so great as is her joy in your love.[221]

Catullus 101

Carried through many nations, and through many seas,[222]
    I have come for this miserable offering, brother,
to endow you with the final service due to death
    and to address your silent ashes in vain.
Seeing as Fortune has torn you yourself away from me,   5
    ah! miserable brother, stolen from me unfairly,
now still, even so, these[223] which in the ancient way of our fathers
    have been presented for offerings, a grim service—
receive them dripping greatly with a brother's tears,
    and for eternity, brother, hail and farewell.[224]   10

220. **Catullus 96**: Calvus had written an elegy on the death of Quintilia (his wife or mistress). The present poem is both a consolation and a meditation on the power of poetry—and love.

221. 96.5–6 **surely . . . love**: As Wray (2001) 52 points out, these last two lines "correct" a line by Calvus himself, "Perhaps the very ashes may find joy even in this" (Latin *forsitan hoc etiam gaudeat ipsa cinis*, fr. 15–16, Courtney [1993] 207); Catullus alludes to the model but turns its speculation into certainty. Such intellectual artistry in a sympathy note may seem out of place to us, but it did not to the ancients.

222. 101.1 **Carried through many nations, and through many seas**: Catullus' brother died near Troy; Catullus probably visited the grave on his way to Bithynia in 57 B.C. This line depicts Catullus' journey in epic terms reminiscent of the *Odyssey* (Odysseus sailed *from* Troy through many nations and many seas).

223. 101.7 **these**: This could refer both to traditional offerings to the dead (such as wine, honey, milk, or flowers) and to the poem itself, a more durable "offering."

224. 101.10 **hail and farewell**: Latin *ave atque vale*; this formula was part of the traditional funerary rite, during which the name of the deceased was called out three times (as "brother" is in this poem). On the poem's relation to Roman funerary ritual and to Catullus' characterization of his own role in society, see Feldherr (2000). As Skinner (2002) 438 observes, "Catullus' lament is also a substitute for performance of cult. . . . [T]he poem is a 'performative' utterance, a statement that accomplishes an effect in and of itself through the very process of being articulated."

Catullus 104

You think that I could hurl abuses at my Life,
    one who is dearer to me than both my eyes?
I couldn't—nor, if I could, would I love so desperately:
    but you, with Tappo,[225] do all monstrous things.

Catullus 107

If ever anything comes to a man who is longing, wishing,
    but hopeless—that is sweet to his spirit indeed!
Therefore this is sweet to me, this is dearer than gold:
    you restore yourself, Lesbia, to me in my longing,
you restore to a longing and hopeless man, on your own you return   5
    yourself to me. Oh day of more radiant note![226]
What happier man lives than me only? Or who will be able
    to name a thing more to be wished in life than this?

Catullus 109

You declare to me, my Life, that this our mutual love
    will be pleasant and last for all eternity.
Great gods, see to it that she be able to promise truly,
    and that she say it sincerely and from the heart,
so we may be allowed for our whole life to continue   5
    this everlasting pact of holy friendship.[227]

Catullus 116 [228]

My mind was hunting eagerly, I kept looking for a way
    to translate the son of Battus' songs for you,
to reconcile you to me, so you would stop attempting
    to fling your vicious shafts against my head;

225. 104.4 **Tappo**: The reference is baffling. Possible candidates are a stock character in Italian farce or an author of scurrilous verses (one Valerius, who seems to have the *cognomen* "Tappo"): see Fordyce (1961).
  226. 107.6 **more radiant note**: See note on 68.148 **more radiant stone**.
  227. 109.6 **pact of holy friendship**: See introduction, "love as *foedus*" and "love as *amicitia*."

I see now this labor was undertaken by me in vain,   5
    Gellius, nor did my prayers here have any weight.
I can dodge those shafts of yours hurled out against *me,*
    but *you* are going to be pinned by mine and punished.[229]

228. **Catullus 116**: It is significant that this, and not poem 109, is the closing poem of the collection. MacLeod (1973) 308 notes that "it is an inverted dedication"; Dettmer (1997) 224–25 shows how it carefully inverts the themes and language of poem 1. Skinner (2003) discusses, among other things, its "professed transfer of allegiance from a Callimachean to an Ennian poetics" (28).

229. 116.8 **but you . . . punished**: As Tatum (1997) 500 observes, "This final line echoes Romulus' fatal last words to Remus in the *Annales* [of Ennius], after the latter had transgressed the city's new wall. In this way Catullus assumes the role of Rome's violent founder, thereby consigning Gellius to play the part of the twin who made himself the ultimate outsider. The switch in status is part of the sting."

Testimonia

SALLUST

The Roman historian Gaius Sallustius Crispus (86–34? B.C.) wrote, among other things, the War with Catiline *and* War with Jugurtha. *His portrait of Catiline's female follower Sempronia shows certain similarities to Clodia, as noted by his medieval commentator ("Scholiast" = "one who writes in the margins").*[1]

Sallust, *Bellum Catilinae* [War with Catiline] 25

But among these was Sempronia, who had often committed many crimes of masculine audacity. This woman was quite fortunate in her birth and her beauty, also in her husband and her children; she was learned in Greek and Latin literature; she played the lyre and danced more elegantly than is necessary for an honest woman; and she engaged in many other activities that are the tools of voluptuousness. But anything and everything were dearer to her than decorum and modesty; you could scarcely tell whether she was less careful with her money or her reputation; she was so enflamed by lust that she propositioned men more often than she

---

1. *Bell. Cat.* 25 **Sempronia**: As Boyd (1987b) 185 observes, "For Sallust, Sempronia is both Catiline's complement and his ironic reverse: both use and abuse the products of *luxuria* to manipulate others, and are themselves its victims; both represent a perversion of the natural order, Catiline by his lack of *virtus* and Sempronia by her possession of its *Ersatz, virilis audacia.*" Despite the elaborate description given here, the identity of this woman is not known; she has no previous or further role in the narrative (aside from a passing reference to her house in §40). See Ramsey (1984) 135–36.

was herself propositioned. But before this [the Catilinarian conspiracy] she had often betrayed her word, repudiated her debt, been an accomplice in murder, fallen headlong through extravagance and poverty. Yet her native wit was nothing to sneeze at; she could compose poetry, make a joke, use language either modest or alluring or wanton; in short, there was much wit and much charm in her.

Scholiast's comment on Sallust's observation that "[Sempronia] danced more elegantly than is necessary for an honest woman":

Ancient documents attest that [Clodia] was eager for dancing more extravagantly and immoderately than was appropriate for a matron.

QUINTILIAN

Marcus Fabius Quintilianus (c. A.D. 35–c. 95) wrote the Institutio Oratoria *("Training in Rhetoric"), a systematic Roman treatment of oratorical theory much influenced by Cicero.*

Quintilian, *Institutio Oratoria* [Training in Rhetoric] 8.6.53

Even orators sometimes use [riddles], as in Caelius' "quadrantaria Clytemnestra"[2] and "Coan in the dining room, Nola in the bedroom."[3]

2. *Inst.* 8.6.53 **"quadrantaria Clytemnestra"**: See note on *Cael.* 62 **usual three-penny exchange**.

3. *Inst.* 8.6.53 **"Coan in the dining room, Nola in the bedroom"**: Saylor (1995) 328–29 explains this elegantly: "The pun was multiple and all the more stinging for its wicked intricacy. Cos suggested the island from which Clodia's transparent silks had come, and therefore the open, vulgar allure of sex; Nola was famous for its impregnable fortress, which had resisted not just Hannibal but a siege by Clodia's own father. Cos also punned with *coitus,* sex, and Nola with *nolo,* or no sex [*nolo* literally = "I don't want to"]. In other words, what the lady lewdly promised at dinner was later frigidly withheld in the bedroom. With a single turn of phrase, and without saying anything explicit, Caelius had managed to suggest that Clodia was not just a temptress but a tease (likely to give poor value even for a quadrans!), to suggest that he had never actually slept with her, and to remind the court of one of her father's military defeats, the siege of Nola." Unlike many fictional works involving Clodia, Saylor's *Venus Throw* is quite accurate in its treatment of Clodia, Caelius, Cicero, and other historical figures. For an assessment of the quality and historicity of Clodia's other "Imaginary Lives," see Wiseman (1975).

Hillard (1981) argues that Caelius' charge of Clodia Metelli's frigidity here is so much at odds with Catullus' portrait of the sexually rampant Lesbia that the two cannot be referring to the same woman: "Whenever they compared notes, little sister Lesbia probably scandalized Clodia Metelli" (154). Yet that a woman should be accused of being both a slut and a prude by embittered (ex-)lovers strikes this reader, at least, as scarcely more improbable than "I hate and I love" (Cat. 85).

PLUTARCH

The Greek biographer and philosopher Plutarch (c. A.D. 46–c. 120) wrote a series of Parallel Lives *pairing prominent Greeks with prominent Romans. "The* Lives, *despite the pitfalls for the historian which have sometimes led to despair about their value as source material, have been the main source of understanding of the ancient world for many readers from the Renaissance to the present day" (OCD).*

Plutarch, *Cicero* 29.1–5

[1] Now, Cicero was a friend of Clodius, and when the Catiline business was going on Cicero made use of him as a most enthusiastic coworker and guardian of his person. But when Clodius was replying to the charge against him by affirming that he had not been in Rome at that time but was staying in places very far away, Cicero bore witness that Clodius had come to him at home and discussed some things with him—which was true. [2] But it appeared that Cicero was not witnessing to this for the sake of the truth, but to defend himself against his own wife, Terentia. [3] For there was enmity between her and Clodius on account of his sister Clodia, because (as Terentia thought) she wanted to marry Cicero[4] and was working this through one Tullus, who was a companion and close friend of Cicero; by constant visits and service to Clodia, who lived nearby, Tullus was making Terentia suspicious. [4] Being harsh by nature and having Cicero under her thumb, she spurred him on to join in the attack on Clodius and bear witness against him. Many of the best and noblest men bore witness against Clodius for perjury, evildoing, bribing the masses, corrupting women. Lucullus produced female slaves who testified that Clodius had had intercourse with his youngest sister when she was married and living with Lucullus. [5] And there was a common belief that Clodius slept with his other two sisters too, of whom Tertia was married to Marcus Rex and Clodia to Metellus Celer. They called her "Quandrantia," because one of her lovers had put copper coins in a purse and sent them to her as silver (they used to call the smallest copper coin a "quadrans"). Because of this sister most of all, Clodius had a bad reputation.

---

4. *Cic.* 29.3 **she wanted to marry Cicero**: That there was something going on between Clodia and Cicero may well be pure fabrication. On the other hand, as Rankin (1969) 504 suggests, "Cicero's hatred in the *Pro Caelio* is not pure and distilled, it still shows by its intensity the attraction that he had once felt, and a horrified fascination." We will never know.

Part II

Clodia's Legacy

Propertius

Sextus Propertius (born 54–47 B.C., died before 2 B.C.), author of four surviving books of elegies, declares his primary subject in the first line of his first poem: "Cynthia first with those eyes of hers captured me in my misery." Yet who this Cynthia was is impossible to say.[1] The modern tendency has been to see her less as a real person and more as a symbol of poetry and the poetic process.[2] Whatever her identity, Propertius is unique among the Roman elegists in placing long, witty, sometimes scathing speeches in her own mouth, giving her (however fictional) a seductive vividness. Like Catullus, Propertius creates a sort of narrative across poems of a stormy affair characterized by passion, betrayal, renunciation, and reunion, interlarded with poems reflecting on male friendship, politics, and mythology. He puts a mischievous spin on Catullus' technique of scrambling the affair's temporal sequence: after what appears to be a final renunciation of Cynthia in 3.24–25, she quite literally comes back from the grave to scold him in 4.7—and in the next poem (4.8), alive and kicking (and scratching and biting), pummels him back into submission and bed.

1. On attempts to identify her as a prostitute, a married woman, a foreigner, or a Roman noblewoman, see Griffin (1985) 27, who concludes, "Surely the trouble is that the alternatives are too narrowly conceived and too sharply opposed." Most likely correct is the assessment of Goold (1990) 9: "No doubt his imagination was fuelled by some model or models who had a historical existence, but his relationship to her or them we cannot know. What we may assert is that Cynthia is Propertius' dream-girl, with an endowment of all that his mind can contrive."

2. As Wyke (2002) 51 argues, Propertius' second book, in particular, "breaks away significantly from the devices of realism, and instead associates Cynthia so intimately with the practice of writing elegy as to undermine her identity independently of that practice." Gold (1993) 88 points out that Cynthia "is identified both by the author himself and by later male critics (ancient and modern) not only *with* his poetry but *as* his poetry."

Propertius 1.1

Cynthia[3] first with those eyes of hers captured me in my misery,
   previously plagued by no desires.
Then did Love hurl down my looks[4] of stubborn disdain
   and pin my head beneath his feet and crush it,[5]
until that wicked boy had taught me to despise decent   5
   girls, and to live with no deliberate plan.
Ah me! For a whole year now this madness has not died down,
   and still I'm forced to put up with hostile gods.[6]

Milanion, Tullus, by fleeing from no hardship, broke
   the savage will of Iasus' pitiless daughter.[7]   10
For now he'd wander out of his mind in Parthenian caves,
   now again he'd go against shaggy beasts;
when he was even dealt a wound from Hylaeus' club,
   he'd groan in pain on the Arcadian cliffs.
Therefore he gained the power to tame the speedy girl: 15
   so much are faith and services[8] worth in love.

---

3. 1.1.1 **Cynthia**: A poetic pseudonym. Apollo and Diana, supposedly born on Mount Cynthus, are sometimes referred to as "Cynthius" and "Cynthia," respectively. "Cynthia" thus recalls both the god of poetry (as Catullus' "Lesbia" recalls a poetess—see note to **Catullus 51**) and his sister: as Richardson (1976) 3 notes, "Her name seems chosen to suggest that she is the triple goddess, Luna, queen of the night, shining and unattainable, Diana, the virgin huntress, and Hecate from the Underworld, patroness of witches."

4. 1.1.3 **hurl down my looks**: As Stahl (1985) 29 notes, "while Cynthia's eyes make Propertius a prisoner, his own eyes are forced down (!)—instead of having a similar effect on her."

5. 1.1.4 **pin my head beneath his feet and crush it**: As Greene (1998) 40 notes, unlike Catullus and Sappho, "Propertius describes the speaker's enslavement to love, not as an internal emotional event, but as an external action that takes place in the world of military conquest." Commager (1974) 24 observes that Love's "placing his feet on him" has a punning second meaning, "imposing the metre of love-elegy," which Ovid amplifies; see note on *Am.* 1.1.4 **snatched away one foot**.

6. 1.1.8 **hostile gods**: Compare Cat. 76.12.

7. 1.1.10 **Iasus' pitiless daughter**: Atalanta (compare Cat. 2.12). Like many poets of his generation, Propertius frequently alludes to mythology, often in roundabout ways; for instance, rather than naming "Atalanta," he says "Iasus' pitiless daughter" and "speedy girl." Such allusions can be wearying to the modern reader forced to rely on footnotes and glossary, but to gloss them in the text would give a misleading impression of Propertius' style. As Gaisser (1977) 381 notes, "Mythology remains something of a stepchild in modern criticism of Propertius," an "embarrassment even to his most sympathetic hearers"—and yet "this very incongruity or irrelevance [of mythological exempla] is in fact a deliberate part of Propertius' poetic technique."

8. 1.1.16 **faith and services**: Latin *fides et benefacta*. This is one of Propertius' only instances of the language of political alliance and reciprocity, such as Catullus uses throughout the Epigrams.

In my case, slow-witted Love does not devise any arts,
    and forgets how to go down his well-known paths as before.
But you, whose task is luring the moon to lead it down
    and performing rites of appeasement on magical hearths,   20
come now, please, and twist the mind of my mistress around
    and see to it that her face turns paler than mine![9]
Then I might believe you have the power to summon
    the Ghosts and the stars with Cytinean songs.[10]

Or you, my friends, who are calling the fallen one back too late,   25
    find out a remedy for a heart that's sick.
Bravely will I suffer both iron and savage fires,[11]
    if anger can just have the freedom to speak its mind.
Carry me through distant lands and through distant seas,[12]
    to a place where not one woman will know my path.   30

Stay home, you to whom the god has lent his ear and said "Yes,"
    and may you always be soul mates in a safe love.
My Venus keeps pestering me throughout the bitter nights,
    and Love is never idle, never fails.
I warn you, avoid this evil: let each hold on to his own   35
    care, and not change beds when love grows familiar.
But if anyone will turn a deaf ear to my warnings, ah,
    what agony when he remembers my words!

Cynthia, however, proves herself the dominant partner. See introduction, "love as *foedus*" and "love as *amicitia*."

    9. 1.1.22 **paler than mine**: Lovers were proverbially pale: see introduction, "love as disease." Propertius is also playing with the ideas of Cynthia as moon goddess (see note on 1.1.1 **Cynthia**) and of quasi-divine, magical powers belonging to poet and mistress: see Zetzel (1996) 91–100.

    10. 1.1.24 **Cytinean songs**: *Am.* 2.1.21–28 alludes to and expands on this Propertian passage.

    11. 1.1.27 **iron and savage fires**: The combination of "iron" (Latin *ferrum*, which often means "sword") and "fire(s)" belongs to several different spheres: war ("fire and the sword" used to attack cities), surgery (the knife followed by cauterization), and slavery (slaves could be both branded and tortured with red-hot iron). Since erotic love is frequently figured as war, disease, and slavery, any of these metaphors could be appropriate here, and there is no need to choose one to the exclusion of the others; see the discussion by Kennedy (1993) 46–63 of "Love's Figures and Tropes."

    12. 1.1.29 **Carry me . . . seas**: Compare Cat. 101.

Propertius 1.3

Just as the Cnossian girl,[13] while Theseus' ship was retreating,
　　lay in a swoon on the abandoned shore;
and as Andromeda, Cepheus' daughter, finally free
　　from the stony cliff, reclined in her first sleep;
and as the Edonian,[14] no less wearied by constant revels,　　　　　5
　　falls on the bank of grassy Apidanus:
so did Cynthia seem to me to breathe soft peace,
　　resting her head on interlocking hands,
as I was dragging my footsteps reeling with plenty of Bacchus,[15]
　　and boys were shaking their torch[16] in the far-gone night.　　　10

I, since I hadn't yet completely lost my senses,
　　attempt to reach her, softly pressing her couch;
and though Love on this side, Liber on that—harsh gods both—
　　were heating my blood with a double flame and commanding me
to try her as she lay, to slide my arm gently beneath her　　　　　15
　　and bring up my hand to steal belated kisses,
yet I had not dared to trouble my mistress's peace,
　　fearing the lash of the savage temper I knew.
But I clung there, piercing her with eyes staring as intently
　　as Argus on the strange horns of Inachus' daughter.　　　　　　20

And now I was loosening the garland from my brow
　　and placing it upon your temples, Cynthia,

---

13. 1.3.1 **Cnossian girl**: Ariadne. Latin conveys the gender of the "Cnossian" by the word ending; the translator must either leave the gender ambiguous or choose an appropriate female noun ("girl," "woman," "maid," etc.).

14. 1.3.5 **Edonian**: See previous note; the Latin "Edonian" here specifies "Edonian female." The reference is to a Thracian Maenad.

15. 1.3.9 **plenty of Bacchus**: Although the surface meaning is simply "I was drunk," the reference to "Bacchus" here alludes to the god's rescue of the abandoned Ariadne—the vignette that opens the poem and which Cynthia will reactivate when she awakens. As Zetzel (1996) 86 points out, "Propertius, perhaps because he is drunk, fondly sees himself as the rescuer; Cynthia clearly sees him as the deserting Theseus."

16. 1.3.10 **boys were shaking their torch**: That is, slave boys were leading drunken revelers home.

and now I was taking pleasure in shaping your fallen tresses,
    now giving furtive apples from my cupped hands:
I was bestowing all these gifts on thankless sleep,   25
    gifts often rolling from your sloping bosom;
and whenever you would breathe a sigh, or stir a little,
    I froze, believing in empty divination—
afraid some nightmare was bringing you strange terrors, or
    some man forcing you to be his against your will: 30
until the moon, hurrying past the parted shutters,
    the busy moon, with light that would have stayed,
opened with its gentle beams her fast-closed eyes.
    Planting her elbow on the soft couch, thus she speaks:

"Finally! Has someone else's scorn sent you back to my bed,   35
    shoved you out and slammed the door behind you?
So where have you been wasting the long hours of *my night,*
    washed up—ah me!—now that the stars are gone?
Bastard! *You* should be the one spending the kind of night
    you keep ordering *me* in my misery to put up with!   40

"For I was just now beguiling sleep with purple thread,[17]
    and again, though weary, with song of Orphean lyre;[18]
all the while, abandoned, I softly bemoaned to myself
    your long and frequent delays as you love another,
till Sleep assailed my languor with his soothing wings.   45
    For my tears that was the final care."

Propertius 1.11

While you're busy dallying, Cynthia, in the heart of Baiae,
    where a causeway lies on Herculean shores,[19]

---

17. 1.3.41 **purple thread**: Weaving in the ancient world symbolized female virtue: one thinks especially of the faithful Lucretia, who sat up late at her weaving while other women were carousing. Purple cloth, on the other hand, often denoted luxury and Eastern exoticism.

18. 1.3.42 **Orphean lyre**: Cynthia is (by her own account) not only as virtuous as Lucretia, but literate and musical as well, and in this stanza she displays her poetic gifts with a vengeance.

19. 1.11.2 **causeway lies on Herculean shores**: Hercules allegedly built a causeway between the Lucrine Lake (near Baiae) and the sea.

and marveling that the waters so recently under Thesprotus'
    kingdom are now close by renowned Misenum,[20]
does the slightest care touch you to bring on nights you remember me?   5
    Does any spot on the edge of your love remain?
Or has some foe or other with simulated flames
    snatched you away, Cynthia, out of my songs—
since often, when her guardian's removed, a girl will backslide,   *15*
    the traitor, and not remember the gods they share?   *16*

I'd rather some cute little skiff, trusting in tiny oars,
    be amusing you upon the Lucrine Lake,   10
or in Teuthras' shallow wave[21] the water easily yielding
    to alternating hands[22] be holding you cloistered,
than that you, softly disposed upon the silent shore,
    be free to hear someone else's flattering whispers!
Not because you're not known to me by tested repute,   17
    but because every love is feared for in this regard.
You'll forgive me, then, if my little book has brought you
    something grim: my fear will take the blame.   20

Oh, I'd be holding no greater vigil for my dear mother,
    nor, without you, do I have any care for my life!
You alone are my home, you alone are my parents, Cynthia,
    you are my every moment of happiness.
Whether I come to meet my friends in sadness or joy,   25
    whatever I'll be, I'll say, "Cynthia was the cause."
But you, just leave foul Baiae behind as soon as you can:
    those shores will be the reason for many a breakup,
shores that have been the enemies of modest girls.
    Oh, damn the waters of Baiae, a plague on love!   30

---

    20. 1.11.3–4 **the waters . . . Misenum**: Thesprotus was king of Epirus, which included the rivers of the Underworld. These rivers supposedly flowed subterraneously into Lake Avernus, which in 37 B.C. was joined to the Bay of Naples (on which Misenum is a promontory) by a canal passing through the Lucrine Lake.
    21. 1.11.11 **Teuthras' shallow wave**: Teuthras was king of Mysia, which sent out a colony to found Cumae (a city on the Bay of Naples). The "shallow wave" has not been identified.
    22. 1.11.11–12 **the water easily yielding to alternating hands**: See Griffin (1985) 88–111 on "The Pleasures of Water and Nakedness," especially 90–91 on this "voluptuous description."

Propertius 1.15

I often feared many hardships from your fickleness, Cynthia,
    and yet I never dreamed of this one: betrayal.
See into what great danger Fortune is hurling me!
    But you are slow to come to me in my fear;
and you can smooth with your hands hair rumpled since last night,   5
    and strive for beauty in long idle hours,
and adorn your breast with oriental gems like a girl
    getting ready to meet a new man looking her best.

Yet not thus had Calypso, stunned by the Ithacan's leaving,[23]
    wept in ages past to the desolate waves: 10
day after day, with hair uncombed, she'd sat in mourning,
    pouring out her complaints to the unjust sea,
and though she was never to see him again after this, she grieved
    in any case, thinking of their long happiness.

Nor thus, when the winds were sweeping away the son of Aeson,   17
    did Hypsipyle stand in her empty chamber in fear:
after that love, Hypsipyle never felt any other,
    once she had melted for her Haemonian guest.   20
Upon her husband's miserable pyre was Evadne's death
    and funeral, glory of Argive chastity.
Alphesiboea took vengeance on her brothers because of her   *15*
    husband, and love broke the bonds of kindred blood.   *16*

Not one of these was able to make you change your ways,
    that you, too, might go down in history.
Stop reminding me now of your treachery with your words,   25
    Cynthia, and don't provoke gods who have forgotten;
Ah, woman all too rash, it's at *my* peril you'll suffer,
    if some worse hardship happens to befall you!

---

23. 1.15.9 **the Ithacan's leaving**: Notice that Propertius does not think to compare Cynthia to Penelope. As Gaisser (1977) 390 notes, this and the following exempla of abandoned mythological heroines "establish a picture of Propertius' role that constitutes an intriguing and perhaps ironic counterpoint to the concern with Cynthia that is the ostensible subject of the elegy."

Sooner will deep rivers flow backward from the sea,
    sooner the year bring its seasons in reverse,   30
than the care for you that's in my heart could ever be changed:
    be anything you want, just not another's!

Let not those eyes of yours appear so cheap to you,
    through which I often believed your treachery![24]
You used to swear by them that if you'd told any lies   35
    they'd fall right out into your hands to catch:
and you can raise these very eyes to face the great Sun,
    and not be trembling with guilt for the wrong you've done?
Who was forcing you to turn pale and blush many colors
    and draw out tears from your reluctant eyes?   40
By which I'm damned now, and I plan to warn lovers like me
    it's not safe to put your trust in any sweet nothings.

Propertius 2.7[25]

Never shall a wife, never a girlfriend part us: 6.41
    you'll always be girlfriend, always be wife to me.
Surely, Cynthia, you were glad when the law was repealed[26]   7.1
    whose enactment once had made us both weep so long,
in case it divided us: although Jupiter himself
    has no power to part two lovers against their will.
"But Caesar is great." Yes, but Caesar is great in arms: 5
    conquered nations count for nothing in love.

---

24. 1.15.33–34 **those eyes . . . treachery**: On swearing by eyes, compare Cat. 82 and *Am.* 3.3.

25. **Propertius 2.7** This poem has been read in opposite ways, as both truly promoting or ironically undercutting its stance of "make love not war"; for interpretation and bibliography, see Gale (1997).

26. 2.7.1 **law was repealed**: This seems to have been a heavy tax on bachelors, which Propertius (allegedly) could not have afforded to pay (and thus he would have had to marry); it was repealed in 28 B.C. The existence and nature of the law are controversial: see Badian (1985), Treggiari (1991) 59-60, and Gale (1997) 89–90. The elegiac genre, of course, presupposes that that there is no possibility of the lover's actually marrying his beloved (if he were to marry her, his poetry would abruptly end).

For sooner would I let my head be cut from this neck
    than I could waste torches at the whim of a bride,[27]
or pass by your threshold, barred now, as a married man,
    looking back with wet eyes as I saw it betrayed.   10
Ah, what slumbers then would my wedding flute sing for you,
    that flute more dismal than the funeral trumpet!
How could I ever furnish sons for the fatherland's triumphs?
    There will be no soldier from my blood.

But if I were following the true camp, that of my girl,   15
    Castor's horse wouldn't be grand enough for me.
From this, indeed, has my glory earned so great a name,
    glory borne to the wintry Borysthenidae.
Cynthia, you alone are my joy—make me alone yours!
    This love will be dearer than even the name of "father."   20

Propertius 2.14

Not so did you rejoice, son of Atreus,[28] in your Dardanian
    triumph, when the great power of Laomedon fell;
nor was Ulysses so happy when, his wanderings over,
    he touched the shores of his beloved Dulichia;
nor was Electra so happy when she saw Orestes safe,   5
    whose false bones she, his sister, had held and wept;
nor was Minos' daughter when she saw Theseus unharmed,
    whose Daedalan path she'd steered with a thread for guide.
What great joys have I harvested in the night just past!
    If there's ever another like that, I'll be immortal.   10

She doesn't try to oppose me with unfair disdain,   *13*
    nor can she sit there hardhearted while I weep;   *14*

---

27. 2.7.8 **waste torches at the whim of a bride**: The text and the meaning of this line pose difficulties. The "torches" (Latin *faces*) could refer either to wedding torches, which Propertius would waste because he would be an ineffectual husband, or to the "flame" of passion (for Cynthia), which would now go to waste. The phrase *nuptae more* (if the text is correct), here "at the whim of a bride," could also mean "in the manner of a bride." See Allen (1992), Gale (1997) 88.

   28. 2.14.1 **son of Atreus**: Agamemnon.

but while I was walking with my neck bowed down like a suppliant,   11
    I was called more worthless than a dry lake.
I wish this option had not been made known to me so late!   15
    Now medicine's being given to a corpse.
The path shone bright before my feet, but I was blind:
    no one, of course, can see when he's madly in love.
I realized this way is more profitable: be scornful, lovers!
    Then whoever said "No" yesterday will say "Yes" today.   20

Others were knocking in vain and calling her their mistress:
    the girl, unmoved, held her head pillowed on me.
This for me is a greater triumph than conquering the Parthians:
    these will be my spoils, my kings, my chariots.
I shall attach great spoils, Cytherea, to your column,   25
    and under my name will be written a poem like this:
I, PROPERTIUS, RECEIVED AS A LOVER FOR A WHOLE NIGHT,
    DO PLACE THESE SPOILS, GODDESS, BEFORE YOUR SHRINE.

Now it's your choice, my Light, whether my ship reaches the shore
    in safety, or founders and sinks among the shoals.   30
And if by chance you've changed toward me because of some wrong,
    then may I fall down dead before your door!

Propertius 2.15

Oh, happy me! Oh, radiant night for me! And oh,
    beloved bed made lucky by my cherished delight!
What a conversation we had, with the lamp beside us,
    and how we wrestled after the light was out!
For now she fought against me with her breasts laid bare;   5
    sometimes she covered herself in her tunic to stall.
When my eyes were drooping in sleep she opened them with her kiss
    and said, "Is this how you lie there, lazybones?"
How we shifted our arms in all different kinds of embraces!
    How long my kisses lingered on your lips!   10

It does no good to wreck Venus by motions that can't be seen:
    if you don't know—eyes are the leaders in love.

Paris himself, it is said, pined away for the naked Laconian[29]
    when she arose from Menelaus' bedroom:
naked, too, did Endymion captivate Phoebus's sister,[30]   15
    and it's said he was naked when he bedded the goddess.
But if, with that stubborn spirit, you go to bed in your clothes,
    you'll feel my hands as your clothing's torn away:
no, more—if anger carries me along even further,
    you'll show your mother your arms all bruised and battered.   20
And sagging breasts aren't holding you back yet from playing the game:
    leave that worry to her who's known childbirth's shame.
While the Fates allow us, let's feast our eyes on love:
    long night is coming for you, and day won't return.

I wish you were willing to bind us in our embrace with a chain[31]   25
    so firmly that no day could ever free us!
Let doves[32] joined together in love be an example to you,
    male and female, a perfect conjugal union.
Whoever seeks the limit of frenzied love is wrong:
    true love doesn't know how to have any boundary.   30

The earth will sooner deceive the plowman with the wrong crop,
    and sooner will the Sun drive on black horses,
and rivers will start to summon their waters back to their source
    and fish will become parched as the deep goes dry,
than I'll be able to shift my pain to another place: 35
    hers will I be in life, I'll be hers in death.

But if she were willing from time to time to grant me nights
    like this, even a year will be long to live.
If she actually gives me many, I'll become immortal in them:
    in one such night *any* man could become a god.   40

---

29. 2.15.13 **naked Laconian**: Helen (the Latin makes her gender clear).
30. 2.15.15 **Phoebus's sister**: Diana.
31. 2.15.25 **with a chain**: Ares (Mars) and Aphrodite (Venus) are caught in bed together, trapped in each other's arms with unbreakable chains, and put on public display by Hephaestus (Vulcan), Aphrodite's husband (the story is told in *Odyssey* 8.266–366). Hermes (Mercury) comments that he would happily endure such public humiliation for a chance to sleep beside golden Aphrodite.
32. 2.15.27 **doves**: On doves as models of amorous monogamy, see Cat. 68.125–28.

If everyone's desire were to lead this kind of life
    and lie with their limbs weighed down by lots of pure wine,
there would be no cruel swords, there would be no ships of war,
    and the sea of Actium wouldn't be tossing our bones,
and Rome, so often attacked on all sides by her own conquests,   45
    would not be weary of loosing her hair in grief.
Rightly can posterity give this praise at least:
    our battles did no harm to any gods.

But you, while the light shines—don't abandon the fruit of life!
    If you give all your kisses you'll give too few!   50
And just as petals have fallen away from withered garlands,
    petals you see strewn everywhere, floating in goblets,
so for us, who now live and breathe so deeply as lovers,
    perhaps tomorrow's fate will seal our days.

Propertius 2.20

Why do you weep with more grief than Briseis abducted? Why do you
    weep, in your fear, with more sorrow than captive Andromache?
And why do you frantically weary the gods about my deception?
    Why do you complain that my faith is so fallen?
Not so shrilly does the funereal bird of Attica[33]   5
    sound her nightly lament in Cecropian leaves,
nor does Niobe, mother of twice six tombs in her pride,
    rain down such a stream of tears from anguished Sipylus.

Even if they should imprison my arms in knots of bronze,
    or your limbs be hidden away in Danaë's home,   10
for your sake, I would break even chains of bronze, my Life,
    and leap the bounds of Danaë's iron home.
My ears are deaf to anything that's said about you:
    just please stop worrying about my sincerity.
By the bones of my mother I swear to you, and the bones of my father 15
    (if I'm lying—oh!—may both Ghosts be hard on me),

---

33. 2.20.5 **funereal bird of Attica**: The nightingale, Philomel.

I will remain with you, my Life, till the final darkness:
one faith, one death, will carry us both away.

But if neither your renown nor your beauty were holding me fast,
the gentleness of your slavery could hold me.   20
Now is the full moon's seventh circle ending its course,
since every street corner's talking about me and you:
meanwhile, not a few times has your door been yielding to me,
not a few times have I gotten a chance at your bed.
Nor has any night been bought me by lavish gifts: 25
whatever I was, that was your heart's great joy.
Though so many men were seeking you, you alone sought me:
can I, now, be forgetful of your care?

If so, may the tragic Furies pursue me, and may you,
Aeacus, damn me at the infernal judgment,   30
and may my punishment fly among the vultures of Tityus,
and may I carry rocks with Sisyphean labor!
Please do not entreat me with suppliant writing tablets:
my final faith will be the same as my first.
This is my lasting glory, that I alone of lovers   35
neither abruptly end nor rashly begin.

Propertius 2.22a

You know many girls all charmed me equally yesterday;
you know many evils come to me, Demophoön.
No crossroads is traversed in vain by the soles of my feet.
O, theater, born all too much for my destruction!
Or if some woman bends her radiant arms with a supple   5
gesture, or pours out a tuneful song from her lips!
Meanwhile, my eyes are searching out a wound for themselves,
if some radiant woman sits with her breast exposed,
or if errant tresses stray upon her faultless brow,
clasped at the crown of her head by a jewel of India.   10

You ask, Demophoön, why I'm so soft for all of them?   13
No love knows the meaning of your question, "Why?"

Why does some man mangle his arms with sacred knives   15
   and get butchered to the Phrygian's crazy rhythm?[34]
Nature has given a defect to everyone at birth:
   Fortune gave *me* always being in love with something.
Though the fate of the singer Thamyras pursue me, I'll never
   be blind to pretty women, my envious friend!   20

But if I seem all shrunken to you, with scrawny limbs,
   you're wrong: the worship of Venus is never hard work.
You're welcome to check this out: often a girl has found
   that my services last for an entire night;
if by chance she'd been cruel enough to say "No" with a look,   *11*
   cold sweat would be pouring down my entire brow.   *12*

Jupiter, for Alcmene, put the twin Bears to sleep,[35]   25
   and heaven was kingless for a doubled night;
he was hardly faint, for all that, when he came to his thunderbolts:
   no love is ever the one to rob its own strength.
So, when Achilles came from the embrace of Briseis,
   did the Phrygians flee Thessalian shafts any less?   30
So, when fierce Hector rose from the bed of Andromache,
   were the Mycenean ships not afraid of war?
Those men had the power to destroy both ships and walls:
   here I'm the son of Peleus, here I'm fierce Hector.

Observe how now the sun, now the moon, does service in heaven: 35
   so for me, too, one girl is not enough.
Let number two hold me and embrace me with passionate arms,
   if ever number one doesn't give me a place;
or if by chance she's become unobliging in my bed,
   then let her know there's another who wants to be mine.   40
For two retaining ropes are better at holding a ship,
   and an anxious mother is safer raising twins.

---

   34. 2.22A.16 **get butchered to the Phrygian's crazy rhythm**: The priests of Cybele, who hailed from Phrygia, were castrated.
   35. 2.22A.25 **put the twin Bears to sleep**: The constellations Ursa Major and Ursa Minor; to prolong his tryst, Jupiter lengthened the night.

Propertius 3.8

Our brawl by the light of yesterday's lamps was delicious to me,
    and all those lashings from your frenzied tongue.
Come on! I want you to make a brazen assault on my hair,   5
    and scratch my face with your beautiful fingernails!
Come on! Threaten to light a fire and burn out my eyes,
    and tear off my shirt to show my naked chest!
When you're raving mad with wine and you knock over the table   *3*
    and hurl full goblets at me with your frenzied hand,   *4*
no question, I'm getting signals here of genuine heat:
    for no woman suffers without a serious love.   10

Whatever woman hurls abuses with ranting tongue—
    she's groveling before great Venus's feet.
If she surrounds herself with a flock of guards as she goes,
    or runs down the middle of the street like a smitten Maenad,
or if crazy nightmares often scare her out of her mind   15
    or a painted girl in a picture moves her to misery,
I'm a true interpreter of these torments of the soul,
    I've learned these are often the signs of a sure love.
No faith is sure if you couldn't turn it into a quarrel:
    may a frigid girl be the fate of my enemies!   20

Let rivals see the wounds all over my nibbled neck:
    let bruises declare that I had my woman with me!
I want to suffer in love, or to hear that you are suffering—
    either to see my own tears, or to see yours,
whenever you send back hidden messages with your eyebrows   25
    or trace with your fingers words that can't be spoken.
I hate the sleep that sobbing sighs don't ever pierce:
    I want to be pale for a wrathful woman—always.

Passion was sweeter to Paris, when he had power to bring
    his own Tyndaris[36] joys amid battles with Greeks: 30

---

36. 3.8.30 **Tyndaris**: Helen. Normally this translation would render the patronymic as "daughter
of Tyndareus," but "his own daughter of Tyndareus" is too unwieldy, and the irony of "his own"

while the Danaans conquer, while savage Hector resists,
    he wages the greatest wars in Helen's lap.
I'll always bear arms—warring either with you or over you
    with rivals: no peace gives me pleasure where you're concerned.
Be glad no woman's equally beautiful: you'd be suffering,   35
    if any were: now, you can be rightly proud.

But on *you,* who wove a snare for my bed, I wish a perpetual
    father-in-law and a house never lacking a mother!
If right now you've been given some chance of stealing a night,
    she gave it annoyed with me, not friendly to you.[37]   40

Propertius 3.24–25[38]

That confidence of yours in your beauty, woman, is false,
    beauty my eyes made all too proud long ago.
Such praises, Cynthia, did my love bestow on you:
    I'm ashamed to have made you famous through my verses.
I often praised you as mingled out of various forms,   5
    so that love thought you to be what you were not;
and so often your color was compared to rosy Dawn,
    when the radiance on your face was all a sham.

What family friends weren't able to turn away from me,
    or Thessalian witch to wash out in the boundless ocean,   10
to this I've been forced not by iron, not by fire, but by being
    shipwrecked

(Latin *suus*) is important. "His own" is precisely what Helen is *not,* in a legal sense; paradoxically, the lack of true ownership (i.e., legal marriage) makes possible the passionate possessiveness that would cause them to call each other "mine."

    37. 3.8.40 **not friendly to you**: As Butrica (1981) suggests, it would appear that Propertius suspects Cynthia of infidelity and is trying to pretend that this is a good thing: "Propertius asserts again and again in exaggerated language that a host of things which might be expected to hurt or offend only give pleasure. The exaggeration of these declarations, their accumulation by simple repetition, the final, unexpected twist and the nature of the curse all show that his protestations are a sham; he minds very much" (30).

    38. **Propertius 3.24–25**: As Goold (1990) 347 notes, "A designed repudiation of 1.1, which it echoes in themes and structure, even to the number of lines."

(I'll tell the truth!) in a very Aegean Sea.
I'd been seized and roasted in Venus's cruel bronze cauldron;
  I'd been bound with my hands behind my back.
Look now, my garlanded keels have just put in to port,   15
  the Syrtes have been passed by, my anchor's cast!

Now at last I've come to myself, exhausted by the surging
  tide, and now my wounds have closed up and healed.
Good Sense (if a goddess you are), I devote myself to your rites!
  My prayers—so many—have slipped deaf Jupiter's mind.   20
I was a laughingstock when tables were set for a party,   25.1
  and anyone could be witty at my expense.
I managed to be a faithful slave to you for five years:
  you'll often bite your nails and mourn my lost faith.

I'm not at all moved by your tears: I've been caught by that art of yours; 5
  it's always an ambush, Cynthia, when you weep.
I'll weep as I say good-bye, but wrong wins out over weeping:
  you aren't allowing a well-matched team[39] to run.
Farewell, threshold, tearful even now at my words,
  and door that my hand never smashed, however angry.   10

But may ponderous old age[40] weight you down with those years
    you've concealed,
  and may the sinister wrinkle invade your beauty!
Then may you desire to pluck out white hairs by the roots,
  now that your mirror's reproaching you with wrinkles.
Locked out yourself in turn, may you endure haughty scorn,   15
  and as an old crone complain of what you yourself did!
Such are the deadly curses my page has sung for you:
  learn to fear the final end of your beauty!

39. 3.25.8 **well-matched team**: Of paired chariot horses (meaning himself and Cynthia).
40. 3.25.11 **ponderous old age**: See note on Tib. 1.6.86 **when our hair is white**.

Propertius 4.7[41]

There are such things as Ghosts. Death isn't the end of all,
    and the pale Shade escapes and conquers the pyre.
For Cynthia appeared[42] to recline upon my couch,
    though recently buried to the last trumpet's drone,
when sleep was hanging over me after the funeral of love,   5
    and I was bemoaning my bed's cold tyranny.
She had with her the very same hair with which she was buried,
    the very same eyes: her dress was charred at the side,
and fire had gnawed at the beryl gem ever on her finger,
    and Lethe's water dissolved the surface of her lips.   10
She sent forth a breathing spirit and voice—and yet her brittle
    hands crackled with a snap of her fingers:

"Traitor, and from whom no girl can expect any better,
    can sleep already have such power over you?
Have the stolen joys of the sleepless Subura slipped your mind,   15
    and my window rubbed smooth by our nocturnal tricks?
How often I let down a rope through it and hung there for you,
    climbing down to your neck hand over hand!
Often our Venus was done at the crossroads, and with breast
    on breast our battles heated up the streets!   20
Alas for the pact we promised, whose deceitful words
    South Winds that would not hear have snatched away!

"But no one called out my name as my eyes were closing in death:
    I could have gained one day if you had called me;

---

41. **Propertius 4.7**: On the many "Structural Correspondences and Thematic Relationships"
between this and the following poem, see Warden (1996). Evans (1971) 53 calls these "an Iliadic
and an Odyssean poem, both focused on Cynthia"; Allison (1980) also notes the echoes in both
poems of certain aspects of the Dido episode from Virgil's *Aeneid*.

42. 4.7.2 **Cynthia appeared**: The apparition of Cynthia's ghost to the sleeping Propertius,
reproaching him for neglecting her proper burial, has an epic model in the apparition of Patroclus
to Achilles in *Iliad* 23: see Margaret Hubbard (1975) 149–51.

nor did a guardian[43] rattle his fissured reed for my sake,   25
    and a broken tile[44] gashed my unprotected head.
Finally, who saw you bent double at my funeral,
    who saw your black toga grow warm with tears?
And if it irked you to pass beyond the gates, you still
    could have ordered my bier to go to that point more slowly.   30
You ingrate! Why didn't you yourself summon the winds?
    Why were my flames not fragrant with perfume?
Even this was too much, to scatter some dime-a-dozen
    hyacinths and hallow my grave with a broken jar?[45]

"Let Lygdamus be burned, let the bar glow hot[46] for that slave: 35
    I knew, when I drank wine pale with treachery.
Though clever Nomas may get rid of her secret potions,
    the fiery shard will declare her hands to be guilty.
She who just now was publicly on sale for cheap nights
    now brushes the ground with the gilded hem of her cloak;   40
with your consent she melted down the gold of my image,   47
    to gain a dowry from my burning pyre.   48
And she repays any girl who chatters about my beauty
    with heavier loads of wool in unfair baskets.
Petale, for bringing a garland to my grave,
    is shackled to a dirty log[47]—an old woman;
and Lalage is hung by her twisted hair and flogged,   45
    because she dared to ask something in my name.

"Still, I'm not scolding you, though you deserve it, Propertius: 49
    in your books, long did I reign supreme.   50

---

43. 4.7.25 **guardian**: A guardian of the corpse was often appointed to ward off evil spirits with the noise of a cleft reed.

44. 4.7.26 **broken tile**: It seems that her head was propped on a broken tile rather than a pillow, but the point of this line is not entirely clear.

45. 4.7.34 **broken jar**: A jar full of wine was customarily broken over the bones after they were burned and before they were collected in an urn.

46. 4.7.35 **bar glow hot**: Let the slave be tortured with a piece of hot metal so he will reveal the plot against Cynthia's life (testimony from slaves was generally extracted under torture).

47. 4.7.44 **a dirty log**: A block of wood was attached to the leg as a punishment and to prevent escape.

By the Fates' song, which no one can roll back, I swear—
    so may the three-headed dog[48] bark softly at me—
I kept the faith. If I am lying, may a viper
    hiss on my tomb and brood upon my bones.

"For two abodes have been allotted along the foul river,   55
    and the whole crowd rows one way or the other.
One wave conveys Clytemnestra's sin, and carries the Cretaness[49]
    who trumped up the wooden monstrosity of a cow.
Look, the other group is borne by a garlanded skiff,
    where the blessed breeze caresses Elysian roses,   60
where faith is plentiful, and where in turbaned choruses
    Lydian plectra sound Cybele's circles of bronze.[50]
Andromeda and Hypermnestra, that wife without guile—
    glorious hearts—relate their histories:
the one complains that her arms were bruised by her mother's chains, 65
    and her hands did not deserve the icy rock;
Hypermnestra tells how her sisters dared a great crime,
    but her heart was too tender for this atrocity.
So with the tears of death we confirm the loves of life:
    I hide in silence your many sins of betrayal.   70

"But now I give you instructions, if by chance you're moved,
    if Chloris's brew hasn't brainwashed you completely:
Let Parthenie, my nurse,[51] lack nothing in her feeble
    old age: she could have been greedy with you but wasn't.
Let not my darling Latris, whose name comes from her service,   75
    hold up the mirror to a different mistress.
And burn for me whatever verses you've composed
    with my name: stop hoarding praises that are mine!

48. 4.7.52 **three-headed dog**: Cerberus.
49. 4.7.57 **Cretaness**: Pasiphaë.
50. 4.7.62 **Cybele's circles of bronze**: Worship of Cybele was loud with tambourines.
51. 4.7.73 **my nurse**: Romans often had lifelong affectionate relationships with their wet nurses (upper-class Roman women rarely breast-fed). This nurse, apparently, was still supervising who gained access to Cynthia in adulthood.

Place ivy[52] on my tomb, that with swelling tendrils it may
    entwine my crumbling bones with its twisted locks.   80

Where foaming Anio falls upon the orchard fields,
    and ivory never yellows, by Hercules' power,[53]
inscribe a poem there worthy of me on a column's center—
    but short, so a traveler hastening from Rome can read it:
HERE IN THE EARTH OF TIBUR GOLDEN CYNTHIA LIES: 85
    YOUR BANKS, ANIO, HAVE RECEIVED FRESH GLORY.

"And do not disregard dreams that come through the Righteous Gate:[54]
    when righteous dreams have come, they carry weight.
At night we wanderers roam, night frees the cloistered Shades,
    and when the bolt's undone even Cerberus strays.   90
At dawn, the laws command a return to Lethe's pool:
    we board, the boatman counts the cargo boarded.
Let others possess you now; soon, I alone will hold you:
    with me you'll be, bones mingled with bones I'll caress."[55]

After she had finished this querulous quarrel with me,   95
    the Shade slipped away from the middle of my embrace.

Propertius 4.8

Hear what routed the well-watered Esquiline tonight,
    when the crowd close by the New Gardens took to their heels,

52. 4.7.79 **ivy**: A symbol of poetic inspiration.
53. 4.7.82 **ivory never yellows, by Hercules' power**: Ivory was said to keep its color better at Tibur, where Hercules was worshipped.
54. 4.7.87 **dreams . . . Righteous Gate**: In the *Odyssey* (19.559–67), Penelope says that true dreams come through gates of horn, false dreams through gates of ivory.
55. 4.7.93–94 **Let others . . . caress**: Michels (1955) 175 calls this couplet "one of the most macabre [Propertius] ever wrote" and observes, "After reading this one would really prefer to agree that

The grave's a fine and private place
But none I think do there embrace."

when a shameful brawl raised a ruckus in a back-street bar—   *19*
    I wasn't there, but my name took quite a hit.   *20*

Lanuvium has long been protected by an ancient serpent:[56]
    an hour on so wondrous a detour's worth your while.
Where the sacred slope breaks off into a blind abyss,   *5*
    there goes in (virgin, beware of all such paths!)
the famished serpent's offering, when he demands his annual
    fodder, and writhes and hisses from the earth's depths.
He snatches the morsels that are held out to him by a virgin: *11*
    the very basket quakes in the virgin's hands.
The girls who are sent down for such a rite turn pale   *9*
    when their hand is rudely grazed by the serpent's mouth.   *10*
If they were chaste, then they return to their parents' embrace
    and the farmers shout, "It'll be a fruitful year!"

Hither my Cynthia was conveyed by close-clipped ponies: *15*
    the reason was Juno—but the real reason was Venus.
Appian Way, tell, please, what a great triumphal procession
    you saw her drive over your stones with unbridled wheels!
She was a sight as she sat leaning over the end of the pole,   *21*
    shamelessly handling the reins amid dirty jokes.
I won't mention the depilated playboy's silk-hung carriage
    and dogs with bracelets around their Molossian necks—
he'll sell his soul for sickening gladiators' mash   *25*
    when a beard, to his shame, takes over his smooth-shaven cheeks.[57]

Since injury was being done to our bed so often,
    I wanted to set up camp on a different couch.
A certain Phyllis is Aventine Diana's neighbor:
    no prize when she's sober, but when she drinks, all charm.   *30*

---

56. 4.8.3 **ancient serpent**: See Janan (2001) 115–16 on various interpretations of this strange opening vignette. As she observes, "The idea of sexuality-as-ordeal summarized by the Lanuvium snake-rite fits the dismally failed eroticism most everyone in the poem suffers" (116).

57. 4.8.25–26 **he'll sell his soul . . . cheeks**: When the growth of body hair destroys his attractiveness, he'll be forced to sell himself as a slave who will risk his life as a gladiator.

The other, Teia, lives among the Tarpeian groves:
 radiant, but one man won't do it for her when she's drunk.
I decided to beguile the night by inviting these over,
 and freshen my love life with Venus I'd never tried.

There was one little bed for the three of us in a hidden garden. 35
 You ask our positions? I was between the two.
Lygdamus was in charge of the cups; there was summer glassware
 and the sweet savor of pure Methymnian wine.
Miletus was the flutist, Byblis the castanetrix
 (artlessly neat, and glad to be pelted with roses), 40
and Biggy[58] himself, contracted narrowly into his limbs,
 was clapping his stunted hands to the boxwood flute.

But though the lamps were full, the flame would not stay still,
 and the table fell upside down upon its trestles.
For me, too, when I'd try for the lucky Venus Throw[59] 45
 at dice, the disastrous Dogs kept leaping up.
They were singing to a deaf man, baring their breasts to a blind one:[60]
 I was totally—ah me!—at Lanuvium's gates;[61]
when suddenly the screeching doorposts sang on their hinge
 and the entrance Lares heard no little thunder. 50

In a flash, Cynthia flings the double doors wide open![62]
 (Her hair wasn't done, but her fury was quite becoming.)

---

58. 4.8.41 **Biggy**: Latin *Magnus,* a name given ironically to a dwarf.

59. 4.8.45 **Venus Throw**: The highest throw in this game of four-sided dice, with each of the four dice showing a different number. (Venus is obviously on Propertius' mind for other reasons as well.) The Dogs was the worst throw, with all of the dice showing a "one."

60. 4.8.47 **a blind one**: Compare the poet's protestation at 2.22A.20.

61. 4.8.48 **at Lanuvium's gates**: As Debrohun (2003) 144 observes, "we are transported away from the party in Rome to a picture of Propertius in the pose of the *exclusus amator* ["locked-out lover"], alone and lonely, uttering a cry of elegiac lament as he waits for Cynthia at the gates of Lanuvium." Debrohun reads *solus* ("alone") rather than *totus* ("totally") in this line, following the major manuscripts; in either case, Propertius shows himself in a private world of his own fantasy. On the ubiquitous theme of the *exclusus amator,* see Copley (1956).

62. 4.8.51 **Cynthia flings the double doors wide open!**: Cynthia's sudden return, and the discomfiture of Propertius and his companions, recall a stock scene from the popular adultery mime, with Cynthia playing the role of the duped husband and Propertius the guilty wife. She

The drinking cup fell to the floor between my slackened fingers,
  and my lips, though they were steeped in pure wine, turned pale.
Her eyes hurl lightning and she rages as much as—a woman: 55
  the sight was no less dire than the sack of a city.
She darts her wrathful nails into the face of Phyllis:
  in terror, Teia shouts, "Neighbors! Water!"[63]
Screams of abuse, full volume, wake up the sleeping citizens,
  and the whole street's echoing with crazy voices.   60
Those girls, their hair all mangled and their tunics torn,
  find shelter in the first bar on the dark street.

Cynthia exults in her spoils and returns triumphant
  and hits me hard in the face with the back of her hand,[64]
and stamps a bruise on my neck and draws blood with a bite,   65
  and strikes my eyes—which deserved it—most of all.
And now that she'd worn out her arms with pummeling me,
  Lygdamus, hiding behind the left leg of the couch,
is rooted out and prays, facedown, to my guardian spirit.[65]
  Lygdamus, I could do nothing: like you, I'd been caught.   70

When I finally came with suppliant hands to make a pact,[66]
  she offered her feet, barely letting me touch them,
and said, "If you want me to pardon this offense you've committed,
  hear what the terms of my settlement will be.
You will not stroll, spiffed up, in the Pompeian shade,[67]   75

---

also resembles the vengeful Odysseus returning to rout the suitors near the end of the *Odyssey*:
see McKeown (1979) 74–75. This reversal of gender roles is in accord with the inverted power
relationships ratified at the end of the poem.

  63. 4.8.58 **"Neighbors! Water!"**: As if there were a fire (a disaster especially dreaded by the
Romans, whose city consisted largely of wooden buildings close together).

  64. 4.8.64 **the back of her hand**: Latin *perversa* ("inverted"), the adjective applied to Cynthia's
hand, can also mean "askew" or "depraved."

  65. 4.8.69 **guardian spirit**: Latin *genius,* thought to preside over each person from birth. A
slave could not worship his master directly but could appeal to his master's *genius.*

  66. 4.8.71 **pact**: Latin *foedera,* plural of *foedus* (Latin sometimes uses plurals with singular
meaning). See introduction, "love as *foedus.*"

  67. 4.8.75 **Pompeian shade**: The colonnade of Pompey in the Campus Martius, later mentioned by Ovid in the *Ars Amatoria* as a choice spot to pick up women.

or when sand is strewn for fun and games in the Forum.[68]
Beware of craning your neck to look up to the top of the theater,[69]
    or an open litter presenting itself to your stare.
Lygdamus most of all, the cause of my whole complaint,
    must be sold and drag double fetters on his feet."   80

She declared her terms: I answered, "I shall abide by the terms."
    She laughed, made proud by the sovereignty I'd offered.
Then she fumigates every place the imported girls
    had touched, and scours the threshold with pure water,
and orders the lamps to be completely changed again,   85
    and touches my head three times with burning sulphur.
And so, when every single cover on the mattress was changed,
    I pledged, and we laid down arms[70] on our well-known bed.

---

68. 4.8.76 **sand is strewn for fun and games in the Forum**: Gladiatorial shows, for which sand was strewn (hence our word "arena," from Latin *harena* = "sand"), were sometimes held in the Forum.

69. 4.8.77 **top of the theater**: Where the women sat; the Vestal Virgins were the only women who sat up front. See note on *Att.* 2.1.5 **giving a place to the Sicilians.**

70. 4.8.88 **laid down arms**: That is, relinquished their "weapons" in anticipation of a more pleasant kind of brawl.

Tibullus

The reputation of Albius Tibullus (born 55–48 B.C., died 19 B.C.), author of
two surviving books of elegies, has suffered in modern times from the acerbic
pronouncement of Sir Ronald Syme: "Augustus' chief of cabinet, Maecenas,
captured the most promising of the poets at an early stage and nursed them
into the Principate. . . . Messalla had to be content with the anaemic Tibullus."[1]
Certainly, Tibullus' mistresses (Delia in book 1, Nemesis in book 2—the plural
says a lot—and also a boy-love, Marathus) do not hold the same sort of grip
over the emotions and imagination as do Lesbia and Cynthia. The idyllic
rural landscape of his fantasies is at odds with the uncompromising urbanity
of Catullus, Propertius, and Ovid;[2] his progressions of thought, which sometimes have the appearance of loosely related vignettes, seem baffling. Yet
readers increasingly appreciate the way in which Tibullus himself, with ironic
wit, undercuts the rural fantasies of his self-abasing poetic persona, and they
have come to see sophistication and structural coherence in both the internal
progressions and the ordering of his poems.[3] The themes of "love as slavery"
and "love as military service" come to full bloom in his elegies.

1. Syme (1939) 460.
2. See Boyd (1984) 275 for bibliography on the "long debate on the realism of Tibullan
landscape." As Bright (1978) 6 points out, "Propertius and Ovid keep in touch with the events of
the world around them and thereby locate Cynthia and Corinna in that world as well. The result is
a concreteness and a believability which Tibullus does not aim at or desire." Elder (1962) 70
notes that Tibullus "elected—surely his own, private, psychological reaction to the Augustan
Revolution—to make his pastoral, idyllic world blurred and hazy, but also to make the actual
world of the City equally indistinct."
3. See, e.g., Elder (1962), Gaisser (1971), Gotoff (1974), Dettmer (1980), Littlewood
(1983), Lyne (1998). As Lee (1990) x observes, "if Propertius is the poet of passion and Ovid of

Tibullus 1.1

Riches—let someone else hoard them in heaps of tawny gold,
    and hold vast acres of cultivated land;
let constant battles with neighboring enemies terrify him,
    and the blare of the martial bugle rout his sleep.
As for me, let my poverty⁴ win me an indolent life,   5
    as long as my hearth burns bright with a constant flame.
When the time is ripe, let me, a man of the country, myself
    plant tender vines and plump apples with nimble hand,⁵
and let Hope not desert me, but always offer me mounds
    of grain and rich new wine in a brimming vat.   10

For I bow in worship, wherever a trunk alone in the fields
    or an old stone at the crossroads has flowery garlands;
and from whatever fruit the new year brings forth for me,
    an offering's placed before the god of the farmer.
Blonde Ceres, may the crown of wheat that hangs before   15
    the doors of your temple be taken from my own field;
and may Priapus, the ruddy guard, be placed in fruit-laden
    gardens to scare off birds with his savage sickle.
And you, Lares, guardians of a field once thriving,
    now impoverished—you too receive your gifts.   20
Then, a slain calf was the peace offering for countless bullocks;
    now, a small lamb is my tiny plot's sacrifice.
A lamb will fall for you, so the country boys can shout
    around her, "Ho, give us good crops and wine!"

---

wit, Tibullus is the poet of feeling." Miller (1999), analyzing "The Tibullan Dream Text," suggests that "[t]he model of the dream, rather than signifying the lack of a clear outline, or a lazy drifting from topic to topic, may instead be read as a measure of the profound emotional complexity of these poems, the subtle and multiple levels of determination that shape their context, and their continuing engagement with the contradictory, the marginal, and the nonlinear" (189).

    4. 1.1.5 **my poverty**: On the alleged "poverty" of elegiac poets, see notes on Cat. 10.23 **old moth-eaten cot** and *Am.* 1.10.11 **Because you're demanding a gift**. As Gaisser (1983) 67 notes, by creating an antithesis between the riches of the soldier and the poverty of the farmer, "Tibullus was able to achieve a contrast with *militia* that was positive and moral by conventional Roman standards."

    5. 1.1.8 **nimble hand**: See Wray (2003), responding in part to Miller (1999) 202–205 (including a survey of previous discussions), on the complex poetic and philosophical resonances of Latin *facilis* (here = "nimble"), whose basic meaning of "easy" can denote both "easy to be worked on" and "creative, makerly."

Now, now let me be able to live content with little,   25
    and not always be committed to a long march,
but avoid the summer rising of the Dog Star under
    the shade of a tree, by a stream of flowing water.
Still, may it be no shame, from time to time, to hold
    the hoe, or to scold lazy oxen with a goad;   30
let me not balk at carrying home a lamb in my bosom
    or a she-goat's offspring its mother forgot and abandoned.

But *you,* you thieves and wolves, be sparing of my tiny
    flock: it's from a great herd you should seek your prey.
It's from here that I ritually purify my shepherd each year   35
    and sprinkle Pales with milk so she'll be kind.
Be with me, gods, and do not scorn the gifts from a pauper's
    table, or from clay vessels[6] as long as they're pure.
Of clay were the goblets the ancient farmer made himself
    at first, and he fashioned them from pliant[7] mud.   40
I'm not asking for our fathers' riches or for the profits
    stored harvests brought our grandfathers of old:
a little crop is enough, it's enough to rest on my bed,
    if I can, and refresh my limbs on my usual couch.

How sweet it is to lie there and listen to the cruel winds   45
    and clasp my mistress[8] in a tender embrace;
or, when the wintry South Wind has poured out icy waters,
    to go to sleep, carefree, by a cheerful fire.

---

6. 1.1.38 **clay vessels**: All artifacts in Greek and Latin poetry—especially cups, bowls, weapons, and textiles—have the potential to make a statement about art in general and their own poem in particular. Putnam (2005) 131 suggests that these clay vessels represent the deceptive simplicity of Tibullus' poetry, "with the aesthetically complex masquerading in the guise of the unsophisticated."

7. 1.1.40 **pliant**: Latin *facilis*; see note on 1.1.8 **nimble hand**.

8. 1.1.46 **mistress**: As Gaisser (1983) 61–62 observes, "The picture of Tibullus' idealized life as *rusticus* (7–48) includes only a single glance at love: near the close of the passage the poet mentions the *domina,* using her chiefly, as critics have recognized, to look ahead to the description of *amor* in the next section." Unlike Propertius (in his Book 1), Tibullus "does not represent himself as essentially or primarily a poet of love, in spite of his use of love as a theme in most of the elegies of the first book" (72).

Let this be my lot; that man deserves to be rich who can bear
    the frenzy of the sea, and the gloomy storms.   50

Oh, all the gold and emeralds in the world be damned,
    rather than any girl weep because of my marches!
For you it's fitting, Messalla,[9] to fight on land and sea
    so your house can display the spoils of the enemy:
as for me, I'm bound and shackled by a beautiful girl,   55
    and I sit there a porter before her pitiless doors.[10]

I don't care about glory, my Delia;[11] if I can just be
    with you, I beg to be called lazy and idle.[12]
Let me look at you, when the last hour has come for me,
    let me hold you, as I die, with my failing hand.   60
You'll weep for me, Delia, too, when I'm laid on the bed to be burned,
    and you'll give me kisses mingled with gloomy tears.
You'll weep: your breast has not been shackled with pitiless iron,
    nor does hard flint stand fast in your tender heart.
From that funeral not a single youth will be able   65
    to carry home dry eyes, not a single maiden.
Please don't cause my Ghost any pain, but spare your loosened
    tresses, Delia, and spare your tender cheeks.[13]

Meanwhile, while the Fates allow, let us join our loves:
    soon Death will come, his head shrouded in shadows,   70

---

    9. 1.1.54 **Messalla**: On the symbolic importance of Messalla as a sort of Freudian superego and father figure, see Johnson (1990). As Van Nortwick (1990) 121 observes, "The mainspring of Roman love elegy is *denial*. The lover/poet defines himself as a denier of certain imperatives associated with manliness in Roman society—he is important for what he is *not*: not a soldier, not aggressive and ambitious, not hard-edged, not brave, and, importantly, not in control of himself or others."

    10. 1.1.56 **before her pitiless doors**: On the perpetually locked-out lover, see note on **Ovid** *Amores 3.7*.

    11. 1.1.57 **Delia**: Like Propertius' "Cynthia," this pseudonym is the feminine form of a cult title of Apollo (see note on Prop. 1.1.1 **Cynthia**). Apuleius (*Apology* 10) says that Delia is the pseudonym of "Plania" (from a family otherwise unknown); Greek *delos*, "clear, evident," is roughly equivalent to Latin *planus*. See Randall (1979) 33. As Lyne (1998) 524 notes, this delayed introduction of Delia and of the theme of love in general "tease the reader; this is a calculatedly different introduction from Propertius' self-presentation."

    12. 1.1.58 **I beg to be called lazy and idle**: See note on Ovid 1.9.1 **Every lover's a soldier**.

    13. 1.1.67–68 **loosened tresses . . . tender cheeks**: Mourning women are conventionally depicted as tearing their hair and clawing their cheeks.

soon sluggish age will creep in and it won't be fitting to love,
  or to whisper sweet nothings with a hoary head.[14]
Now is the time for fickle Venus, when it's no shame
  to break down doors, it's a joy to stir up brawls.
Here I'm an excellent captain and soldier: you, standards and trumpets,   75
  go far hence[15]—bring wounds to greedy men,
bring riches, too: I, from the mound I've gathered here,[16]
  carefree, shall look down on wealth, and look down on hunger.

Tibullus 1.6

You always show me a fawning face so I'll be drawn in,
  but you're grim and harsh to me then in my misery, Love.
Savage one, why do you bother with me? Great glory, is it,
  for a god to have laid an ambush for a man?
For the nets are spread for me; devious Delia now, in secret,   5
  is keeping some man warm in the silence of night.

She denies it, of course, on oath, but it's hard to believe:
  to her husband she's always denying the same about me.
I in my misery taught her how to deceive her guardian:
  now I'm undone—alas!—by my own device.   10
I taught her, then, how to make up excuses to sleep alone;
  then, how to open the door with silent hinge;
then, I gave juices and herbs to make the bruise disappear
  that mutual Venus makes with the pressing of teeth.

But you, unwary husband of a deceiving girl,   15
  keeping an eye on me, too, so she'll do no wrong,

---

14. 1.1.71 **hoary head**: Shea (1998) 8 notes, "Flowing hair at the funeral finds its echo in the white hair that makes an aged lover appear ridiculous." Compare note on 1.6.86 **when our hair is white**.

15. 1.1.76 **go far hence**: See note on Cat. 27.5 **go away**.

16. 1.1.77 **from the mound I've gathered here**: Lyne (1998) 533 suggests that to Propertius' romantic abnegation of wealth "Tibullus responds with plump, complacent, almost bourgeois, and certainly funny prudence."

beware lest she visit young men for frequent conversations,
    or lie with her breast uncovered by drooping fold,
or deceive you with a nod, and draw with her fingertip
    in wine,[17] and trace out notes on the table's surface.   20
If she goes out often, be worried, or if she says she'll go see
    the Good Goddess's rites unapproachable by males.
But if you'd trust *me,* I alone would follow her to the altar;
    then I'd not have to worry about my eyes.[18]

Often, as if I were judging her gems and her signet ring,   25
    on that pretext, I remember, I touched her hand.
Often for *you* I conjured up sleep with pure wine—but *I,*
    in triumph, drank sober cups, since I'd put in water.
I didn't hurt you on purpose: forgive me as I confess.
    Love ordered me. Who could bear arms against the gods?[19]   30
I am the one—and I'm not ashamed now to speak the truth—
    at whom your dog was barking all night long.

What good is a tender wife to you? If you don't know how
    to guard your goods, the lock's on the door for nothing.
She's holding you, but sighing for other loves not there,   35
    and suddenly she pretends she's got a headache.
But you should entrust her to *me* to guard; I won't refuse
    savage whips,[20] or shrink from shackles for my feet.
Then may ye go far hence, you who dress your hair artfully
    and whose toga flows drooping down with effusive fold;[21]   40

---

17. 1.6.19–20 **draw . . . in wine**: For this and other love signals, compare *Am.* 2.5.15–20.

18. 1.6.24 **I'd not have to worry about my eyes**: It was thought that the Good Goddess would strike blind any males who observed her rites.

19. 1.6.30 **Who . . . gods?**: As Smith (1913) 314 observes, "Tibullus is, of course, quite aware that his excuse is insufficient. Indeed the flippant insertion of the trivial commonplace as a prelude to the following disclosures intensifies, as was intended, the cold mockery of the entire passage."

20. 1.6.38 **savage whips**: In a variation on the "love as slavery" theme, Tibullus imagines himself as an actual slave guardian of the wife.

21. 1.6.39–40 **dress your hair . . . effusive fold**: On styled hair and loose tunics as a sign of effeminate dandyism, see Corbeill (1996) 159–69.

and whoever meets us, so he can steer clear of being accused,
    should stand far away or take another path.

Thus does the god himself command it be done, the great priestess
    prophesied thus to me with voice divine.
She, when she's driven on by Bellona's impulse, fears neither   45
    the searing flame nor tortuous whips[22] in her frenzy;
she herself gashes her own arms with an axe and, uninjured,
    splatters the goddess with an outpouring of blood,
and stands with her side pierced by a spit, stands with wounded breast,
    and sings of the events the great goddess foretells: 50
"Refrain from violating the girl whom Love is guarding,
    lest, through great harm, you regret that you learned too late.
Lay a finger on her, and your wealth will run out like the blood
    from my wound, and as these ashes are tossed by the winds."

For you, too, my Delia, she declared some penalty or other: 55
    yet if you should be guilty, I pray she'll be mild.
It's not for *your* sake I'm lenient to you, but because your mother,
    golden[23] old lady, melts me and conquers my wrath.
She leads me in to you in the darkness,[24] and with fear and trembling,
    secretly, silently, she joins our hands.   60
Glued to the door, she waits for me at night, and far off
    she recognizes the patter of my feet as I come.
Live a long life for me, sweet old lady: I'd wish to contribute
    my own years to yours, if only it were allowed.

22. 1.6.46 **tortuous whips**: The orgiastic rites of the goddess Bellona included such physical tortures. As Putnam (1973) on 45–46 notes, "There are several suggestive links between Bellona and the poet himself."

23. 1.6.58 **golden**: As Gaisser (1971) 211 points out, this apparently tender epithet doubles as an ironic reminder that Delia's mother, "like Delia, does not perform her services for free." The pun represents Tibullus' technique throughout the elegy: "Tibullus sets up a situation or makes a statement that is apparently naïve or sentimental. . . . Then, almost immediately, he begins to undermine his sentimental picture by juxtaposing it with incongruous or contradictory elements. The result is a very subtle, but nonetheless powerful, irony" (215).

24. 1.6.59 **She leads me in to you in the darkness**: Delia's mother here is a strange blend of conventional procuress and parent arranging a real marriage: compare note on Cat. 68.143–44 **Still . . . father's hand**.

You I'll always love, and your daughter because of you: 65
    whatever she does, no matter, she's of your blood.
Just teach her to be chaste,[25] although no fillet confines
    her hair with its band nor a lengthy robe her feet.[26]

For me, too, let there be tough terms: let me not be able
    to praise any woman without her attacking my eyes;   70
if it seems I've done any wrong, let me be dragged by the hair
    and flung face down in the middle of the street.
I never could want to strike you, but if such madness possessed me,
    then I would wish I had never had any hands.[27]
And please be chaste, not through cruel fear, but with faithful heart;   75
    let the love we share keep you safe for me while I'm gone.

But she who was faithful to no one, afterward, wasted by age and
    penniless, pulls twisted thread with trembling hand,
and fastens firm the leashes on a rented loom
    and draws and scours handfuls of snowy wool.   80
Throngs of young men rejoice in their hearts to see her and say
    the old crone deserves to bear so many evils;
Venus, high up on lofty Olympus, watches her weeping
    and shows how harsh she is to the unfaithful.
Let these curses fall on others; Delia, let us be   85
    a model of love, both of us, when our hair is white.[28]

25. 1.6.67 **chaste**: By "chaste" here he means, of course, "unfaithful to her husband with no one but me."

26. 1.6.67–68 **fillet . . . her feet**: The hair fillet and long robe were marks of the respectable Roman married woman. As Lyne (1980) 159 points out, these lines "clearly imply that she was not married in the full and official legal sense."

27. 1.6.74 **never had any hands**: On the wounding of a mistress and consequent blaming of hands, compare *Am.* 1.7.1–4.

28. 1.6.86 **when our hair is white**: This would appear to be a direct reversal of 1.1.71–72. The elegiac poet has a tricky paradox to resolve: he wants to get across the idea that "we must seize the moment and love now, while we are young," which includes the implicit or explicit threat, "soon you'll be old and undesirable" (see, e.g., Prop. 3.25.11–18); on the other hand, he wants to protest that his love is, and hers should be, everlasting.

Tibullus 2.4

Here I see my slavery and mistress waiting for me:
    and now farewell, renowned ancestral freedom!
Yes, dismal slavery is my fate, I'm held fast by chains,
    and Love never loosens the shackles for me in my misery.
And whether I deserved it or did no wrong, he burns me.   5
    I'm burning—oh!—cruel girl, take the torches away!

Oh, if only I could stop feeling this agony,
    I'd rather be a stone on an icy mountain,
or a rocky crag that stands exposed to frenzied winds,
    for the shipwrecking wave of the desolate sea to pound!   10
Now day is bitter, the shadow of night is bitterer still:
    now every moment is dripping with acrid gall.

My elegies are no help, nor Apollo, author of song;
    with hollowed palm she's constantly asking for bribes.[29]
Muses, get ye far hence,[30] if you do a lover no good;   15
    I'm not your worshipper so I can sing of wars,
nor do I tell of the paths of the Sun, or how the Moon
    turns her horses and trots back when she's finished her circle.
Easy access to my mistress is what I'm seeking through songs;[31]
    Muses, get ye far hence if they don't do the trick.   20

No, I've got to come up with the gifts through slaughter and crime,
    so I don't lie there lamenting before a locked house;
or I'll seize the ornaments hanging high in a sacred shrine!
    Yes, Venus, before all the rest, is the one I should pillage.
She's the one who suggests wicked crime and gives me a grasping   25
    mistress; let *her* feel sacrilegious hands.

---

29. 2.4.14 **bribes**: See note on *Am.* 1.10.11 **Because you ask for a gift**.
30. 2.4.15 **get ye far hence**: See note on 1.1.76 **go far hence**.
31. 2.4.19 **easy access . . . through songs**: On poetry as a tool for seduction (and the poet's consequent rejection of other themes), compare *Am.* 2.1.21–38.

Damn him, whoever it is that collects green emeralds
     and stains the snowy sheep with Tyrian dye.[32]
Both Coan robe[33] and gleaming pearl from the crimson sea
     give additional reasons for avarice to girls.   30
It's these things that made them wicked; these made the door feel
          the lock
     and the dog begin to be guardian of the threshold.
But if you should offer a hefty bribe, the guardian's conquered,
     the locks don't stop you, and even the dog keeps mum.[34]
Alas, whatever divinity gave the greedy girl beauty,   35
     what good he superimposed on many evils!
From this comes the sound of bawlings and brawls—in short, this is why
     the god Love is now roaming around with a blot on his name.

But you, who lock the door on lovers done in by a bribe—
     may wind and fire snatch away your ill-gotten gains!   40
Better, let young men cheer as they watch you go up in flames,
     and no one lift a finger to put out the fire.
Or if Death comes for you, there won't be any to grieve
     or to give the offerings for your funeral rites.
But the one who was good and *not* greedy, though she live
          for a hundred   45
     years, will earn tears before her burning pyre;
and some older man, in reverence for his ancient love,
     will place garlands every year on her mounded tomb,
and will say as he departs, "May your sleep be gentle and deep,
     and the earth be light on your bones as you rest in peace."   50

---

32. 2.4.28 **Tyrian dye**: On the moral connotations of this deep-purple dye, see note on Prop.
1.3.41 **purple thread**.

33. 2.4.29 **Coan robe**: See note on *Inst.* 8.6.53 **"Coan in the dining room, Nola in the
bedroom."**

34. 2.4.31–34 **It's these things . . . keeps mum**: Of these lines, Gotoff (1974) 247 observes,
"there is a special wit and self-serving irony about the speaker using satiric commonplaces to
bemoan, not immorality in general, but a particular situation disadvantageous to the pursuit of his
amatory goals."

The truth is, in fact, what I'm telling—but for me, what good is the truth?
  It's on *her* terms that I must cultivate love.
Nay, more—if she should command me to sell my ancestral home,
  go under another's control and placard, Lares![35]
Whatever Circe, whatever poison Medea possesses,   55
  and whatever herbs the land of Thessaly bears,
and when Venus breathes love into the unbroken herds, whatever
  hippomanes[36] drips from the loins of a lustful mare,
if only my Nemesis[37] look upon me with a kindly face,
  let her mix in a thousand more herbs—I'll drink!   60

35. 2.4.54 **go under another's control and placard, Lares!**: That is, "be sold, house!" The "placard" (*titulum*) was a notice of sale; Tibullus addresses his Lares ("household gods") as representing his home.

36. 2.4.58 **hippomanes**: A Greek word meaning "horse madness"; this liquid was thought to be effective as a quasi-magical aphrodisiac.

37. 2.4.59 **Nemesis**: Tibullus' girlfriend in his second book of elegies. Like the goddess of "Retribution" after whom she is named (compare Cat. 50.20–21), she is a tough customer: as Murgatroyd (1994) xvii–xviii notes, "The name connotes power and pain, and there are sombre associations in the fact that the deity was the daughter of Night."

Ovid

AMORES

Publius Ovidius Naso (43 B.C.–A.D. 17), author of the Amores *("Loves" or "Love Affairs") and many other surviving works* (Ars Amatoria, Heroides, Metamorphoses, Fasti, Tristia, Epistulae Ex Ponto, Ibis), *is one of the most beloved and influential of Roman authors. As Barbara Boyd has aptly demonstrated, the* Amores *present parallel (and intersecting) narratives: the journey of the* amator *("lover") into and out of love and the journey of the* poeta *("poet") through and beyond love elegy.*[1] *Ovid's mistress, Corinna, is an idealized literary construction even more obviously than other poets' mistresses; the poet's true love, it would seem, is his own Muse. Like the orators in the legal profession for which he was trained, he is determined to explore love from every angle—and in leaving no stone unturned manages to bury the body along the way.*[2]

---

1. Boyd (1997). Though the *Amores* were Ovid's first published work, various reincarnations of the poetic persona and generic rules he created there resound throughout his poetry; for instance, his poems written from exile (he was banished from Rome in A.D. 8 by Augustus, partly because of his supposedly immoral poetry) show him as an *exclusus amator* ("locked-out lover") trying to gain admission to Rome. See, e.g., Holzberg (2002), especially 176–98, and Harrison (2002). For the uncertainty concerning date and manner of publication—Ovid claims that there was originally a five-book edition, for instance—see Boyd (2002a) 110–15.

2. Kenney (1990) xvii nicely summarizes the consequences of Ovid's work: "The effect may be compared with that intended by Professor Morris Zapp in David Lodge's brilliant novel *Changing Places,* whose projected definitive edition of Jane Austen was not designed to enhance the understanding and enjoyment of her books but to put a stop once and for all to the production of any further garbage on the subject. After the *Amores* it was simply no longer possible to write love-elegy: Ovid had dealt the genre its death-blow."

Ovid *Amores* 1.1

Arms,[3] in weighty measure, and violent wars I was making
    ready to write, my material fitting my meter.[4]
The second line of verse was equal; it is said
    that Cupid laughed and snatched away one foot.[5]

"You savage boy, who gave you this right over poetry?   5
    We poets are the Muses' crowd, not yours.
What if Venus should filch the armor of blonde Minerva,
    blonde Minerva fan the lighted torch?[6]
Who could approve of Ceres reigning in mountainous woods,
    of fields tilled under the quivered virgin's sway?[7]   10
Who could arm Phoebus of the lovely locks with a piercing
    spear, while Mars was plucking the Aonian lyre?
You already have a great and all-too-powerful kingdom:
    why are you hunting new work, ambitious boy?
Or is everything everywhere yours? Yours the Helicon valley?   15
    Even for Phoebus, now his own lyre's in danger?

---

3. 1.1.1 **Arms**: The first word or phrase of any ancient text was often used as its title. Virgil's
Aeneid, the Latin paradigm of martial epic (i.e., a long narrative poem about war), was referred to
as his *arma virumque* ("Arms and the Man") from its opening phrase. With intentional irony, Ovid
pretends that he first set out to write another *Aeneid,* giving the collection we call the *Amores*
("Love Affairs") a "title" that is the opposite of their real subject. The contrast—and sometimes the
parallel—between *amor* ("love") and *arma* ("arms, weapons, war") is a prevailing motif throughout Ovid's poetry: see Hinds (1992).

4. 1.1.2 **my material fitting my meter**: The Romans, and especially Ovid, were highly sensitive to issues of form and genre—that is, how the "meter" and structure of a poem are suited (or
not suited) to the "material" or subject matter (see next note).

5. 1.1.4 **snatched away one foot**: One metrical foot, a small section of a line of verse; for
instance, "To be | or not | to be: | that is the | question" comprises five "feet." The hexameter, a line
of verse consisting of six feet, was typically the meter of epics, the kind of poem Ovid claims to be
about to write. When Cupid snatches one foot, he changes the poem's meter to elegiac couplets,
which consisted of a hexameter (six feet) followed by a pentameter (five feet). Elegy was typically
the meter of funeral laments and love poetry. Wordplay involving metrical feet and human feet
appears often in Ovid's poems, especially at their beginnings, as when he sends his first poem
from exile to Rome, the only "feet" with which he can approach his beloved city (*Tristia* 1.1.16).

6. 1.1.8 **fan the lighted torch**: That is, what if Minerva, goddess of (among other things)
war, should take over Venus' business of wedding torches? (This is the first of three couplets
about pairs of gods ludicrously exchanging jobs.)

7. 1.1.10 **quivered virgin's sway**: Diana's, that is, that of the goddess of the hunt, who was
often depicted with a quiver full of arrows.

When my new page had started out fine with its first verse,
    the one that came after it shortened my strings.[8]
And I've got no material suited to lighter meters,
    either a boy or a girl with long, styled hair."[9]   20

So I'd complained, when right away from his loosened quiver
    he plucked an arrow made for my destruction
and forcefully bent the bow in a crescent with his knee
    and said, "Receive, O poet, a work to sing!"
Miserable me![10] That boy's arrows were well aimed.   25
    I'm burning, and Love reigns supreme in my unattached heart.[11]
Let my work rise in six-foot lines, fall back in five;
    iron wars, along with your meter, farewell.
Encircle your blonde temples with myrtle from the shore,[12]
    Muse to be warbled with lines of eleven feet!   30

Ovid *Amores* 1.5

Hot it was, and day had completed its middle hour;
    I laid my limbs to rest on the middle of the bed.[13]

---

8. 1.1.18 **shortened my strings**: Latin *nervus* (pl. *nervi*, here = "strings") has an astonishing range of meanings: "sinew," "muscle," "nerve" (literal and figurative), "bowstring," "lyre string," "penis," "power," "literary abilities," etc. On Ovid's allusion here to Propertius' use of *nervi* with this last meaning, see Keith (1992) 339. (The astute reader will perhaps notice that I have succumbed to the temptation to shorten the line, which Ovid does not do but might possibly have approved.)

9. 1.1.20 **a girl with long, styled hair**: Not coincidentally, in Latin as in English, "style" (Latin *comere*) can refer to both hair and writing. As Keith (1994) 28 notes, "Ovid characterizes elegy's subject matter with an epithet that evokes the stylistic attributes of elegiac poetry. . . . The adjective *compta* ["styled"] gestures toward the Alexandrian aesthetic principle of refinement and elegance favored by Ovid." (Ovid is not the first to conflate hairstyle and poetic style: see, e.g., Zetzel [1996], Oliensis [2002].) In this his first published poem, Ovid emphasizes the literary nature of his *amor*—a word that can mean "love," "god of Love," "object of love," and "poem about love."

10. 1.1.25 **Miserable me!**: See introduction, "Love after Lesbia."

11. 1.1.26 **Love reigns supreme in my unattached heart**: Although some take "unattached" here to mean "*previously* unattached" (i.e., before Love got to it), the paradox of being in love but not with anyone in particular accords better with Ovidian wit and the lighthearted, satirical tone of the *Amores*. See McKeown (1989) 27–28, Hardie (2002a) 30.

12. 1.1.29 **blonde temples with myrtle from the shore**: The "temples" of the head, that is. Myrtle was the tree sacred to Venus. Crowns made from various kinds of leaves often indicated some important quality or achievement of the wearer (the laurel wreath for athletic victory, the oak wreath for saving citizens in battle, etc.).

13. 1.5.1 **middle of the bed**: Those who lie in the *middle* of the bed generally do not expect company, as Lyne (1980) 261 points out.

Half of the shutter was open, the other half was closed;
    almost the kind of light that's found in forests,
the kind of twilight that dimly gleams as Phoebus is fleeing,   5
    or when night has gone, but day not yet arisen.
That is the light that ought to be offered to blushing girls,
    where timid shame can hope for a place to hide.

Look! Corinna comes, draped in an unbelted tunic,[14]
    radiant, divided hair cloaking her neck[15]—   10
such as lovely Semiramis is said to have entered
    her chamber, and Laïs, beloved of many men.
I ripped off her tunic—it was too see-through to do much damage,
    but still, she fought to be covered with her tunic.
Because she fought like one who has no desire to win,   15
    she was won with no difficulty by her own betrayal.
As she stood before my eyes, her covering cast aside,
    there was no blemish[16] anywhere on her whole body.
What shoulders, what kind of arms they were that I saw and touched!
    The curve of her breasts—how fit it was to caress!   20
How flat and smooth her belly under her chiseled chest!
    How great, how fine[17] her flank! What a youthful thigh!
Why linger on each detail? I saw nothing not to be praised,
    and pressed her naked body to mine all the way.

Who doesn't know the rest? Exhausted, we both fell asleep.   25
    May many a noon turn out that way for me!

14. 1.5.9 **unbelted tunic**: Fear (2000) 224–25 notes the ironic dissonance between the modest "blushing girls" of line 7 and Corinna's meretricious demeanor, emphasized in her loosened clothing. Corinna is a "texual female constructed to ensnare the reader" (227) as she seduces the (narrative persona of the) poet.

15. 1.5.10 **radiant, divided hair cloaking her neck**: It is unclear whether the word "radiant" here refers to Corinna's neck or to Corinna herself; most translators take it as modifying "neck." But the line beginning "**radiant, divided**" (*candida dividua*) echoes the "epiphany" of Lesbia, the "**radiant divinity**" (*candida diva*) of Cat. 68.70: see Hinds (1987) 8 on the implications of this echo.

16. 1.5.18 **blemish**: Latin *menda* generally refers to mistakes in writing; Ovid is the only ancient author to apply it to a physical defect. See McKeown (1989) 116.

17. 1.5.22 **How great, how fine**: The Latin phrase (*quantum et quale*) resembles the formula used to describe gods and goddesses when they appear in their full size and beauty. For instance, at *Aeneid* 2.591–92, Venus appears to her son Aeneas "confessing herself a goddess, as fine

Ovid *Amores* 1.7[18]

If I've got any friend here—put my hands in bonds
   (they deserve chains) till all this madness is gone:
for madness moved my reckless arms[19] against my mistress;
   my girl weeps, wounded by my frenzied hand.
Then, I could have violated my own dear parents   5
   or taken savage whips to the holy gods!

Well? Didn't Ajax, too, lord of the sevenfold shield,
   capture and slaughter herds throughout the broad fields,
and Orestes, champion of father against mother, wicked avenger,
   dare ask for weapons against the secret goddesses?[20]   10
Therefore I was able to tear her well-combed hair?
   Nor did rumpled hair not suit my mistress—
so lovely she was! Like this, I should say, Schoeneus' daughter
   harried the Maenalian beasts with her bow;
like this did the Cretaness[21] weep that the South Winds had borne   15
   headlong false Theseus' promises and sails;
thus—except her hair had fillets[22]—did Cassandra
   lie prostrate in your temple, chaste Minerva.

Who would not call me "insane"? Who would not call me "barbarian"?
   She, nothing: her tongue was held back by trembling fear.   20

(*qualis*) and as great (*quanta*) as she customarily appears to the heaven-dwellers" (*confessa deam, qualisque videri/caelicolis et quanta solet*). See Hinds (1987) 10–11.

    Aeneas' meetings with his mother, incidentally, sometimes have a mischievously erotic undercurrent: see Reckford (1996). It is possible that Ovid's overtly sexual encounter with his "goddess" in the forestlike half-light alludes to Aeneas' quasi-erotic forest encounter with Venus in *Aeneid* 1.314–410. On Virgilian echoes in *Am.* 1.5, see Nicoll (1977).

    18. **Ovid *Amores* 1.7**: See introduction, "love as war."

    19. 1.7.3 **arms**: Latin *bracchia*, meaning the "arms" of the body, not (as in English) "weapons."

    20. 1.7.10 **secret goddesses**: The Furies.

    21. 1.7.15 **the Cretaness**: Ariadne. The mythological exempla here resemble those in Prop. 1.3, but the reader should recall that there the girlfriend's disarray is due to sleep, not (as in the present poem) to the poet's beating.

    22. 1.7.17 **except her hair had fillets**: This is a "correction" of the portrait of Cassandra with "scattered tresses" (*passis . . . crinibus*) in Virgil's *Aeneid* 2.403–404: see Boyd (1997) 124. Davis (1980) 425–16 suggests that "Ovid chooses to describe her with her priestly fillet in place for no other reason than to render his simile inappropriate. Why? In order to make a joke out of the use of mythological *exempla* generally and to add to the mock tragic tone of this poem in particular."

But her face, though silent, hurled reproaches nonetheless;
   with tears on her wordless lips she declared me guilty.
I wish my arms had sooner fallen off of my shoulders;
   I'd have done better by lacking part of myself!
The frenzied strength I had was to my own cost, and I   25
   myself was mighty for my own punishment.

Handmaids of slaughter and crime, what have I to do with you?
   Sacrilegious hands, take the chains you deserve!
So, if I'd struck the least, plebeian citizen, I'd be
   punished—but I'll have greater rights over my mistress?   30
Tydeus' son[23] left the worst example of wickedness:
   he was the first to strike a goddess; I, second.
And he was less guilty: I wounded one whom I claimed to love;
   Tydeus' son was savage against an enemy.

Go now, the victor, prepare your splendid trimphal procession,   35
   gird your hair with laurel and pray to Jove,
and let the throng of attendants who'll be following your chariot
   shout "Ho! This valiant man has conquered—a girl!"
Let the sad captive walk before you, her hair unbound,
   all radiant—if her wounded cheeks allowed it.   40
It would have been better for her to be bruised by the pressing of lips,
   for her neck to bear the mark of affectionate teeth.

Finally, if I was swept along like a swollen torrent
   and blinding anger had made me its own prey,
wouldn't it have been enough to shout at the timid girl   45
   without my thundering too-relentless threats,
or shamelessly to have torn her tunic[24] from top to middle
   (at the middle, her belt would have come to her rescue)?

---

23. 1.7.31 **Tydeus' son**: Diomedes, who wounds the goddess Aphrodite on the battlefield in
Iliad 5.
24. 1.7.47 **torn her tunic**: Compare the playful "fight" in *Am.* 1.5.13–16.

But as it was, I could bear to rip out her hair from her brow—
    man of iron!—and mark her noble cheeks[25] with my nails.   50

She stood there in shock, the blood drained from her chalk-white face,
    like the marble blocks hewn out of the Parian cliffs;
I saw her limbs hang lifeless, and her body tremble,
    as when a breeze is ruffling the poplars' tresses,
as when a slender reed is quivering with gentle Zephyr,   55
    or the water's surface ripples with a warm South Wind;
and her tears, hanging so long in her eyes, flowed down her face,
    as water drips from snow that's cast aside.[26]
Then did I first begin to feel that I was guilty;
    it was my blood, the tears that she was shedding.   60
Still, three times[27] I tried to lie at her feet as a suppliant;
    three times she pushed away the hands she feared.

But you, do not hesitate (revenge would lessen my pain)
    to fly at my face immediately with your nails;
and do not spare my eyes, and do not spare my hair!   65
    Anger gives strength to hands however weak.
Or at least, so such grim signs of my wickedness won't remain,
    compose your hair again[28] and put it in place!

25. 1.7.50 **noble cheeks**: Latin *ingenuas genas* (the wordplay is impossible to convey in English). The word *ingenuus* (here = "noble," whence our "ingenuous") literally means "freeborn, not a slave."

26. 1.7.51–58 **She stood there . . . cast aside**: On this densely allusive passage, see Boyd (1997) 124–30. The comparison of a woman to a marble statue "has admirable predecessors" (126): Euripides' Medea (*Medea* 26), Catullus' Ariadne (64.61), Callimachus' Niobe (*Hymn to Apollo* 22, 24), and Virgil's Dido in the Underworld (*Aeneid* 6.471).

27. 1.7.61 **three times**: The motif of three attempts and failures is common in epic poetry.

28. 1.7.68 **compose your hair again**: See note on 1.1.20 **a girl with long, styled hair**. Like "style," "compose" (Latin *componere*—the verb here is *recomponere,* "compose again") can refer both to writing and to personal grooming. Is this line the lover's humorously transparent attempt to assuage his guilt by removing the visible signs of his wrongdoing? Or is it part of the poet's reflection on the power of art to transform violence into a thing of beauty? On the poem's teasing ambiguities, see Sharrock (2002) 157.

Ovid *Amores* 1.9

Every lover's a soldier,[29] and Cupid's got his own camp;
    Atticus,[30] trust me—every lover's a soldier.
The age that's fit for war is right for Venus as well.
    A senile soldier, a senile love's a disgrace.
The same kind of spirit captains seek out in a valiant soldier,   5
    a pretty girl seeks in the man for her alliance.[31]
Both are awake all night; each one lies down on the ground—
    one guards his mistress's door, the other, his captain's.
A long march is the soldier's duty; send out the girl,
    a strenuous lover will track her to the end of the earth.   10
He'll take on mountains with hostile slopes and rivers doubled
    by rain, he'll crush down piles of heaped-up snow,
and when he's about to tackle the sea, he won't use the swollen East
    Wind as excuse, or wait for the right stars for rowing.

Who but a soldier or a lover will endure both the cold   15
    of night and a mixture of snow and heavy rain?
One is sent as a spy against the hated foe;
    one keeps his eyes on his rival as if on a foe.
One holds mighty cities, one his harsh girlfriend's threshold
    in siege; one breaks down gates, the other, doors.   20
It often was advantageous to massacre the foe in his sleep
    and slaughter the unarmed throng with a well-armed troop;
thus did the fierce squadrons of Thracian Rhesus fall,
    and you deserted your master, captive steeds.[32]

---

29. 1.9.1 **Every lover's a soldier**: This elegy's depiction of love as a strenuous occupation contrasts paradoxically with the conventional notion that love arises from and encourages idleness (*otium*): compare, for instance, Cat. 51.13 and Tib. 1.1.53–58. The entire elegy takes the form of a *comparatio* or elaborate comparison, one of the standard exercises in the schools of rhetoric where Ovid was trained (and perhaps was still attending when the *Amores* were composed). The joke is that the usual comparison was between not *lovers* and soldiers, but *lawyers* and soldiers; compare *Cael.* 11. See McKeown (1995).

30. 1.9.2 **Atticus**: The identity of this man is unknown; see McKeown (1989) 260. It would be pleasing to see here an allusion to Cicero's lifelong correspondent and hence to Cicero himself.

31. 1.9.6 **alliance**: Latin *socius* can refer both to an ally in war and to a partner in marriage.

32. 1.9.24 **captive steeds**: A prophecy declared that if the horses of Rhesus (an ally of the Trojans) should drink from the river Xanthus, Troy would never fall; in *Iliad* 10, Odysseus and Diomedes sack the Thracian camp by night—an unusual and sneaky tactic—and capture the horses.

Lovers, to be sure, make use of the slumbers of husbands   25
   and ply *their* weapons whenever the foe's asleep.
To slip through the hands of guards and throngs of sentinels
   is ever the task of the soldier and the lover in misery.
Mars is doubtful, and Venus uncertain; the vanquished rise up,[33]
   and those you would say could never be brought down fall.   30
Therefore, whoever was calling love "laziness"—he should shut up!
   Love is for one of enterprising character.

Great Achilles is burning for Briseis taken away—
   while you can, Trojans, crush the Argives' strength!
Hector would march to battle from Andromache's embrace,   35
   and his wife was the one to give his head its helmet.
The captain of captains, Atreus' son, when he saw Priam's daughter,[34]
   they say, stood stunned at the Maenad's free-flowing hair.
Mars, even, when caught in the act, felt the blacksmith's chains;[35]
   no story was more notorious in heaven.   40

I myself was born idle and fit for undisciplined leisure;
   bed and shade had made my spirit soft.
Care for a beautiful girl has startled me out of my sloth
   and ordered me to earn soldier's wages in its camp.
Therefore you see me alert and waging nocturnal wars.   45
   Whoever wants not to be lazy—let him love!

Ovid *Amores* 1.10

Like her who, carried off from the Eurotas in Phrygian ships,
   became the cause of war[36] for her husbands two;
like Leda, whom the cunning adulterer deceived
   by hiding among white feathers in a counterfeit bird;

33. 1.9.29 **the vanquished rise up**: A double entendre only slightly less obvious than "weapons" in line 26.
34. 1.9.37 **Priam's daughter**: Cassandra, who became the mistress of Agamemnon. See note on 1.7.17 **except her hair had fillets**.
35. 1.9.39 **blacksmith's chains**: See note on Prop. 2.15.25 **with a chain**.
36. 1.10.2 **cause of war**: Helen, whose adulterous affair with the "Phrygian" Paris caused the Trojan War.

like Amymone wandering in arid Argos, as the urn   5
    was pressing down the locks on the top of her head—
such were you: on your account I feared the eagle
    and bull and whatever Love made out of great Jove.
Now all my fear is gone,[37] and my soul's distraction is healed,
    and that beauty of yours does not take hold of my eyes.   10
Why have I changed, you ask? Because you're demanding a gift:[38]
    that's grounds for forfeiting all your charm for me.
While you were guileless, I loved your soul along with your body;
    now your figure is marred by your mind's defect.
Love is both a child and nude—he has spotless youth   15
    and no clothes, to show how innocent he is.
Why are you ordering Venus' child to sell himself for money?
    He hasn't got a pocket to hold his money!
Neither Venus nor Venus' son is fit for fierce arms:
    it doesn't suit peaceful gods to earn soldier's wages.   20
The prostitute's for sale to anyone for a fixed price,
    and seeks miserable wealth by hiring out her body;
but still, she curses the command of her greedy pimp,
    and does through compulsion what you are doing at will.

Take as an example the animals lacking reason: 25
    what a disgrace, if beasts have a gentler nature!
A mare doesn't ask a stallion for a gift, or a cow ask a bull,
    or a ram go after a ewe buttered up by a gift.
Woman alone exults in stripping the spoils from a man,
    she alone leases out nights, she alone is leased   30
and sells what's a pleasure for both of them, what both were after,
    and sets the price by how much she likes it herself.

---

37. 1.10.9 **Now all my fear is gone**: If the opening catalog of mythological heroines leads the reader to expect something along the lines of Prop. 1.3, this line abruptly deflates that expectation.

38. 1.10.11 **Because you're demanding a gift**: See James (2001) on "The Economics of Roman Elegy." James suggests that the elegiac mistress is "a fictional construct based upon the courtesan of New Comedy—that is, she is an elegant, educated woman who has no financial security and thus must earn her own living while she can" (224). Elegiac lovers, seeking to extract sexual favors without payment, "attempt to ignore, as much as possible, the social status of their beloveds, so they must convert the generic, professional mercenary behavior of their beloveds into individual character flaws (which, not coincidentally, provide an excellent source for elegiac laments)" (226).

The Venus that will bring equal joy to both of the two—
    why is one party selling her, the other buying?
Why should that pleasure be a loss for me, a gain for you,   35
    which woman and man get by moving together as allies?
It's wrong for hired witnesses to sell perjuries,
    it's wrong for a chosen juror's purse to lie open;
a disgrace to plead with purchased tongue[39] for miserable defendants,
    a tribunal making big money's a disgrace;   40
a disgrace to add to ancestral wealth with earnings from bed,
    and to prostitute one's own beauty for a profit.
Thanks are due and deserved for things that haven't been bought;
    no thanks are felt for a wickedly rented bed.
Once the price is paid, the renter has paid for everything;   45
    that debtor is no longer at your service.

Pretty women, refrain from setting a price for a night:
    sordid booty comes to no good end.
The bargain she'd struck for Sabine armbands wasn't worth
    having armor crush the sacred Virgin's head;[40]   50
with a sword a son pierced through the womb from which he'd sprung,
    and a necklace[41] was the cause of this punishment.
And yet, it's not unseemly to ask a *rich* man for a gift:
    he's the one who's got plenty of gifts for the asking.
Pluck the low-hanging grapes from his luxuriant vines;   55
    let the generous field of Alcinous[42] yield its fruit!

Let the poor man pay you in service, and zeal, and fidelity;
    let each bestow all he has upon his mistress.

---

39. 1.10.39 **disgrace to plead with purchased tongue**: This sentiment may sound odd to a society accustomed to paying lawyers. In ancient Rome, however, there were no professional "lawyers" like ours today: upper-class men were expected to plead cases for their friends for mere gratitude, not monetary compensation. Such gratitude often did lead to tangible rewards (see introduction, "Patrons and Clients"), but the bald exchange of money was considered unacceptable.

40. 1.10.50 **sacred Virgin's head**: The Vestal Virgin Tarpeia, according to some versions of the legend, betrayed Rome to attacking Sabine warriors, requesting as a bribe "whatever they had on their arms"; she was hoping for golden bracelets but received instead a crushing torrent of shields.

41. 1.10.52 **necklace**: Eriphyle was bribed with a necklace to persuade her husband (who foresaw his own death) to fight against Thebes; her son killed her in revenge.

42. 1.10.56 **generous field of Alcinous**: In the *Odyssey* this king rules over a never-never land whose fields bear fruit several times a year.

To celebrate deserving girls in my poems is also
    my present: the one I desire gets fame through my art.   60
Clothing will be torn, jewels and gold will be smashed;
    the fame my poems will bring will last forever.
It's *being asked* for a bribe that I hate and despise, not *giving* one;
    what I refuse when you ask, just stop wanting—I'll give![43]

Ovid *Amores* 2.1

This one, too, is my doing—Naso, from wet Paeligni;
    I'm that poet of my own naughtiness.[44]
This one, too, was Love's order. Stay far, far hence, ye serious:[45]
    you're no fit audience for tender lines.[46]
I should be read by the girl heating up at her bridegroom's beauty,   5
    and the boy getting his first twinge of that thing called "love";
and some youth, wounded by the same bow[47] as I am now,
    should recognize telling signs of his own flame,
and say, standing there in amazement, "Who tipped off that poet
    to tell the story of my own misfortunes?"   10

I had dared, I remember, to sing of wars in heaven
    and hundred-handed Gyes (I had plenty of voice),
how Earth took her bad revenge, and lofty Ossa piled
    on Olympus carried steep Pelion on its back:[48]

---

43. 1.10.64 **just stop wanting—I'll give!**: As McKeown (1995) 310 notes, "He wittily subverts all that has gone before by this revelation that he does not actually suffer from conventional elegiac *paupertas* ["poverty"], but rather from a sensitive ego."

44. 2.1.2 **naughtiness**: Latin *nequitia,* like our "*naught*iness," has an etymological connection with "nothing"; on Ovid's possible wordplay here, problematizing his own identity and connecting himself with Odysseus (who identifies himself as "No one" to the Cyclops in *Odyssey* 9), see Buchan (1995) 78–83.

45. 2.1.3 **Stay far, far hence, ye serious**: See note on Cat. 27.5 **go away.**

46. 2.1.4 **tender lines**: See note on Cat. 35.1 **tender poet.**

47. 2.1.7 **wounded by the same bow**: As Califf (1997) notes, the Latin word for "bow" in the ablative case, *arcu,* is an anagram of *cura* ("care," specifically, "the passion of love"). Ovid's phrase *saucius arcu* may thus allude to Virgil's *saucia cura* ("wounded by care," *Aeneid* 4.1), a phrase applied to Dido after she falls in love with Aeneas: "The weapons of war are the weapons of love, and the cares of love are a subject for epic and elegy alike" (605).

48. 2.1.11–14 **wars in heaven . . . on its back**: The Gigantomachy, or fight between Giants and Olympian gods, represents the kind of bombastic epic that the poets of tender subjects avoid. They frequently claim to be writing or intending to write such epics but then to be interrupted

I held the clouds in my hands, and Jove, and the thunderbolt   15
    for him to hurl so well on his heaven's behalf.
My girlfriend closed her door! I dropped Jove and the thunderbolt;
    Jupiter himself slipped out of my mind.
Jupiter, please forgive me: your weapons don't help me at all;
    the closed door has a greater bolt[49] than yours.   20

I've taken up my weapons again—light, flattering elegies:
    gentle words have softened hard-hearted doors.
Songs[50] bring down the horns of the blood-red moon, and summon
    the snowy horses of the Sun in its course;
song has made serpents burst apart with their jaws ripped open,   25
    and water turn and run back up to its spring;
songs have made doors give way, and the bolt inserted in
    the doorpost—though hardwood—has been conquered by song.

What good will fleet Achilles do for me if I sing him?
    How will Atreus' sons, one and two, plead my case,   30
and the man who lost as many years in wandering as war,[51]
    and pitiful Hector, dragged by Haemonian horses?
But when a tender girl's good looks are repeatedly praised,
    she herself comes to the poet as payment for song!
Now that's a terrific deal. Farewell, illustrious names   35
    of heroes: your gratitude's not the kind for me.
Girls, make your lovely faces available for my songs,
    which glowing Love keeps dictating to me.

Ovid *Amores* 2.4

I would not dare to mount a defense of my faulty character
    and take up false arms on behalf of my defects.

---

either by some outside force or by a recognition of their own deficiencies. Ovid's "I had plenty of voice" eliminates the latter possibility.

    49. 2.1.20 **greater bolt**: Had Ovid been writing in English, there can be little doubt that he would have exploited the double meaning of "bolt" as "thunderbolt" and "door bolt"; Latin *fulmen* ("bolt" here) means only "thunderbolt."

    50. 2.1.23 **Songs**: See introduction, *carmen,* and note on Prop. 1.1.24 **Cytinean songs**.

    51. 2.1.31 **man who lost ... war**: Odysseus.

Yes, I confess—if it does any good to confess one's wrongs;
    I madly attack my crimes now that I've confessed them.
I hate what I am, and I can't—though I want to—*not* be what I hate: 5
    alas, how heavy to bear what you want to lay down!
For my strength is failing me, and my authority over myself;[52]
    I'm swept away like a boat tossed by rushing water.

The beauty that invites my loves[53] is not specific:
    there's a hundred reasons why I'm always in love.   10
If there's some woman demurely casting her eyes to the ground,
    I'm on fire—that modesty's laid an ambush for me;
If there's some saucy one, I'm entranced that she's not uncouth
    and promises to be supple on a soft bed.
If one seems harsh and imitates the rigid Sabines,[54]   15
    I think she's willing but hiding it deep down;
if you're accomplished, you charm me with your rare set of skills;
    if you're unpolished, your guilelessness is charming.
There's one who'd say Callimachus' poems are uncouth compared
    to mine: one I charm is instantly charming herself.   20
There's even one who'd find fault with me as poet—and my poems:
    that makes me long to hoist up the faultfinder's thigh.
One strides softly? Her motion ensnares me! The other is rigid?
    But a man's touch will be able to make her softer!
This one sings sweetly and modulates her voice with such ease,   25
    I wish I could steal some kisses from her as she sings;
this one strokes the querulous strings[55] with nimble thumb:
    who could *not* be in love with hands so accomplished?

---

52. 2.4.7 **authority over myself**: The language here plays on the Roman formula for legal independence; see introduction, "*Patria Potestas.*"

53. 2.4.9 **my loves**: Latin *meos amores* is plural in form but often singular in meaning ("my love"); here Ovid seems to be reactivating the literal sense. *Amores* can mean "loves," "love affairs," and "love poetry." As Keith (1994) 33 notes, "Like Corinna, many of these *puellae* can be read as incarnations of the aesthetic principles that inform Ovid's elegies."

54. 2.4.15 **rigid Sabines**: Soon after the founding of Rome, the (all-male) Romans invited the neighboring Sabines to a festival and stole their young women; when the Sabine parents protested and made war on Rome, the women intervened, protesting that they loved their new husbands, and thus ensured Rome's continuation (see Livy 1.9–10). Sabine women became synonymous with old-fashioned virtue.

55. 2.4.27 **querulous strings**: The adjective *querulus,* "querulous" or "complaining," is a tag for the genre of love poetry, or in this case love songs played on the lyre.

That one's charming by her gestures, rhythmically bending her arms
    and twisting her tender flank with supple skill: 30
not to speak of myself (since everything gets me excited),
    put Hippolytus there—he'll turn into Priapus!
You, because you're so tall, are equal to the ancient heroines,
    and in your magnitude you can take up the whole bed.
That one's handy by her shortness. I'm seduced by both: 35
    tall and short fit right in with my desire.
She's ungroomed? You think what proper grooming could do for her!
    Dressed up? She got her adornments on display!
A radiant girl will ensnare me, a golden one will ensnare me;
    even a dark complexion can make a nice Venus.   40
If dusky locks are hanging down on her snowy neck,
    Leda was admired for her black hair;
or if they're gold, Aurora was charming with her saffron locks:
    my love adapts itself to all the old stories.
Youth turns me on, maturity gets me excited too: 45
    one's better looking, the other's charming through character.
Finally, all the girls anyone in the whole City might like,
    my love's ambitious for them,[56] every one!

Ovid *Amores* 2.5

No love is worth it—begone with you, O quivered Cupid!—
    that my most fervent prayer keeps being for death.
My prayer is for death, when I remember you've done me wrong,
    O, girl created for my everlasting ruin!
No intercepted tablets lay bare your deeds to me,   5
    nor do gifts given in secret make the charge.
If only my accusation were such that I couldn't win!
    Miserable me! Why is my case so good?
Happy the man who bravely dares to defend what he loves,
    whose girlfriend is able to say, "I didn't do it!"   10
He's a man of iron, he's too much in love with his own pain,
    who seeks the bloody palm[57] through proving her guilt.

56. 2.4.28 **ambitious for them**: Compare 1.1.14.
57. 2.5.12 **bloody palm**: That is, the palm branch of victory, achieved painfully through proving himself right about his girlfriend's infidelity.

I myself in my misery saw your crimes,[58] when you thought
    I was sleeping—stone sober, though the wine was set out.
I saw you speaking volumes with the twitch of an eyebrow;[59]   15
    there was a whole conversation in your nods.
Your eyes did not keep silence, nor did the table scribbled
    with wine, nor did your fingertips fail to form letters.
I noticed that what you said was bearing hidden messages,
    and your words were charged to stand for certain signals.   20

Now most of the guests had gone, the table was deserted,
    one or two young men were lying about:
it was then that I actually saw you sharing wicked kisses—
    it's clear to me that they were the tongue-weaving kind!
Not the kind a sister would give her upright brother,   25
    but an easy girlfriend would give her eager lover;
the kind Diana, we may be sure, did *not* give Phoebus,
    but Venus often gave to her own Mars.[60]
"What are you doing?" I shout. "Where are you squandering *my* joys?
    I'll lay owner's hands on my rightful property!"[61]   30
These are held jointly by you with me, by me with you:
    why's some third party getting in on those goods?"

These were my words, and what pain told my tongue to say; but she—
    purple shame[62] spread over her guilty face,
as the sky glows with color, when Tithonus' wife is turning it softly   35
    pink, or a girl when she feels her new bridegroom's gaze;

58. 2.5.14 **your crimes**: Latin distinguishes between "you (pl.)" and "you (sg.)"; the "your" here is plural (= "y'all's," which decorum prevents the translator from using), though "you" in the previous line is singular. In the following lines Ovid uses both singular and plural forms.

59. 2.5.15 **speaking volumes with the twitch of an eyebrow**: As McKeown (1979) 76 notes, "Ovid plays the role of the *cultus adulter* ["clever adulterer"] in *Amores* 1.4, giving erotodidaxis to the *puella* on how to dupe her *vir* ["husband"] at a banquet; in 2.5, he exploits the same situation, but achieves variety by portraying himself in the role of the duped *vir.*" The clever adulterer deceiving the stupid husband was the quintessential theme of Roman mime; see note on Prop. 4.8.51 **Cynthia flings the double doors wide open!**

60. 2.5.28 **her own Mars**: See note on Prop. 3.8.30 **Tyndaris**.

61. 2.5.30 **rightful property**: In this and the next couplet, Ovid is playing on Roman legal formulae involving possession and ownership.

62. 2.5.34 **purple shame**: On the many literary models for and implications of the complex multiple simile that follows, see Boyd (1997) 109–17.

as roses sparkle in the embrace of lilies, or
 the Moon in distress[63] when her horses are under a spell,
or Assyrian ivory that a Maeonian woman has dyed
 so that it can't turn yellow from length of years;   40
to these (or something like them) was that color most similar,
 and never had she happened to look more beautiful.

She stared at the ground: to stare at the ground became her well;
 her face was full of gloom: the gloom was becoming.
My impulse was to tear her tresses just as they were   45
 (and they were well combed) and attack her tender cheeks.
As I saw her face, my valiant arms fell to my side;
 my girl was defended by weapons of her own.
I who had just been fierce now fell on my knees and begged her
 not to give inferior kisses to *me*.   50
She laughed and gave me the very best, from the heart, the kind
 that could shake the three-pronged spear from Jove in his wrath.

I'm wracked with anxiety that the other got ones this good;
 his better not have been from that same vintage!
Even these were better by far than what *I* taught her,   55
 and she seemed to have acquired some new skill.
That they were all-too-delicious—that's bad!—and that your entire
 tongue was received by my lips and mine by yours.
Still, it's not this alone that grieves me, I'm not just complaining
 that her kisses were close (though I *do* complain they were close): 60
those could not have been taught anywhere except in bed.
 Some teacher or other's gotten a very sweet deal.

Ovid *Amores* 2.6

The parrot, flying mimic[64] from India Land of Dawn,
 has died: go flock to his funeral, ye birds!

---

63. 2.5.38 **Moon in distress**: Compare Prop. 1.1.19–22, with note on 1.1.22 **paler than mine**.
 64. 2.6.1 **The parrot, flying mimic**: As Hinds (1987) 7 points out, that the parrot is described as an *imitatrix* ("imitator," here = "mimic") signals Ovid's "imitation" here of Cat. 3 on the death of Lesbia's sparrow. The similarity between birds and poets is an implicit theme in this poem

Go, ye righteous wingèd, and beat your breasts with your wings
    and score your tender cheeks with rigid claw;
let bristling plume be torn instead of mournful hair,   5
    and let your songs resound as the final trumpet.
That crime you complain about, Philomel, of the Ismarian king—
    that complaint of yours has been fully discharged by its years;
divert yourself to the miserable funeral of a rare bird:
    Itys is a great cause of grief, but an old one.   10

All ye who suspend your course in the liquid air,
    but you before the others, friend turtledove: grieve.
There was full harmony between you throughout your life
    and your long and stubborn faith stood firm to the end.
What the youth from Phocis[65] was to Argive Orestes—this   15
    the turtledove was to you, parrot, while he could.
Yet how does that faith of yours, how the beauty of your rare color,
    how does your voice ingenious at changing sounds,
how does it help that the gift of you was a joy to my girl?
    Yes, glory of birds, you lie unhappily dead.   20
You with your feathers could make brittle emeralds seem dull,
    wearing your crimson beak tinged with rosy saffron.
No bird in the land was better able to simulate voices:
    you rendered words so well with your stammering sounds.

It was envy that snatched you away. *You* made no fierce wars;   25
    you were a talker and a lover of gentle peace.
It took very little to satisfy you, and for love of talk
    you couldn't spare your mouth for many foods:
the nut was your morsel, and soporific poppy seeds,
    and liquor of simple water drove out your thirst.   30
Look, quails are always battling amongst themselves and live on—
    perhaps that's why they often become old ladies.

---

and elsewhere in Ovid: see, e.g., *Fasti* 1.441–50, where the fate of birds punished for telling the truth mirrors the poet's own in exile. As Boyd (1987a) 206 suggests, "The parrot of *Am.* 2.6 sees itself as an elegiac lover; its words at death and its epitaph cast Corinna into the role of the bird's elegiac *domina*."

   65. 2.6.15 **youth from Phocis**: Pylades, whose friendship with Orestes was proverbial.

The ravenous vulture lives on, and the kite, drawing circles through
    the air, and the jackdaw, prophet of rainy weather;[66]
the crow lives on, too, hateful to armor-bearing Minerva,[67]   35
    that one scarcely to die in nine generations.

But he has died, the loquacious mirror of human speech,
    the parrot, a present brought from the end of the earth.
Best things are usually stolen first by greedy hands;
    worse things remain complete in all their parts.   40
Thersites saw the grim funeral of the son of Phylacus[68]
    and Hector was already ash while his brothers lived on.
Why should I mention the girl's righteous prayers for you in her fear,
    prayers swept out to sea by the gusty South Wind?
The seventh dawn had arrived—there would be none to follow—   45
    and the Fate stood over you, her distaff now empty;[69]
yet words did not cling numbly on your lazy palate:
    your tongue cried out as it died, "Corinna, farewell!"

Under Elysium's hill stands a grove of shady black ilex,
    and the earth is moist and green with undying grass.   50
If there's any credence in doubtful things, that is called the place
    of the righteous wingèd, from which obscene birds are barred:
there the innocent swans are pastured far and wide,
    and the long-lived phoenix, always a single bird;
there the very bird of Juno[70] unfurls her feathers,   55
    and the frisky dove gives kisses to her eager mate.[71]

---

66. 2.6.34 **prophet of rainy weather**: The jackdaw was considered a harbinger of bad weather.

67. 2.6.35 **hateful to armor-bearing Minerva**: In *Metamorphoses* 2.547–64, Ovid relates how Minerva punishes the crow for being a tattletale.

68. 2.6.41 **Thersites . . . Phylacus**: In the *Iliad* Thersites is called the ugliest man in the Greek army, which in the ancient world implied moral turpitude as well. Protesilaus, the son of Phylacus, was the first Greek killed in the Trojan War.

69. 2.6.46 **her distaff now empty**: The traditional picture is of three Fates who spin, even out, and cut the thread representing a person's life; the distaff holds the raw wool or flax from which the thread is spun.

70. 2.6.55 **bird of Juno**: The peacock; the "eyes" in its tail were said to have come from the hundred-eyed monster Argus, whom Juno sent to guard Io, as Ovid relates in *Metamorphoses* 1.622–723.

71. 2.6.56 **frisky dove gives kisses to her eager mate**: On the amorous, monogamous dove, compare Cat. 68.125–28. Cahoon (1984) 30 notes, "Here, in line 56, appears the only affectionate and tender sexual exchange of the *Amores*."

The parrot, welcomed among these in their sylvan home,
    attracts the righteous wingèd to his words.
A barrow covers his bones, a barrow big for his body,
    where a tiny stone's got a poem that fits it just right: 60
FROM THE MONUMENT ITSELF, YOU CAN GATHER I PLEASED
    MY MISTRESS.
MY MOUTH WAS ACCOMPLISHED IN SPEAKING MORE THAN A BIRD.

Ovid *Amores* 2.7

So I'm always going to be put in the dock for some new crime?
    Though I win, it's annoying to keep on having to fight.
If I've glanced up at the highest row in the marble theater,[72]
    you pick out one from the crowd to make you sore.
Or if a radiant woman's eyed me with silent face,   5
    you claim her face is giving out silent signals;
if I've praised any woman, you head for my miserable hair with
    your nails;
    if I blame one, you think I'm covering up some crime.
If my color's good, the word is I'm cold, even to you;
    if it's bad, I'm dying of love for someone else.   10

And I could wish my conscience were saying I'd done you wrong;
    those who've earned their punishment bear it calmly.
As it is, you're lashing out blindly, and by believing it all
    for no reason, you're keeping your wrath from carrying weight.
See how slowly the long-eared donkey of wretched fortune   15
    plods along, broken down by constant whippings!

Look, here's a new accusation: Cypassis, skilled at adorning,
    is charged with having polluted her mistress's bed.
Gods forbid, if I'm itching to sin, that a vulgar girlfriend
    of despicable fortune should turn me on!   20

---

72. 2.7.3 **highest row in the marble theater**: See note on Prop. 4.8.77 **top of the theater**.

What free man could wish to enter the conjugal clasp
    of a slave-Venus,[73] and to hug a back cut by the whip?
Furthermore, she's devoted to adorning your hair,[74]
    and a servant who pleases you by her accomplished hands.
Sure, I'd ask your handmaid because she was faithful to you!   25
    Why else, but to have rejection added to exposure?
I swear by Venus and by her child of flighty bow:
    I'm not in the dock for a committed crime![75]

Ovid *Amores* 2.8

Perfect at arranging hair in a thousand positions,[76]
    but worthy, Cypassis, to comb goddesses alone,
and whom I've found to be not uncouth through a pleasant intrigue,
    fit for your mistress, indeed, but fitter for me—
who tipped her off about that alliance we made with our bodies?   5
    How did Corinna find out you did it with me?
So, did I blush, then? Did I slip up in a single word
    and give telltale signs to point to our furtive Venus?
What if I did contend that a man who could misbehave
    with a handmaid must be out of his proper mind?   10

73. 2.7.21–22 **free man . . . slave-Venus**: Slaves were incapable of contracting legal marriages; to emphasize the absurdity of Corinna's accusation, Ovid uses the technical term *conubia* (here = "conjugal clasp"), which can literally mean "the right to marry."

74. 2.7.23 **she's devoted to adorning your hair**: The term *operata est* (here = "she's devoted") often refers to religious ceremonies; Ovid implies that Corinna is a divinity and Cypassis her votary. Compare the "epiphany" of Corinna in 1.5.

75. 2.7.28 **I'm not in the dock for a committed crime**: Note the cleverly evasive ambiguity of this line, pointed out by Ahern (1987). Though most translators and commentators interpret the Latin to mean "I'm on trial for a crime that has not been committed," the fluidity of Latin word order allows "not" to refer to "on trial" as well as to "committed" (i.e., Ovid may be saying "I'm not on trial for the crime I did, in fact, commit").

76. 2.8.1 **positions**: Latin *modus* has numerous meanings: "measure," "manner," and "position," but also "metrical rhythm" and even "poetic verse." Ovid's use of the word in the first and last lines of this poem reflects his proclivity for wordplay involving women's hair and poetic composition (see notes on 1.1.20 **a girl with long, styled hair** and 1.7.68 **compose your hair again**).

(The Thessalian[77] burned for the beauty of Briseis, a handmaid;
   Phoebas, a slave girl, was loved by the Mycenean chief.[78]
I'm not greater than Tantalus' son,[79] not greater than Achilles;
   why think what's fit for a king a disgrace for me?)

Nevertheless, as she fixed her wrathful eyes upon you,   15
   I saw you turn bright red all over your cheeks.
But with how much more presence of mind, you may recall,
     did I swear
   an oath by the great divinity of Venus!
(You, goddess, please, please order the warm South Winds to sweep
   a pure soul's perjuries out to the Carpathian sea!)   20
Pay me back for these services rendered, brunette Cypassis,
   by making a sweet deal: do it with me today!
Why do you shake your head and trump up new fears, you ingrate?
   To have satisfied one of your masters is sufficient.
But if you're fool enough to say "No," I'll squeal, and confess   25
   what we did, and turn informer on my own crime,
and where I was with you and how many times, I'll tell the mistress,[80]
   Cypassis, and in how many and what positions![81]

Ovid *Amores* 3.3

Go on, believe there are gods: she swore, and broke her promise,
   and all the beauty she had before is still there!
Hair as long as she had before she became a perjurer—
   still just as long, after her blow to the gods!
Radiant she was, her radiance bathed in a rosy glow,   5
   before: that glow still shines on her snowy face.

77. 2.8.11 **Thessalian**: Achilles.

78. 2.8.12 **Phoebas ... Mycenean chief**: Phoebas was another name for Cassandra, the Trojan princess who became the concubine of Agamemnon, king of Mycene, when the Trojan women were enslaved after the war.

79. 2.8.13 **Tantalus' son**: Agamemnon was actually the grandson of Tantalus. As McKeown (1998) 163 notes, "Tantalus' notorious inability to keep secrets (see on 2.2.43f.) possibly gives the periphrasis special point here."

80. 2.8.27 **the mistress**: Ovid does not specify *whose* mistress, his or Cypassis'.

81. 2.8.28 **what positions**: See note on 2.8.1 **positions**.

Her foot was tiny: the shape of her foot is the daintiest.
    She was tall and lovely: tall and lovely she stays.
Her eyes were full of light: they sparkle like stars, those eyes
    through which she often lied to me,[82] the traitor!   10

Yes, even the gods are eternally looking the other way
    when girls swear falsely, and beauty's got divine power.
Just recently she swore, I remember, both by her own eyes
    and by mine—and mine were the ones that got hurt!
Tell me, gods, if she'd deceived you and gotten away with it,   15
    why was I paying for someone else's guilt?
(But you didn't bat an eye about Cepheus' virgin daughter,
    commanded to die for a mother unlucky in her beauty.)
Isn't it enough that I found you to be weightless witnesses,
    while she laughs about fooling you gods and me too, scot-free?   20
So she can pay for her perjury through punishment of me,
    am I, deceived, to be the deceiver's victim?

Either "god" is a name without substance, and feared in vain,
    and moves the peoples through foolish credulity,
or, if there is any god, he's in love with tender girls: 25
    his orders, naturally, are that *they* can do anything.
Against us men, Mars equips himself with his death-dealing sword,
    at *us* heads Pallas's spear from unvanquished hand,
against *us*, Apollo's pliant bow is bent into shape,
    at *us* Jove's lofty hand aims his thunderbolt.   30
Against pretty girls, the gods are afraid to strike back when they're hit,
    and they're scared for no reason of those who were not scared
        of them.
Why does anyone bother to place righteous incense on altars?
    Really, we men should show a bit more spunk!
Jupiter hurls his fire at sacred groves and citadels—   35
    but the shafts he's sent he forbids to strike perjuring girls!

---

82. 3.3.10 **through which she often lied to me**: On swearing by eyes, see note on Cat. 82.1 **owe you his eyes**.

So many deserved to be hit: only wretched Semele burned.
    Her punishment came from offering her services.
(But if she'd snuck herself away from her lover as he came,
    the father would not have done mother's work in Bacchus.[83])   40

Why am I griping and hurling abuses at all of heaven?
    Gods, too, have eyes; gods, too, have a heart.
If I myself were a god, I'd let a woman's treacherous
    mouth deceive my divinity scot-free.
I myself would swear that girls were swearing the truth,   45
    and I wouldn't be known as one of those killjoy gods.
But you, even so—make use of their gift more sparingly,
    girl, or at least, please give my eyes a break!

Ovid *Amores* 3.7[84]

So wasn't the girl a beauty? So wasn't she well groomed?[85]
    So wasn't she, in fact, the girl of my dreams?
Yet I held her to no effect, completely wilted—just lay there
    a dead weight, a scandal, on the impotent bed,
and couldn't, for all my desire—for all the girl's equal desire—   5
    make use of the pleasuring part of my withered loins.

She, indeed, slid under my neck her ivory arms
    more radiant[86] than the Sithonian snow,

---

83. 3.3.40 **father would not have done mother's work in Bacchus**: After Bacchus' mother, Semele, was accidentally incinerated by Jupiter's thunderbolt (she had been tricked into asking to see her lover in his divine form), Jupiter took the unborn infant Bacchus from her womb and sewed him into his own thigh to complete the gestation.

84. **Ovid *Amores* 3.7**: For a persuasive interpretation of why Ovid would write a poem "celebrating" his own impotence, see Sharrock (1995), especially 157: "the sexual and poetic impotence which the poem celebrates are a reflection on the nature of elegy, doomed as it is to a perpetual 'failure' through which it achieves success. The lover must—paradoxically—be weak to be strong, yield to win, and even fail as a lover to succeed as a poet, for the classic paradigm of elegy is the locked-out lover."

85. 3.7.1 **well groomed**: Latin *cultus* (here = "groomed") is yet another word that can refer both to personal grooming and "polished" poetic style.

86. 3.7.8 **more radiant**: This and many other details echo, and reverse, the successful encounter in *Am.* 1.5.

and thrust in grappling kisses with her greedy tongue,
   and placed her naughty thigh beneath my thigh,   10
and whispered sweet nothings to me, and called me lord and master,
   and all the other words that everyone likes.
And yet my member, as if it was poisoned with icy hemlock,
   the slouch, failed to execute my proposal.
I lay there a lifeless trunk,[87] a phantom, a useless weight;   15
   it wasn't clear whether I was a body or a ghost.

What old age is in store for me—if old age *is* in store—
   when even youth is unable to measure up?
My years shame me: oh, what's the point of being a youth and a man?
   My girlfriend found me neither youthful nor manly!   20
Thus the eternal priestess[88] rises to go to the righteous
   flames, and a sister revered by her dear brother!
But the other day blonde Chlide twice, thrice radiant Pitho,
   thrice was Libas satisfied by my services;
I remember in one short night Corinna demanded for me   25
   to supply her a full nine times,[89] and I succeeded!
So now my body's wilting, doomed by Thessalian poison?
   Now songs[90] and herbs are impairing me in my misery,
or a witch has cursed my name with scarlet wax[91] and driven
   a slender needle through the middle of my liver?   30
Assaulted by songs, Ceres withers to a sterile stalk,
   waters dry up when their springs are assaulted by songs;
acorns fall from oaks, grapes fall from vines when they're sung to,
   and apples glide down without anyone touching them.

---

87. 3.7.15 **lifeless trunk**: On the theme of impotence as death, of poet and of phallus, see Thomas (1993) 134–35.

88. 3.7.21 **eternal priestess**: The Vestal Virgins tended the fire at the city's hearth; their virginity was guarded so carefully that they were buried alive if discovered to have lost it. The epithet "eternal" is transferred from the flame to its keeper.

89. 3.7.26 **nine times**: Compare Cat. 32.8.

90. 3.7.27–28 **Thessalian poison? Now songs**: See introduction, *carmen,* and note on Prop. 1.1.24 **Cytinean songs**.

91. 3.7.29 **scarlet wax**: That is, made an effigy of Ovid out of wax and stuck pins in it like a voodoo doll. Such "binding spells" were widespread in the ancient world: see Gager (1992).

What prevents muscles, too, from failing through magic arts?   35
    Maybe that's the reason my flank gets limp.
Shame was there too, the very shame for the deed made it worse;
    that was a second reason for my failure.

But what a girl she was I saw so much of, and touched!
    The way she's touched by her own tunic, too!   40
At her touch the Pylian[92] could become young again,
    and Tithonus grow stronger than his years.
She had fallen into my lap—but no man fell into hers.
    What prayers can I make anymore for future desires?
I think even the great gods are kicking themselves for the gift   45
    that they offered me and I used so disgracefully.
I longed to be let in, yes—and let in I was!
    to kiss her—I could! to lie by her—I did!
What was the point of such a fortune for me, of kingship not used?
    Only to make a rich miser of me, hoarding wealth!   50
So in the midst of the waves the betrayer of secrets[93] thirsts,
    and he's got apples he can never touch.
Does anyone rise at dawn from beside a tender girl
    in a state to approach the holy gods right away?

But wasn't she, in fact, charming, didn't she spend her best   55
    kisses on me, and rouse me with all her resources?
That girl could move solid oaks, and rigid adamant,
    and deaf boulders,[94] by whispering her sweet nothings:
surely she was worthy to move the living, and men—
    but then I was neither alive nor a man as before.   60
What good can it do, if Phemius sings his song to deaf ears?
    What good does a painting do miserable Thamyras?

92. 3.7.41 **the Pylian**: Nestor, the quintessential old codger, was from Pylos.

93. 3.7.51 **betrayer of secrets**: Tantalus; see note on 2.8.13 **Tantalus' son**. In light of his own betrayal of Corinna in 2.8, is Ovid by this allusion suggesting that his punishment in 3.7 is just?

94. 3.7.57–58 **solid oaks . . . deaf boulders**: Orpheus, the quintessential poet, was said to be able to move trees and rocks with his poetry. See note on 3.7.1 **well groomed**.

But what delights did my private fantasies not devise!
   What techniques did I not fashion and plan![95]
And yet my member just lay there as if prematurely dead,   65
   disgracefully, more wilted than yesterday's rose.

Now—look here!—it's virile and vigorous out of season,
   now it's clamoring for its business and battle.
Why don't you hang your head in shame there, worst part of myself?
   I've been tricked this way before, too, by your promises.   70
You betray your master; because of you, caught unarmed,
   I have incurred grim losses with great disgrace.
Even this part my girl did not disdain to rouse up
   gently, moving her hand solicitously;
but after she sees that it can't be raised by any arts   75
   and lies there prostrate, oblivious of her,
"Why do you insult me?" she says. "You're sick! Who ordered you
   to lay your limbs unwillingly on my bed?
Either the Aeaean poisoner's cursing you, piercing some woolen
   doll, or you've come worn out by another love."   80
In a flash, she leapt down, draped in her ungirdled tunic—
   her tripping along in bare feet was so becoming!—
and so her maids could not find out she hadn't been touched,
   she covered up this sorry affair with water.[96]

Ovid *Amores* 3.11b[97]

They struggle to pull my fickle heart in different directions—
   love this way, hate that;[98] but I think love wins.

---

   95. 3.7.64 **What techniques did I not fashion and plan!**: Once again, the vocabulary here applies both to sexual positions and to literary composition; on the ambiguity of Latin *modus* (here = "technique"), see note on 2.8.1 **positions**.
   96. 3.7.84 **covered up this sorry affair with water**: What this means is not entirely clear; perhaps she simulated the aftereffects of intercourse by taking a bath or performing other ablutions.
   97. **Ovid *Amores* 3.11b**: This poem was originally considered part of the previous poem, and the lines are numbered accordingly.
   98. 3.11b.34 **love this way, hate that**: Compare the succinct expression of this idea in Cat. 85.

{I'll hate if I can; if not, I'll love unwillingly: 35
    no bull loves the yoke; but what he hates, he's still got.}[99]
I flee from your baseness, your beauty calls back me as I flee;
    I'm repulsed by your wicked ways; your body I love.
This way I can't live with you, and I can't live without you—
    it seems I don't even know what I should pray for.   40
I could wish you were either less beautiful or less wicked:
    such a fine shape won't do for such evil ways.
Your deeds deserve hate, your loveliness cries out for love:
    miserable me, she's got more power than her vices!

Oh, spare me, by our bed's conjugal laws, by all the gods   45
    who keep handing themselves over to you to deceive,
and by your loveliness, like a great divinity to me,
    and by your eyes, which have stolen away my own.
Whatever you'll be, you'll always be mine; only choose whether
    you'd like me to like it, too, or to love by compulsion.   50
I'd rather spread out my sails, and make use of following winds,
    so I'll like loving her whom I'm forced to love like it or not!

Ovid *Amores* 3.15

Find a new prophet,[100] mother of the tender Loves!
    This is the final turning post grazed by my elegies;[101]
these were my doing, a son of the Paelignian fields
    (nor were my "cherished delights" unbecoming for me)—
long-time heir of rank (if it makes any difference) from my ancestors,   5
    not just made knight by a whirlwind tour in the army.

Mantua takes pride in Vergil, Verona in Catullus;
    I'll be called "glory of the Paelignian race,"

---

    99. 3.11b.35–36: Most modern editors believe these lines to be an interpolation, that is, an addition by someone other than Ovid.

    100. 3.15.1 **a new prophet**: Ovid and others like to exploit the ambiguity of Latin *vates,* which literally means "prophet" but often refers to a "poet." Both roles are appropriate to describe Ovid's relationship to Venus.

    101. 3.15.2 **final turning post grazed by my elegies**: See note on *Cael.* 75 **stuck on the turning post**. Poetic composition is often compared to a chariot race.

which love for its own freedom had driven to honorable war
    when Rome was in anxious fear of the allied troops.[102]   10
And some sojourner, gazing upon the walls of watery
    Sulmo, which enclose few acres of ground,
will say, "You who were able to produce so great a poet,
    however small you are, I call you great."

Cultured boy, and cultured boy's Amathusian mother,[103]   15
    pluck up your golden standards from my field;
horned Lyaeus has rattled with a heavier thyrsus:[104]
    by great steeds must his greater field be struck.
Unwarlike elegies, congenial Muse, farewell,
    bound to live after my death a surviving work!   20

102. 3.15.10 **allied troops**: The Paeligni had fought against Rome during the Social War.

103. 3.15.15 **Amathusian mother**: See note on Cat. 68.18 **sweet bitterness**.

104. 3.15.20 **horned Lyaeus has rattled with a heavier thyrsus**: Lyaeus is another name for Bacchus/Dionysus, the god of tragedy; the thyrsus was an ivy-covered wand brandished by his votaries. Ovid means that the god is summoning him to write tragedy, which he in fact did, though his *Medea* is no longer extant.

Martial

Marcus Valerius Martialis (born A.D. 38–41, died 101–104), best known for his three books of epigrams, was an avid reader and imitator of Catullus. Unlike Catullus, who tends to maintain a consistent tone throughout each individual epigram,[1] Martial is a master of what Bernard Knox has aptly called the "Scorpion's Sting,"[2] the surprise punch line (7.14 below is a choice example). Yet Martial's reading of Catullus, in some sense remaking the proto-epigrammatist in his own image, was profoundly influential in the Renaissance and beyond.[3] The poems presented here comprise all those in which Martial alludes to Catullus' "Sparrow"; for better or worse, no one who has read them will be able to recapture the unfortunate bird's lost innocence.

Martial 1.7

The "Dove," cherished delight of my Stella[4]—
I'll say it even in Verona's hearing,

---

1. Elder (1972) 63 remarks on "Catullus' tendency to state his theme at the start of a poem, in contrast with a Horace, as Keats contrasts in this respect with a Wordsworth."
2. Bernard Knox (1989) 176–81.
3. As Gaisser (2002) 374 observes, "Catullus presents a persona of himself that is so vivid, sympathetic, and realistic that it persuades his readers to believe in its sincerity and to empathize and identify with it—or rather to identify it with themselves"; Martial casts Catullus as a "popular and racy epigrammatist" like himself.
4. 1.7.1 **cherished delight of my Stella**: An allusion to Cat. 2.1; Martial's friend Stella has written a "Dove" poem to rival Catullus' "Sparrow" poem.

Maximus[5]—has beaten Catullus' sparrow.
My Stella's greater[6] than your Catullus by
as much as a dove is greater than a sparrow.   5

Martial 1.109

Issa's naughtier[7] than Catullus' sparrow,
Issa's purer than the kiss of a dove,
Issa's friskier than any girl,
Issa's dearer than the gems of India,
Issa's the cherished delight, the puppy of Publius.   5
If she whines, you'll think that she is speaking;
she is sensitive to his grief and joy.
Resting on his neck, she lies and sleeps
in such a way that not a sigh is heard;
and when compelled by urges of the belly   10
she's not betrayed the sheets with a single drop,
but rouses him with her coaxing paw and warns him
to put her down,[8] and asks to be lifted up.
Such great modesty dwells in this chaste pup
that she knows nothing of Venus; nor can we find   15
a husband worthy of so tender a girl.
Lest her final day should steal her totally,

---

5. 1.7.3 **Maximus**: This name, the superlative of *magnus* (see next note), appears not to designate any real individual. It is an appropriate lead-in to the measuring contest in the next two lines.

6. 1.7.4 **greater**: Latin *maior* is the comparative of *magnus*, which can mean both "great" and "big." Whether or not Cat. 2 intends an obscene double entendre (see note on Cat. 2.1 **Sparrow**), the point of the present poem is greatly enhanced if one assumes that Martial read (or purported to read) Catullus in this way. For bibliography see Thomas (1993) 137–38. Martial's reading (or purported reading) became central to the way Catullus was read in the Renaissance and beyond.

7. 1.109.1 **Issa's naughtier**: Howell (1980) 335 notes that "Issa" is "the vulgar form of *ipsa* ["herself": see note on Cat. 3.7 **"herself"**], used in the sense of *domina*, and often employed as a term of endearment." For "naughtiness" (*nequitia*) with sexual connotations, compare *Am.* 2.1.2; Martial's use of the word here again suggests his salacious reading of Catullus' sparrow poems (though the puppy is later called "chaste" and "ignorant of Venus," 14–15).

8. 1.109.13 **to put her down**: Howell (1980) 337 explains, "It seems that the dog is just put on the floor, and not put outside, but the Romans were not particular about their floors: there were plenty of slaves to clean them."

Publius is painting a portrait of her,
in which you'll see so similar an Issa
that she is not so similar to herself.   20
In short, put Issa right beside the portrait:
either you'll think that both of them are real,
or else you'll think that both of them are painted.

Martial 4.14

Silius, glory of the Castalian sisters,
you who crush the perjuries of the barbarian
fury with your mighty mouth, and make the
treacherous wiles of Hannibal and the faithless
Carthaginians yield to the great Africani[9]:   5
Laying aside your gravity a little,
while frivolous December[10] is busy rattling
its coaxing dice here and there in the risky dice box,
and *tropa's* playing[11] with naughtier knucklebones,
put your leisure in my Muses' hands.   10
Smooth that frown and lighten up as you read
my little books just dripping with risqué jokes.
In this way, perhaps, did tender[12] Catullus
dare to send his "Sparrow" to great Maro.[13]

9. 4.14.5 **great Africani**: Scipio Africanus defeated Hannibal. The plural *Africani* appears to be a poetic exaggeration.

10. 4.14.7 **frivolous December**: The Saturnalia, a festival beginning on December 17, was the "merriest festival of the year" (*OCD*): gifts were exchanged, slaves and masters switched roles, and in general standards of decorum were relaxed.

11. 4.14.9 *tropa's* **playing**: This game involved tossing knucklebones into a hole or jar.

12. 4.14.13 **tender**: See note on Cat. 35.1 **tender poet**.

13. 4.14.14 **"Sparrow" to great Maro**: That is, send his "Sparrow" poems (which probably refers to the whole Polymetric collection) to the poet Vergil (Publius Vergilius Maro)—at least, this is the surface meaning. Vergil would have been about sixteen at the time of Catullus' death (c. 54 B.C.). This leaves three possibilities: (1) Martial was unaware that Vergil was so much younger than Catullus; (2) Martial knew that Vergil was much younger, but chose to ignore this in order to make his point about an erotic poet (the epithet "tender" emphasizes this) sending light verse to an epic poet; (3) Martial was aware of the age difference and reveled in the naughty implications of a thirty-year-old man "sending a Sparrow" to a young adolescent boy, the ideal ages for the sort of liaison Catullus has with the boy Juventius. (If there were any doubt about Martial's willfully obscene interpretation of the Catullan Sparrow, the ending of 11.6—another

Martial 7.14

Unspeakable villainy, Aulus, has befallen my girl:
    she's lost her plaything and her cherished delight—
not the kind that tender Catullus' girlfriend wept,
    Lesbia, bereft of her sparrow's naughtiness,[14]
or the one sung by my Stella[15] that Ianthis wept,   5
    whose black dove flits about in Elysium.
My Light is not captured by trifles, nor by loves like that,
    nor do such losses move my mistress's heart:
she has lost a boy who numbered twice six years,
    whose prick had not yet reached a foot and a half.   10

Martial 11.6

On the old Scythe-bearer's well-oiled days,[16]
in which King Dice Box holds supreme command,
unless I'm mistaken, cap-wearing Rome,[17] you allow
some fun with verses that aren't full of labor.
You smiled: so it's allowed, we're not forbidden.   5
Go away,[18] ye pallid cares, far hence!
I shall say whatever comes to mind
without lugubrious excogitation.
Boy, mix me some drinking cups half and half,[19]
such as Pythagoras used to give to Nero[20]—   10
mix them, Dindymus, but keep them coming.

"Saturnalian" poem—would clear it up.) One can only hope that Silius, in a spirit of Saturnalian amnesty, would forgive the insult.

    14. 7.14.4 **her sparrow's naughtiness**: See note on 1.109.1 **Issa's naughtier**.

    15. 7.14.5 **the one sung by my Stella**: On this dove's relationship to Catullus' sparrow, see 1.7.

    16. 11.6.1 **the old Scythe-bearer's well-oiled days**: The Saturnalia (see note on 4.14.7 **frivolous December**). The god Saturn was depicted with a scythe.

    17. 11.6.3 **cap-wearing Rome**: During the Saturnalia, as a symbol of the festival's unusual "freedom," Romans wore a felt cap called the *pilleus,* generally worn by former slaves as a sign of their manumission.

    18. 11.6.6 **Go away**: See note on Cat. 27.5 **go away**.

    19. 11.6.9 **half and half**: That is, half wine and half water. This was a relatively strong brew, by Roman standards.

    20. 11.6.10 **Pythagoras used to give to Nero**: Pythagoras was one of the emperor's Greek servants, presumably an attractive adolescent Ganymede figure also available for other activities.

Sober, I can do nothing; when I drink,
fifteen poets come rushing to my rescue.
Now give me kisses—and make sure they're Catullan:
if they'll be as many as he said,   15
I'll give *you* the Sparrow of Catullus![21]

21. 11.6.16 **the Sparrow of Catullus**: Shackelton Bailey (1993) 9 observes, "Clearly with an obscene double sense here, but that is M's contribution. Catullus meant no such thing, nor is M. likely to have thought he did." See note on 4.14.14 **"Sparrow" to great Maro**.

Glossary

Adjectives ending in "-an" (e.g., "Tusculan") may be listed under the corresponding place or person (e.g., "Tusculum").

This glossary relies heavily on the following works:

Austin (1960)
Garrison (2004)
Goold (1990)
OCD
OLD
Shackleton Bailey (1965–70), (1988), (1993), (1995), (1999)

The easiest place to find further information on figures of any importance is the *OCD*. Roman men will normally be listed with the *nomen* first, the *praenomen* last (see introduction, "Names"). For instance, "Appius Claudius Pulcher" appears in the *OCD* as "Claudius Pulcher, Appius." For a list of *praenomina* and abbreviations, see entry "*Praenomen.*"

If English line numbers differ from Latin, they are listed English/Latin.

Names that are alluded to but not stated are listed in [ ]. Patronymics ("son/daughter of X") are the most common form of periphrasis; these are listed under both father and child. For instance, Latin "Pelides," meaning "son of Peleus" and referring to "Achilles," is listed under both "Peleus" (Prop. 2.22A.34) and "Achilles" (Prop. 2.22A.[34]).

Achilles: Greatest Greek hero of Trojan War (from Phthia in Thessaly); refused to fight when Agamemnon took away his slave-wife Briseis, causing Greeks temporary defeat; reentered battle after best friend killed by Trojan Hector (Prop. 2.22A.29, [34]; *Am.* 1.9.33, 2.1.29).

Acme: Greek woman in love with Septimius (Cat. 45.1, 45.2, 45.10, 45.22/21, 45.23).

Actium: Promontory in northwest Greece, site of naval battle that ended the civil war between Antony/Cleopatra and Octavian (31 B.C.), establishing Octavian as supreme ruler of the Roman world; his propaganda cast this as a foreign war by emphasizing Cleopatra's role (Prop. 2.15.44).

Adriatic: Sea between Italy and Balkan peninsula (Cat. 4.6, 36.15).

Aeacus: Son of Jupiter; a judge of the Underworld (Prop. 2.20.30).

Aeaea: Island where Circe lived (*Am.* 3.7.79).

Aedile: Third-ranking Roman magistrate; four elected annually in late Republic (two "curule," two "plebeian"); responsible for city administration and public games.

Aegean Sea: Sea between Greece and Turkey (Prop. 3.24.12).

Aeson: Father of Jason (Prop. 1.15.17).

Africa: Continent; Roman province (*Cael.* 73).

Africani: *See* note on Mart. 4.14.5 **great Africani** (Mart. 4.14.5).

Africanus: *See* note on *Q. fr.* 2.3.3 **Africanus** (*Q. fr.* 2.3.3).

Agamemnon: Leader of Greek troops during Trojan War (*Am.* [1.9.37], [2.1.30], 2.8.[12], [13], [2.14.1]).

Agrarian Law: Law involving redistribution of land to the benefit of Pompey's veterans; partially opposed by Cicero (*Att.* 2.1.3, 6).

Ajax: Greek hero of the Trojan War; after losing contest for Achilles' armor to Odysseus, went crazy and slaughtered a flock of sheep, thinking they were men, then committed suicide in shame (*Am.* 1.7.1).

Alcinous: *See* note on *Am.* 1.10.56 **generous field of Alcinous** (*Am.* 1.10.56).

Alcmaeon: Son of Eriphyle, whom he killed to avenge his father's death; husband of Alphesiboea (Prop. [1.15.15]; *Am.* [1.10.51]).

Alcmena: Mother of Hercules (Prop. 2.22A.25).

Alexander (1): Alexander the Great (356–323 B.C.), king of Macedonia who conquered Greece, the Persian Empire, and Egypt.

Alexander (2): *See* note on *Att.* 2.22.7 **Alexander** (*Att.* 2.22.7).

Alexandria: Capital city of Egypt on Mediterranean coast west of Nile delta, founded by Alexander the Great; cosmopolitan seat of learning, with largest library in ancient world; "Alexandrian" poetry (a modern term) refers to the slender, elegant, allusive style associated with Callimachus (*Q. fr.* 2.3.2; *Cael.* 23, 24, 51).

Allius: Friend of Catullus who offered his house as a trysting spot (Cat. 68.41, 50, 66).

Allobroges: Highly Romanized tribe in Gaul with whom Catiline had dealings (*Att.* 2.1.3).

Alphesiboea: Wife of Alcmaeon, who deserted her; avenged herself by killing her brothers (in Propertius' version; in usual version her brothers kill Alcmaeon) (Prop. 1.15.15).

Alps: Mountains forming northern border of Italy (Cat. 11.9).

Amalthea: Nymph who nursed the infant Zeus (*Att.* 2.1.11).

Amastris: City in Bithynia (Cat. 4.13).

Amathus: Town in Cyprus, sacred to Aphrodite/Venus (Cat. 36.14).

Amathusia: Epithet of Venus, "from Amathus" (Cat. 68.51; *Am.* 3.15.15).

Amator: Latin "lover"; a fictional construct not to be confused with the actual author, despite use of first person.

Ameana: Girlfriend of Mamurra (Cat. [43.1]).

Amicitia: Latin "friendship"; *see* introduction, "love as *amicitia.*"

Amphitryon: Husband of Hercules' mother, often called Hercules' father (though his real father was Jupiter) (Cat. 68.112).

Amymone: Woman seduced by Neptune/Poseidon when she went to get water (*Am.* 1.10.5).

Ancon: Town on Adriatic coast, sacred to Venus (Cat. 36.12).

Andromache: Wife of Hector (Prop. 2.20.2, 2.22A.31; *Am.* 1.9.35).

Andromeda: Princess chained to a rock for sacrifice to a sea monster when her mother Cassiepia boasted excessively about her own beauty; rescued by Perseus (Prop. 1.3.3/4, 4.7.63; *Am.* [3.3.17]).

Anio: River on which Tibur stands (Prop. 4.7.81, 86).

Antimachus: Greek poet of fifth–fourth century B.C. whom Callimachus ridicules for prolixity (Cat. 95.8).

Antisthenes: Greek philosopher (c. 455–360 B.C.), founder of the Cynic school; wrote two dialogues entitled "Cyrus," the second of which had the alternate title "Concerning Kingship" (*Att.* 12.38a.2).

Antium: City on the coast south of Rome; Cicero had a house there (*Att.* 2.1 [heading], 1, 2.9 [heading], 4, 2.12.2).

Antius: Politician (Cat. 44.10).

Antony: Marcus Antonius, "Mark Antony" (c. 83–30 B.C.), member of Second Triumvirate; took command of East while Octavian took command of West. Alliance turned to enmity (*see* Cleopatra), leading to civil war culminating in Battle of Actium (*Att.* 14.8.1).

Aonian: Of Aonia, region of central Greece containing Mount Helicon, the Muses' home (*Am.* 1.1.12).

Apidanus: River in Thessaly (Prop. 1.3.6).

Apollo: God of the sun and poetry, twin brother of Diana; *see also* Phoebus (*Q. fr.* 2.3.3; Tib. 2.4.13; *Am.* 3.3.29).

Appian Way: Road running northwest from Capua to Rome; oldest and best known of roads leading to Rome (*Att.* 2.12.2; Prop. 4.8.17).

Appius: Appius Claudius Pulcher (praetor 57 B.C.), elder brother of Clodius (*Att.* 2.22.2).

Appius Claudius the Blind: Appius Claudius Caecus ("The Blind"), censor in fourth–third century B.C.; "the first live personality in Roman history" (*OCD*). Opposed peace with Pyrrhus; built Appian Way and first aqueduct (*Har.* 38; *Cael.* 33–35).

Apuleius: Writer and orator (c. A.D. 125–170), author of *Apology, Metamorphoses* (or *Golden Ass*), *Florida,* etc.

Arabs: Nomadic people living in Arabia (Cat. 11.5).

Arcadia: Rural region of central Greece (Prop. 1.1.14).

Argives: People of Argos; often used to mean "Greeks" (Cat. 68.88; Prop. 1.15.22; *Am.* 1.9.34, 2.6.15).

Argos: Ancient Greek city-state in Peloponnesus (*Am.* 1.10.5).

Argus: Hundred-eyed monster sent by Juno to guard Io (Prop. 1.3.20).

Ariadne: Daughter of Minos; helped the Athenian Theseus, with a thread, find his way out of the labyrinth (where he defeated the Minotaur imprisoned inside it); ran away with Theseus, who abandoned her on an island; Bacchus found and married her (Prop. [2.14.7]; *Am.* [1.7.15]).

Aristotle: Greek polymath (384–322 B.C.), arguably the most influential figure in Western intellectual history (*Att.* 2.1.1).

Arpinum: Town in Latium, birthplace of Marius (1) and Cicero; Cicero had a villa there (*Att.* 2.14.2, 12.42.3).

Arrius: Social climber; possibly orator Quintus Arrius (Cat. 84.1/2, 84.11).

Asia: "The continent of Asia or such parts of it as were known to the ancients, the East; (spec.) Asia Minor" (*OLD*) (Cat. 46.6).

Asicius: *See* note on *Cael.* 18 **arrival of king Ptolemy** (*Cael.* 23, 24).

Asinius Marrucinus: Napkin thief, brother of Pollio (Cat. 12.1).

Assyrian: Of Assyria, a part of Mesopotamia (Cat. 68.144; *Am.* 2.5.39/40).

Astura: Small island joined to the Italian mainland, south of Antium; Cicero had a house there (*Att.* 12.38a [heading], 13.26.2).

Atalanta: Beautiful and swift-footed girl, exposed at birth and brought up in the wild. Promised to marry the man who could beat her in a footrace and lost the race because she stopped to pick up golden apples thrown by her future husband (Cat. [2.12]; Prop. 1.1.[10], [15]; *Am.* [1.7.13]).

Athena: *See* Minerva.

Athenio: *See* note on *Att.* 2.12.2 **Athenio the standard-bearer** (*Att.* 2.12.2).

Athens: Leading city of Greece (*Att.* 2.1.2).

Atius Balbus: Marcus Atius Balbus; *see* note on *Att.* 2.12.1 **our friend Gnaeus, the colleague of Atius Balbus** (*Att.* 2.12.1).

Atratinus: Lucius Sempronius Atratinus, prosecutor of Caelius (*Cael.* [1], 2, 7).

Atreus: Father of Agamemnon and Menelaus (Prop. 2.14.1; *Am.* 1.9.37, 2.1.30).

Attica: Region of Greece containing the city of Athens (Prop. 2.20.5).

Atticus (1): Titus Pomponius Atticus (110–32 B.C.), wealthy, cultured *eques,* lifetime friend of Cicero (his sister Pomponia married Cicero's brother Quintus). Lived in Athens from 85 to mid-60s B.C., where he studied Epicurean philosophy, among other things. Had Cicero's works copied and distributed. Cicero's "Letters to Atticus," published under the reign of the emperor Nero (54–68 A.D.), are one of the most extensive and important sources for the history of the late Republic (*Att.* 2.9.4, 2.12.4; *Q. fr.* 2.3.7; also headings of multiple letters).

Atticus (2): *See* note on *Am.* 1.9.2 **Atticus** (*Am.* 1.9.2).

Augustus: Roman statesman (63 B.C.–A.D. 14); first emperor of Rome, responsible for its transformation from Republic to Empire. Born "Gaius Octavius"; became "Gaius Julius Caesar Octavianus" ("Octavian") when adopted by his grand-uncle Caesar in 45 B.C.; named "Augustus" ("revered, having authority") in 27 B.C. following his "Restoration of the Republic" (generally hailed as the beginning of the Roman Empire). As heir of Caesar, fought against Caesar's assassins (as part of Second Triumvirate); after years of rivalry and civil war with Antony, finally beat him at Actium and became ruler of Roman world. Instituted numerous reforms and was patron, directly or indirectly, of many poets and artists (Prop. [2.7.5]).

Aulus: Aulus Pudens; pederast, friend of Martial (Mart. 7.14.1).

Aurelius: Friend/enemy/rival of Catullus, otherwise unknown (Cat. 11.1, 16.2).

Aurora: Goddess of dawn (*Am.* 2.4.43, [2.5.35]).

Aventine: Hill of Rome famed for its shrine of Diana (Prop. 4.8.29).

Bacchus: Greek Dionysus; god of wine, drama, etc.; often used to mean "wine" (Prop. 1.3.9; *Am.* 3.3.40).

Baiae: *See* note on *Cael.* 27 **who's seen Baiae** (*Att.* 14.8.1; *Cael.* 27, 35, 38, 47, 49; Prop. 1.11.1, 27, 30).

Balbus (1): Lucius Cornelius Balbus, manager (with Oppius) of Caesar's affairs; wrote to Cicero on Caesar's behalf (*Att.* 12.44.3, 12.47.1, [14.8.1]).

Balbus (2): Lucius Herennius Balbus, prosecutor of Caelius (*Cael.* 25, 27, 49, 53, 56).

Battle of Actium: *See* Actium.

Battus: First king of Cyrene (Cat. 7.6, 116.2).

Bellona: Goddess of war (Tib. 1.6.45).

Bestia: Lucius Calpurnius Bestia, father of Atratinus; *see* note on *Cael.* 1 **son of a man ... prosecuted already** (*Q. fr.* 2.3.6; *Cael.* [1], [16], 26, [76]).

Bibulus: Marcus Calpurnius Bibulus, consul in 59 B.C. with Caesar; hostile to both Caesar and Pompey (*Att.* 2.14.1; *Q. fr.* 2.3.2, 4).

Biggy: Dwarf at Propertius' party (Prop. 4.8.41).

Bithynia: Country on the Black Sea where Catullus served on the staff of praetor Memmius (Cat. 10.6, 31.6/5).

Black Sea: Large inland sea between Europe and Asia Minor (Cat. 4.9).

Bona Dea: "Good Goddess," whose rites, held once a year at the home of the chief magistrate in Rome, were open only to women; *see* Clodius (Tib. 1.6.22).

Borysthenidae: Dwellers on the Borysthenes River (modern Dnieper, long river flowing into Black Sea) (Prop. 2.7.18).

Briseis: Slave-woman captured in war who fell to Achilles' share when spoils were divided; Agamemnon claimed her when his own woman was taken, thus causing Achilles' anger in the *Iliad* (Prop. 2.20.1, 2.22A.29; *Am.* 2.8.11).

Britain: Britain (i.e., England, Wales, and Scotland) (Cat. 45.23/22).

Briton: Inhabitant of Britain (Cat. 11.11/12).

Brutus: Marcus Junius Brutus (c. 85–42 B.C.), leader of the conspiracy to assassinate Caesar after the latter was declared perpetual dictator. Committed suicide after losing the second Battle of Philippi, and "revered by many as the last defender of Roman freedom" (*OCD*). Married first to Claudia, daughter of Appius Clodius Pulcher (Clodius' brother), then to Porcia, daughter of Cato. "Cicero admired but never liked him" (*OCD*) (*Att.* 12.38a.1, 14.8.1, 2).

Byblis: Castanetrix for Propertius' party (Prop. 4.8.39).

Byzantines: Inhabitants of Byzantium (*Att.* 14.8.1).

Byzantium: Greek city on European side of Bosporus (strait between European and Asian Turkey); subsequently called Constantinople and (now) Istanbul.

Caecilian: *See* note on *Cael.* 37 **Caecilian one** (*Cael.* 37).

Caecilius (1): Poet, contemporary of Catullus; apparently wrote "Mistress of Dindymon" (Cat. 35.1/2, 35.17/18).

Caecilius (2): Quaestor, otherwise unknown (*Att.* 2.9.1).

Caelius: Marcus Caelius Rufus (c. 88–48 B.C.), defendant in the *Pro Caelio*. Son of an *eques*, did his "apprenticeship in the Forum" (*tirocinium fori*) under Cicero and Crassus. Known for dissolute lifestyle; in 59 B.C., successfully prosecuted Cicero's colleague in consulate of 63 B.C.. Was involved in murder of Alexandrian embassy opposing restoration of Ptolemy XII; prosecuted for *vis* ("seditious violence") but acquitted through Cicero's ingenious speech blaming everything on Clodia (April 56 B.C.) (Cat. 58.1, 69.1, [71.1], 77.1; *Cael.* passim; *Inst.* 8.6.53).

Caesar (1): Gaius Julius Caesar (100–44 B.C.), great military leader and ruler, member of First Triumvirate; wrote brilliant memoirs, which survive, of his leadership in Gallic War (Roman conquest of Gaul, 58–51 B.C.) and Civil War (against Pompey, 49–48 B.C.). Instituted many reforms, including the Julian calendar (still used) and partial cancellation of debts, but was assassinated in Senate (15 March 44) when he declared himself perpetual dictator and aspired to divinity (*Att.* 2.1.6, [2.9.2], 2.12.2, 12.41.4, 13.26.2, 12.52.2; Cat. 11.10, 93.1).

Caesar (2): = Augustus (Prop. 2.7.5).

Callimachus: Alexandrian poet of third century B.C., known for his learned, slender, elegant poems (Cat. [106.2]; *Am.* 2.4.19).

Calvus: Gaius Licinius Macer Calvus, poet and orator, friend of Catullus (Cat. 50.1, 50.8, 96.2).

Calypso: Nymph who loved Odysseus and kept him nearly ten years on her island, offering to make him immortal; he refused and went back to his wife, Penelope (Prop. 1.15.9).

Camilli: *See* three listings under "Furius Camillus" in *OCD*; famous family of Roman statesmen active in fourth century B.C. (*Cael.* 39).

Campus: Campus Martius, originally large field outside Rome where athletics and military maneuvers were practiced, increasingly filled with temples, monuments, etc. (*Cael.* 11).

Caninius: *See* Rebilus.

Capaneus: Husband of Evadne; killed during attack on Thebes (Prop. [1.15.21]).

Capitol: Hill of Rome, containing famous temple of Jupiter (*Att.* 2.1.7).

Carinae: Fashionable quarter of Rome (*Q. fr.* 2.3.7).

Carpathian Sea: Sea between Crete and Rhodes (*Am.* 2.8.20).

Carteia: Town on coast of southern Spain (*Att.* 12.44.3).

Carthaginians: People of Carthage, a city on the north coast of Africa; Rome's enemy in the Punic Wars (Mart. 4.14.5/4).

Cassandra: Daughter of Priam; given gift of prophecy by Apollo in exchange for promised sexual favors but then refused him, so he cursed her with never being believed; took refuge in Minerva's temple but was dragged from it and raped during sack of Troy; became mistress of Agamemnon and was killed along with him by Clytemnestra (*Am.* 1.7.17).

Cassiepia: Mother of Andromeda (Prop. [4.7.65]; *Am.* [3.3.18]).

Castalia: Fountain on Mount Parnassus, haunt of the Muses (Mart. 4.14.1).

Castor: Twin son (with Pollux) of Jupiter and Leda; patron of sailors (*Q. fr.* 2.3.6; Cat. 4.27, [37.2], 68.65; Prop. 2.7.16).

Catiline: Lucius Sergius Catilina (d. 62), patrician demagogue who organized a conspiracy exposed by Cicero (63 B.C.); left Rome to join his veterans, defeated and killed in January 62 B.C. *See* note on *Fam.* 5.2.8 **inflicted capital punishment on others without a hearing** (*Att.* 2.1.3; *Cael.* 10–15; *Cic.* 29.1).

Cato: Marcus Porcius Cato Uticensis, "Cato the Younger" (95–46 B.C.). As tribune designate, made powerful speech in Senate to ensure the execution of Catiline's coconspirators (63 B.C.). As tribune, alienated *equites* by refusing to allow revision of Asian tax contracts. In 59 B.C. opposed Caesar and was imprisoned, but Clodius removed him to oversee annexation of Cyprus. In 52 B.C. abandoned constitutional principles and supported Pompey's election as sole consul; fought on Pompey's side in civil war and rallied Pompey's army after his defeat at Pharsalus (48 B.C.). Committed suicide after defeat at Thapsus (April 46 B.C.) rather than accept Caesar's pardon, "an act which earned him the undying glory of a martyr" (*OCD*) (*Att.* 2.1.8, 10, 2.9.1, 2, 12.41.4, 12.44.1).

Catullus: Roman poet; *see* introduction to "Catullus" (Cat. 6.1, 7.10, 8.1, 12, 19, 10.25, 11.1, 13.7, 44.2/3, 46.4, 49.4, 51.13, 58.2, 68.27, 135, 71.1, 76.5, 79.2, 3, 82.1; *Am.* 3.15.7; Mart. 1.7.3, 4, 1.109.1, 4.14.13, 7.14.3, 11.6.15, 17).

Catulus (1): Quintus Lutatius Catulus (consul 102 B.C.), war hero (*Cael.* 78).

Catulus (2): Quintus Lutatius Catulus (d. 60 B.C.), friend of Cicero and supporter of his conservative political agenda (*Att.* 2.14.2; *Cael.* 59, 70).

Cecrops: Legendary king of Athens (Prop. 2.20.6).

Celer: Quintus Caecilius Metellus Celer (consul 60 B.C.), husband of Clodia; died suddenly in 59 B.C., causing rumors that she had poisoned him (*Fam.* 5.1, 5.2; *Att.* 2.1.4, 5, [8]; *Cael.* 34, 59, [60]).

Celtiberia: District in central Spain, with mixture of Celts and Iberians (Cat. 37.18).

Censor: Roman magistrate; two elected every five years for eighteen-month office; revised roll of citizens, supervised public contracts, and issued decrees as guardians of morals.

Cepheus: Father of Andromeda (Prop. 1.3.3; *Am.* 3.3.17).

Cerberus: Three-headed dog who guarded the entrance to the Underworld (Prop. 4.7.[52], 90).

Ceres: Goddess of agriculture; often used to mean "grain" (*Att.* 2.12.2, 4; Tib. 1.1.15; *Am.* 1.1.9, 3.7.31).

Chlide: Woman with whom Ovid (i.e., Ovid's *amator*) has slept (*Am.* 3.7.23).

Chloris: Alleged to be Propertius' mistress after Cynthia's death (Prop. 4.7.72).

Chrysippus: Vettius Chrysippus, freedman who served as an architect for Cicero (*Att.* 13.29.1).

Cicero (1): Marcus Tullius Cicero, Roman orator, statesman, philosopher, and epistolographer (106–43 B.C.); *see* "Cicero: Introduction" (Cat. 49.2; *Cic.* 29.1–5).

Cicero (2): Marcus Tullius Cicero (junior), son of Cicero (1) (*Att.* 2.9.4, 2.12.4, 12.52.1).

Cinna: Gaius Helvetius Cinna, poet, friend of Catullus (Cat. 10.29 [English only], 30).

Circe: Enchantress-goddess who turned men into animals with her potions and wand (Tib. 2.4.55; *Am.* [3.7.79]).

Cisalpine: *See* Gaul.

Claudia (1): Alternate spelling of Clodia; *see* note on *Fam.* 5.2.6 **Claudia** (*Fam.* 5.2.6).

Claudia (2): Vestal Virgin who protected her father, Appius Claudius Pulcher (consul 143 B.C.), from attack when people tried to prevent him from celebrating his triumph (*Cael.* 34).

Cleopatra: Cleopatra VII (69–30 B.C.), last and best known of the Ptolemies (Macedonian kings and queens of Egypt after its conquest by Alexander the Great). Mistress of Caesar, brought by him to Rome (46–44 B.C.), to dismay of Romans; later mistress of Antony, who lived with her openly after 37 B.C., leaving his wife Octavia (Augustus' sister). Committed suicide shortly after battle of Actium; demonized by Augustan propaganda as symbol of degenerate East (*Att.* [14.8.1]).

Clodia: *See also* Claudia, Lesbia, Ox-Eyes (*Att.* [2.1.5], 12.38a.2, 12.42.1–2, 12.41.3, 12.43.3, 12.44.2, 13.26.1, 12.47.1, 2, 12.52.2, 13.29.2, 14.8.1; *Q. fr.* 2.3.2; *Cael.* passim, especially 1–2, 18–20, 30–38, 47–70, 75–76, 78; "Cicero: Speeches (Excerpts)" and "Testimonia," passim).

Clodius: Publius Clodius Pulcher, "Publius," "Little Beauty" (c. 92–52 B.C.). Prosecuted Catiline in 65 B.C. but was in cahoots with the defense (according to Cicero). Infiltrated the all-female rites of the Bona Dea in drag in December 62 B.C.; alienated from Cicero when the latter gave evidence against him in May 61 B.C., though Clodius was acquitted (through bribery, according to Cicero). In March 59 B.C., transferred to *plebs,* with Caesar presiding as Pontifex Maximus (high priest). Elected tribune in 58 B.C.; instituted many measures, including free grain for *plebs* (whose favor he courted, casting himself as a *popularis*) and condemnation of people who had put citizens to death without trial, thus ensuring Cicero's exile. Turned against Pompey, but changed attitude after Triumvirate was reconfirmed at Luca (56 B.C.), and by violence helped secure joint consulship of Pompey and Crassus in 55 B.C.. Murdered by Milo in 52 B.C.; his clients among the *plebs* burned the Senate house as his pyre. *See also* Lesbius (*Att.* 2.1.4, [5], 2.9.1, 3, 2.12.2, 2.22.1, [2], 4, [2.23.3]; *Q. fr.* 2.3.2, 4; *Dom.* [25, 26, 92]; *Har.* [9, 38, 39, 42]; *Sest.* [16, 39, 116]; *Cael.* 17, [32], [35], [60], [78]; *Cic.* 29.1–5).

Clodius Patavinus: Unknown (*Att.* 12.44.3).

Clytemnestra: Wife of Agamemnon, whom she killed upon his return from Troy (*Inst.* 8.6.53; Prop. 4.7.57).

Cnidus: Town in southwest Asia Minor where Aphrodite/Venus was worshipped (Cat. 36.14/13).

Cnossos: City of Crete ruled over by King Minos (Prop. 1.3.1/2).

Coan: Of Cos (island in the Aegean off the coast of southwestern Turkey), known for its luxurious see-through cloth (*Inst.* 8.6.53; Tib. 2.4.29).

Cognomen: A "nickname," supposedly designating a distinguishing characteristic of oneself or one's family; sometimes obscure and insulting (e.g., Calvus = "Bald," Brutus = "Stupid").

Comum: *See* New Comum.

Corcyra: Modern Corfu, island in the Ionian Sea (*Att.* 2.1.1).

Corinna: Greek poetess (dates unknown: sometime between sixth and third centuries B.C.); pseudonym of Ovid's girlfriend (*Am.* 1.5.9, 2.6.48, 2.8.6, 3.7.25).

Corinth: City in northeastern Peloponnesus, known as cosmopolitan center of trade (*Att.* 2.1.11).

Cornelius: Cornelius Nepos, celebrated historian and biographer (Cat. 1.3).

Crassus: Marcus Licinius Crassus (d. 53), known as wealthiest man in late Republic after he made a fortune in proscriptions of Sulla. Defeated slave revolt of Spartacus (72–71 B.C.), but Pompey took credit. Supported Catiline at first but stopped when Catiline turned to revolution and canceling debts. Caesar persuaded him to be reconciled with Pompey, and the three became the First Triumvirate. Supported Clodius after Caesar left for Gaul (59 B.C.) but later dropped him as too ambitious. Tried to conquer Parthia; against unfavorable omens, crossed the Euphrates River and was killed, leading to further deterioration in relationship of Pompey and Caesar and ultimately civil war (*Att.* [2.9.2], 2.22.5; *Q. fr.* 2.3.2–4; *Cael.* 9, 18, 23).

Crete: Large island in the Mediterranean off southeastern coast of Greece (Prop. 4.7.57).

Cumae: Coastal town west of Naples (*Att.* 13.29.3).

Cupid: God of love, son of Venus (Cat. 3.1, 13.12, 36.3, [45.8, 45.17], 68.133; *Am.* 1.1.4/3, [22, 25–26], 1.9.1, 1.10.[15], [19], [2.1.3, 38], 2.5.1, 2.7.27, 3.15.[1], [15]).

Curii: Family of Roman statesmen, active in third century B.C.; known for austerity similar to that of Fabricii (*Cael.* 39).

Curio (1): Gaius Scribonius Curio (senior, consul 76 B.C.); supported Clodius, hostile to Caesar; Cicero wrote pamphlet against him (and Clodius) but denied authorship when he needed Curio's help in exile (*Q. fr.* 2.3.2, 4).

Curio (2): Gaius Scribonius Curio (junior, tribune 50 B.C.), friend of Clodius, but joined his father in supporting the Optimates in the 50s (*Att.* 2.12.2).

Cusinius: Marcus Cusinius, praetor in 44 B.C., named governor of Sicily by Antony; co-owner of property Cicero considers buying (*Att.* 12.38a.2, 12.41.3).

Cybele: Great Mother goddess (*Cael.* [1]; Cat. [35.14], [35.18]; Prop. 4.7.62).

Cyclades: Archipelago in southern Aegean Sea (Cat. 4.7).

Cyllenean: Of or near Mount Cyllene in Arcadia (Cat. 68.109).

Cynthia: Pseudonym of Propertius' girlfriend; *see* note on Prop. 1.1.1 **Cynthia** (Prop. 1.1.1, 1.3.8, 22, 1.11.1, 8, 23, 26, 1.15.2, 26, 2.7.3, 19, 3.24.3, 3.25.6, 4.7.3, 85, 4.8.15, 51, 63).

Cypassis: Slave of Corinna (*Am.* 2.7.17, 2.8.2, 22, 28/27).

Cyrene: City in northeastern Libya, birthplace of Callimachus (Cat. 7.4).

Cyrus: King of Persia in the sixth century B.C. who conquered most of central Asia (*Att.* 12.38a.2).

Cytherea: Epithet for Venus/Aphrodite (from Cythera, island between Peloponnesus and Crete, chief center for her worship) (Prop. 2.14.25).

Cytina: City in Thessaly (Prop. 1.1.24).

Cytorus: Mountain in Bithynia, famous for boxwood (Cat. 4.11, 4.13).

Daedalan: Of Daedalus, the quintessential clever inventor, most famous for building the labyrinth (Prop. 2.14.8).

Danaans: Greeks (from Danaus) (Prop. 3.8.31).

Danaë: Princess of Argos; imprisoned by father Acrisius in a bronze tower; Jupiter nevertheless visited and impregnated her by pouring through the bars in a shower of gold (Prop. 2.20.10, 12).

Danaus: Ancient Greek king; *see* Hypermnestra.

Dardanian: Trojan (from Dardanus, first Trojan king) (Prop. 2.14.1).

Delia: First named girlfriend of Tibullus; *see* note on Tib. 1.1.57 **Delia** (Tib. 1.1.57, 61, 69/68, 1.6.5, 55, 85).

Delos: Island on which Apollo and Diana were born (Cat. 34.8/7).

Demophoön: Pseudonym of a friend of Propertius (Prop. 2.22A.2, 13).

Demosthenes: Greatest Athenian orator (384–322 B.C.) (*Att.* 2.1.3).

Diana: Goddess of moon, hunt, and Underworld; twin sister of Apollo; *see also* Luna (Cat. 34.1, 34.3; Prop. [2.15.15], 4.8.29; *Am.* [1.1.10], 2.5.27).

Dicaearchus: Greek philosopher; *see* note on *Att.* 2.12.4 **Dicaearchus** (*Att.* 2.12.4).

Dindymon: Mountain in Phrygia sacred to goddess Cybele (Cat. 35.14).

Dindymus: Probably pseudonym of friend of Martial (Mart. 11.6.11).

Dio: *See* note on *Cael.* 18 **arrival of king Ptolemy** (*Cael.* 23, 24, 51).

Diomedes: Greek hero of Trojan War; wounded Aphrodite and Ares on battlefield (*Am.* [1.7.31], [34]).

Dog Star: Latin *Sirius,* star whose rising in August was associated with parching weather (Tib. 1.1.27).

Dolabella: Publius Cornelius Dolabella; married Cicero's daughter against Cicero's wishes and divorced her in 46 B.C. (*Att.* 13.29.2).

Drusus: Marcus Livius Drusus Claudianus, praetor in 50 B.C., owner of property Cicero considers buying (*Att.* 12.38a.2, 12.41.3, 12.44.2, 13.26.1).

Dulichia: Ionian island often treated by poets as synonymous with Ithaca, Odysseus' home (Prop. 2.14.4).

Durrachium: Town on coast of Illyria, east of Adriatic Sea (Cat. 36.15).

East Wind: Latin *Eurus*; proverbially stormy (*Am.* 1.9.13–14/13).

Edonian: Thracian (the Edoni were a Thracian tribe) (Prop. 1.3.5).

Egnatius: Lover of Lesbia with a killer smile (Cat. 37.19).

Electra: Daughter of Agamemnon and Clytemnestra; sister of Orestes; she was separated from him in infancy and thought him dead (Prop. 2.14.5).

Elysium: Realm of the blessed in the Underworld (Prop. 4.7.60; *Am.* 2.6.49; Mart. 7.14.6).

Empire: Period of Roman history following the end of the Republic (27 B.C.).

Endymion: Son of Jupiter; loved by Diana (Prop. 2.15.15).

Ennius: Quintus Ennius (239–169 B.C.), often considered greatest early Roman poet, author of tragedies, epic, etc.

Eques: *See* Knight.

Eriphyle: *See* note on *Am.* 1.10.52 **necklace** (*Am.* [1.10. 51]).

Esquiline: Hill of Rome, crossed by three aqueducts (Prop. 4.8.1).

Euripides: Athenian tragic playwright (c. 480–c. 406 B.C.).

Eurotas: River of Sparta (*Am.* 1.10.1).

Evadne: Wife of Capaneus; immolated herself on his funeral pyre (Prop. 1.15.21).

Faberius: Caesar's secretary (*Att.* 12.27.1, 13.29.1, 2).

Fabius: *See* note on *Att.* 2.1.5 **Fabius**.

Fabricii: Family of Roman statesmen; Gaius Fabricius Luscinus, censor in third century B.C., known for austerity, famously expelled an ex-consul from the Senate for possessing silver tableware (*Cael.* 39).

Fabullus: Friend of Catullus (Cat. 12.17, 13.1, 13.14).

Falernian: Finest Roman wine (Cat. 27.1).

Favonius: Roman politician, "admirer and excessive imitator of Cato (Uticensis), especially in rude forthrightness" (*OCD*) (*Att.* 2.1.9, 12.44.3; *Q. fr.* 2.3.2).

First Triumvirate: *See* note on *Att.* 2.9.2 **three exorbitant men**.

Flaminius: *See* note on *Att.* 12.52.1 **Montanus owes Plancus** (*Att.* 12.52.1).

Flavius: Friend (or enemy) of Catullus, otherwise unknown (Cat. 6.1).

Formiae: Town on west coast of Italy; Cicero was killed in his villa there (*Att.* 2.9.4, 2.14.2; Cat. 43.5).

Forum: Forum Romanum, central public square of Rome; Cicero emphasizes it as site of law courts (as in our word "forensic"), love poets as site of flirtation

(*Att.* 2.1.5, 2.22.3; *Q. fr.* 2.3.6; *Har.* 39; *Cael.* 3, 11, 12, 18, 21, 35, 42, 67; Prop. 4.8.76).

Furies: Greek "Erinyes," goddesses of vengeance (Prop. 2.20.29; *Am.* [1.7.10]).

Furius: Friend/enemy/rival of Catullus, possibly poet Furius Bibaculus (Cat. 11.1, 16.2).

Gaius Antonius: Gaius Antonius Hybrida, Cicero's colleague as consul in 63 B.C.; *see* note on *Cael.* 15 **accusing another man of conspiracy** (*Cael.* [15], 74, [78]).

Gaius Arrius: Neighbor of Cicero at Formiae (*Att.* 2.14.2).

Gaius Caesernius: *See* note on *Cael.* 71 **the condemnation of Marcus Camurtius and Gaius Caesernius** (*Cael.* 71).

Gaius Carbo: Gaius Papirius Carbo (d. 119 B.C.); orator and politician, considered one of the murderers of Publius Cornelius Scipio Aemilianus Africanus Numantinus (*Q. fr.* 2.3.3).

Gaius Cato: *See* note on *Q. fr.* 2.3.1 **Gaius Cato** (*Q. fr.* 2.3.1, 3, 4).

Gaius Coponius: Friend of Dio (*Cael.* 24).

Gaius Cornelius: Unknown (*Q. fr.* 2.3.5).

Gallic: Of Gaul (*Att.* 2.1.11; Cat. 11.11).

Gaul: Region corresponding to northern part of Italian peninsula ("Cisalpine"), to southeastern part of modern France, or to modern France and Belgium (*see* OLD s.v. "Gallia") (*Fam.* 5.1 [heading]; *Q. fr.* 2.3.4; *Att.* 14.8.2).

Gellius: Lucius Gellius Poplicola, rival and enemy of Catullus; ally of Clodius and later of Antony (Cat. 74.1, 91.1, 116.6).

Gnaeus: *See* Pompey.

Gnaeus Domitius (1): Gnaeus Domitius Calvinus, presider over court for Bestia's trial; possibly identical with Gnaeus Domitius (2) (*Q. fr.* 2.3.6).

Gnaeus Domitius (2): Presider over court for Caelius' trial; possibly identical with Gnaeus Domitius (1) (*Cael.* 32).

Gnaeus Lentulus Vatia: Gnaeus Cornelius Lentulus Vatia, owner of the gladiatorial school from which Spartacus escaped (*Q. fr.* 2.3.5).

Gnaeus Nerius: Informer (*Q. fr.* 2.3.5).

Gnaeus Pompeius: *See* Pompey.

Golgi: Town in Cyprus, sacred to Aphrodite/Venus (Cat. 36.14).

Good Goddess: *See* Bona Dea.

Gyes: Hundred-armed Giant who fought in the Gigantomachy ("battle between gods and Giants") (*Am.* 2.1.12).

Haemonian: Thessalian (Prop. 1.15.20; *Am.* 2.1.32).

Hannibal: Carthaginian general whom the Romans fought in the Second Punic War (218–202 B.C.); one of Rome's most dangerous enemies (Mart. 4.14.4).

Harpocrates: Egyptian sun god (Cat. 74.4).

Hebe: Goddess of youth; became Hercules' wife when he was made a god (Cat. 68.116).

Hector: Chief Trojan hero in Trojan War; killed by Achilles, who had his horses drag Hector's dead body around the walls of Troy (Prop. 2.22A.31, 34, 3.8.31; *Am.* 1.9.35, 2.1.32, 2.6.42).

Helen: Greek woman who left her husband, Menelaus, and went to Troy with Paris, causing Trojan War (Cat. 68.87; Prop. 3.8.[30], 32; *Am.* [1.10.1]).

Helicon: Mountain in central Greece sacred to Apollo and the Muses (*Am.* 1.1.15).

Hercules: Greatest Greek hero; forced to undergo many labors at the command of the inferior Eurystheus; ultimately was made a god and married Hebe (*Cael.* 76; Prop. 1.11.2, 4.7.82).

Hippolytus: Son of Theseus; worshipped Diana and scorned Venus/Aphrodite (i.e., rejected sexual love), who punished him gruesomely (*Am.* 2.4.32).

Hirtius: Aulus Hirtius (consul 43 B.C.), supporter of Caesar; notorious epicure (*Att.* 12.41.4, 12.44.1, [14.8.1]).

Homer: Greek poet (probably eighth–seventh century B.C.), composer of *Iliad* and *Odyssey.*

Hortensius: Quintus Hortensius Hortalus, poet and orator, chief rival of Cicero; known for flowery "Asiatic" style of oratory (Cat. 95.3).

Hylaeus: Arcadian centaur who attacked Atalanta; she killed him after Milanion, in defending her, had been wounded by him (Prop. 1.1.13).

Hymen: God of weddings (Cat. 62.5, 62.10, 62.19, 62.25, 62.31, 62.38, 62.48, 62.66).

Hypermnestra: Only one of the fifty daughters of Danaus who refused to kill her husband on her wedding night (Prop. 4.7.63, 67).

Hypispyle: Queen of Lemnos, beloved and deserted by Jason (Prop. 1.15.18, 19).

Hyrcani: People living on southeastern shore of Caspian Sea (Cat. 11.5).

Ianthis: Poetic name for Stella's wife, Violentilla ("Little Violet"; Greek *ion* means "violet") (Mart. 7.14.5).

Iasus: Father of Atalanta (in some versions) (Prop. 1.1.10).

Iberia: Spain (Cat. 37.20).

Idalium: Town in Cyprus sacred to Aphrodite/Venus (Cat. 36.12).

Inachus: Father of Io (Prop. 1.3.20).

India: *See* note on Cat. 11.2 **India** (Cat. 11.2; Prop. 2.22A.10; *Am.* 2.6.1; Mart. 1.109.4).

Interamna: Modern Terni, town in central Italy (*Att.* 2.1.5).

Io: Woman whom Jupiter slept with then turned into a cow to hide her from Juno; Juno knew and sent Argus to guard her and a gadfly to torment her (Prop. [1.3.20]).

Ionian Sea: Sea to the west of Greece (Cat. 84.11, 84.12).

Ipsitilla: Potential lover of Catullus (Cat. 32).

Ismarian: Thracian (from Mount Ismarus, in Thrace) (*Am.* 2.6.7).

Isocrates: Greek orator (436–338 B.C.), known for elegant, elaborate style (*Att.* 2.1.1).

Issa: Puppy (Mart. 1.109.1–5, 19, 21).

Ithaca: Greek island; home of Odysseus (Prop. 1.15.9).

Itys: *See* Philomel (*Am.* 2.6.10).

Jason: Leader of the Argonauts; *see* Hypsipyle, Medea, Pelias (Prop. 1.15.[17], [19]).

Jerusalemarian: *See* note on *Att.* 2.9.1 **Jerusalemarian bestower of plebeian status** (*Att.* 2.9.1).

Jove: *See* Jupiter.

Junia: Wife of Lepidus and half-sister of Brutus (*Att.* 14.8.1).

Juno: Jupiter's wife, queen of the gods (Cat. 34.13/12, 68.138; Prop. 4.8.16; *Am.* 2.6.55).

Jupiter (= Jove): King of the gods (*Dom.* 92; Cat. 1.7, 4.20, 7.5, 34.6, 68.140, 72.2; Prop. 2.7.3/4, 2.22A.25, 3.24.20; *Am.* 1.7.36, 1.10.[4], 8, 2.1.15, 17, 18, 19, 2.5.52, 3.3.30, 35).

Juvenal: Decimus Junius Juvenalis (c. A.D. 60–c. 140), Roman author; wrote *Satires.*

Juventius: Adolescent boy; *see* note on Cat. 48.1 **Juventius** (Cat. 48.1).

Knight: Latin *eques* (pl. *equites,* "horsemen," from traditional role in supplying Roman cavalry), members of well-to-do social class below senators; *see* introduction, "Social Classes" (*Att.* 2.1.7, 8; *Cael.* 3–5; *Am.* 3.15.6).

Laconian: Of Sparta (city-state in Peloponnesus), home of Helen and Menelaus (Prop. 2.15.13).

Laïs: Famous Greek prostitute (*Am.* 1.5.12).

Lalage: Slave of Cynthia (Prop. 4.7.45).

Lamiae: Family friends of Cicero; Lucius Aelius Lamia was exiled in 58 B.C. for helping Cicero (*Q. fr.* 2.3.7).

Lanuvium: Small town twenty miles southeast of Rome on the Appian Way; famed for its shrine of Juno Sospita (*Att.* 12.41.1, 12.43.1, 12.44.3, 13.26.2; Prop. 4.8.3, 48).

Laodamia: Wife of Protesilaus; grieved so much that the gods allowed her to see him after his death for three hours, after which she killed herself (Cat. 68.73/74).

Laomedon: Father of Priam (Prop. 2.14.2).

Lares: Gods of hearth and home (Prop. 4.8.50; Tib. 1.1.19/20).

Larius: Lake (modern Lago di Como) on which New Comum borders (Cat. 35.4).

Latona: Mother of Apollo and Diana (Cat. 34.5).

Latris: Slave of Cynthia; her name means "Service" (Prop. 4.7.75).

Leda: Wife of Tyndareus, mother of Castor, Pollux, Helen, and Clytemnestra; Jupiter in the form of a swan slept with her (*Am.* 1.10.3, 2.4.42).

Lentulus (1): Cornelius Lentulus Spinther (senior); *see* note on *Q. fr.* 2.3.1 **changed clothes** (*Q. fr.* 2.3.1, 4).

Lentulus (2): Cornelius Lentulus Spinther (junior); *see* note on *Att.* 12.52.2 **Spinther getting a divorce?** (*Q. fr.* [2.3.1]; *Att.* 12.52.2).

Lepidus: Marcus Aemilius Lepidus (d. c. 12 B.C.), member of the Second Triumvirate (*Att.* [14.8.1]).

Lesbia: Catullus' pseudonym for Clodia (Cat. 5.1, 7.1, 43.7, 51.7, 58.1, 58.2, [70.1], 72.2, 75.1, [76.23], 83.1, 86.5, 87.2, 92.1, 92.2, 107.4, [109.1]; Mart. 7.14.4).

Lesbius: Pseudonym of Clodius; *see* note on Cat. 79.1 **Lesbius is beautiful** (Cat. 79.1).

Lesbos: Large island in the Aegean Sea; home of Sappho.

Lethe: River in the Underworld; drinking from it caused amnesia (Prop. 4.7.10, 91).

Libas: Woman with whom Ovid (i.e., Ovid's *amator*) has slept (*Am.* 3.7.24).

Liber: "Free One," cult title of Bacchus (Prop. 1.3.13).

Libya: Country on north coast of Africa (Cat. 45.6).

Licinian: *See* note on *Q. fr.* 2.3.7 **Licinian house near Piso's lake** (*Q. fr.* 2.3.7).

Licinius: *See* Calvus.

Little Beauty: Nickname of Clodius; *see* note on *Att.* 2.1.4 **Little Beauty** (*Att.* 2.1.4, 2.22.1).

Lucceius: Lucius Lucceius, friend of Cicero; ran for consul in 60 B.C. with Caesar, providing money for both, but was defeated by Bibulus; wrote a contemporary history and was asked by Cicero to glorify his deeds in a special monograph (*Att.* 2.1.9; *Cael.* 51–55).

Lucina: Goddess of childbirth, usually associated with Juno or Diana (Cat. 34.13).

Lucius Cossinius: Friend of Atticus and Cicero (*Att.* 2.1.1).

Lucius Crassus: Lucius Licinius Crassus (consul 95 B.C.), statesman whose oratorical style Cicero admired (*Att.* 14.8.1).

Lucius Herennius: *See* Balbus (2).

Lucius Lucceius: *See* Lucceius.

Lucius Tullius Montanus: Friend of Marcus Cicero (Cicero's son); accompanied him to Athens (*Att.* 12.52.1).

Lucretius: Titus Lucretius Carus (c. 96–55 B.C.), author of *De Rerum Natura* ("On the Nature of Things"), an Epicurean didactic epic poem.

Lucrine Lake: *See* note on Prop. 1.11.3–4 **the waters . . . Misenum** (Prop. 1.11.10).

Lucullus: Lucius Licinius Lucullus (consul 74 B.C.), statesman and military leader, husband of one of Clodia's sisters (whom he divorced for adultery); notorious epicure (*Cic.* 29.4).

Luna: "Moon," name for Diana as moon goddess (Cat. 34.16; *Am.* 2.5.38).

Luperci: Fraternity who conducted the festival of the Lupercalia, which included odd fertility rites such as running around the Palatine in loincloths and striking women with goat-skin thongs (*Cael.* 26).

Lyaeus: "Liberator," epithet of Bacchus (*Am.* 3.15.17).

Lydia: Country in Asia Minor; origin of "Lydian mode" in music (Cat. 31.13; Prop. 4.7.61).

Lygdamus: Slave of Cynthia (Prop. 4.7.35, 4.8.37, 68, 70, 79).

Maenad: Female follower of Bacchus, engaging in wild revelry on the mountains (*Har.* 39; Prop. [1.3.5], 3.8.14; *Am.* 1.9.38).

Maenalus: Mountain range in Arcadia (*Am.* 1.7.14).

Maeonian: Of Maeonia, the eastern part of Lydia; traditional birthplace of Homer (*Am.* 2.5.39/40).

Malian: Of Malis, in southern Thessaly (Cat. 68.54).

Mamurra: Henchman of Julius Caesar; from Formiae (Cat. [43.5]).

Manius: A friend of Catullus (Cat. 68.11, 30).

Mantua: Town in northern Italy; birthplace of Vergil (*Am.* 3.15.7).

Marcius Rex: Quintus Marcius Rex (consul 68 B.C.), statesman and military leader, husband of Tertia (*Cic.* 29.5).

Marcus Caelius: Father of Caelius (*Cael.* 3, [4], [9], [18], [73], [79–80]).

Marcus Camurtius: *See* note on *Cael.* 71 **the condemnation of Marcus Camurtius and Gaius Caesernius** (*Cael.* 71).

Marcus Crassus: *See* Crassus.

Marcus Marcellus: Orator, praised (along with Caesar) by Cicero (*Brutus* 248–51); may have been Clodius' colleague as curule aedile (*Q. fr.* 2.3.1).

Marcus Metellus: Mentioned as giver of gladiatorial shows; otherwise unknown (*Att.* 2.1.1).

Marcus Scaurus: Marcus Aemilius Scaurus (d. 89 B.C.), last great leader of the Senate; opposed Saturninus (*Sest.* 39).

Marcus Tullius (1): *See* Cicero.

Marcus Tullius (2): *See* note on *Q. fr.* 2.3.5 **one Marcus Tullius** (*Q. fr.* 2.3.5).

Marius (1): Gaius Marius (c. 157–86 B.C.), great military leader, New Man, and first to call up property-less volunteers for the army (who would thus be more dependent on him, their general); adversary of Sulla; marched on Rome with his own army after Sulla did.

Marius (2): *See* note on *Att.* 14.8.1 **Marius** (*Att.* 14.8.1).

Maro: *See* Vergil.

Marrucini: People living on Adriatic coast (*Cat.* 12.1).

Mars: God of war (*Am.* 1.1.12, 1.9.29, 39, 2.5.28, 3.3.27).

Martial: Roman poet; *see* introduction to "Martial."

Maximus: *See* note on Mart. 1.7.3 **Maximus** (Mart. 1.7.3).

Medea: Enchantress from Colchis (on Black Sea), held up as example of murderously passionate barbarian woman. Helped Jason acquire the Golden Fleece, ran away with him, killed her brother and scattered his remains to distract pursuers, and got Pelias' daughters to kill him; when Jason married someone else, Medea killed the new bride and her own children (by Jason) in revenge (*Cael.* 18; Tib. 2.4.55).

Memmius: Gaius Memmius (praetor 58 B.C.), governor of Bithynia when Catullus was there (57–56 B.C.); literary connoisseur and patron (*Att.* 2.12.2; Cat. [10.10, 12/13]).

Menelaus: King of Sparta; husband of Helen and younger brother of Agamemnon; Trojan War was fought to get Helen back after she ran away with (or was abducted by) Trojan Paris (Prop. 2.15.14; *Am.* [1.10.2], [2.1.30]).

Messala: Marcus Valerius Messalla Corvinus (64 B.C.–A.D. 8), Roman public figure; as consul in 31 B.C. with Octavian, fought in Battle of Actium; patron of Tibullus and young Ovid (Tib. 1.1.53).

Metellus (1): *See* Celer.

Metellus (2): *See* Nepos.

Methymnian: Of Methymna, a city on Lesbos famed for its wine (Prop. 4.8.38).

Milanion: Atalanta's lover (Prop. 1.1.9).

Miletus: Flutist for Propertius' party (Prop. 4.8.39).

Milo: Titus Annius Milo (d. 48 B.C.). As tribune in 57 B.C., worked for Cicero's recall and organized gangs to combat those of Clodius; had Clodius killed in 52 B.C. Prosecuted for *vis* ("seditious violence") under legislation passed by Pompey; Cicero tried to defend him but was so intimidated by Pompey's troops that he could not give a good speech (the *Pro Milone* we have was written later). Exiled and killed when he attempted (along with Caelius) to raise rebellion among the poor in Italy (*Q. fr.* 2.3.1, 2, 4).

Minerva: Goddess of war, wisdom, weaving, etc.; identified with Greek Athena; *see also* Pallas (*Dom.* 92; *Am.* 1.1.7, 8, 1.7.18, 2.6.35).

Minos: King of Cnossus (on Crete); father of Ariadne (Prop. 2.14.7).

Minotaur: Monstrous half-man, half-bull; *see* Pasiphaë.

Misenum: Promontory on the Bay of Naples (Prop. 1.11.4).

Molo: Teacher of rhetoric in Rhodes (*Att.* 2.1.9).

Molossian: Of the Molossi, a tribe on the west coast of Greece famed for their breed of dogs (Prop. 4.8.24).

Moon: *See* Luna.

Mucia: Wife of Pompey, half-sister of Celer (*Fam.* 5.2.6).

Muse: Goddess of poetry and other arts (Cat. 68.7; Tib. 2.4.15, 20; *Am.* 1.1.6, 30, 3.15.20; Mart. 4.14.[1], 10).

Mustela: One of Scapula's heirs (*Att.* 12.44.2, 12.47.1).

Mycene: Ancient Greek city ruled by Agamemnon (Prop. 2.22A.32; *Am.* 2.8.12).

Naples: City on southwest coast of Italy (*Cael.* 23).

Nasica: Publius Cornelius Scipio Nasica, tribune prosecuted for bribery in 60 B.C. (*Att.* 2.1.9).

Naso: "The Nose," *cognomen* of Ovid (*Am.* 2.1.2).

Nemesis: Goddess of retribution; pseudonym of girlfriend of Tibullus (Cat. 50.20, [68.77]; Tib. 2.4.59).

Nepos: Quintus Caecilius Metellus Nepos, brother of Celer; *see* note on *Fam.* 5.1 **Quintus Metellus Celer** (*Fam.* 5.1.1, 5.2.[1], 6–10; *Att.* 2.12.2).

Neptune: God of the sea (Cat. 31.2).

Nero: Roman emperor in A.D. 54–68; known for vanity, artistic pretensions, and philhellenism (Mart. 11.6.10).

Nestor: Aged, garrulous former warrior and advisor of Greeks during Trojan War (*Am.* [3.7.41]).

New Comum: Town one hundred miles west of Verona, originally "Comum," renamed "New Comum" when Julius Caesar settled colonists there (Cat. 35.4/3–4).

New Gardens: Gardens on the Esquiline (Prop. 4.8.2).

New Man: Man who becomes consul without having ancestors who were consuls.

Nicaea: City in Bithynia (Cat. 46.5).

Nile: River in Egypt (Cat. 11.7/8).

Niobe: Daughter of Tantalus; when she boasted that her twelve children were more numerous and beautiful than Apollo and Diana, they killed all her children in revenge, and she turned into a stone statue that wept eternally (Prop. 2.20.8).

Nola: City in southern Italy; *see Inst.* 8.6.53 **"Coan in the dining room, Nola in the bedroom"** (*Inst.* 8.6.53).

Nomas: Slave of Cynthia (Prop. 4.7.37).

Numerius Numestius: *See* note on *Att.* 2.22.7 **Numerius Numestius** (*Att.* 2.22.7).

Octavius: Gaius Octavius, father of man who would be Augustus (*Att.* 2.1.12).

Odysseus: Latin "Ulysses"; Greek hero of Trojan War; protagonist of Homer's *Odyssey*, which tells of his ten years of wanderings and return to his home (and wife Penelope) on Ithaca (Prop. [1.15.9], 2.14.3; *Am.* [2.1.31]).

Oetaean: Of Oeta, a mountain in Thessaly associated with the hot springs at Thermopylae; *see* note on Cat. 62.7 **Oetaean flames** (Cat. 62.7, 68.54).

Olbia: Town on the east coast of Sardinia (*Q. fr.* 2.3.7).

Olympus: Mountain on borders of Thessaly and Macedonia; said to be home of gods (Cat. 62.2; Tib. 1.6.83; *Am.* 2.1.14/13).

Oppius: Gaius Oppius, manager (along with Balbus) of Caesar's affairs; wrote to Cicero on Caesar's behalf (*Att.* 12.44.3).

Optimates: The "best men" (also called *boni*, "good men"), name for conservatives of late Republic who wanted to preserve the power of the senatorial aristocracy against encroachment by *populares.*

Orcus: God of the Underworld (Cat. 3.14).

Orestes: Greek hero who killed his mother, Clytemnestra, in revenge for her killing his father, Agamemnon; pursued by Furies, finally freed when Athena set up a law court that decided in his favor (Prop. 2.14.5; *Am.* 1.7.9, 2.6.15).

Orpheus: Quintessential poet/singer; could move beasts, trees, and stones with his song (Prop. 1.3.42).

Ossa: Mountain in Thessaly (*Am.* 2.1.13/14).

Ostia: City at the mouth of the Tiber (*Sest.* 39).

Otho (1): Lucius Roscius Otho, possibly identical with Otho (2); *see* note on *Att.* 2.1.3 **Otho**.

Otho (2): Roscius (?) Otho, possibly identical with Otho (1); one of Scapula's heirs (*Att.* 12.38a.1, 12.42.1, 12.43.3, 12.44.2).

Ovid: Roman poet; *see* introduction to "Ovid: *Amores.*"

Ox-Eyes: Cicero's nickname for Clodia; *see* note on *Att.* 2.9.1 **Ox-Eyes** (*Att.* 2.9.1, 2.12.2, 2.14.1, 2.22.5, 2.23.3).

Padua: Town in Italy at mouth of Po River (Cat. 95.6).

Paeligni: Romanized tribe of central Italy; inhabited Sulmo, the birthplace of Ovid (*Am.* 2.1.1, 3.15.3, 8).

Paetus: Lucius Papirius Paetus, friend of Cicero (*Att.* 2.1.12).

Palatine: Hill of Rome, site of expensive, fashionable homes (*Cael.* 18, 78).

Pales: Goddess of flocks and herds (Tib. 1.1.36).

Palla: *See* note on *Cael.* 23 **that part of the case** (*Cael.* 23).

Pallas: Minerva (*Am.* 3.3.28).

Parcae: The Fates, who spun the thread of destiny for each person at birth (Cat. 68.85; *Am.* 2.6.46).

Parian: Of Paros, island in Cyclades famed for its white marble (*Am.* 1.7.52).

Paris: Trojan prince who seduced and/or abducted Helen, causing Trojan War (Cat. 68.103; Prop. 2.15.13, 3.8.29; *Am.* [1.10.2]).

Parthenian: Of Parthenius, a mountain in Arcadia (Prop. 1.1.11).

Parthenie: Cynthia's nurse (Prop. 4.7.74).

Parthians: Asian people, known for treachery (especially shooting arrows backward on horseback), whom Romans fought unsuccessfully for years; Augustus achieved diplomatic victory over them in 20 B.C. (Cat. 11.6; Prop. 2.14.23).

Pasiphaë: Wife of Minos; fell in love with a bull (in punishment for Minos' not sacrificing it to Neptune), slept with it using wooden cow contraption, and gave birth to Minotaur (Prop. [4.7.57]).

Paulus: Lucius Aemilius Paulus (consul 50 B.C.); originally supporter of Cicero but "purchased" by Caesar. Declared his younger brother Lepidus a public enemy and was consequently named in the proscriptions, but escaped (*Att.* 14.8.1).

Peleus: Father of Achilles (Prop. 2.22A.34).

Pelian: From Mount Pelion (*Cael.* 18).

Pelias: King of Iolcus, city near Mount Pelion; ordered Jason (rightful heir to his throne) to seek Golden Fleece, thus launching the expedition of the Argonauts. When Jason returned with Medea, she persuaded Pelias' daughters to cut him in pieces (they thought he would be rejuvenated).

Pelion: Mountain in Thessaly (*Am.* 2.1.14).

Peloponnesus: Large peninsula forming southern part of Greece.

Pelops: A Byzantine; *see* note on *Att.* 14.8.1 **Byzantines . . . Pelops** (*Att.* 14.8.1).

Petale: Slave of Cynthia (Prop. 4.7.43).

Pharnaces: Clerk of Atticus (*Att.* 13.29.3).

Phemius: Singer in the *Odyssey* (*Am.* 3.7.61).

Pheneus: Town in Arcadia with underground channels (Cat. 68.109).

Philippics: Series of speeches by Demosthenes against Philip of Macedon; term later applied to Cicero's speeches against Antony (*Att.* 2.1.3).

Philomel: Athenian princess; raped by her sister Procne's husband, Tereus (king of Thrace), who cut out Philomel's tongue to prevent her telling; wove a tapestry depicting the crime; Procne killed her own son Itys in anger at Tereus; Philomel turned into a nightingale, Procne a swallow (vice versa in some versions), Tereus a hoopoe (Prop. [2.20.5]; *Am.* 2.6.7).

Philotimus: Freedman of Terentia (*Att.* 12.44.3).

Phocis: Country of central Greece; home of Pylades (*Am.* 2.6.15).

Phoebas: "Woman inspired by Phoebus," i.e., Cassandra (*Am.* 2.8.12).

Phoebus: Apollo (Prop. 2.15.15; *Am.* 1.1.11, 16, 1.5.5, 2.5.27).

Phrygia: "A country comprising part of the centre and west of Asia Minor; (poet.) Troy" (*OLD*) (Cat. 46.4; Prop. 2.22A.16, 30; *Am.* 1.10.1).

Phylacus: Father of Protesilaus (*Am.* 2.6.41).

Phyllis: Loose woman at Propertius' party (Prop. 4.8.29, 57).

Picenum: Region on eastern side of central Italy (*Q. fr.* 2.3.4).

Piso: *See* note on *Q. fr.* 2.3.7 **Licinian house near Piso's lake** (*Q. fr.* 2.3.7).

Pitho: Woman with whom Ovid (i.e., Ovid's *amator*) has slept (*Am.* 3.7.23).

Plancus: *See* note on *Att.* 12.52.1 **Montanus owes Plancus** (*Att.* 12.52.1).

Plato: Greek philosopher (c. 437–347 B.C.); "The safest general characterization of the European philosophical tradition is that it consists of a series of footnotes to Plato" (Alfred North Whitehead) (*Att.* 2.1.8).

Plutarch: Greek biographer and philosopher; *see* "Testimonia."

Poeta: Latin "poet."

Pollio: Gaius Asinius Pollio, orator and historian, founder of Rome's first public library c. 30s B.C. (Cat. 12.6).

Pollux: *See* Castor (Cat. [4.27], [37.2], 68.65).

Pompeii: Town on Bay of Naples (*Att.* 2.1.11).

Pompey: Gnaeus Pompeius Magnus ("The Great"), Roman statesman and military leader (106–48 B.C.). Won victories for Sulla in 83 B.C.; consul with Crassus in 70 B.C. In 67–66 B.C. waged successful war against pirates in Mediterranean, then given provinces in Asia; defeated Mithridates IV, annexed Syria, settled Judea, and laid foundation for Roman organization of East. In 62 B.C. returned, disbanded army, held triumph; wanted land for veterans and ratification of arrangements in East. Divorced wife Mucia, half-sister of Metellus (Clodia's husband), for adultery with Caesar; reconciled to Caesar through Crassus in 60 B.C. Formed coalition and married Caesar's daughter Julia in 59. Clodius attacked him in 58–57 B.C.; accordingly, Pompey helped secure Cicero's recall in 57 B.C. When Julia died in 54 B.C., strain between Pompey and Caesar increased, further mounting with death of Crassus in 53 B.C. Was appointed sole consul in 52 B.C. (after Clodius' murder) with backing of Cato. Defeated by Caesar at battle of Pharsalus in 48 B.C.; fled to Egypt and was stabbed to death as he landed. *See also* Sampsiceramus (*Fam.* 5.2.6, *Att.* 2.1.6, [2.9.1, 2], 2.12.1, 2.22.2, 5, 6, 12.44.3; *Q. fr.* 2.3.1–4; Prop. 4.8.75).

Pomponia: Sister of Atticus, wife of Cicero's brother Quintus (*Att.* 2.1.11).

Pomponius: *See* Atticus.

Pontianus: Unknown (*Att.* 12.44.2).

Pontus: The Black Sea and the region adjoining it (Cat. 4.13).

Populares: "Men of the people"; demagogues (according to their enemies) of late Republic who wanted to break power of senatorial aristocracy.

Posidonius: Stoic philosopher (c. 135–c. 51 B.C.), ran school in Rhodes that "became the leading centre of Stoicism, and a general mecca not only for intellectuals, but for the great and powerful of the Roman world such as Pompey and Cicero" (*OCD*) (*Att.* 2.1.2).

Postumia: Possibly mistress of Caesar (Cat. 27.3).

Praenomen: A "first name" (for Roman men); there were twenty-odd possibilities, with only about a dozen in common use, generally abbreviated in writing: Appius (App.—used only by the Claudian family), Aulus (A.), Gaius (C.— reflecting original pronunciation of "C" as "G"), Gnaeus (Cn.), Decimus (D.), Lucius (L.), Marcus (M.), Publius (P.), Quintus (Q.), Sextus (Sex.), Titus (T.), and Tiberius (Ti.).

Praetor: Second-ranking Roman magistrate; eight elected annually (until Caesar increased number to twenty); presided over courts, etc.

Praetuttians: A people of Picenum, region in middle of Adriatic coast of Italy that was Caelius' birthplace (*Cael.* 5).

Priapus: God of procreation, depicted with a huge erect phallus; set up in gardens as a guardian and scarecrow (Tib. 1.1.17/18; *Am.* 2.4.32).

Propertius: Roman poet; *see* introduction to "Propertius" (Prop. 4.7.49).

Propontis: Modern Sea of Marmara, between European and Asiatic Turkey (Cat. 4.9).

Proscriptions: "Black lists" of prominent men to be killed and their property confiscated; first round was by Sulla in 82–81 B.C., second by the Second Triumvirate in 43–42 B.C. Octavian allowed Cicero to be proscribed by Antony in 43 B.C.

Protesilaus: First man killed in the Trojan War; was punished by the gods for failing to sacrifice before setting up his house (Cat. 68.74; *Am.* [2.6.41]).

Ptolemy: *See* note on *Cael.* 18 **arrival of king Ptolemy.**

Publician: Belonging to one Publicius, presumably; Cicero considers buying the "Publician place," but it is not to his liking (*Att.* 12.38a.2).

Publius (1): *See* Clodius.

Publius (2): Friend of Martial (Mart. 1.109.5, 18).

Publius Asicius: *See* Asicius.

Publius Clodius: Prosecutor of Caelius (*Cael.* 27).

Publius Licinius: *See* note on *Cael.* 61 **Publius Licinius here** (*Cael.* 61–66).

Puella: Latin "girl," often used to mean "girlfriend," "romantic interest."

Pupinian: Clan of Gnaeus Nerius (*Q. fr.* 2.3.5).

Puteoli: City near Naples on southwest coast of Italy (*Cael.* 23).

Pylades: Best friend of Orestes (*Am.* 2.6.15).

Pylos: City in Peloponnesus; home of Nestor (*Am.* 3.7.41).

Pyrrhus: King of Epirus (in western Greece); fought against the Romans (280–75 B.C.). After winning a battle but incurring heavy losses, said to have remarked, "One more such victory over the Romans and we shall be utterly lost," source of our term "Pyrrhic victory" (*Cael.* 35).

Pythagoras: *See* note on Mart. 11.6.10 **Pythagoras used to give to Nero** (Mart. 11.6.10).

Quaestor: Lowest-ranking Roman magistrate (election meant admission to Senate); twenty elected annually; oversaw financial matters, etc.

Quinta Claudia: *See* note on *Cael.* 34 **Quinta Claudia** (*Cael.* 34).

Quintia: Pretty woman (Cat. 86.1).

Quintilia: Wife or mistress of Calvus (Cat. 96.5/6).

Quintilian: Roman writer on oratory; *see* "Testimonia."

Quintilis: Month of Roman calendar renamed "July" after Julius Caesar (*Att.* 2.1.11).

Quintius: Rival of Catullus (Cat. 82.1).

Quintus: Quintus Tullius Cicero (senior), brother of Cicero (*Q. fr.* 2.3 [heading]; *Cael.* [78]).

Quintus Catulus: *See* Catulus (2).

Quintus Cicero: Quintus Tullius Cicero (Junior), son of Quintus Catulus (*Att.* 13.29.3).

Quintus Metellus: *See* Celer.

Quintus Pompeius: Governor of Africa in 61 B.C. (*Cael.* 73).

Quirinalia: Feast of Quirinus, the name for the deified Romulus; held on February 17 (*Q. fr.* 2.3.2, 4).

Ravidus: Rival of Catullus (Cat. 40.1).

Rebilus: Gaius Caninius Rebilus, appointed *consul suffectus* (i.e., fill-in for one who died in office) by Caesar for one day in 45 B.C.; co-owner of property Cicero considered buying (*Att.* 12.41.3, 12.44.3).

Remus: Brother of Romulus (Cat. 58.5).

Republic: Period of Roman history between expulsion of kings (509 B.C.) and Augustus' assumption of imperial power, often dated to his misnamed "Restoration of the Republic" (27 B.C.).

Rhamnusian: Of Rhamnus, a Greek town famous for its statue of Nemesis (Cat. 68.77).

Rhesus: Thracian ally of Priam during Trojan War; *see* note on *Am.* 1.9.24 **captive steeds** (*Am.* 1.9.23).

Rhine: River forming border between Gaul (modern France) and Germany (Cat. 11.11).

Rhodes: Large island in Aegean Sea (*Att.* 2.1.2, 9; Cat. 4.8).

Romulus: Founder of Rome; killed brother, Remus (*Att.* 2.1.8; Cat. 49.1).

Rostra: Speakers' platform at Rome.

Rufus: *See* Caelius.

Sabine: Name of area northeast of Rome; *see* note on *Am.* 2.4.15 **rigid Sabines** (Cat. 44.1, 44.4, 44.5; *Am.* 1.10.49, 2.4.15).

Sagae (or Sacae): Nomadic tribe of northern Iran (Cat. 11.6).

Sallust: Roman historian; *see* "Testimonia."

Sampsiceramus: Syrian ruler and nickname of Pompey; *see* note on *Att.* 2.14.1 **Sampsiceramus** (*Att.* 2.14.1, 2.23.2).

Sappho: Greek poetess from island of Lesbos; wrote lyric love poetry to girls and women, seventh–sixth century B.C. (Cat. 35.17/16).

Sardinia: Large mountainous island in central Mediterranean, Roman province but never fully Romanized (*Q. fr.* 2.3.7).

Satrachus: River in Cyprus (Cat. 95.4).

Saturn: Father of Jupiter (Mart. [11.6.1]).

Saturninus: Lucius Appuleius Saturninus (quaestor 105 B.C.); embittered by losing quaestorship, turned against ruling oligarchy; as tribune, had hostile candidate for consulship murdered and incited riot in popular assembly (*Sest.* 39).

Scapula: Quinctius (?) Scapula, deceased owner of property Cicero wanted to buy (*Att.* 12.38a.2, 12.41.3, 12.52.2).

Schoeneus: Father of Atalanta (in some versions) (*Am.* 1.7.13).

Scholiast: Writer of commentary in margins (often) of ancient texts.

Sebosus: Neighbor of Cicero at Formiae, friend of Catulus (2) (*Att.* 2.14.2).

Second Triumvirate: Official alliance of Octavian, Antony, and Lepidus (43 B.C.), formed to restore order after murder of Caesar; instituted proscriptions, including that of Cicero.

Semele: Mother of Bacchus; *see Am.* 3.3.40 **father would not have done mother's work in Bacchus** (*Am.* 3.3.37).

Semiramis: Ancient queen of Babylon, known for her beauty (*Am.* 1.5.11).

Sempronia: Female follower of Catiline (*Bell. Cat.* 25).

Senate: Governing body of Roman Republic, consisting of magistrates and ex-magistrates.

Senian: *See note on Cael.* 61 **Senian baths** (*Cael.* 61–62).

Septimius: Roman man in love with Acme (Cat. 45.1, 45.13, 45.21, 45.23).

Serapis: Egyptian god of healing (Cat. 10.27).

Servilius: Publius Servilius Isauricus, Roman politician who as praetor in 54 B.C. supported Cato (and married his niece) but in 48 B.C. became consul with Caesar; betrothed his daughter to Octavian (*Att.* 2.1.10; *Q. fr.* 2.3.2).

Sesterce: Unit of Roman money, very roughly equivalent to a modern quarter.

Sestius: Publius Sestius (tribune 57 B.C.), worked for Cicero's recall and was successfully defended by him in *Pro Sestio* (56 B.C.); notorious bore (*Q. fr.* 2.3.5, 6; Cat. 44.10, 44.19, 44.20).

Sextus: Sextus Pompeius Magnus (c. 67–36 B.C.), younger son of Pompey; one of Octavian's greatest foes, finally defeated and killed in 36 B.C. (*Att.* 14.8.2).

Sextus Cloelius: Henchman of Clodius (*Att.* [2.12.2]; *Dom.* 25; *Cael.* 78).

Sicily: Largest island in Mediterranean, Roman province (*Att.* 2.1.5).

Sicyon: Greek town west of Corinth (*Att.* 2.1.10).

Silius (1): Publius Silius (praetor before 51 B.C.), owner of property Cicero considered buying (*Att.* 12.41.3, 12.44.2, 12.52.2).

Silius (2): Gaius Silius Italicus (c. A.D. 26–102), author of extant epic on war with Hannibal (Mart. 4.14.1).

Sinuessa: Town in central Italy; Cicero had a house there (*Att.* 14.8 [heading], 1).

Sipylus: Mountain in Lydia where Niobe turned to stone (Prop. 2.20.8).

Sirmio: Peninsula twenty miles from Verona; site of Catullus' family villa (Cat. 31.1, 31.12).

Sisyphean: Of Sisyphus, king of Corinth, condemned in the Underworld eternally to push a rock uphill and have it roll back down as soon as it reached the top (Prop. 2.20.32).

Sithonian: Thracian (Sithonii were a Thracian tribe) (*Am.* 3.7.8).

Smyrna: Poem by Cinna; *see* Cat. 95.

Social War: War between Italian "allies" (*socii*) and Rome (91–88 B.C.), resulting in full Roman citizenship for Italians.

Solonium: District of Italy near Lanuvium, a town about twenty miles south of Rome (*Att.* 2.9.1).

South Wind(s): Latin *Notus*; often shown carrying away unfulfilled promises (*Am.* 1.7.15/16, 56, 2.6.44, 2.8.19/20).

Spaniards: Inhabitants of Spain (*Att.* 14.8.2).

Spinther: *See* Lentulus (2).

Standard: Wooden pole capped with an eagle; held at head of Roman army, like our flag.

Stella: Lucius Arruntius Stella, friend and patron of Martial; writer of elegies (Mart. 1.7.1, 4, 7.14.5).

Straits: Straits of Messina, narrow channel between Sicily and Italian mainland (*Att.* 2.1.5).

Stymphalian: Of Stymphalus, a town in Arcadia with man-eating birds killed by Hercules (Cat. 68.114/113).

Subura: Crowded lower-class quarter of Rome; where Cynthia lived (Prop. 4.7.15).

Suetonius: Gaius Suetonius Tranquillus (c. A.D. 70–c. 130), Roman biographer.

Suffenus: Poetaster (Cat. 22.1, 22.20/19).

Sulla: Lucius Cornelius Sulla Felix (c. 138–79 B.C.), military leader and politician, lieutenant and later adversary of Marius (1). When deprived of military command, was first to take his army and march on Rome (88 B.C.); instituted several reforms of Roman Senate and courts (most reversed after his death); first to engage in proscriptions (82–81 B.C.).

Sulmo: Town in central Italy; birthplace of Ovid (*Am.* 3.15.12/11).

Syria: Country in western Asia including modern Syria, Lebanon, and Palestine region; known for perfumes and other luxury items (Cat. 6.8, 45.22, 84.7).

Syrtes: Two gulfs on the North African coast considered dangerous for their shoals and shifting currents (Prop. 3.24.16).

Tantalus: Legendary king in Asia Minor; notorious offender against gods (betrayed secrets of gods, or distributed gods' food and drink to mortals, or cooked his own son Pelops and served him to gods); punished by being eternally "tantalized" in Underworld with food and drink just out of his reach (*Am.* 2.8.13, [3.7.51]).

Tappo: *See* note on Cat. 104.4 **Tappo** (Cat. 104.4).

Tarpeia: Vestal Virgin who betrayed the Capitol; "Tarpeian groves" = Capitoline hill (Prop. 4.8.31; *Am.* [1.10.50]).

Teia: Loose woman at Propertius' party (Prop. 4.8.31, 58).

Terentia: First wife of Cicero (*Att.* 2.1.4, 2.12.4; *Cic.* 29.2–4).

Tertia: One of Clodia's sisters; married to Marcius Rex (*Cic.* 29.5).

Teuthras: *See* note on Prop. 1.11.11 **Teuthras' shallow wave** (Prop. 1.11.11).

Thamyras: Singer who boasted that he could win a contest even if Muses opposed him; they blinded him and took away his skill (Prop. 2.22A.19; *Am.* 3.7.62).

Themis: Goddess of justice (Cat. 68.154/153).

Theophanes: Gnaeus Pompeius Theophanes, hanger-on of Pompey (*Att.* 2.12.2).

Theophrastus: Greek philosopher; *see* note on *Att.* 2.9.2 **Theophrastus** (*Att.* 2.9.2).

Thermopylae: "Hot Gates," a narrow pass in Thessaly between Mount Oeta and the Malian Gulf (Cat. 68.54).

Thersites: Greek warrior in Trojan War; *see* note on *Am.* 2.6.41 **Thersites . . . Phylacus** (*Am.* 2.6.41).

Theseus: Greek hero; *see* Ariadne (Prop. 1.3.1, 2.14.7; *Am.* 1.7.16/15).

Thesprotus: King of Epirus in northwestern Greece (Prop. 1.11.3).

Thessaly: Region of northern Greece, known for its witches; home of Achilles (Prop. 2.22A.30, 3.24.11; Tib. 2.4.56; *Am.* 2.8.[11], 13, 3.7.27).

Thrace: Country in southeastern part of Balkan Peninsula (Cat. 4.8; *Am.* 1.9.23).

Three Taverns: *See* Tres Tabernae.

Thyonian: Epithet of Bacchus, whose mother was sometimes called Thyone; hence, "wine" (Cat. 27.7).

Tiber: Major river running through Rome (*Cael.* 36).

Tibullus: Roman poet; *see* introduction to "Tibullus."

Tibur: Small town on Anio River in Sabine hills (Cat. 44.1, 44.3/2, 44.5; Prop. 4.7.85).

Tithonus: Husband of Aurora; she obtained eternal life for him but forgot to ask for eternal youth, so as he aged he shriveled into a grasshopper (*Am.* 2.5.35, 3.7.42).

Titus: *See* Atticus.

Titus Coponius: Friend of Dio (*Cael.* 24).

Tityus: Giant pinned down in the Underworld over nine acres, punished by being eternally devoured by vultures (Prop. 2.20.31).

Trebonius: Gaius Trebonius, appointed *consul suffectus* (i.e., fill-in for one who died in office) in 45 B.C.; supported Caesar but then participated in his assassination; co-owner of property Cicero considered buying (*Att.* 12.38a.2, 12.41.3, 12.43.3).

Tres Tabernae: "Three Taverns," station on the Appian Way south of Lanuvium (*Att.* 2.12 [heading], 2).

Tribune: One of ten Roman officials elected annually from nonpatricians (*see* introduction, "Patricians and Plebeians"); had wide powers, such as convening popular assembly, introducing legislation, and vetoing any law or senatorial decree.

Trinacrian: Of Sicily ("Trinacria"), site of the volcanic Mount Aetna (Cat. 68.53).

Triton: Sea god (*Att.* 2.9.1).

Triumph: Parade honoring victorious Roman war leader.

Triumvirate: *See* First Triumvirate, Second Triumvirate.

Trivia: Name for Diana as Underworld goddess (*see* note on Cat. 34.15 **Trivia**) (Cat. 34.15).

Trojan: Inhabitant of Troy (*Am.* 1.9.34).

Trojan Horse: Huge wooden horse concealing Greek soldiers within; Trojans brought it inside Troy, thus causing the city's downfall after ten years of war (*Cael.* 67).

Troy: City in Asia Minor where Trojan War was fought (Cat. 68.89, 90, 99).

Tullia: Daughter of Cicero.

Tullus (1): Friend of Cicero (*Cic.* 29.3).

Tullus (2): Friend of Propertius (Prop. 1.1.9).

Tusculum: Fashionable resort town in Latium, fifteen miles southeast of Rome; Cicero had a villa there (*Att.* 2.1.11, 2.9.4, 12.41.1, 3, 12.43.1, 3, 12.44.3, 13.26.1, 2, 13.29.1).

Tydeus: Father of Diomedes (*Am.* 1.7.31, 34).

Tyndaris: Helen, daughter of Tyndareus (Prop. 3.8.30).

Tyrian: From Tyre (city on coast of Syria), famous for its purple dye; *see* note on Prop. 1.3.41 **purple thread** (Tib. 2.4.28).

Ulysses: *See* Odysseus.

Underworld: Abode for spirits of the dead, who continued a shadowy existence enjoying reward or punishment for their life on earth.

Urii: Town in Italy associated with Venus (Cat. 36.13/12).

Varro: *See* note on *Att.* 2.22.4 **Varro** (*Att.* 2.22.4).

Varus: Friend of Catullus (Cat. 10.1, 22.1).

Vatinius: Publius Vatinius, political ally of Caesar; attacked in speech by Calvus and defended (successfully) by Cicero in 54 B.C. (*Att.* 2.9.2).

Venus: Goddess of sexual love; *see* note on Cat. 86.6 **all the Venus** (*Cael.* 52; Cat. 3.1, 13.12, 36.3, 68.5, 86.6; Prop. 1.1.33, [2.14.25], 2.15.11, 2.22A.22, 3.8.12, 3.24.13, 4.8.34, 45; Tib. 1.1.73, 1.6.14, 83, 2.4.24, 2.4.57, 4.8.16; *Am.* 1.1.7, 1.9.3, 29, 1.10.17, 19, 33, 2.4.41, 2.5.28, 2.7.22/21, 27, 2.8.8, 18, [19], 3.15.[1], [15]; Mart. 1.109.15).

Veranius: Friend of Catullus (Cat. 9.1, 12.17).

Vergil: Publius Vergilius Maro (70–19 B.C.), Roman poet; author of *Eclogues, Georgics,* and *Aeneid*; name often spelled "Virgil" after the Renaissance because he was the *virga* ("rod") that guided Dante through the Inferno and Purgatory (*Am.* 3.15.7; Mart. 4.14.14).

Vergilius: Probably Gaius Vergilius Balbus, governor of Sicily during Cicero's exile; one of Scapula's heirs (*Att.* 13.26.1).

Verona: Provincial town in northeastern Italy; Catullus' birthplace (Cat. 35.3, 68.28/27; *Am.* 3.15.7; Mart. 1.7.2).

Vestal Virgins: Priestesses who tended the sacred hearth (Vesta was goddess of the hearth) at Rome; accorded many special privileges but punished with burial alive if virginity violated.

Vestorius: Gaius Vestorius of Puteoli (town on Bay of Naples), friend of Cicero's concerned with his business affairs (*Att.* 13.29.3).

Vettius: *See* note on *Cael.* 71 **wicked Vettian assault . . . old penny story** (*Cael.* 71).

Virgil: *See* Vergil.

Volusius: Poetaster, author of "Annals" (Cat. 36.1, 36.20, 95.6).

Vulcan: Greek Hephaestus, lame-footed god of fire and metallurgy; husband of Venus (Cat. [36.6/7]; *Am.* [1.9.39]).

Zephyr: West Wind; proverbially warm and gentle (Cat. 46.3; *Am.* 1.7.55).

Bibliography

Adams, J. N. 1982. *The Latin Sexual Vocabulary.* Baltimore: Johns Hopkins Univ. Press.

Ahern, Charles F., Jr. 1987. "Ovid, Amores 2.7.27f." *CJ* 82: 208–209.

Allen, Archibald. 1992. "Propertius 2.7 on Love and Marriage." *AJP* 113: 69–70.

Allison, June W. 1980. "Virgilian Themes in Propertius 4.7 and 8." *CP* 75: 332–38.

Arkins, Brian. 1983. "Caelius and Rufus in Catullus." *Philologus* 127: 306–11.

Austin, R. G., ed. 1960. *M. Tulli Ciceronis Pro M. Caelio Orationis.* 3rd ed. Oxford.

Axer, Jerzy. 1989. "Tribunal-Stage-Arena: Modeling of the Communication Situation in M. Tullius Cicero's Judicial Speeches." *Rhetorica* 7: 299–311.

Badian, E. 1985. "A Phantom Marriage Law." *Philologus* 129: 82–98.

Baker, Robert J. 1983. "Catullus and Sirmio." *Mnemosyne* 36: 316–23.

Booth, Joan. 1997. "All in the Mind: Sickness in Catullus 76." In *The Passions in Roman Thought and Literature,* edited by Susanna Morton Braund and Christopher Gill, 150–68. Cambridge.

Boyd, Barbara Weiden. 1984. "*Parva Seges Satis Est*: The Landscape of Tibullan Elegy in 1.1 and 1.10." *TAPA* 114: 273–80.

———. 1987a. "The Death of Corinna's Parrot Reconsidered: Poetry and Ovid's *Amores.*" *CJ* 82: 199–207.

———. 1987b. "*Virtus Effeminata* and Sallust's Sempronia." *TAPA* 117: 183–201.

———. 1997. *Ovid's Literary Loves: Influence and Innovation in the Amores.* Ann Arbor: Univ. of Michigan Press.

———. 2002a. "The *Amores*: The Invention of Ovid." In *Brill's Companion to Ovid,* edited by Barbara Weiden Boyd, 91–116. Leiden, Boston, and Cologne: E. J. Brill.

———, ed. 2002b. *Brill's Companion to Ovid.* Leiden, Boston, and Cologne: E. J. Brill.

Braund, Susanna Morton, and Christopher Gill, eds. 1997. *The Passions in Roman Thought and Literature.* Cambridge.

Bright, David F. 1978. *Haec Mihi Fingebam: Tibullus in His World.* Leiden: E. J. Brill.

Briscoe, John. 1971. Review of *Catullan Questions,* by T. P. Wiseman. *JRS* 61: 303–304.

Brunt, P. 1965. "Amicitia in the Late Roman Republic." *PCPhS* 11: 1–20.

Buchan, Mark. 1995. "Ovidius Imperamator: Beginnings and Endings of Love Poems and Empire in the *Amores.*" *Arethusa* 28: 53–85.

Burnand, Christopher. 2004. "The Advocate as a Professional: The Role of the *Patronus* in Cicero's *Pro Cluentio.*" In *Cicero the Advocate,* edited by Jonathan Powell and Jeremy Paterson, 277–89. Oxford.

Butrica, James F. 1981. "Propertius 3.8: Unity and Coherence." *TAPA* 111: 23–30.

Cahoon, Leslie. 1984. "The Parrot and the Poet: The Function of Ovid's Funeral Elegies." *CJ* 80: 27–35.

Cairns, Francis. 2005. "Catullus 45: Text and Interpretation." *CQ* 55: 534–41.

Califf, D. J. 1997. "*Amores* 2.1.7–8: A Programmatic Allusion by Anagram." *CQ* 47: 604–605.

Camps, W. A. 1961. *Propertius: Elegies, Book I.* Cambridge.

———. 1965. *Propertius: Elegies, Book IV.* Cambridge.

———. 1966. *Propertius: Elegies, Book III.* Cambridge.

———. 1967. *Propertius: Elegies, Book II.* Cambridge.

Cape, Robert W., Jr. 2002. "Cicero's Consular Speeches." In *Brill's Companion to Cicero: Oratory and Rhetoric,* edited by James M. May, 113–58. Leiden, Boston, and Cologne: E. J. Brill.

Caston, Ruth. 2006. "Love as Illness: Poets and Philosophers on Romantic Love." *CJ* 101: 271–98.

Clarke, Jacqueline. 2003. *Imagery of Colour and Shining in Catullus, Propertius, and Horace.* New York: Peter Lang.

Clausen, Wendell. 1972. "Callimachus and Latin Poetry." In *Approaches to Catullus,* edited by Kenneth Quinn, 269–84. Cambridge (= *GRBS* 5 [1964] 181–96).

———. 1988. "Catulliana." *BICS* Suppl. 51: 13–17.

Clauss, James J. 1995. "A Delicate Foot on the Well-Worn Threshold: Paradoxical Imagery in Catullus 68b." *AJP* 116: 237–53.

Commager, Steele. 1974. *A Prolegomenon to Propertius.* Norman: Univ. of Oklahoma Press.

Copley, Frank Olin. 1947. "*Servitium amoris* in the Roman Elegists." *TAPA* 78: 285–300.

———. 1956. *Exclusus Amator: A Study in Latin Love Poetry.* Ann Arbor: Univ. of Michigan Press.

———. 1972. "Catullus, 35." In *Approaches to Catullus,* edited by Kenneth Quinn, 173–84. Cambridge (= *AJP* 74 [1953] 149–60).

Corbeill, Anthony. 1996. *Controlling Laughter: Political Humor in the Late Roman Republic.* Princeton, N.J.: Princeton Univ. Press.

———. 1997. "Dining Deviants in Roman Political Invective." In *Roman Sexualities,* edited by Judith P. Hallett and Marilyn Skinner, 99–128. Princeton, N.J.: Princeton Univ. Press.

———. 2005. "*O singulare prodigium!* Ciceronian Invective as Religious Expiation." *Prudentius* 37: n.p.

Courtney, Edward. 1993. *The Fragmentary Latin Poets.* Oxford.

Craig, Christopher P. 1989. "Reason, Resonance, and Dilemma in Cicero's Speech for Caelius." *Rhetorica* 7: 313–29.

———. 1993. *Form as Argument in Cicero's Speeches: A Study of Dilemma.* Atlanta: Scholars Press.

———. 1995. "Teaching Cicero's Speech for Caelius: What Enquiring Minds Want to Know." *CJ* 90: 407–22.

D'Arms, John H. 1970. *Romans on the Bay of Naples: A Social and Cultural Study of the Villas and Their Owners from 150 B.C. to A.D. 400.* Cambridge, Mass.: Harvard Univ. Press.

Davis, John T. 1980. "*Exempla* and Anti-*exempla* in the *Amores* of Ovid." *Latomus* 39: 412–17.

Day, Archibald A. 1938. *The Origins of Latin Love-Elegy.* Oxford.

Debrohun, Jeri Blair. 2003. *Roman Propertius and the Reinvention of Elegy.* Ann Arbor: Univ. of Michigan Press.

Dettmer, Helena. 1980. "The Arrangement of Tibullus Book 1 and 2." *Philologus* 124: 68–82.

———. 1997. *Love by the Numbers: Form and Meaning in the Poetry of Catullus.* New York: Peter Lang.

Dufallo, Basil. 2001. "Appius' Indignation: Gossip, Tradition, and Performance in Republican Rome." *TAPA* 131: 119–42.

Dyson, Julia T. 1997. "Birds, Grandfathers, and Neoteric Sorcery in *Aeneid* 4.254 and 7.412." *CQ* 47: 314–15.

———. 2001. *King of the Wood: The Sacrificial Victor in Virgil's Aeneid.* Norman: Univ. of Oklahoma Press.

———. 2007. "The Lesbia Poems." In *A Companion to Catullus,* edited by Marilyn B. Skinner, 254–75. Malden, Mass., and Oxford: Blackwell.

Edwards, Catharine. 1993. *The Politics of Immorality in Ancient Rome.* Cambridge.

———. 1997. "Unspeakable Professions: Public Performance and Prostitution in Ancient Rome." In *Roman Sexualities,* edited by Judith P. Hallett and Marilyn Skinner, 66–95. Princeton, N.J.: Princeton Univ. Press.

Elder, J. P. 1962. "*Tibullus: Tersus Atque Elegans.*" In *Critical Essays on Roman Literature: Elegy and Lyric,* edited by J. P. Sullivan, 65–105. Cambridge, Mass.: Harvard Univ. Press.

———. 1972. "Notes on Some Conscious and Subconscious Elements in Catullus' Poetry." In *Approaches to Catullus,* edited by Kenneth Quinn, 41–76.
Cambridge (= *HSCP* 60 [1951] 101–36).

Erskine, Andrew. 1997. "Cicero and the Expression of Grief." In *The Passions in
Roman Thought and Literature,* edited by Susanna Morton Braund and
Christopher Gill, 36–47. Cambridge.

Evans, S. 1971. "Odyssean Echoes in Propertius IV.8." *G&R* 18: 51–53.

Fantham, Elaine, Helene Peet Foley, Natalie Boymel Kampen, Sarah B. Pomeroy,
and H. A. Shapiro, eds. 1994. *Women in the Classical World.* Oxford.

Fear, Trevor. 2000. "The Poet as Pimp: Elegiac Seduction in the Time of Augustus."
Arethusa 33: 217–40.

Feeney, Denis C. 1992. "'Shall I compare thee . . . ?': Catullus 68b and the Limits
of Analogy." In *Author and Audience in Latin Literature,* edited by Anthony J.
Woodman and Jonathan Powell, 33–44. Cambridge.

Feldherr, Andrew. 2000. "*Non inter nota sepulcra*: Catullus 101 and Roman Funerary
Ritual." *CA* 19: 209–31.

Ferguson, John. 1988. *Catullus.* Greece & Rome, New Surveys in the Classics,
No. 20. Oxford.

Fitzgerald, William. 1995. *Catullan Provocations: Lyric Poetry and the Drama of
Position.* Berkeley, Los Angeles, and London: Univ. of California Press.

Fordyce, C. J. 1961. *Catullus.* Oxford.

Fraenkel, Eduard. 1972. "*Vesper Adest* (Catullus LXII)." In *Approaches to Catullus,*
edited by Kenneth Quinn, 195–209. Cambridge (= *JRS* 45 [1968] 1–8).

Gager, John G. 1992. *Curse Tablets and Binding Spells from the Ancient World.*
Oxford.

Gaisser, Julia Haig. 1971. "Structure and Tone in Tibullus, I, 6." *AJP* 92: 202–16.

———. 1977. "Mythological *Exempla* in Propertius 1.2 and 1.15." *AJP* 98: 381–91.

———. 1983. "*Amor, rura* and *militia* in Three Elegies of Tibullus: 1.1, 1.5 and
1.10." *Latomus* 42: 58–72.

———. 1993. *Catullus and His Renaissance Readers.* Oxford.

———. 2001. *Catullus in English.* London: Penguin.

———. 2002. "Picturing Catullus." *CW* 95: 372–85.

Gale, Monica R. 1997. "Propertius 2.7: *Militia Amoris* and the Ironies of Elegy."
JRS 87: 77–91.

Gardner, R. 1958. *Cicero Vol. XIII: Pro Caelio, De Provinciis Consularibus, Pro
Balbo.* Cambridge, Mass.: Harvard Univ. Press.

Garrison, Daniel H. 2004. *The Student's Catullus.* 3rd ed. Norman: Univ. of Oklahoma Press.

Geffcken, Katherine A. 1973. *Comedy in the Pro Caelio, with an Appendix on the
In Clodium Et Curionem.* Wauconda, Ill.: Bolchazy-Carducci.

George, David B. 1991. "Catullus 44: The Vulnerability of Wanting to Be Included."
AJP 112: 247–50.

Godwin, John. 1995. *Catullus: Poems 61–68.* Warminster, UK: Aris & Phillips.

———. 1999. *Catullus: The Shorter Poems.* Warminster, UK: Aris & Phillips.

Gold, Barbara K. 1993. "'But Ariadne Was Never There in the First Place': Finding the Female in Roman Poetry." In *Feminist Theory and the Classics,* edited by Nancy Sorkin Rabinowitz and Amy Richlin, 75–101. New York and London: Routledge.

Goold, G. P. 1983. *Catullus.* London: Duckworth.

———. 1990. *Propertius: Elegies.* Cambridge, Mass.: Harvard Univ. Press.

Gotoff, Harold C. 1974. "Tibullus: *Nunc Levis Est Tractanda Venus.*" *HSCP* 78: 231–51.

———. 1986. "Cicero's Analysis of the Prosecution Speeches in the *Pro Caelio*: An Exercise in Practical Criticism." *CP* 81: 122–32.

———. 1993. "Oratory: The Art of Illusion." *HSCP* 95: 289–313.

Gratwick, A. S. 2002. "*Vale, Patrona Virgo*: The Text of Catullus 1.9." *CQ* 52: 305–20.

Greene, Ellen. 1998. *The Erotics of Domination: Male Desire and the Mistress in Latin Love Poetry.* Baltimore: Johns Hopkins Univ. Press.

Griffin, Jasper. 1985. *Latin Poets and Roman Life.* London: Duckworth.

Griffith, R. Drew. 1996. "The Eyes of Clodia Metelli." *Latomus* 55: 381–83.

Hallett, Judith P. 1984. "The Role of Women in Roman Elegy: Counter-Cultural Feminism." In *Women in the Ancient World: The Arethusa Papers,* edited by John Peradotto and J. P. Sullivan, 242–62. Albany: State Univ. of New York Press.

Hallett, Judith P., and Marilyn Skinner, eds. 1997. *Roman Sexualities.* Princeton, N.J.: Princeton Univ. Press.

Hardie, Philip. 2002a. *Ovid's Poetics of Illusion.* Cambridge.

———, ed. 2002b. *The Cambridge Companion to Ovid.* Cambridge.

Harrison, Stephen. 2002. "Ovid and Genre: Evolutions of an Elegist." In *The Cambridge Companion to Ovid,* edited by Philip Hardie, 79–94. Cambridge.

Hillard, T. W. 1981. "*In triclinio Coam, in cubiculo Nolam*: Lesbia and the other Clodia." *LCM* 6: 149–54.

Hinds, Stephen. 1987. "Generalising About Ovid." *Ramus* 16: 4–31.

———. 1992. "*Arma* in Ovid's *Fasti.*" *Arethusa* 25: 81–149.

———. 1998. *Allusion and Intertext: Dynamics of Appropriation in Roman Poetry.* Cambridge.

Holland, Tom. 2003. *Rubicon: The Last Years of the Roman Republic.* New York: Random House.

Holzberg, Niklas. 2002. *Ovid: The Poet and His Work.* Translated by G. M. Goshgarian. Ithaca and London: Cornell Univ. Press.

Howell, Peter. 1980. *A Commentary on Book One of the Epigrams of Martial.* London: Athlone Press.

Hubbard, Margaret. 1975. *Propertius.* New York: Scribner.

Hubbard, Thomas K. 1984. "Catullus 68: The Text as Self-Demystification." *Arethusa* 17: 29–49.

Hutchinson, G. O. 2003. "The Catullan Corpus, Greek Epigram, and the Poetry of Objects." *CQ* 53: 206–21.

James, Sharon L. 2001. "The Economics of Roman Elegy: Voluntary Poverty, the *Recusatio,* and the Greedy Girl." *AJP* 122: 223–53.

Janan, Micaela. 1994. *"When the Lamp Is Shattered": Desire and Narrative in Catullus.* Carbondale and Edwardsville: Southern Illinois Univ. Press.

———. 2001. *The Politics of Desire: Propertius IV.* Berkeley, Los Angeles, and London: Univ. of California Press.

Johnson, W. R. 1990. "Messalla's Birthday: The Politics of Pastoral." *Arethusa* 23: 95–113.

Keith, Alison M. 1992. "*Amores* 1.1: Propertius and the Ovidian Programme." *Latomus* 217: 327–44.

———. 1994. "*Corpus Eroticum*: Elegiac Poetics and Elegiac Puellae in Ovid's *Amores*." *CW* 88: 27–40.

Kennedy, Duncan F. 1993. *The Arts of Love: Five Studies in the Discourse of Roman Love Elegy.* Cambridge.

Kenney, E. J. 1990. Introduction to *Ovid: The Love Poems.* Translated by A. D. Melville. Oxford.

King, Charles. 2003. "The Organization of Roman Religious Beliefs." *CA* 22: 275–312.

Kleiner, Diana E. E., and Susan B. Matheson, eds. 1996. *I Claudia: Women in Ancient Rome.* Austin: Univ. of Texas Press.

———. 2000. *I Claudia II: Women in Roman Art and Society.* Austin: Univ. of Texas Press.

Knox, Bernard. 1989. *Essays Ancient and Modern.* Baltimore: Johns Hopkins Univ. Press.

Knox, Peter E. 1984. "Sappho, fr. 31 and Catullus 51: A Suggestion." *QUCC* 46: 97–102.

Krostenko, Brian A. 2001. *Cicero, Catullus, and the Language of Social Performance.* Chicago and London: Univ. of Chicago Press.

Lee, Guy. 1990. *Tibullus: Elegies.* Leeds: Francis Cairns.

Leen, Anne. 2000–2001. "*Clodia Oppugnatrix*: The *Domus* Motif in Cicero's *Pro Caelio*." *CJ* 96: 141–62.

Leigh, Matthew. 2004. "The *Pro Caelio* and Comedy." *CP* 99: 300–35.

Littlewood, R. J. 1983. "Humour in Tibullus." *ANRW* II.30.3: 2128–58.

Lowry, Michèle. 2006. "*Hic* and Absence in Catullus 68." *CP* 101: 115–32.

Lyne, R. O. A. M. 1979. "*Servitium Amoris*." *CQ* 29: 117–30.

———. 1980. *The Latin Love Poets from Catullus to Horace.* Oxford.

———. 1998. "Propertius and Tibullus: Early Exchanges." *CQ* 48: 519–44.

MacLeod, Colin W. 1973. "Catullus 116." *CQ* 23: 304–309.

———. 1974. "A Use of Myth in Ancient Poetry." *CQ* 24: 82–93.

MacMullen, Ramsay. 1982. "Roman Attitudes to Greek Love." *Historia* 31: 484–502.

Martin, Charles. 1992. *Catullus.* New Haven and London: Yale Univ. Press.

May, James M. 1988. *Trials of Character: The Eloquence of Ciceronian Ethos.* Chapel Hill and London: Univ. of North Carolina Press.

————, ed. 2002. *Brill's Companion to Cicero: Oratory and Rhetoric.* Leiden, Boston, and Cologne: E. J. Brill.

McGinn, Thomas A. J. 2004. *The Economy of Prostitution in the Roman World: A Study of Social History and the Brothel.* Ann Arbor: Univ. of Michigan Press.

McKeown, J. C. 1979. "Augustan Elegy and Mime." *PCPhS* 25: 71–84.

————. 1989. *Ovid: Amores. Text, Prolegomena, and Commentary in Four Volumes.* Vol. II, *A Commentary on Book One.* Leeds: Francis Cairns.

————. 1995. "*Militat omnis amans.*" *CJ* 90: 295–304.

————. 1998. *Ovid: Amores. Text, Prolegomena, and Commentary in Four Volumes.* Vol. III, *A Commentary on Book Two.* Leeds: Francis Cairns.

Michels, Agnes Kirsopp. 1955. "Death and Two Poets." *TAPA* 86: 160–79.

Miller, Paul Allen. 1999. "The Tibullan Dream Text." *TAPA* 129: 181–224.

————. 2002. "Why Difference Matters: Catullus and Contemporary Theory." *CW* 95: 425–31.

Murgatroyd, Paul. 1994. *Tibullus: Elegies II.* Oxford.

Newman, John Henry Cardinal. 1999. *The Idea of a University.* Washington, D.C.: Regnery.

Nicholson, John H. 1994. "The Delivery and Confidentiality of Cicero's Letters." *CJ* 90: 33–63.

————. 1997. "Goats and Gout in Catullus 71." *CW* 90: 251–61.

Nicoll, W. S. M. 1977. "Ovid, *Amores* 1.5." *Mnemosyne* 30: 40–48.

Noonan, J. D. 1979. "*Mala Bestia* in Catullus 69.7–8." *CW* 73: 155–64.

Oliensis, Ellen. 1997. "The Erotics of *amicitia*: Readings in Tibullus, Propertius, and Horace." In *Roman Sexualities,* edited by Judith P. Hallett and Marilyn Skinner, 151–71. Princeton, N.J.: Princeton Univ. Press.

————. 2002. "Feminine Endings, Lyric Seductions." In *Traditions and Contexts in the Poetry of Horace,* edited by Anthony J. Woodman and Denis C. Feeney, 93–106. Cambridge.

Osgood, Josiah. 2005. "Cicero's *Pro Caelio* 33–34 and Appius Claudius' *Oratio de Pyrrho.*" *CP* 100: 355–58.

Peradotto, John, and J. P. Sullivan, eds. 1984. *Women in the Ancient World: The Arethusa Papers.* Albany: State Univ. of New York Press.

Pomeroy, Arthur J. 2003. "Heavy Petting in Catullus." *Arethusa* 36: 49–60.

Pomeroy, Sarah B. 1975. *Goddesses, Whores, Wives, and Slaves: Women in Classical Antiquity.* New York: Schocken Books.

Powell, Jonathan, and Jeremy Paterson, eds. 2004. *Cicero the Advocate.* Oxford.

Putnam, Michael C. J. 1972. "Catullus' Journey (*Carm.* 4)." In *Approaches to Catullus,* edited by Kenneth Quinn, 136–45. Cambridge (= *CP* 57 [1962] 10–19).

————. 1973. *Tibullus: A Commentary.* Norman: Univ. of Oklahoma Press.

————. 2005. "Virgil and Tibullus 1.1." *CP* 100: 123–41.

Quinn, Kenneth. 1970. *Catullus: The Poems.* London: Bristol Classical Press.

————, ed. 1972. *Approaches to Catullus.* Cambridge.

————. 1999. *The Catullan Revolution.* 2nd ed. London: Bristol Classical Press.

Rabinowitz, Nancy Sorkin, and Amy Richlin, eds. 1993. *Feminist Theory and the Classics.* New York and London: Routledge.

Ramage, E. S. 1985. "Strategy and Methods in Cicero's *Pro Caelio.*" *A&R* 30: 1–8.

Ramsey, J. T. 1984. *Sallust's Bellum Catilinae.* Atlanta: Scholars Press.

Randall, J. G. 1979. "Mistresses' Pseudonyms in Latin Elegy." *LCM* 4: 27–35.

Rankin, H. D. 1969. "Clodia II." *AC* 38: 501–506.

————. 1976. "Catullus and Incest." *Eranos* 74: 113–21.

Rauk, John. 1997. "Time and History in Catullus 1." *CW* 90: 319–32.

Reckford, Kenneth. 1996. "Recognizing Venus I: Aeneas Meets His Mother." *Arion* (3rd series) 3: 1–42.

Reynolds, L. D. 1983. *Texts and Transmission: A Survey of the Latin Classics.* Oxford.

Reynolds, L. D., and N. G. Wilson. 1991. *Scribes and Scholars: A Guide to the Transmission of Greek and Latin Literature.* 3rd ed. Oxford.

Richardson, L., Jr. 1976. *Propertius: Elegies I–IV.* Norman: Univ. of Oklahoma Press.

Richlin, Amy. 1981. "The Meaning of *irrumare* in Catullus and Martial." *CP* 76: 40–46.

————. 1992. *The Garden of Priapus: Sexuality and Aggression in Roman Humor.* Rev. ed. Oxford.

————. 1993. "Not before Homosexuality: The Materiality of the *Cinaedus* and the Roman Law against Love between Men." *JHS* 3: 523–73.

Riggsby, Andrew M. 1999. *Crime and Community in Ciceronian Rome.* Austin: Univ. of Texas Press.

————. 2002a. "Clodius/Claudius." *Historia* 51: 117–23.

————. 2002b. "The *Post Reditum* Speeches." In *Brill's Companion to Cicero: Oratory and Rhetoric,* edited by James M. May, 159–95. Leiden, Boston, and Cologne: E. J. Brill.

————. 2004. "The Rhetoric of Character in the Roman Courts." In *Cicero the Advocate,* edited by Jonathan Powell and Jeremy Paterson, 165–85. Oxford.

Rosenmeyer, Patricia A. 2001. *Ancient Epistolary Fictions: The Letter in Greek Literature.* Cambridge.

Ross, David O., Jr. 1969. *Style and Tradition in Catullus.* Cambridge, Mass.: Harvard Univ. Press.

————. 1975. *Backgrounds to Augustan Poetry: Gallus, Elegy and Rome.* Cambridge.

Salzman, Michele Renee. 1982. "Cicero, the *Megalenses* and the Defense of Caelius." *AJP* 103: 299–304.

Saylor, Steven. 1995. *The Venus Throw.* New York: St. Martin's Paperbacks.

Shackleton Bailey, D. R. 1965–70. *Cicero's Letters to Atticus.* 7 vols. Cambridge.

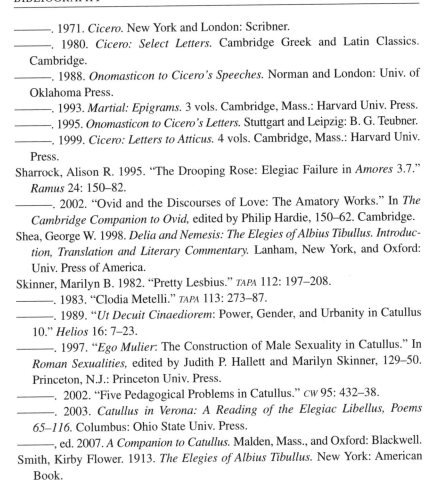

———. 1971. *Cicero*. New York and London: Scribner.

———. 1980. *Cicero: Select Letters*. Cambridge Greek and Latin Classics. Cambridge.

———. 1988. *Onomasticon to Cicero's Speeches*. Norman and London: Univ. of Oklahoma Press.

———. 1993. *Martial: Epigrams*. 3 vols. Cambridge, Mass.: Harvard Univ. Press.

———. 1995. *Onomasticon to Cicero's Letters*. Stuttgart and Leipzig: B. G. Teubner.

———. 1999. *Cicero: Letters to Atticus*. 4 vols. Cambridge, Mass.: Harvard Univ. Press.

Sharrock, Alison R. 1995. "The Drooping Rose: Elegiac Failure in *Amores* 3.7." *Ramus* 24: 150–82.

———. 2002. "Ovid and the Discourses of Love: The Amatory Works." In *The Cambridge Companion to Ovid*, edited by Philip Hardie, 150–62. Cambridge.

Shea, George W. 1998. *Delia and Nemesis: The Elegies of Albius Tibullus. Introduction, Translation and Literary Commentary*. Lanham, New York, and Oxford: Univ. Press of America.

Skinner, Marilyn B. 1982. "Pretty Lesbius." *TAPA* 112: 197–208.

———. 1983. "Clodia Metelli." *TAPA* 113: 273–87.

———. 1989. "*Ut Decuit Cinaediorem*: Power, Gender, and Urbanity in Catullus 10." *Helios* 16: 7–23.

———. 1997. "*Ego Mulier*: The Construction of Male Sexuality in Catullus." In *Roman Sexualities*, edited by Judith P. Hallett and Marilyn Skinner, 129–50. Princeton, N.J.: Princeton Univ. Press.

———. 2002. "Five Pedagogical Problems in Catullus." *CW* 95: 432–38.

———. 2003. *Catullus in Verona: A Reading of the Elegiac Libellus, Poems 65–116*. Columbus: Ohio State Univ. Press.

———, ed. 2007. *A Companion to Catullus*. Malden, Mass., and Oxford: Blackwell.

Smith, Kirby Flower. 1913. *The Elegies of Albius Tibullus*. New York: American Book.

Stahl, Hans-Peter. 1985. *Propertius: "Love" and "War": Individual and State under Augustus*. Berkeley, Los Angeles, and London: Univ. of California Press.

Starr, Raymond J. 1987. "The Circulation of Literary Texts in the Roman World." *CQ* 37: 213–23.

Stowers, Stanley K. 1986. *Letter Writing in Greco-Roman Antiquity*. Philadelphia: Westminster Press.

Sullivan, J. P., ed. 1962. *Critical Essays on Roman Literature: Elegy and Lyric*. Cambridge, Mass.: Harvard Univ. Press.

Syme, Ronald. 1939. *The Roman Revolution*. Oxford.

Tatum, W. Jeffrey. 1997. "Friendship, Politics, and Literature in Catullus: Poems 1, 65 and 66, 116." *CQ* 47: 482–500.

———. 1999. *The Patrician Tribune: Publius Clodius Pulcher*. Chapel Hill and London: Univ. of North Carolina Press.

———. 2003–2004. "Elections in Rome." *CJ* 99: 203–16.

Thomas, Richard F. 1986. "From *Recusatio* to Commitment: The Evolution of the Vergilian Program." *PLLS* 5: 61–73.

———. 1993. "Sparrows, Hares, and Doves: A Catullan Metaphor and Its Tradition." *Helios* 20: 131–42.

Thomson, D. F. S. 1964. "Catullus 95.8: 'Et Laxas Scombris Saepe Dabunt Tunicas.'" *Phoenix* 18: 30–36.

———. 1997. *Catullus*. Toronto: Univ. of Toronto Press.

Trapp, Michael. 2003. *Greek and Latin Letters: An Anthololology with Translation*. Cambridge.

Treggiari, Susan. 1991. *Roman Marriage: Iusti Coniuges from the Time of Cicero to the Time of Ulpian*. Oxford.

———. 1996. "Women in Roman Society." In *I Claudia: Women in Ancient Rome*, edited by Diana E. E. Kleiner and Susan B. Matheson, 116–25. Austin: Univ. of Texas Press.

Tuplin, C. J. 1981. "Catullus 68." *CQ* 31: 113–39.

Van Nortwick, Thomas. 1990. "*Huc Veniet Messalla Meus*: Commentary on Johnson." *Arethusa* 23: 115–23.

Wallace-Hadrill, Andrew. 1996. "Engendering the Roman House." In *I Claudia: Women in Ancient Rome*, edited by Diana E. E. Kleiner and Susan B. Matheson, 104–15. Austin: Univ. of Texas Press.

Walters, Jonathan. 1997. "Invading the Roman Body: Manliness and Impenetrability in Roman Thought." In *Roman Sexualities*, edited by Judith P. Hallett and Marilyn Skinner, 29–43. Princeton, N.J.: Princeton Univ. Press.

Warden, J. 1996. "The Dead and the Quick: Structural Correspondences and Thematic Relationships in Propertius 4.7 and 4.8." *Phoenix* 50: 118–29.

White, Peter. 1993. *Promised Verse: Poets in the Society of Augustan Rome*. Cambridge, Mass.: Harvard Univ. Press.

Wilder, Thornton. 1948. *The Ides of March*. New York: Harper.

Williams, Craig A. 1999. *Roman Homosexuality: Ideologies of Masculinity in Classical Antiquity*. Oxford.

Williams, G. 1962. "Poetry in the Moral Climate of Augustan Rome." *JRS* 52: 28–46.

Wills, Jeffrey. 1996. *Repetition in Latin Poetry: Figures of Allusion*. Oxford.

Winterbottom, Michael. 2004. "Perorations." In *Cicero the Advocate*, edited by Jonathan Powell and Jeremy Paterson, 215–30. Oxford.

Wiseman, T. P. 1969. *Catullan Questions*. Leicester: Leicester Univ. Press.

———. 1975. "Clodia: Some Imaginary Lives." *Arion* (new series) 2: 96–115.

———. 1985. *Catullus and His World: A Reappraisal*. Cambridge.

Woodman, Anthony J., and Denis C. Feeney, eds. 2002. *Traditions and Contexts in the Poetry of Horace*. Cambridge.

Woodman, Anthony J., and Jonathan Powell, eds. 1992. *Author and Audience in Latin Literature*. Cambridge.

Wray, David. 2001. *Catullus and the Poetics of Roman Manhood.* Cambridge.

———. 2003. "What Poets Do: Tibullus on 'Easy' Hands." *CP* 98: 217–50.

Wyke, Maria. 2002. *The Roman Mistress: Ancient and Modern Representations.* Oxford.

Zetzel, James E. G. 1996. "Poetic Baldness and Its Cure." *MD* 36: 73–100.